LETTERS
FROM THE
EMPIRE

The simple life is what I want;
To drill the wily Gurkha again, to shoot, fish, draw T.A.
(D'you know what that is, by the way?
Travelling allowance, ten bob a day).

AMH

'I wish mamma would not talk rot about burning villages, etc; there is a damn sight too much of that spirit abroad without finding it in a respectable family. I don't think any decently intelligent people are unnecessarily cruel, but confess that if there's any burning, killing, or ravaging to be done I prefer that we should do it to someone else rather than allow them to do it to us.'

LETTERS FROM THE EMPIRE

A Soldier's Account of the Boer War and the Abor Campaign in India

Researched and transcribed by
Yvonne Wagstaff and Sheila Shaw
Edited and annotated by
Stephen Morris

SPELLMOUNT

First published 2011 by Spellmount, an imprint of
The History Press
The Mill, Brimscombe Port
Stroud, Gloucestershire, GL5 2QG
www.thehistorypress.co.uk

British Library Cataloguing in Publication Data.
A catalogue record for this book is available from the British Library.

ISBN 978 0 7524 6518 0

Typesetting and origination by The History Press
Printed in the EU by The History Press

Contents

Foreword

In 1996, my brother told me that he had found a letter written twenty-five years previously by our father's sister, to say that an ancestor had been a priest in East Bridgford, Nottinghamshire. When a business meeting he had been attending in Nottingham finished early, he decided to explore. Imagine his amazement to find that it was our great-great-grandfather, Rev. Richard William Hutchins (1872–1859). I immediately began to research the family, and for five years made many visits to Record Offices, checking the Census, BMDs, professional bodies and Army records, tracing members of the family in the hope of finding any still alive, and wrote up many biographies including Allan's. I looked up wills and the beneficiaries named, and learnt that a cousin, Sara Cutforth, was indeed alive and living in the Lake District. After contacting her, she invited me and my sister Sheila to visit her, and told us she was in possession of seventeen trunks of family letters which she was happy to let us see. So armed with a photocopier, and packs of paper, we spent a most fascinating day or two making copies of letters, some written by our great grandfather to George his brother, and in a trunk labelled A.M.H., all the letters Allan had written home. These were written on both sides of flimsy paper, and the ink had often leaked through the pages making them very difficult to decipher. Sara allowed us to copy them however, also his diaries.

Sadly, Sara died the following year, but she had been so very pleased to know that the archive of letters and photographs had been accessed by us, and knowledge of the family passed on. At Sara's memorial service we met her three children, and they allowed us to borrow five trunks in order to examine and record the contents before returning them.

We felt that Allan's letters were so detailed and well written that they deserved a wider audience, and so we transcribed them, painstakingly, for publication.

In one letter to his sister Ada Sybil, Allan says 'Papa has taken up literature, has he? My salaams! I've occasionally thought of doing a bit that way myself, if I had time, but it's not an uncommon aspiration, is it?'

Well, posthumously, Allan has indeed got himself into print.

Yvonne Wagstaff

Introduction

Allan Marriott Hutchins was born in Carmarthen on 14 September 1879 and died in Dibrughar, Assam, north-east India on 3 December 1911. There, at the very edge of the British Empire on the banks of the Brahmaputra river, he died a European death – from pneumonia – and was buried in Christian ground with Arum lilies growing round the headstone. In Almora (many miles from Dibrughar in the hills above Delhi) Allan's brother officers recorded his passing on a tablet in the old hill station church. A replica of it hangs on the north wall of the lovely church of St Mary's in Welshpool:

To the memory of
Captain Allan Marriot Hutchins
3rd Queen Alexandra's Own Gurkha rifles
who died at Dibrugarh on 3rd December 1911
from pneumonia contracted on the Abor Expedition aged 32 years.

And there, in just a few words below crossed Kukris, the story might have ended. Allan died a bachelor and five years later his parents died too – within hours of one another and each ignorant of the other's passing. The elegant, late-Regency house in Welshpool (Clive House) that was the Hutchins' family home – and a happy one too – was sold and the contents auctioned. Allan's older brother George (always known as D'Oyly) acquired the sobriquet 'horrid' for insisting his sisters bid for lots. Soon the Great War engaged every family in new, more appalling losses.

After the death of their parents the oldest daughter, Aida Sybil (Billy), carefully preserved her father's papers including Allan's diaries, correspondence, photographs and miscellaneous items. Billy moved to London taking with her trunks containing all these and other family mementos. She played viola for the South London Symphony Orchestra and until her death at 92, worked assiduously to create a family archive. The trunks stayed in the family and a new generation opened them from time to time to dress up in a native hat and read about dangerous incursions into the African veldt. Some contents grew worn and scuffed but the papers were left to gather dust.

The trunks were passed down on Billy's death to her niece, Sara Cutforth, residing in Keswick in the Lake District where she lived until her death in 2006; they are now in the keeping of Sara's family. Allan's descendants and researchers for this book, the sisters Sheila and Yvonne, met Sara at a moment when she had begun annotating the papers. Yvonne, engaged in researching her family's history, asked if she and Sheila could visit Sara in Keswick and explore the fabled archive.

'What we found,' says Yvonne, 'was breathtaking, seventeen trunks packed with papers, photographs and letters.' Another long journey north ensued, and longer trips to South Africa and India following in Allan's footsteps. Never mind that he had died almost 100 years before, his letters and diaries brought the man vividly to life not only for the family but for people Sheila and Yvonne met along the way: the keeper of the little museum in Ceres, the historians and owners of the bookshop in Graaff Reinet, one of whom was close to tears listening to Allan's story, and the hoteliers fascinated by the story of the man who had been a guest 100 years before.

A big part of the archive comprises a collection of papers and artefacts from Allan's short but adventurous life. Some are the things a proud parent would keep: school reports, letters homes from postings in Africa and India, magazine cuttings. Some are records of a father keen to see his son progress: copies of letters written to Allan's superiors in pursuit of rank and appointment. Others letters, despairingly, enquire how his son died and the replies received are there. At some point an unknown hand returned Allan's diaries and they too went in the trunks, along with his jottings to friends and cousins – including things not for his mother's eyes.

Sheila and Yvonne opened the trunks and began to read – and read. Allan's handwriting (criticised in his reports from Newtown County Intermediate School as 'very bad'), often written on both sides of flimsy paper, was not always easy to decipher. Copies of his father's letters were in a bolder hand on quality notepaper and easier to follow. They found his father's coveted Q badge awarded for shooting at Bisley. There was an order for 30 pairs of football boots (for the men) from Brown and Co in Welshpool and telegrams to home from Aldershot ('Leave till Tuesday night'). There were some maddening gaps and obscure references in the narrative but the urge to piece together the story of Allan's life proved irresistible. This book is the result.

The papers and photographs describe Allan's entire career as a soldier and an officer in the British Empire at its height – and on the cusp of a great fall. More than that, they show us what Allan was like as a man: brave, modest and hard-working, who would not suffer fools but was generous and likeable. A school master says of him 'the boy cannot write' and yet his letters home are alive with humour, affection and intelligence. He decribes in detail skirmishes of the Boer War and his time in India, the excitement, routine and discomforts of life in exotic lands and the cast of sharply drawn characters with whom he shares the privations and pleasures of an overseas posting. He is a cool observer of men and their failings (including his own) and though he is in thrall to adventure, he is modest about his achievements and feigns cowardice: 'personally I stayed with the mules, hoisted the Red Cross on a waggon, got inside, and gave out I was the Doctor.'

A.C. Benson (who wrote 'Land of Hope and Glory') described Allan's generation as 'well-mannered, well-groomed, rational, manly boys, smiling politely at anyone who finds matter for serious interest in books, art or music' but, as his writing shows, Allan is more complicated and more interesting than that. No doubt as a child he dressed up to celebrate Victoria's Golden Jubilee and as a boy avidly read *King Solomon's Mines* ('I am laid up here at Durban with the pain in my left leg ... ever since that confounded lion got hold of me') but a few years later when he and his generation found themselves fighting over the real diamond mines of the Transvaal, cracks in the Empire – and the very idea of the Empire – were beginning to show. We shall never know what Allan thought of it all. He had a low opinion of certain senior officers and political appointees, freely expressed in writings home, but his complaints were few. Like all good soldiers Allan got on with the job and, had he lived, would no doubt have carried with him that same sense of duty to the poppy fields of France.

1

Hutchins' Military Service

Allan Hutchins was educated to London University Matriculation standard at The Grammar School in Newtown, Montgomeryshire, and on leaving in December 1893, was articled to his father's civil engineering practice. Within the year he had joined 'K' (Llanidloes) Company of the 1st Hereford R.V.C. Shrewsbury, of which his father was the Lieut. Colonel. He proved to be an exceptional shot, winning the National Rifle Association Medal, and was a bugler in the regiment. In 1897 he was commissioned as Lieutenant in the 5th Battalion South Wales Borderers.

In 1900 he resigned his commission and volunteered for active service against the Boers as a trooper in one of the squadrons of Yeomanry raised by Sir Watkin Williams-Wynn. In South Africa, Britain's 'small wars' army was in danger of being overwhelmed by the Boers who not only objected to British designs on the self-governing Afrikaaner colonies of the Transvaal and the Orange Free State, but whose rebellious farmer army had Her Majesty's forces on the run. Allan became Trooper 8384 in the 49th Company, Montgomeryshire Imperial Yeomanry. The Imperial Yeomanry was the volunteer force recruited for the South Africa War that later became the Territorial Army and comprising, says Thomas Packenham in *The Boer War*, 'the fox hound masters, riding farmers and horse masters of the shires [in] a rush to abandon the fox in pursuit of the Boer.' It was merged with the TA in 1909.

Allan's Attestation Papers show he applied for Short Service (one year with the colours) on 16 January 1900, aged 20 years and 4 months. At 5 feet 9.5 inches tall, he weighed 154 lbs with a chest measurement of 33.5 inches (expanding to 35.5 inches), with light coloured hair, fair complexion and grey eyes.

The 49th embarked at Haverford West on the Montrose on 12 March 1900 and sailed the next day. The ship (with six stowaways on board, 'one a Russian Jew, about 11 years old, who has been helping himself to watches, money etc' – Lce. Cpl. Critten, 31st Co Imp Yeomanry) arrived at Table Bay via Las Palmas on 6 April and the 49th were immediately assigned to the 9th Battalion, Imperial Yeomanry along with the Pembrokeshire and Denbighshire companies. Allan was recommended for a line commission but, barely three months after arriving, in July 1900 he contracted enteric at Vet River, Orange River Colony, and was invalided home. In November, after he had recovered and with only three months of his engagement to run, he was discharged at his own request and, after 287 days in the ranks, enlisted as a Second Lieutenant in the 5th V.B. South Wales Borderers. In January 1901 he was again recommended for a line commission. He was appointed Second Lieutenant in the South African Imperial Yeomanry and then, as temporary captain, he took out a Yorkshire section (E) of the Imperial Yeomanry to Blandsfontein, Transvaal.

Thereafter Allan was with Doran's Flying Column in Cape Colony, South of Orange River, coming into daily contact with the Boers. In August 1901 he was appointed temporary transport officer of the Column, in his mind an appointment of dubious privilege and no joy ('I don't like it at all'). He was with a detachment that came within a whisker of capturing General Smuts and at Middlepost in which three of his brother officers were killed; he was left with nothing but a revolver and the remnants of his hot-weather uniform. Given command of the rearguard, he led a retreat of 70 miles in 36 hours without further losses.

In May 1902 a delegation of Boer leaders signed the proffered peace treaty in Pretoria. In September 1902 Allan was gazetted out of the South African Imperial Yeomanry and as an honorary Lieutenant left the country 'where every inhabitant is about half civilised, and everything in the way of civilization reminds one of tinned meat' and transferred to the Montgomeryshire Imperial Yeomanry. But not for long. He sat the Infantry, Militia and Yeomanry Competitive Examination and coming second in his entry, became the first officer to pass from Yeomanry to regulars. His Yeomanry commission had lasted 1 year and 222 days and for his service in South Africa he was awarded two medals and five clasps.

In July 1903 Allan arrived in India, still the jewel in the crown of empire but also a troubled, sprawling and gloriously diverse land where Curzon, as Viceroy, sought to turn back the rising tide of nationalism by playing Muslim against Hindu, province against province in the great game of divide and rule. For an officer in the British Army, India was both feast and famine, a difficult and sometimes hostile country (mostly due to climate) but immensely rewarding too, where roads and bridges could be built, new frontiers mapped and where a man could keep servants, ride, hunt and play polo. Following one year's attachment to the Leicestershire Regiment, Allan transferred to the Indian Army, the 73rd Carnatic Infantry, on 18 July 1904. A year later he joined the 3rd Gurkhas and was promoted to Lieutenant. On 14 March 1909, he was appointed Second Assistant Commandant to the Lakhimpur Military Police stationed at Sadiya. In August 1910, eighteen months before he would have attained that rank by length of service, Allan was gazetted Captain in the 3rd Queen Alexandra's Own Gurkha Rifles (attached to Lakhimpur Military Police). In November he played a key part in a punitive expedition against the Daphla tribe, successfully maintaining lines of communications in the dense, unexplored jungle between Tibet and Assam. Here, at the very fringes of the British Empire, Allan succumbed to pneumonia.

2

The Victorian
Family Hutchins

Allan was the fourth of six children born to George Albert Hutchins and Eliza Hutchins. Allan's father was the youngest son of Richard William Hutchins, Rector of St Peter's in East Bridgford, Nottinghamshire, a Fellow and later, in 1819, vice-president of Magdalen College, Oxford, in the last days before nineteenth century reforms would shake Oxford to the core. His mother, Eliza Anne Jones, was the youngest daughter of Alderman Benjamin Jones and his wife Laura of Guildhall Square, Carmarthen. George Albert Hutchins was born at the rectory on 12 November 1841 and educated at Magdalen College School, Oxford. The greater part of St Peter's parish was in the patronage of Magdalen College.

George Albert Hutchins and Eliza had four daughters and two sons: George D'Oyly followed by Marianna Emily, Elsie Adelaide, Allan Marriott, Aida Sybil and Nina. All the children were born in Carmarthen except for Marianna who was born in Spanish Town, Jamaica. We don't know much of Eliza (also known as Toosie or Lalla). Photographs of her show an unsmiling woman with rather sad eyes, a high forehead, broad, determined jaw and full cheeks – the well defined features passed on to her four daughters. George Albert is slightly built but strong-looking and sporting a finely waxed moustache. For 12 years the couple jointly owned, managed and edited the *Carmarthen Journal*, also known as 'The Thunderer' for its robust views. They appear to be the quintessentially severe Victorian parents but perhaps appearances deceive. Allan's writing home is loving, affectionate and irreverent, redolent of a childhood spent mucking about in the garden, making fun of his sisters, doting and being doted upon. 'Best love and luck, dear Kittens, From your affectionate br'er … Your young man is a jolly lucky devil, anyhow, though I says-it-as-shouldn't. Best love and lots of luck to both of you, and tell him I looks towards him and likewise bows.' In obituaries George Albert is described as 'A man of most amiable disposition', 'always so cheery and optimistic' with 'winning kindness and charming courtesy'.

Like Allan, his father George Albert loved sport, particularly archery and hunting (he rode with the Belvoir Hunt); his school certificates for prizes in swimming and diving survive to this day. Like Allan, George Albert sought adventure. On leaving school he began military training but quit at 18, in 1859, on the death of his father, Richard, ('being unable to bear the expenses of a cavalry regiment'). The following year he joined the auxiliary forces and took articles as a civil engineer under Joseph Cubitt and John Wright. It was an extraordinary time to be an engineer, especially in Britain where a coming together of science, ingenuity and capital was forging an indomitable world power. George Albert's own career and achievements are an essay of the age: railway building for the Manchester and Milford Railway, the Carmarthen and Cardigan Railway, bridges in Yorkshire for the Great Northern Railway; in Wales, hospitals, police stations, schools and metalled roads. In 1867 he travelled to India to build canals for the Madras Irrigation and Canal Company. Four years later, he and Eliza moved to Jamaica where he designed and built the Rio Cobre canal and dam. After five years this dynamic and gifted man – now father of two young children – was defeated by the Caribbean climate and, in poor health, returned with his family to Wales. He was appointed Borough Engineer, Architect and Surveyor for Carmarthen and later County Surveyor for Cardiganshire; in 1890 he joined Montgomeryshire County Council. From 3, Guildhall Square, Carmarthen, the family moved to Clive House, Welshpool, Montgomeryshire in 1890, a mansion house now functioning, by co-incidence, as offices for the Montgomeryshire Council Highways Department. His work remains today in several bridges including the Rheidol Bridge at Aberystwyth and the single-span, bowspring bridge over the Dyfi; he built in the wells and pipes that supply Carmarthen with fresh water, numerous roads, public buildings and schools throughout the counties.

The army and military matters remained George Albert's great interest and he was one of the founders of the 5th Volunteer Battalion, South Wales Borderers. He was one of the first to receive the volunteer decoration and was awarded the Diamond Jubilee medal. In later life he was always known as Colonel Hutchins. On returning from Jamaica he joined the 1st Battalion Pembrokeshire regiment, and later transferred to the 1st Herefords, the regiment that Allan would later join with his father as Lieutenant-Colonel.

George Albert was an expert shot and at Bisley, featured on the King and Queen's prize list eight times, earning a prestigous 'Q' to his name in the army list. In 1884 he published 'Hints on Rifle Shooting' under the name of 'Outis' and in 1907, a Gold Medal essay, 'The Supply of Officers for a National Army on a Voluntary Basis'. He was involved in training the Montgomeryshire contingent and testing the rifles for the Imperial Yeomanry – amongst them Allan – on their departure for the war in South Africa, in January 1900.

The first born son, George (Doy), was to become a senior civil servant in the Ministry of Munitions but it was Allan who shared his father's enthusiasms. Like his father he was articled as an engineer (to his father's department) and joined the volunteer forces. Like his father he was an excellent shot (in 1894 he won a National Rifle Association prize and was entered for the Queen's Prize) and no doubt it was to his father and commanding officer, that Allan turned for advice at the outbreak of war. Should he resign his commission as Lieutenant with the 1st Herefords so that he might join the ranks of Yeomanry enlisting to fight in South Africa? There could be only one answer.

Perhaps the old man, 'the Colonel', came to live his life vicariously through his son's –
the hunting, riding, shooting apple of his eye. Copies of letters written by him to senior
officers in both the regular and volunteer forces show him pursuing, with unabashed
nepotism, Allan's promotion and well-being. He wrote to the shipping line in Liverpool
asking for reassurance that his son had arrived safely in India; he wrote to officers in the
field asking that his son should not be forgotten and filed their replies:

> Dear Colonel Hutchins,
>
> I am just off for 3 or 4 days patrol but the colonel has promised to forward your
> son's application for a commission.

Allan begged his father to desist and in letters home he gently admonishes those correspondents who address him as 'captain' before he is gazetted: 'Remember I'm only a
lieutenant now, please.'

Allan is withering about senior officers who he believes are not up to the job, and
critical of self-regarding political appointees. One can only ponder how his mother,
and his father who had tried so hard to promote his son's interests, reacted to news of
his death. Surviving letters between Mrs Hutchins and the service doctor who treated
Allan at his death are sorrowful and stoic and it is not hard to imagine her sitting at the
desk in the study of Clive House in the winter chill, wondering for what purpose her
son died, alone and thousands of miles from home.

> Dear Sir,
>
> I would be extremely obliged if you are able to give me a few details of my dear
> son's death … who I understand died in the hospital at Dibrughar after a dreadful
> journey down from the Abor country …

Five days before he died in December 1916, in a letter to Billie (Aida Sybil) the Colonel
mentions that the temperature in his bedroom was 32 degrees – freezing point. He
and Eliza both died of 'flu within hours of each other; it is believed Eliza died without
knowing her husband had already gone. The following day, Eliza's sister, Laura, who was
visiting, also died of the same.

3

South Africa

The Republics are determined, if they must belong to England, that a price will
have to be paid which will stagger humanity.
President S.J.P. Kruger

It is much to be feared that it is Mr Kruger and his ignorant people who will in
the end be 'staggered' at the butcher's bill.
The Navy and Army Illustrated, *October 1899*

Looking back the Boer War appears as a bloody foretaste of how future wars would
come to be fought: armies fighting bitter battles with powerful weaponry and civilians
as unwilling victims of a world laid waste. The Boer commandos, outnumbered, well
armed and driven, would lead a merry dance to a massive invading force. Guerrilla warfare, scorched earth, concentration camps – South Africa was a martial proving ground
of vileness. Even the new British battledress – the khaki having replaced the regimental
peacock – was a portent of things to come.

It began with imperial necessities. A foothold at the Cape (commandeered to secure
a stopping off point for India-bound ships) had become a British colony – seized from
the Dutch who, with characteristic fervour, between 1836 and the early 40s made the
Great Trek north in search of new land and self-governance. Bitter dispute followed
and constant skirmishes. An Afrikaaner nation emerged when in 1852 and 1854 Britain
recognised the two Boer republics of the Transvaal and Orange Free State.

There the story may have ended, had not children playing on the banks of the Orange
River uncovered a pocketful of shiny stones. Three years later, in 1870, diamond-bear-
ing rock was discovered on a farm belonging to Johannes de Beer. A year later 50,000
people were living roughshod in a camp that was to become Kimberley, site of the
'biggest hole in the world' more than a mile in circumference and a tourist attraction
(Thomas Hardy wrote about his visit). Thereafter 50,000 people per year flooded into
the diamond fields. Companies moved in, mechanised and monopolised until De Beers

Consolidated Mines, under control of an Englishman, Cecil John Rhodes, was producing 90 per cent of the world's diamonds worth £15 million per year by 1898. Both black Africans and Boers claimed the land and with sleight of hand the British settled the matter by annexing Kimberley to Cape Colony.

Then, in 1886, gold was discovered in the Witwatersrand south of Pretoria in Transvaal. It would prove to be the biggest gold-bearing reef ever discovered, over 30 miles long. Overnight, President Paul Kruger's 'ramshackle' Republic of Transvaal became a honey-pot for white adventurers; and Johannesburg – 'Monte Carlo imposed on Sodom and Gomorrah' – was born.

Kruger, the old warhouse, had not made the Great Trek northwards for half a million godless outsiders ('Uitlanders') to emasculate his Boer nation. And though he might not be able to rid Transvaal of its fortune-seeking immigrants he could at least deny them the franchise. It was the excuse Cecil Rhodes, now Prime Minister of Cape Colony, needed in order to intervene. The great game for the mastery of Africa now had new and higher stakes and Rhodes' Imperial ambition, for a railway and unbroken sphere of influence from Egypt to the Cape, included 'the richest spot in the world'. 'If we wait,' he wrote to one of his fellow mine owners in August 1895, 'with its marvellous wealth Johannesburg will make South Africa an independent republic.'

With the covert support of the British Government Rhodes and his fellow 'Randlord', Leander Jameson, launched an armed attack on Kruger's forces. It was a disaster. Jameson's 500 men were defeated and captured outside Johannesburg. In London, the government denied knowledge of the affair; Rhodes was dismissed and Joeseph Chamberlain as Colonial Secretary (who survived the crisis) addressed the House in words that would prove prescient: 'A war in South Africa,' he said, 'would be a long war, a bitter war and a costly war.' But as Chamberlain knew, there was no going back. Kruger stood in the way of British ambitions in the Transvaal where, as *The Times* correspondent William Stead noted, Victoria 'reigns but does not rule'. Without securing voting rights for British subjects there was no other legitimate way to get rid of Kruger. Sir Alfred Milner, British High Commissioner in South Africa, put it succinctly in a letter to Chamberlain: 'I should be inclined to work up a crisis [so that] we shall have to fight.'

The crisis came soon enough. Throughout 1899 British forces gathered along the borders of Transvaal and the Orange Free State and in September a corps of 10,000 men embarked for the Cape. In October Kruger issued his ultimatum to the British government: withdraw or we are at war. How perfectly he played into British hands. The fight that Britain had so wanted was presented to her and forces – and public opinion – were mobilised. General Sir Redvers Buller was chosen to lead an army to 'teach those Dutch farmers a lesson'. In Glasgow, London, and Liverpool troops marched to cheering crowds. At Waterloo the *Daily Mail* described how 'the police were swept aside and men borne shoulder high.'

In the public imagination and in the minds of the boys who volunteered the adventure would 'be all over by Christmas'. The first action of the war would make them think again: a disciplined and well-armed commando of Boers captured an armoured train carrying guns to the British garrison at Mafeking. On October 14 the British garrison (commanded by Baden-Powell) was surrounded by Boers and besieged. The Boer forces brought up a Creusot 94-pounder and poured shells onto the town.

Kruger's 'farmers' were ready for war. Four years earlier the Jameson Raid had transformed Kruger's thinking and, with the threat of war hanging like a cloud over the Republic, he had armed and organised his people. From a gleeful Germany, he had bought 37,000 rifles from the Krupps works; from France, artillery guns. In 1899 Boer men from 16 to 60 mobilised – each with a horse, a saddle and bridle, a rifle and 30 rounds and each assigned to commando groups of 500 to 2000 men.

In the troopships making the 6000-mile journey from Britain were the officers and men who, at best, had only ever fought 'small wars against natives' and whose experience defined the Imperial adventure: a succession of skirmishes, often bloody, settled by force and secured by divide and rule. Kitchener of Khartoum, the great player in the Imperial adventure, was Chief of Staff long before he fought another white man. When, in 1900, Germany could mobilise an army of 3 million men, Britain had 316,000 regulars to police an Empire upon which, as every schoolboy knew, the sun never set.

South Africa would call upon huge numbers of British soldiers, 450,000 by war's end, to fight no more than 35,000 Boers. The traditional British dislike of a large standing army meant Britain would be dependent on reservists in any large-scale conflict and so it proved. Whereas Germany (for example) had an army of one million regulars in 1900, Britain had one million reservists in local volunteer units. And though Cecil Rhodes might bluster about the 'inferiority' of other races, the reality was self-evident to those at the recruiting stations: the English working class was under-nourished, unhealthy and – in the army – under-paid. Wolseley complained that the army would never be any good while 'we pay our soldiers according to rates for unskilled labour'. The poor physical shape of the Tommy surprised the Boers. 'How I was disillusioned,' wrote one, 'they were small, and some had the naked bully beef slapped in their pockets so that the grease oozed through. They had neither, it seemed, the accent nor the gait of Christians.' (R. W. Schikkerling, *Commando Courageous*); another was blunter: 'An Englishman on a horse always reminds me of a wooden clothespin.'

Meanwhile, even before the first of Buller's corps had disembarked, a force of hardened regulars led by Sir George White lost 1200 men trying to break out of Ladysmith. Kimberley and Mafeking were besieged. Near Magersfontein on the Modder River, Methuen lost 500 men in an ambush by an enemy who then vanished under cover of darkness. In one week in December 1899 British forces suffered three defeats to a mobile guerrilla enemy who 'don't believe in frontal attacks', who used the bleak kops to best advantage and pounded the enemy with artillery and small arms fire. The British public mourned and the newspapers fumed. Black Week, as it became known, had seen the Guards and the Highland Brigades thrashed by the 'farmers'. There was no longer talk of a punitive expedition – this was a twentieth-century war that would have tragic consequences for South Africa.

In France and Germany the press gloated over British defeats. The *Daily Mail* demanded retribution and Buller demanded 50,000 more men, 8000 of whom should know how to ride. Upon receiving news of Black Week, Victoria was said to have remarked 'We are not interested in the possibilities of defeat.' (Earlier she had chastised her grandson, Kaiser Wilhelm II, for his communiqué to Kruger celebrating the defeat of the Jameson raiders). Britain gritted her teeth and crowds poured into the recruiting offices. The new Imperial Yeomanry were raised by county around a core of existing volunteer units. Drawn from the middle classes of the shires, the hunt masters, the riding farmers and the landed classes, in many cases small companies with rich benefactors, such as the Duke of Cambridge's Own, paid their own passage and donated their pay to the Widows and Orphans Fund. Officers and men, according to the Royal Warrant; would 'bring their own horses, clothing, saddlery and accoutrements … The men to be dressed in Norfolk jackets, of woollen material of neutral colour, breeches and gaiters, lace boots, and felt hats. Strict uniformity of pattern will not be insisted on.' Thirty-four MPs and peers enlisted. Buller was withdrawn and replaced by Lord Roberts as Commander-in-Chief, with Kitchener as Chief of Staff.

For twenty-year-old Allan, already a Lieutenant in his father's 1st Hereford RVC and a competent horseman, the time had come – it was an irresistible opportunity for adventure. No doubt with his father's blessing and with his mother's acquiescence, Allan resigned his commission to become Trooper 8384 in the 49th Company, Montgomeryshire Imperial Yeomanry.

A Note about Mail

On Christmas Day 1898 the *Imperial Penny Post* began. Correspondents throughout the Empire could send a letter (weighing half an ounce or less) to all corners – except, initially, the Australasian Colonies and the Cape. The Cape adopted it in 1899 and at the peak of the conflict around one million letters weekly were sorted and delivered by the South African Army Postal Corps. A bugle call in camp signalled the arrival.

Christian De Wet, the Boer Commando, captured a mail train and burned 1500 mailbags. He would not allow his burghers to destroy mail addressed to British officers – this he did himself.

Beneficent organisations from around the world sent parcels to the soldiers and the women and children held in concentration camps. The *Anglo-Boer War Album* cites an incident in which a case of women and children's clothing intended for distribution amongst refugees ended up at the front. Col. Gordon had the contents distributed to impoverished families on nearby farms.

From the beginning of the war the British censored combatants' mail from Transvaal and Orange Free State and later PoW mail in Cape and Natal. Censorship did not apply to Cape Colony until late 1900 and was not universally applied – which may explain why much of Allan's writing survives.

The Correspondence

This boy's writing skills leave much to be desired.
Allan's end of term report, Newtown Grammar School

The troopships bring us one by one
At vast expense of time and steam.
Rudyard Kipling

The poor fellows were in a perfect frenzy of delight and excitement at the idea of going to the front. They swarmed over the deck, climbed into every available bit of rigging … and roared waved and screamed to the echo.
Private Tucker's Boer War Diary

Those were still the days when we all expected a magic termination to the war, and as we neared Cape Town a tragic despair seized most of the subalterns lest we should arrive too late, and be returned ignominiously as unnecessary. How little any of us really knew …
V. Brooke-Hunt, A Woman's Memories of War

★ ★ ★

The Budget Letter Card, protected under the Patent Act
[postmarked Welshpool 15 March, 1900]
Wednesday
Off Holyhead

Dear People,

Sir Watkin Williams–Wynn has not left us yet, but is going off today and will take this. Everything fine so far. We pulled out from river about 10 last night and anchored 'til this morning when we sailed about 8 a.m. Feeling very fit as yet, but a few have already succumbed. Pretty comfortable but not much room. You should see us in our hammocks at night. You couldn't see an inch of the floor from the ceiling, we're so close. The great drawback is having so little room to put your things. The grub is very fair, three meals a day and meat at all of them. The canteen is not open yet. The breeze is pretty cold on deck but I keep warm all right.

No more time.
Best love
Allan

Montrose,
Sunday March 25 1900

Dearest People,

I am writing this, or rather commencing to write this in hospital, having been inoculated on Friday. The hospital consists of the after deck of the ship, where we are all ranged round like sardines. The first lot that were done fared badly since no arrangements had been made for them, so when they began to feel ill, they had nowhere to go, and it seems the great thing to lie down and keep quiet as soon as you are done.

Jimmy was of the first batch, but Charlie and I looked after him and he didn't get it as bad as some. They do it in your side, just above the hip. First they rub you violently with some hard thing I didn't care about looking at, and then they stick a syringe with a spike about the thickness of a knitting needle about a yard and a half into you and squirt. It is not supposed to take effect for about 3 hours, but I went and laid down and in an hour had shivers and heats and felt deathly sick. However in about half an hour it wore off and I've scarcely felt anything since, except of course your side is awfully sore all over. Charlie isn't going to be done. Its awfully hot. We expect to cross the line tomorrow. I am only wearing pyjamas all day now.

On the horse decks it is simply awful. How the poor brutes stand it I don't know. We do all our work there in the simple costume of a pair of slacks. We have only lost three or four so far.

Las Palmas is awfully pretty. I did enjoy the time we had there. It was so funny to see all the Antonios come alongside in their boats and sell cigars and fruit, so many for a 'bob'. This was a great word of theirs, and so was 'Oiright'. The little kids could dive like billy ho. You chuck some sixpences in the water and they go in and fetch them up. We coaled there and I never saw such a mess in my life. Not a word of warning was given us, and lots of fellow's kits were ruined. You couldn't go into our mess room. We all went out on deck that night and stopped there. Next morning we pitched all our kits up and our place was cleaned. It was a perfect picture that morning to see all the fellows on deck three parts naked and as black as soot. Some couldn't get clean for days. However that's over, but it was miserable for about two days.

The weather has been quite calm ever since we started, but we haven't seen as much of the sun the last 2 or three days as you might expect.

(Wednesday afternoon) I came back to work on Monday mid-day, and we 'crossed the line' that afternoon in the ancient and approved manner. The ship's officers were all arrayed in suitable costumes with Father Neptune at their head, and assisted by a gang of our fellows as catchers, and the crew as duckers, laid hands on everyone irrespective, and first administered a pill of soap with other nastiness in it. Each was then lathered impartially all over the face, head and shoulders with a large brush and a fearsome yellow mixture of which the only ingredient I'm sure of was Stockholme Tar. He was then sheared with an enormous jagged wooden razor and then tipped backwards into the bath, where he was left to the mercies of the crew who ducked him about six times and then shot him into a windsail through which he had to crawl all the way while the hose played on his retreating figure. After that, if alive, he was at liberty to wash, which was highly necessary and took a bit of doing. I enjoyed it all thoroughly as I was still too sore to be done. I scored there. Inoculation is not a bad thing sometimes.

Messrs. Elder, Dempster have presented us each with two large tins of tobacco. Very kind, I'm sure. One of the reat disadvantages of this boat is the way things get collared. You can't leave a thing a minute but somebody bones it. It's simply beastly and everybody moans about it. If anyone gets caught he will get a warm time. I've not lost much except my sponge bag and one towel but I'm exceptionally lucky.

Another horse overboard today. We have changed our programme for stables now. We start sharp at 5 a.m. and clean out, go down and exercise the horses, and get everything done before breakfast.

Calm, or rather still. The sea has had a bit of a popple on for the last day or so but you can't feel it in a boat this size. I'm blooming now as sweetly as ever having got over the intoxication. I've just finished 'The King's Mirror' which I never had an opportunity of reading at home. I don't think much of it.

How are you all at home? I should like to hear from you, but I suppose I can't for some time. I hope George and The Walky Bird are again at peace, and that Podgie still violins constantly, and that dear old Tootsie still keeps her end up all right. I am writing to Billy also, and want you to send all my letters round to Betty, Roney, Billy, D'Oy and anybody else you think suitable. I think I shall write to all of you by turns, and get you to adopt this plan, but of course be sure of the contents being of a suitable nature.

(Wednesday 4th April) We expect to make land tomorrow afternoon, but don't suppose we shall land till Friday. I can't say if there is anything in it, but the rumour was that we are to go to Stellenbosch, about 25 miles from Cape Town. The time has been same as usual lately except that we are always having marching orders parade; a blooming nuisance. The weather has been good all along, the boat having a bit of a roll the last day or two; not much but enough to make the soap fly. We haven't had a bad time all through, though some of the arrangements might have been better. The great difficulty has been the canteens, both wet and dry. What with short hours of opening, irregularity of same, lack of proper stores and one thing and another, it has been almost impossible to get anything you want. At present the only things obtainable at the dry canteen are ship-biscuits and soap. We shan't be sorry to land.

We all had to give up our revolvers when we came on board and told that we should have them for practice, and ammunition allowed to us, but that is the last we have seen of them. We don't know whether we shall have them back or not.

I think between Billy's letter and this you'll be able to make out something about it all. Send yours to her, Betty, etc.

Goodbye dear Toosie, George, Podgie, Becky and all the members of the family too numerous to mention.

Bestest love all round from

Allan

28th March 1900
At sea
H.M. TRANSPORT
Elder Dempster Liner 'MONTROSE'

Dearest William,

It has occurred to me that it is not any too soon for me to write and congratulate you on your little bit. You may have thought me very slow in not doing so before, but the fact of the matter is that whenever I thought of your so-creditable success, a sort of paralysis took me and I couldn't write. However, dear, we'll forgive each other for that. I am now taking the opportunity of doing it and do do it very 'earty.

I'm on the briny at present, about 8 or 9 hundred miles south of the line. It's pretty hot, but the sea looks very much what it does at Aberystwyth on a cheap day trip; except now and again little fishes take to themselves wings and whizzle about over the top of the water. They are much smaller than what I thought, being only two or three inches long, and they won't stop to talk. It's great fun when we see dolphins and porpoises. These latter are so called from the fact that they keep porping up and down and out of the water. We touched at Las Palmas, you know, which of course any Matriculashers knows is a Grand Canary; very pretty island indeed, with any amount of gentlemen speaking the Spanish language but otherwise with a strong look of Antonio Borelli about them. They came forth in tribes in boats and said, 'You want banana? Twenty five a bob', or, 'I give vair' good seegar – you want good seegar for smoke?' One confiding yeoman lowered a fiver to one of them in trust while he inspected a glass he thought of buying. Antonio immediately started with a furious rush, and the fiver, for the beautiful shore of his Gran Canaria. A steam launch intercepted him though, and the fellow got his £5 back, though he didn't deserve it. The little kids diving for sixpences shied into the water and fetched them up very smartly!

I was inoculated for enteric the other day. The doctor jabbed a sort of spike into my side about a hinch and a 'arf and then squirted. I then went to hospital for three days but didn't feel very bad. Your side gets awfully sore all over though.

How are you getting on in sunny France? I hope you don't dance the can-can more than is absolutely necessary. You should ask the head boss how it's properly done though? Do your little native friends appreciate the honour of Matriculashon? I suppose you have to rough it a bit, and there you have my sympathy.

One thing, though, that I never appreciated before, was having a certain amount of space to shy things about. Here we live, eat and sleep in a mess room in which, when we sit down to the table, we are pretty close. When we hang our hammocks you can't see the floor from above and the whole of your personal belongings have to be put in a rack made of laths, with very wide openings, nailed to the bottom of the deck beams. You are allowed about a square yard, of which your viz-a-vee, (as Nelly P. would say), has to have half. In this you must keep your kitbag, cloak, boots, belts, dirty linen, and everything you require for immediate use, as your kit bag is so ingeniously constructed that it is impossible to get so much as a clean pocket handkerchief out without emptying all the rest on the floor, a dem' nuisance.

I am now writing on the horse deck at a porthole, and a very weird looking stoker discourses the while to me in an accent belonging to no one of the earthly world that I can discover. There is the dearest old nigger stoker on board who comes and talks with me at times. He's a fine chap, all wool and teeth. He can jabber Spanish too, like blazes.

Things get very monotonous on board but we have a fair amount of work. We get up at 4.30 and go to bed about 9. We have lost a fair amount of horses; I daresay about a dozen by the time we reach the Cape which we hope to do about Thursday, which I think will be April 6th. No one will be sorry, as too much 'Montrose' is apt to pall. I have been given my revolver back to clean, with orders to hand it in again. We do all our work there in the simple costume of a pair of slacks. It will be kept for me until my discharge. Very kind, I'm sure.

Your old Brer,
Allan

★★★

[Date and place missing]

Foggy and so also next morning, with a biggish sea running. You could only see about a hundred yards from the boat when all of a sudden we came on two steamers which had been in collision a short time before. One was the 'Mexican', outward bound from the Cape, and the other the 'Wingfield', with the Northumberland Yeomanry on board. The first had a great hole in her side, and the 'Wingfield' bow was a W sideways shape, and all skew-whiff. We stayed by them a long time and picked up a boatful of men from both ships; some were yeomen and some part of the crew of the 'Mexican'. They had been rowing about in the fog for hours. At last we came on, leaving the Wingfield' to tow the 'Mexican' back to the Cape where we arrived that night.

It was perfectly lovely next morning coming into Table Bay. The hills are enormous – great rocks with the mist all round the bottoms and the sun on the tops looked scarcely earthly. The town, or rather what we can see of it, looks awfully pretty. The Bay is full of ships and steamers. There are almost half-a-dozen troop ships waiting to get in, among them the 'Wingfield' who had to abandon the 'Mexican' and got here soon after us. We are expecting to disembark every minute. We have to march about four miles to Maitland Camp.

I got a paper yesterday, the *Cape Times*, but nothing in it except the Prince of Wales being shot at.

[On 5 April 1900 the Prince of Wales was shot at by a 16-year-old Belgian boy as the royal train left Brussels for Denmark. The would-be assassin, Sipido, said he was revenging the thousands of deaths in South Africa. The Prince, the future Edward VII, and the Princess Alexandra were unharmed. At the outbreak of war the British Empire was linked by a unique underwater network of telegraph cables. Like never before, the telegraph and mass printing gave newspaper readers news of world events as they happened.]

Arrival

At all the stations were small camps and pickets of bronzed and bearded soldiers
and on the platforms could be seen many Officers newly arrived from England,
distinguished by their brand-new uniforms, nearly all carrying the inevitable Kodak.
S. Wilson, South African Memories

Disembarkation must have come as a day of great hardship to the Yeomanry, unfit-
ted as they were for it, after the lazy life on board, for after unloading they had to
walk leading their horses some miles out of their destination, pitch their camp,
water and see to their horses and perform many inevitable duties.
V. Brooke-Hunt, A Woman's Memories of the War

Tuesday night: 10th.
I must now fill up to date and post to catch the mail. We did not disembark till Sunday mid-day after all, and in full marching order and leading horses, marched nearly
six miles with one halt of about three minutes. It made me whacked, I can tell you.
We just touched on one big street of Cape Town and the rest was all outskirts. We are
right outside, at Maitland Camp. It is pretty rough out here. We are fourteen in a tent,
and our grub consists of a pound of bread and a tin of tea in the morning, (which
bread lasts you all day), a pound of meat for dinner and a tin of tea for tea. There is
a good canteen, both wet and dry; but rather expensive, as most things are here. We
don't have any plates or forks or knives or such luxuries so our mess tins and combination knives and forks come in very useful. We have very little time to ourselves,
being at something or other from 6 a.m. in the morning till 6 at night. I had my first
wash and hair brush since I have been in camp, today. The horse lines are, of course,
open air. We are taking our own horses I think. How long we stop here I can't say
but I don't think more than about a fortnight. Nobody knows when they are really
going as they have a pleasant little way of ordering camp to be struck and every man
marched out in full marching order on the way to the front and then pitching them
back after a mile or so. However, most companies seem to get off in the time I mention. One or two have left since we came.

I am writing this in the 'Soldiers Home' – a sort of missionary place made of tin where
you can write and smoke and get T.T. drinks very cheap: a most desirable sort of place and
cram full. We have a parade in marching order in the morning at 6.30 which means having
all our blankets rolled on the horse's back, so it's rather a question how to get ready.

I got your letter etc. all right yesterday; was I pleased to have 'em. It was awfully
nice to hear so soon. Thanks, Podgie, so much for the rosettes and pin and George, also,
for the photies. I hope you both, and dear Toosie, are well as it leaves me at this present.
I feel awfully fit. I was awfully sorry about missing George, but we did say Good-bye
before, and I hope Toosie caught him all right at the bottom of the gang plank.

At present we are on a sort of sandy flat just within sight of the sea and Cape Town and under Table Mountain, which sticks up like a gurt rock. We are not allowed outside the camp except on pass which is from 4 p.m. till 10 p.m. so I don't expect to see a great deal of Cape Town proper. Charlie heard from Harry yesterday. He is up Bloemfontein way, where we expect to go shortly.

Billy will be angry to hear you can buy very nice grapes here from 3d. a pound. Ah Ha! They are about the cheapest things you can buy.

We are all very fit and jolly as can be. In fact it's rather fun being here, and thinking of Volunteer Camp, we used to call that roughing it once! It is not so very hot here and it is pretty warm at nights. We had some new horses today, Australian b[r]umbies. It's awful fun: when you put the heel ropes on them first, they fairly throw somersaults. Breaking them will take a bit of doing as they all seem pretty old 'uns.

Now dear people, a final farewell and with best love and kisses all round,
Yours very affect.
Allan

★★★

April 28th 1900
Stellenbosch
Saturday

Dearest People,

I got your letter of 5th today and very glad I was. It was great news, and I was very happy to hear of Kitty's engagement.

Charlie Elwell and I and Jim form a sort of brotherhood. Jim has had about enough of soldiering but I and Charlie are as merry as gingo. You see they have moved us from Maitland up here; partly because Maitland was not as healthy as it might be and partly because you can do field firing here. We fired 25 rounds each today, much to the alarm of a little buck of some species and one or two semi-tame ostriches. Kirkby thought the buck was a jackal. He gets on fairly well here. Though he is far from being an ideal officer, he is certainly the most useful in the company. He gets very excited in the attack and swears and squeals like a rabbit. It's rather funny.

We marched here from Maitland in two easy stages, bivouacking the night we left, camping near the road at a place called Durban Road. It was a fine fun. The horses were linked and Charlie and I made a fire and slept by it like stones, though it rained some in the night. One drawback was that the commissariat had overlooked such a detail as food for the men and we had nothing with us except cold tea, but we managed to sneak off and raise some cheese and biscuits at a roadside store, so we managed all right. We are about 5 miles from Stellenbosch which is, I think, about 30 miles from Cape Town. The Stellenbosch range of hills is one of the most wonderful views possible. It seems simply a chain of gigantic crags, as sharp and jagged as a saw. I don't know whether they are climbable or not but they don't look it.

We had a dog chasing an ostrich round the horse lines today. The ostrich went like an express train; it was one of the funniest sights imaginable. You know we are practically on active service now and expect to be really so in a very short time. We were allowed to bring absolutely no luggage here except what we carry on the saddle. We have our wallets in front with a change of underclothing and small necessaries; on top of these a pair of breeches and pair of boots and your cloak over all. Behind, we carry a spare coat, and a pair of puttees rolled in your waterproof sheet. Your blanket is folded under the saddle to do duty as a numnah. Draped picturesquely round different parts of the saddle are picketing pegs and ropes, heel ropes, nosebag, mess tins and two great forage nets. Also rifle bucket and shoe case, etc. This, with you arrayed in bandolier, haver-sack, waterbottle, belt and bayonet, field-glasses and your trusty gun, completes your full marching order, which means that the horse carries every stick you possess.

Charlie has gone to Stellenbosch tonight to see Miss Tichner, who used to stay at the Walkers. She lives there.

This camp is the Remount depot for all the cavalry regiments and there are an enormous lot of horses and mules here. We have to ride a mile and a half to water the horses. The farm where we water them belonged five years ago to one of the Sergeants in the Newtown Company.

I mentioned Durban Road just now, I have been there before, on picket duty. There is a small bridge which the Boer sympathisers have threatened to blow up, so there is always a picket there. Once or twice the sentries have been potted at and once they did a bit of potting. It is a grand job in fine weather as it is a very pretty little spot and you sleep in the open but, although very fine on the day we got there, it rained heavily early the next morning and continued nearly all day, so when we reached camp again we were drenched through and through. It was Easter Sunday, by the way.

I did G.M.P., [Garrison Military Police], with Parker the other night at Observatory Road Station from Maitland to Capetown. It is in the Observatory Gardens, which are one of the very pretty suburbs to Capetown; or rather Mowbray is, and the gardens are in Mowbray, which you might imagine was a suburb of London, with its shops and electric lights, and also trams. It was only about a mile from the camp and Charlie and I used to sneak off there of an evening without leave. It's a very pretty little place.

Washing here is not much of an enjoyment as you have to do it in one long trough in which the water is only changed at long intervals. You can get a swim though, by walking about two miles. There was a ripping swimming bath in the Observatory Gardens and we often used to go there but now no more 'las. It's not many times that I have seen my feet on the dark continent of South Africa. As far as I have seen it is not a pretty country, but sometimes you get a very fine view of great hills. I have scarcely seen a blade of grass but what it is like later on, I don't know. Of course, it is the beginning of winter now.

We don't have much reliable news from the front here. They know it sooner in London.

I think we shall do a day or two route marching shortly and then entrain for the front. What ho!

I hope I shall hear again from you soon and that everything goes on alright at home.

Send this letter around the family circle since I can't write to all at once, and it is very wearisome to write the same news twice over.

Very best love to all the family from
Your affectionate
Allan

★★★

Almost a month passes before we catch up with Allan. In the following long letter home he describes the emptiness of the battleground: 'not a human or other being for miles' and the looting of food and arms from abandoned farms. Two months later De Wet and 250 commandos would make a miraculous escape from British forces and so become the legendary vanishing Boer described in this ditty by an unknown British cavalry officer:

We have good reason to believe
Their force is large or small
And furnished with some fifty guns
Or else no guns at all.

De Wet, a brilliant escapologist in the eyes of the British public, later wrote 'It was impossible to think of fighting – the enemy's numbers were far too great – our only safety lay in flight.'
The looting of farmhouses was sanctioned by Roberts, Commander-in-Chief, who declared that any buildings harbouring the enemy were to be burned and that burghers would swear allegiance to the Union flag or be taken as prisoners. (If they broke their oath they would be executed.) Farmhouses and machinery were damaged beyond repair (especially wagons which could be used by commandos), domestic and farm animals and poultry were killed and trunks, bedding, clothing, private correspondence piled onto bonfires. It was both a humanitarian catastrophe and a measure of Roberts' desperation to break the enemy's resolve. Milner blamed Roberts for the want of a coherent military strategy and in a letter to Salisbury's new Conservative government predicted disaster should the war – the war that Roberts said was practically over – continue thus. Milner's mood could hardly have been buoyed when in November 1900 Kitchener replaced Roberts as C-in-C – he thought even less of K.
At least Roberts' farm-burning achieved a significant change in Boer strategy. Botha and Steyn with De Wet, Smuts and De la Rey agreed that the war should be carried to Cape Colony and Natal, British territories where the resident Afrikaners could be mobilised against the British and join the Boers in a war of liberation
Allan's description of a land of 'dead horse' (in this case where Methuen had fought the Battle of Modder River five months before) was familiar to all combatants and no doubt painful for Allan, who loved horses. 'The beasts, horses and oxen, are strewn about, dead and putrid, and deserters say that the stench from their rotting carcasses is unbearable' wrote Capt

*L March Philips at Kitchener's kopje, where De Wet and Cronje put up terrific resistance
before De Wet fled and Cronje was captured. Allan's description of horses and a railway
accident in which many mounts were lost is noted in his letter of November 12 1901.*

*Allan has much to say about the quality of the officers and his disdain for petty
discipline would remain with him always. Frustrated by an invisible enemy and with time
to dwell upon their circumstances, he laments the 'dodging round the district, disarming,
patrolling etc.' He also says 'there is a lot of enteric about'; soon after he is felled by it.*

Bloomfontein
24th May 1900

Dear People,

At long last I have a chance of writing home and letting you know how and what I have
been doing. Things have moved pretty fast since I last wrote you from Wellington. I am
never very good at exact dates but it was, I think, on the Friday night after I wrote last
that I entrained for this place. At least it was here we landed but they didn't tell us where
we were going until we got there. We travelled all Friday night, Saturday, Sunday and
arrived on Monday midday. The journey was pretty awful – 8 of us in a narrow 3rd class.
No racks, no cushions and no room. A good many got in 2nd and 1sts. And these were
pretty well off, especially the 2nds as you can get 6 good bunks in these. The horses were
in trucks and got pretty well bashed about. One corpsed.

The country we crossed was almost entirely the Great Karoo; an awful place. Nothing
but little kopjes which cut off any view. Stony, sandy ground with little stunted green
bushes growing over it. Not a human or other being for miles. It looks like a disused
cabbage garden. Occasionally you see a few ostriches, sheep and here and there a Kaffir
hut. After De Aar it got a bit better and after Nervals Pont we got into the Free State
where you pass a farm every few miles. We passed the scene of the fighting: Dewsberg,
Colesbury, etc., rather uninteresting country to look at. When we got here we found a
high plain with the usual kopjes round it and innumerable camps. Ours is about a mile
from the station. The feature of the place seems to be dead horse. They lie about everywhere, round and between the camps and hum little songs to themselves. There is a lot
of enteric about but we are all very well.

We pitched our tents and stayed there that night. Next day we were inspected by
General Kelly Kenny [in command of 6th Division]. Next day we dispatched before sunrise on a flying column towards Boshof to protect the Engineers who were constructing
or repairing the telegraph line. The nearest Boers were about 300 strong … We left our
camp at Bloomfontein with all sick men, sick horses etc. and did 2 days forced march
to Abraham's Drift on the Modder River, not far from the Modder River battle. We
marched sometimes along the road and sometimes across the veldt, marching about 20
miles per day and bivouacking at night near water. Bully beef and biscuits was the usual
fare but we commandeered some sheep and had fresh mutton. We had lots of scouting
and patrolling, etc., to do and the horses were living on chaff, bran, etc. We left a sort of

base at Abraham's Drift and went on to some farm where we made ourselves at home. Our scouts saw some Boers leaving it so we scoffed every blooming thing we could lay hands on, including a large and healthy flock of geese and some chickens. Officers, men and the nigger ambulance drivers chased those miserable geese off the plain together. Charlie, Jim and I did ourselves proud having a chicken and a share of a goose to ourselves. Charlie is a great man at cooking. He cooked those birds grand. We make our fires of wood and cow-dung. We always have a fire of our own when bivouacking and make tea and soup and fry liver, etc., which we get from a particular friend of ours, one of the cooks. We also get dripping, etc. from him which, seeing the butter is 2/- a pound and hard to get at that, is a great thing. We enjoyed ourselves pretty well [on] that expedition.

It is pretty cold sleeping out at night: butter that is running at 5 is frozen hard at 7 in the evening. Another thing that hits us pretty hard is getting no bread. Biscuits take a bit of eating. We have rather bad teeth all three of us; if anything, mine are the best.

We took a lot of arms from the farms and started home: three days march, so as to reach here in time for the Queen's Birthday [24 May]. We got here in good time and took part in a review in which the Imperial Yeomanry took the right of the line, altho' there were both cavalry and artillery present. We marched past by squadrons and I was in the right troop of the leading squadron so got a good view of the aristocracy. We were rather glad to get back because we wanted to wash our clothes and get bread and write home. We found a mail waiting for us: your letter of the 7th April comes to hand, much to my delight. Just before we started, I had a letter from Kitty through someone at Port Elizabeth who wrote me a very kind letter offering me all kinds of hospitality. I am totally unable to make out the name – everything points to its being Mr. Beck but it doesn't look in the least like that. More like W. C. Beck but even that won't work. I shall have to reply somehow but it is rather awkward. I haven't had a chance yet.

I don't know what they are going to do with us now; we are having a rather welcome rest today and yesterday, in honour of the Queen's Birthday, we had jam and cheese served out. We are doing ourselves proud at present. Charlie got news just before he left that he had been selected for a commission, provided he passed the medical. He went to the doctor and all went well till he looked at his teeth, when the doctor said he would send a report to the authorities but was sorry he could not recommend him. He has heard nothing more hitherto. It is beastly rough for him.

I am writing this in the guard tent, having been put on guard last night. I hope you will be able to read it but have my doubts. We hear all sorts of strange rumours about the war and us, but definite news is the rarest thing about. We have given up all hope of seeing any fighting and the great idea is to get out of all this as soon as possible. Really when you come to think of it, we have been treated disgracefully. The authorities induce a lot of young fellows to join in the hope of seeing a bit of service and so get a body of men (who are *practically* trained) to do police duty at a rate of pay which is merely a fraction of the amount which they would have to pay for men who enlisted for the purpose. We are all heartily dissatisfied with the whole business. We shall probably remain here dodging round the district, disarming, patrolling etc. till everything is over. And the petty restrictions that our officers put on us is sickening. You must know that we have far less liberty than any ordinary private in the army. This is due chiefly to our own officers, who are really the rottenest lot ever born. Bobby Wynn [Captain Robert Williams-Wynn] and Gordon [the adjutant] are about the only ones who are any good at all. Howard, [the Colonel] is an old woman. At Wellington, for instance, as soon as we arrived from the march everything was put out of bounds except the camp, a patch of waste land about 8 or 10 acres in size. The only thing to drink was the river water which we were strictly forbidden to drink and which, immediately after, was given us to drink in the watercart. There was nothing to eat excepting bully beef and biscuits. Another little way they have if we have a few hours spare time is to order some parade in the middle of it so as to make it of no use. Rifle inspection or something of that sort. After falling in and waiting for about ¾ of an hour to be inspected, we are told the officers must have gone away somewhere and we shall be inspected some other time, etc.

We have heard from Harry once or twice; he has been in action and is having a good time. Our great day is mail day. Letters from home are a great excitement. Toosie needn't worry about my wardrobe, I manage finely on what I've got. Besides I have a lot of things I've never worn at Cape Town; as for the little comforts you so kindly suggest, any little thing is acceptable such as chocolate. Tobacco I am pretty well provided with, also jams. I don't think it would pay to send but on occasion sticks of chocolate or a bit of home-made toffee or cake would be fine if not too heavy. As for coin, I think the best way, (if you have a bob or two to spare now and again), I think a P.O. is negotiable. But I can manage fairly well tho' things are expensive.

I have had a couple of sketches from Poppy but when to write and thank her, I don't know. It is as much as I can do to write home and keep you all informed of our doings. I owe scores of letters but I don't know when to write them.

Thank you all very much for your letters. George is becoming a very military man, what with Yeomanry and Volunteers. I'm glad to hear that you are all doing well, and that Billy is having a good time; as to the photos, I have some left so the family had better distribute the others at their discretion. It's rough that Kitty is going to live so far away but I suppose it can't be helped. I like the look of him very much. I hope to hear from you all again soon and will wind up for the present.

Best love all round and remember me to everyone,
Yrs. Affectly,
Allan

★★★

In May 1900 combined forces comprising Plumer's Rhodesian Mounted Regiment, a flying column of mostly African volunteers led by Col Mahon – a young Irishman who had excelled in Egypt – and Canadian troops finally broke the seven-month siege of Mafeking, held by Baden-Powell. Strategically, the town was insignificant but the raising of the siege was another defeat for a demoralised enemy. Roberts now marched on Pretoria hoping to draw the Boers into a major battle. At Doornkop near Johannesburg a smaller Boer force dug in and was overwhelmed. On 31 May Roberts took Johannesburg and on 5 June, 65km to the north, he entered Pretoria, the capital of Transvaal.

Allan writes about receiving the news on parade. Already, on 1 June, Kruger had suggested surrender to a furious Steyn (President of the Orange Free State). Steyn had already lost his capital but he would fight, he said, 'to the bitter end'. News of Boer successes gave new heart to a campaign of increasing harassment of British supplies and communications. In the Free State Piet de Wet (brother of Christiaan) captured 530 Imperial Yeomanry of the 13th Battalion at Lindley. It was a terrible humiliation, not least because the 13th comprised the Duke of Cambridge's Own and three Irish companies whose men came from the wealthiest, most influential families and were nicknamed 'Millionaires' Own'. In the same week Christiaan De Wet cut the railway to Pretoria and took 500 prisoners. By destroying railways and telegraph lines the Boers made supplying and commanding the larger British forces a logistical nightmare. In June, winter in the Karoo, the men of the Yorkshire Imperial Yeomanry were without winter clothes; dressed in rags, they made uniforms of 'sheep skin with the hair on', sacks and wagon tarpaulins.

In the Transvaal, Louis Botha raised 4000 men and met 20,000 under Roberts at Diamond Hill, east of Pretoria. Botha couldn't win but he fought for two days and with only minor casualties made a tactical withdrawal.

Roberts knew that if the British were going to win the war they would have to defeat Botha in Transvaal and de Wet in the Free State – and expected to take terrible reprisals against civilian collaborators.

11th June 1900
Smalldeel

Dear Old Folks,

I am so sorry that such gaps are occurring again in my correspondence. Don't think it is because I don't think of you all over there. We have been on the march again you see and you have no time or opportunity to write.

On the 28th of last month an escort of the 49th I.Y., of which I was one, marched into Bloemfontein and formed up opposite the house of the Governor, General Prettyman, who presently emerged with his staff and was received with a salute. He then proceeded with his escort to the Market Square which was filled with troops and the inhabitants. He took up his position facing the Club and just under the flagstaff. There were a few of the principal inhabitants of the town facing him inside the soldiers. He then, after the usual salute, read Lord Robert's Proclamation annexing the Free State as the Orange River Colony. Oh, how my buzzum swelled with pride as I sat my noble steed, (Shakespeare), which wasn't mine but borrowed. As he concluded, the Royal Standard was broken out from the flagstaff and the whole square broke out into vociferous cheering. A salute of 21 guns was also fired from a hill just above the town. There were lots of cameras and cinematographs going, so you may very likely see some of them. If you do, look for the flagstaff with the Governor under it and the mounted men close behind which are us. Count five from the left of the line (the men's proper left) and you have me; four you have Charlie; first or second from the other end, Jim. So there you are.

On the 31st we left Bloemfontein for a place called Buttfontein under Col. Lloyd of Aston with the West Riding Regiment and we marched by easy stages till we got there. We always started early though, turning out at 5 every morning. We had one days rest on the way and one at Buttfontein, one about 2 ½ miles from it as that was the nearest we ever got from it. We left next morning and made one march of it to Vet River which is on the railway. Our camp is there still but I am out on a patrol of 20 men and am going on up tomorrow somewhere.

It's fine to hear about Pretoria isn't it. I suppose it will all be over soon and a good job too.

How are all of you dear people? I think I got a letter dated May 4th from you at Bloemfontein but I am afraid I have lost it. Keep writing as often as possible; it's such a pleasure to get letters from home. We have not had a mail now for a fortnight.

I was thinking today how the country is looking your way now. I can imagine you sitting in the shade with the hay getting ready to cut. Out here it's pretty cool in the daytime and it freezes every night. I always keep warm enough at night though, though lots of fellows complain of the cold.

For the first time Charlie, I and Jim are temporarily separated. Jim is on another patrol up in this direction, I am here and Charlie's at Vet River. It rather rubs me as I haven't got any money bar one quid left in my belt, which I don't touch.

Well, I'm feeling very longing to see you all again, and I daresay I shall try and manage it soon. Don't George think he had better make arrangements for placing a small some of oofticki in the Standard Bank of South Africa so that I might take a run up to Johannesburg and see if there is a job to be picked up when I am discharged? The war may close suddenly see, and I am unprepared.

Very best love to all, especially Toosie and George,
From your affectionate
Allan

★★★

A letter from Father

Clive house,
Welshpool
June 21st, 1900

My dearest old boy,

We were delighted to get your letter of May 24th on Saturday last (16th inst.) telling us of your march towards Bishof and back to the Queen's Birthday Parade at Bloemfontein. I expect they will now be giving you some real work to do and not be keeping you hanging around any of those beastly fever-holes.

The reason of my long silence is that I have been doing 28 days training with the 15th Yeomanry Brigade at Wynastry, attached to the Montgomeryshire Yeomanry Cavalry. We had an awfully jolly time and, personally, I had plenty of hard work, first of all in pitching the camp for the Brigade and then in musketry and other Regimental duties. The Camp was in the Farm field – the flat beyond the river from the monument where you and I one day were observing a Bugler 'tootling' forth his lays, whilst we were walking along by the aforesaid monument. You know you cross from the latter, over a deep wooded dingle and river (an old dam) in the direction of the Railway goods yard.

There were 90 men's Bell tents, 27 for servants – and saddlery and guards, 19 for officers, besides 3 officers' marquees and six hospital marquees. Enough to accommodate about 1500 regular troops in active service so that our 360 (odd) yeomen have plenty of room to kick about in. I had a pretty stiff job in getting them all into line properly – especially as the C.O. had all the distances and interval changes just as we began our work.

One day at musketry, to my surprise Paul and Webb and Hughes of the Llanidloes Company of 1st Herefords introduced themselves to me – saying they were the last of my old Llanidloes recruits and, being so, had joined the Yeomanry. By the way, Lewis Lloyd has had a direct Commission in the Devons. I fear Charlie's chances are not good on account of his teeth and eyesight. The last I heard of Hal Kirkby is that he has his Commission in the Lancashire Fusiliers and is likely to go to China. He and the 1st to 5th V/B S.W.B. [South Wales Borderers] volunteers company were in action at the Rand Rifles fight with the S.W.B.'s and behaved very steadily under fire. One or two men were slightly wounded – one in the leg, I think in the puttee.

Our camp at Wynestry was very jolly. The unit officers were Col Sir Watkin Williams-Wynn; Colonel Arthur Wynn, Major; myself (special); Captains Williams, Vaughan, Hope, Graham; Lieuts. Anwyl, Dugdale, George Mayther – and I am pleased to say the latter turned out a very smart officer and took to soldiering wonderfully well, and D.Masters.

The Denbighs were – C.O. Captain Ormrod; also Davies-Cooke; Owen-Williams; Frank Cotton. Lieut. Piercy; Dr. R. Williams; Vet. Howatson. Altogether as nice a lot as I have been in Mess with, full of fun and last but no means least, as you know in your old guvnor's estimation, gentlepeople. So I really enjoyed myself. We had a good old field firm day on the last Thursday at a place called Eoglwysey belonging to Sir Watkin [Herbert Lloyd Watkin Williams-Wynn, 7th Baronet, Lord Lieutenant of Montgomeryshire] at a place which I had chosen out the day before and, thank the Lord, we all returned without even a horse or even more, a sheep having been shot. Fancy hundreds of future Yeomen, blazing away Enfield dumdums, in boxes full, generally speaking, into space without hitting anything but the improvised targets.

By the way, to show the skill in marksmanship of the 'casual' yeoman, at Llangollen Range I allowed a wandering 'Brebis' to stand behind the target whilst 20 individual shots were being fired, without his being converted into a silent but serviceable 'mouton'. After that I began to understand the reason why it takes a tin of bullets to kill a man on active service. Merely want of education. Look at the other side of the picture! I had for two days at Llanyinyech about 60 smart young yeomen from Liverpool (Denbighs), who had never fired out of a carbine before, for individual and collective firing. First I coached them in the firing exercise, then in individual firing – got them all thro' that – then a little coaching and much swearing before and at volleys and they averaged (from 600 and 300 yards) 40 to 60 per cent of hits. I really felt proud and I felt I could have done wonders with those boys on active service.

We go into camp at Salisbury Plain on the 19th July to 3rd August with the S.W. Brigade, I think via Ludgershall, so I hope to have a chance of admiring the graves of those of my ancestors who repose there under the name HUTCHINS. An old cock of the family, one Giles Hutchins, was Member of Parliament for that important village in the reign of Queen Elizabeth, and I believe the respected old buffer was buried there. It's not very far you know from Penton Lodge, Andover, where Uncle Allan [my] used to live sometime in the 40s. That's the property, no doubt you can remember my constant complaint about disappearing in Chancery (called a friendly suit) [a far from congenial dispute over the property and to whom it was to be bequeathed, reminiscent of *Bleak House*].

The hay is very forward this year and a very heavy crop with us. We are 'loosing' Trow and horses into it next week.

Enclosed in this will be a Post Office Order for 20/- and we shall send you a pound of chocolate by same parcel post.

Best love my dearest old boy and best wishes for your health and happiness and safety from your ever loving old governor,

G.A. Hutchins

P.S. I see a serving corporal has had a direct Commission from Imp. Yeo. so I am having another try for you.

★★★

Hospital notes from the siege of Ladysmith show how starvation and disease were more effective than Boer guns at cutting down the garrison: 10,500 admissions from a garrison of 13,500. There were three field hospitals in the town but most typhoid victims were despatched to Intombi Camp in no man's land. Built for 300, the camp was nursing 2000 by January 1900 and losing 10 to 20 men per day. As food ran out the cavalry horses were slaughtered and eaten. The besieging Boers polluted the garrison's water supply with animal carcasses, thus multiplying dysentery.

At Bloemfontein British forces brought typhoid with them, having picked it up by drinking untreated water. Within a month of taking the town in March 1900, 1000 men had died of fever. In the whole war, of 21,000 British dead, only 8000 died of wounds caused in battle.

Allan now announces the death of Rayner, and describes the loss at Lindley of most of the 46th Company. There is a monument to the Yeomanry who died there, on 31 May 1900, on what became Yeomanry Hills.

21/6/00
Winburg
Orange River Colony

Dear Col. Hutchins,

I send you just one line to say your son, Allan, is seedy, but I am happy that he is getting on alrightly – I was off on detachment for 9 days and he was one of my party and on the 3rd day he complained of feeling unwell, so I struck him off duty and sent him to Vet River where our doctor was quartered and he sent him to Bloemfontein where he is in hospital with a mild attack of enteric fever. Poor Elwell is also there and Pritchard-Rayner, but we have heard they are all doing well, so I expect they will all shortly be invalided home and you may expect to see your son before very long.

We had a very trying time for the last two weeks as we had a force of 800 or 900 Boers around us and my command consisted of 70 Yeomanry and although the enemy attacked Land River 20 miles from us, they didn't tackle us, but our patrolling work was very heavy as we had to be out night and day. We are now moved here and there is a force of 7000 Boers in the district.

Yours sincerely,
R. W. W-Wynn

★★★

Volks Hospital,
Bloemfontein
25th June 1900

Dearest Folks,

I am writing this to you from hospital, having had a touch of enteric; but am all right now. I am getting up tomorrow. I had been feeling very dicky most of the last march we had but kept pegging away in the hope I should get better. The most distressing symptom was that I tired so awfully quickly that I found it very difficult to get through my work and I had no appetite. Charlie was ill too, and under the doctor all the while, but I didn't want to go sick. (By the way, I don't know what Charlie has told his people, so don't mention it unless you hear from them first). Jim looked after Charlie till we had been at Wet River two or three days, when he was ordered off on a patrol. I then took up his duties till I, a day or two later, was ordered off on patrol also, to Smaldeel, where I wrote you last from. By this time Charlie was almost quite right again.

At Smalldeel, we had a lot of night work to do and after a couple of days of it, two or three of the fellows persuaded me to go sick. I reported myself to Kirkby who was in charge, and he sent me off to Vet River by the first train to see the doctor. I rode on top of a load of sleepers. Its not far. When I got to Vet River, I found they had just shifted camp up to a kopje about a mile off. There was a wagon still left on the old camp ground (which is close to the railway) and the doctor, who put me on the wagon and started me off for the new camp. When we got about half a mile I saw them carrying someone on a stretcher from the old camp to the railway (there is no station you can call as such) I asked who it was and they said 'Elwell'. I hopped down and raced back and found it was Charlie right enough, but not so bad as it looked. He had had a relapse, and was going to wait in a shed, along with Rayner (who has also got it) for an ambulance train to take them down the line.

I stayed with him some time, and then the doctor packed me off to camp on a bullock wagon which was handy. Next morning was all alarms and rumours and standing to arms and the doctor sought me out about 10 o'clock (he and the orderlies had been sublimely unconscious of my existence till then) and told me to start off to walk back to the station. All the kit I could take was my cloak and one blanket. Where the rest is now, heaven only knows, but I've got some fresh clothes here so shan't be inconvenienced as regards that.

I pegged off to the station accordingly (about 1½ miles) and got there all right. There was an ambulance train waiting there, going up, a brand new train but as communication had been interrupted by the Boers up Kroonstadt way, instead of going on, it picked up me, Charlie and Rayner, and about a dozen others belonging to other regiments, and took us back to Bloemfontein. It was comfortable on board the train, and they were good to us. Every man was given a bag containing a suit of pyjamas, a pair of shoes, sponge bag, sponge, soap, toothbrush, and hairbrush and towel. I was rather bad that night. I don't know about the others as I haven't seen either of them since I got into the train. I only know they are with me.

When we got here, we were taken out on stretchers and by the greatest luck in the world, the three of us, and about half a dozen others, were sent up to a private hospital, a real hospital with proper wards, nurses, beds etc. When you think what all the chances were, we went to a military hospital to live in marquees, our luck is simply tremendous. I've only been in about 10 days, and I'm getting up tomorrow. The name of the hospital is Volks Hospital, Bloemfontein. It's Dutch, as you see, but nearly all the nurses, etc., are English. I have a dear old doctor, a Frenchman, one of the leading practitioners of the place.

The treatment I got when I first arrived was strict instructions to lie quiet and was fed on slops, a cupful of milk, beef tea, coffee, arrowroot, soup, etc., every two hours or so. This goes on till your temperature comes down to normal when, after three or four days, they begin to give you light grub. At present my grub consists of maigera [a sort of thick arrowroot], tea, and bread and butter for breakfast, good unstrained soup, rice and mince, and custard pudding for dinner, and for tea the same as breakfast. I get lots of slops in between as well. In three or four days I hope to get on full diet, when you do well. Charlie is not quite so forward as me, they tell me, (he is in another ward and I don't see him, but the nurses are very good and keep us informed about each other) although his temperature wasn't as high as mine was. When I get convalescent, I don't know what they will do with me. They may very likely send me to the Cape, or some other place to convalesce. The Regiment is at Winburg and I don't expect get their mails very regular.

The best thing will be for you to write to me c/o Ernest Beck, Esq., Box 188, The Post Office, Port Elizabeth, whom I will keep informed of my address. I can't get any money till I rejoin the Reg't. so wish George would send me a P.O.A. A parcel would also be very acceptable and I venture to suggest the contents, seeing how often you've asked me what I want. Some plain chocolate, a small box of cigarettes, a little tobacco, some home-made toffee, and fill up with some of Toosie's nice cakes. You might, also, please, put in an indelible pencil or two if you please. Now, there is a large order for you. Send it all to Mr. Beck and I expect it will reach me all right.

My programme for the future is uncertain. I am determined to be home in the Spring to see Kitty. If the war lasts long, getting on to Christmas, I should come home with the Company. If on the other hand, it finishes in the course of a month or so, I think I shall wing my flight to Johannesburg, where I have sanguine hopes of being able to earn enough to bring me home and send me out again. I shall require a little money for a start though, I am afraid, if you people can scratch it up. The fare from the Cape to Johannesburg is about £7, I understand. Living there costs about £8 a month, board and lodging. I hope I can do it cheaper by going into diggings. The above is boarding house rates. What pay I should get I don't know. At the worst, I think I could get about £25 a month as assistant in a store, if I couldn't get a respectable job at once. (Which reminds me, please send my instruments to the Yeomanry Stores, Cape Town, to be left till called for). So you see, dear people, I probably shan't starve in Johannesburg. If you can scrape some money together, please put it down to me in the Standard Bank of Africa, Cape Town. Kitty has promised me £5.

Jim is the only man of our subsection left sound. Little Atkinson got enteric soon after we got here, and then Charlie succumbed and then me. Hutton (the officer of the Gun Section) and Bates (the Vet) got it some time ago. 3 others have also got it. Most of these are somewhere round Bloemfontein but I don't expect many had the luck we did.

And now to turn to pleasant subjects. How are all you dear old things at home? I wish I were there with you all. I tell you, for one thing, I begin to yearn for the fleshpots of Egypt. When I think of lamb and mint sauce, green peas, new potatoes, gooseberry tart, etc., I fairly curl up. By Jove it is a time since I've had a decent meal. Never mind. I shall be there some day and shan't I expect you to fatten me up! You hurry up with that pencil. My mouth is watering.

I suppose you have cut the hay by this time, and are beginning to find mushrooms in the field.

★★★

Friday 29th.

I am up now and on full diet, and have walked into Bloemfontein (about ¾ mile) yesterday and today. I don't know what will become of me shortly. I may be sent down to the Cape and invalided home. If I had been worse I probably should be, but since I've pulled round so quickly can't say. I have seen Charlie several times, every day in fact; he gets up and sits in the sun now, but isn't nearly so well as I am, although his temperature was never as high as mine; but he says he didn't have enteric at all and that it was diphtheria, but he must be making a mistake over the last as he never had any of the symptoms of diphtheria. I must ask his nurse about it. She is a nipper and looks after him very well. His ward has ever so much a better time than ours, which is a very big one and I must say is rather neglected. It is left too much to a great stupid Dutch orderly but we get by. (I refer to myself and a Royal Engineer who has been in the next bed to me, and has recovered step by step along with me. He came in same day as me (15th) and got up same day and changed his diet all along same as me).

Rayner is pretty bad. He has a complication (pleurisy) and has been having a pretty thin time. I was sent to sit with him yesterday but he would insist that I shouldn't be made a martyr of so strongly that I had to leave him as he has to be kept quiet. Poor old buffer. He asked me the date and when I told him the 28th, it turns out it was his 28th birthday.

Best love all round from
Your affectionate,
Allan

★★★

5th July 1900
Volks Hospital,
Bloemfontein

Dearest Podgie,

You have been the most faithful of my correspondents I think, and it is about time you had a letter from the field of war, so to speak. There are one or two items of news since last week. In the first place, poor old Rayner died here on the 1st of this month. He had enteric, pleurisy and pneumonia. It was the latter that did it. I used to go and sit with him until two days before he died. Bobby Wynne came down the day before and came to see me and Charlie also. One of the last things old Rayner did was to ask after Charlie and me. Charlie went in to sit with him on the second day he (Charlie) got up and overdid it and in consequence is back in bed and on liquid diet again. Fortunately, he is coming round much quicker than expected. I hope he will hurry up as I want to get down to the Cape and (with luck) home. I am getting as strong as anything again, but what worries me is, that although they tell you to grub up and get strong again, they don't give us half enough grub now we are convalescent. For breakfast we get tea, a small go of porridge, and either bread and butter or bread and jam. On one occasion they omitted both the butter and the jam and we had what is known as bread and bread. Well personally speaking, I don't find bread and butter at all satisfying, especially with the enormous appetite one develops after a liquid diet. Dinner would be all right provided there was more of it, but it is brought up, your allowance, on a plate, and there are no second helps. A fair sized slice of meat, a little potato and cabbage (as a rule) and some rice, is the allowance, with a small go of soup one day and a small go of pudding the next. Tea is tea and either bread and butter or bread and jam. To make matters worse, the orderlies who feed with us, are given chops, sausages, stewed chicken, etc at tea and breakfast. In consequence, I have spent my last cent in going down to Bloemfontein and getting grub. But I have now been to the matron and arranged that I am to have the same grub as the orderlies and pay for it. I don't know how much yet, but I expect I shall have to have assistance from the poor bank, since at present I am penniless, though expecting a pay soon (about 30/-), and everything is awfully expensive in Bloemfontein.

If you haven't despatched the things I asked for in my last by the time you get this you ought to be smacked, since every day is an object. For one thing, I may be on the boat for home when they arrive, so please don't delay. As to the money for the bank, if I come home I shan't want it but I may want some to pay my bill here.

By Jove they do stick it on in Bloemfontein. Eggs 3/- a dozen, butter 2/6 a lb., bread 6d. a small loaf, tea 6d. a cup, English biscuits about 2/- a lb., English tobacco 9d. an ounce, matches (those small boxes of safety matches; you never see any others) 6d. a dozen. Everything just about double home or Cape Town prices. In the country on the march I've given as much as 2/- for a decent sized loaf of bread, and the country stores are the devil. They will charge you a penny a piece for biscuits. But eggs and milk you can get cheap from the Kaffir kraals As a rule, I avoid washing my things myself, since a kaffir does it very cheaply.

I was awfully glad to get your letters. The worst of it is, they all have to go up to Winburg, where the company is now, before they can be sent to me but, of course, now they will go to M. Beck as we arranged in my last letter.

No, dear Podgie, I am nowhere near Johannesburg, nor likely to be, until I come out, as I hope to do, next year. The cholera belt did not turn up with the letter but the day before yesterday I saw about five of our mailbags going from here to Winburg so I am hoping for something shortly. [A cholera belt is a flannel or silk girdle or cummerbund worn to protect against cholera, orginating with the British Army in India. The idea was that chills on the abdomen made one susceptible to the disease, as well as dysentery, diarrhoea and other gastrointestinal ailments.]

I congratulate you most heartily on your job, especially as you get such a screw. It's a fine thing and ought to suit you well.

I want to write a lot of letters by this mail. I have tomorrow and Saturday morning so I must write hard, if I can cadge some note paper. A nurse gave me this, but I don't like to ask her for more as I don't know whether it was her own property or the hospital's.

I saw a fellow I knew the other day working at the mailbags. He was an Irishman, one of the 45th who came across with us. He and about half a dozen others had for different causes been left behind, and the other day the whole of their company was shot or taken prisoner at Lindley, so those 6 are the only survivors at present.

I have lost my belt with my two knives, knife, fork and spoon, etc. They took it off in the ambulance train but I can't learn that anybody has seen it up here. It's very annoying. The solitary remaining quid had been taken out in time, however, and is now safely spent.

No more paper but much love to all,
Allan

8th July 1900

Sir,

I beg respectfully to apply for an extension of sick furlough, and enclose a doctor's certificate to that effect.

My present furlough is for a period of one month and expires on 22nd inst. I have received £4 advance furlough money.

I should be obliged for a further advance if you can kindly grant my application since my health will not allow me to undertake duty at present.

Allan M. Hutchins

★★★

Volks Hospital,
Bloemfontein
Thursday July 12th 1900

Dear People,

Still here and blooming, and Charlie up again I'm glad to say. Unfortunately, am short of cash. Any members of our regiment who come down, as two or three have done on duty and business, tell us that everything is arranged and that my kit and both our pays and a lot of luxuries that have been sent out, and our mails, etc. are all going to be sent us very shortly. We wait and wait but nothing except an occasional letter ever comes. I have received the cholera belt and many thanks therefore. I have managed to get hold of a few letters much delayed that had gone astray. I managed to dig them out after much enquiry at several places.

There is practically no news this last week. It has been very nice and warm in the daytime: wonderful weather for the time of year.

I am hoping for some more letters shortly. Write up, dear people, and even if there isn't much news, don't let that deter you.

I can't get on at all at writing this morning as life here does not give one much to talk about and Charlie is sitting next to me and people conversing all round so I will abandon the attempt for the present.

★★★

Volks Hospital
Bloemfontein

Dear Maude and Doy,

At last I write a letter to you and the only excuse in the long delay is that until now I have written no letters except to home which same I tried to do every mail but it didn't come off by a long way. Now being laid up here, a strong and healthy convalescent, after a slight touch of enteric, I am working off arrears of correspondence. As this is my first letter to you, I think I should give you a slight sketch of my doings since I left England. Don't expect anything exciting as we have never been near the front and never seen a Boer unless he was some poor devil that had gone astray and ran away like the devil when he saw us a couple of miles off.

We had a perfect voyage out. After convalescing here a while, how long I can't say but wish I could, we shall in all probability be sent down to the Cape and then awa' for home. I think I shall then have a bit of a holiday, part of which I hope you will have me to spend with you, and then return to the office 'til the following summer so that I shall see Kitty in the spring. Then I hope to come out again for, though I am far from prepossessed by S. A. as a country, I think that there is a bit of cash to be made in Johannesburg and I like cash, you know. Bloemfontein is expensive at present. It consists of hospitals principally; that is to say, improvised or temporary hospitals. This is the only permanent one and also the only non-military one although the government keeps it going and sends lots of soldiers here. What I meant was the doctors, nurses, etc., are civilian.

How are you both and the bouncing boy? Tell him how his Uncle Allan has slain many a Boer and marched from Bloemfontein to Pretoria dripping blood from every step. I hope to see you all soon and then can tell you more as the sword comes handier to me than the pen.

Yours affectionately,
Allan

★★★

With his father canvassing for his son's promotion, Allan is recommended for a line commission. However, and only three months after arriving in South Africa, in July 1900 he is evacuated by troopship. In September the Yeomanry surgeon examines Allan at home in Welshpool and finds him 'somewhat feeble'. In November 1900 and with only three months of his engagement to run, he is discharged at his own request. George is unhappy with his son's decision but Allan immediately enlists as a Second Lieutenant in the 5th V.B. South Wales Borderers.

From Captain Robert Williams-Wynn
49th Company (9th Battn.)
Imp. Yeomanry

To Lt Col GA Hutchins
Clive House
Welshpool
1st August 1900

Dear Colonel Hutchins,

I am just off on 3 or 4 days patrol but the Colonel has promised to forward your son's application for a commission. I hope he will get it – he has worked very well out here and his going down to hospital has been a loss to us in every way – I heard from him a few days ago and expect the next thing will be that he has started for home. We have had plenty of work round here chasing the Free State Kommando under De Wet and preventing them breaking out again. So far we have not let them thro' on this side, etc.

Yours sincerely,
R. W. Wms. Wynn

★★★

18th September 1900
Welshpool

I hereby certify that I have examined Lce. Corpl. A. M. Hutchins of 49th Co. Imp. Yeomanry and find he is in a somewhat feeble state of health, following an attack of Enteric Fever and in my opinion is not fit to resume his duties at present.

(signed) Francis E. Marston
Surgeon
Mon. C. Yeo. Cavalry

★★★

Welshpool
26th 1900

Dear Captain Wynn,

Could you kindly tell me if my son was recommended for a direct commission by the C.O. 9th Battalion?

Yours sincerely,
G. A. Hutchins

★★★

From Captain Robert Williams-Wynn
49th Company (9th Battn.)
Imp. Yeomanry

To Lt Col G A Hutchins,
Clive House,
Welshpool
Rustenberg
October 29th 1901

Yes — Your son was recommended by C.O. and by self.

Yrs
R. W. Wms. Wynn

★★★

23 Sherriff Road,
West Hampstead, N. W.
Wednesday

Dear George,

I'm sorry you took on so about me taking my discharge. Why didn't you tell me distinctly that I wasn't to if you didn't want me to? If I'd thought you would have cut up so about it, I would have stopped in that damned pigsty till Judgement day but as it was, after thinking it out, I thought I was doing the best thing.

Are you sure you must be in the Army before you can get the outfit allowance? It seems contrary to common sense, and besides, for the matter of that, I *was,* at the time of application, and my discharge doesn't take effect till the 29th. If they haven't settled the business by then, they never will.

I return your form herewith. I have signed it, under protest, because you asked me to, but remember I strongly dislike having a commission in the battn. and shan't do any drills or go into camp with them, nor get any uniform. You can do what you like with the form, but I hope you won't send it in. I can't see what good it will do at all.

Thank you very much, old chap, for sending up my things so promptly. It was very good of you to take so much trouble, but don't bother to send anything more by post, they come just as well by train. Perhaps you won't mind sending on the rest when they come. I believe there ought to be more handkerchiefs, a collar or two, and one or more white shirts. Of the things that you didn't send, the blue suit is the one that I can do best without.

I and Maude [Doy's wife] had a bob'sworth at the Hippodrome the day before where we saw 'Siberia'. This afternoon we went to the Lyric [gallery] and saw Floradora. Simply ripping! Florence St. John, Ada Reeve, Willy Edwin, Sydney Barraclough, etc. Ada Reeve was splendid. I'm going to Terry's on Friday (stalls again) and to a friend of Johnny's tomorrow night (very nice fellow). C.J.V. on Saturday. You see, I'm doing very well.

Now, dear old man, good-bye. I'm sorry to have upset you. Come up soon with Toosie and thanks very much for all the trouble you've taken.

Best love to you and all of them from
Your erring son,
Allan

★★★

A Commission

Imperial Yeomanry
16 Great George Street
Westminster SW
9 February 1901

2nd Lieut AM Hutchins
5th VB S. Wales Borderers
Clive House
Welshpool

Sir,

I have the honour to inform you that your appointment to the Imperial Yeomanry as a Second Lieutnant has been samctioned by the Secretary of State for War and will appear in an early Gazette.

You should report yourself without delay to the Officer Commanding the Imperial Yeomanry at Aldershot on Thursday next the 14th instant showing him this letter.

★★★

Clive House
Welshpool
February 10th 1901
To Col. E Pryce-Jones MP

My Dear Colonel,

I see by the papers that the WO are sending out 10,000 Yeomanry instead of 5,000 as in first orders. Do you think it would be any use asking the DAAG Imp. Yeo. again about a commission for my son, Allan, in the Imp. Yeo.? We have heard nothing of his application which you were kind enough to recommend and hand in the last week in January and I see by the papers that Mr Marshall Dugdale's son – 2nd Lieut. in the Mont. Yeomanry of last year – has already had his commission and been ordered to Aldershot. He is so keen on going and I should like him to have a little show after his bad luck last time in getting enteric just as the fun was beginning.

Yours sincerely,
G A Hutchins

★★★

Officers were expected to acquire and pay for their uniform and kit. Allan later wrote that his was 'an object of admiration and encomium from all beholders' and showed more restraint than some, as this order from Kitchener shows:

> The C-in-C South Africa desires to impress on officers in command of mobile columns that the object of such columns is mobility; that he has learned that such forces carried about with them furniture, kitchen ranges, pianos and harmoniums which nullify that object; these articles must be handed over to the nearest stores.

Col. Doran, under whom Allan was to serve, was much criticised for compromising mobility with a mass of equipment and wagons. As Allan says, he was 'too slow to catch worms'.

20 February 1901
Clive House,
Welshpool

Dearest George and family,

I live here safe and sound at 112 Victoria Road, as per invoice, and hope you are all the same.

This is chiefly a business letter, so let's get to work. Firstly, will you please send me some corks (otherwise rhino) as funds is getting low again. The chief items they've gone on are cabs (2/- + 2/6), fares (9/- + 3/-), buses (innumerable), rails (2/- + 2/-), tips (legion), and D'Oy and I and Johnnie went to the Pavilion last night (5/-). Now, as to yesterday's doings. The first thing was that George Evans had spoilt my serge again by putting a fearful collar on it all skew-whiff, so my first proceeding on leaving Doys was to get to his (Doys) tailor and get him to put it right. From there to the Stores. Went round and round it and thought it very expensive. I enquired the price of all the things I wanted and put 'em down. By the time I'd finished it was about one or half past, and I went down to Lawn & Alders and compared the prices. By the time this was over, it was about half past three and I was beginning to get hungry, so I went to a modest looking restaurant and got stuck half-a-dollar for a not very good lunch. However I had a rest, a smoke and a good think which was much needed. The Army and Navy seemed so dear and George had so shaken my confidence in Lawn & Alders, and was so keen on the A&N himself, that I couldn't decide what to do for some time. However, at last I determined to go to the A&N and order there the things that had to be chosen and left the others to George's discretion. Full particulars enclosed.

Firstly, I had to get there. It was getting on and the Stores close at 6; a thick fog pervaded the streets and so I had to call a swift cab into requisition and landed about 4.30. The first thing I ordered was my breeches, which work out to £2. 13. 0. This bill is separate from the others, for some reason. I arranged to be fitted on Saturday but whether I can go or not I dunno yet.

The field cap the brutes rushed me 9/6 for and as I was bound to have it then, I had to grin and bear it. It and the breeches are considered as paid for, so they only gave me the duplicate bills.

Another separate thing is shooting boots, which I had to get from the Auxiliary, which is separate. You will have to send them a cheque direct before they will send the boots to me. The price was 25/- but I see from the bill they charged me 2/6 for half doz pairs of laces I ordered and -/6 for postage. I then bought the following to await address and come together; sweater 6/9, 3 cholera belts @ 1/4, 6 towels @ 1/6 ½, 3 neckerchiefs @ /3, 3 prs socks @ 1/1 ½, flannel bags 14/-, puttees 5/-, notebook 5/2.

The rest remains for you. I append comparative prices. The devils said that they would make me a pair of brown gauntlets for 19/6 but, unless you can get them cheaper than that somewhere, I won't have 'em as they are nowise necessary.

Yours,
Allan

★★★

Allan landed once more in South Africa on 10 April 1901. Meanwhile, Roberts had returned to England at the end of 1900 to an earldom and a generous pension, proclaiming the war 'practically over', and handing command to Kitchener. It was a poisoned chalice. The Boer cities had fallen and the last big battle, at Dalmarutha, had gone to Buller and yet, galvanised by Botha, the Boers now pursued a relentless guerrilla war on the veldt, cutting communications and railway lines and harrying the British forces.

One particular problem Roberts had faced and Kitchener inherited was what to do with surrendering Boers and their families. Returning them to their farms had failed – too many took up arms once more – so instead, Roberts created three camps where they and their families might be safely concentrated. Kitchener now created another 43 camps, near railway lines, and there detained not only the 'hands uppers' who had surrendered, but families of kommandos still in the field. At the same time, in an attempt to flush the enemy, Kitchener gave orders 'to denude the country of forage and supplies' and lay waste anything and everything that might help the enemy. If the kommandos could no longer gain food and shelter from families on the veldt, voluntarily or by force, then the guerrilla war would collapse.

It was a response that would come to haunt the British. To the Boers at least, and to the Germans and French, it was now a war of extermination. Without proper medical care or sanitation the concentration camps became death camps for thousands of white women and children – 28,000 all told. Africans too, witnessed the destruction of their homes and animals, crops and possessions and with nowhere to go, they also were delivered to British camps. Allan was to experience first hand what 'scorched earth' looked and smelled like; by the end of the war more than 30,000 farms had been destroyed.

The Feather Market,
Port Elizabeth
13/4/01

Dear People,

We were ordered round here from Capetown and, arriving yesterday, have just disembarked. The place we are in is a big hall where all the good ladies of the place are filling us full of sandwiches and pineapples in the most kind way.

We are going to Springfontein this afternoon some time. I don't know what to do exactly about letters but I think William Watson & Co. ought to be about the mark. I shall communicate with them; I think that's the best. I am very well and hope that everybody at home is the same. I wish that I could hear from you shortly, but I'm afraid it will be some little time before I do.

I was orderly officer today and I tell you I've had to sweat since 4.30 this morn. We're taking all our baggage up to Springfontein with us.

The carbine met with great admiration from everybody. I did a good deal of shooting on board ship and was much pleased with the weapon.

Give my best love to all our friends and acquaintances and remember me kindly all round.

Goodbye all, and best love
From yours affectionately,
Allan

★★★

With every Boer town in British hands and Kruger in exile, Jan Smuts, who at 31 was
already an experienced State Attorney in Kruger's republic, rejected a negotiated peace
and urged the Boers to fight on – taking the war to the British by invading Cape Colony
and the Orange Free State. In this new and brutal phase Smuts the lawyer became a
determined and charismatic military strategist and rebel leader who, with Gideon Scheepers,
Kritzinger, Fouche and Malan – and with huge self-belief – sought to incite an unstoppable
insurrection in British-held territory. Smuts himself led a kommando of 340 men into the
Cape.

The 5th Lancers intercepted Kritzinger's Kommando at the Naauwpoort/Dettar railway
line near Hanover. In daylight and through a storm of bullets from the blockhouses,
Kritzinger's men – who had vowed to follow him 'to heaven or hell' – stormed the railway
line in advance of an armoured train. Cronje believed the British would never leave the
railway and focused much attention on cutting the lines of communication.

In June 1901 Kitchener gave General J.D.P. French supreme command for combating
guerrilla warfare in the Cape and French responded by building lines of fortified, defensible
blockhouses, of the type Roberts had built to protect the lines of communication and
especially the railways. More than 8000 were built, with 50,000 men protecting them, in a
line stretching to Wellington in the Western Cape. Nevertheless, 'The country is entirely in
their hands.'

Elandsfontein.
Sunday afternoon, 21/4/01

Dearest old folks,

We are here now, after having been in the train until yesterday morning when we got
out here. We had a very uneventful journey up, although the country from Cradock
up simply stinks of Boers. I never understood it at home, how the war was lasting so
long, but now I begin to see. The country is entirely in their hands. We simply hold
the railway which gives us all we can do, since every stretch of, say, 20 miles has a blow
up about twice a week on an average. Of course there are posts with entrenchments
and blockhouses all the way up, at the sidings and bridges, but they can't do anything.
Generally, by going five miles from one of them into the veldt, you are in the middle of
the Boers. No drivers will run a train after sunset. Of course there are no very big kommandos left, though we passed within 15 miles of about 3 or 4 of about 400 and over.
The war may last two or three years yet.

This place is the Yeomanry depot up here. It is only about 10 miles from Johannesburg,
and is the junction for that place. Some of the drafts are being split up and some kept
here. What's to be done with us, I don't know, but expect to be split up in a day or so. I
will let you know as soon as I hear anything definite. I've already been degraded to the
rank of 2nd Lt. So has everybody.

You might find out from Cox whether they will collect the Colonial allowance for
me, will you please?

Bobby Wynne is on Chesham's staff at Johannesburg and I hope to see him soon. There are several other of the 49th round here, including Poulson (from Leighton) who is all right, and lots of others I know. They have mostly got fat jobs.

I have my tent kit, etc., at present and am doing very well. I have the best kit of anyone here, I believe. Lewis, my man, is very good too. He is very obliging and industrious. The only thing is that he's a bit slow and forgets where he puts things, etc., but I'm lucky to have him. I may go to the Yorkshire battn. but can't say for certain.

I will leave this letter for the present since I've about worked off my news stock. However there will very likely be fresh developments tomorrow, so goodnight till then.

22nd.

My section was all split up today and I was left here, unattached, the men all going to their various companies. I shall very likely be here a week or two, worse luck. The only thing that bothers me is that my servant went too, and I have to break in another to my ikey little ways. Dam' nuisance. I'd quite got to like the silly old fool.

Lord Kitchener inspected us this afternoon and in his staff I espied dear old Bobby, but had no chance of making my presence known to him as they went off immediately after.

I hope as how everybody is well and in good health as it leaves me at present, though a bit worried over settling things up. However it's 'all in the seven' I suppose, and I think I will leave off for the night now.

23rd.

I'm writing this in the post office at Johannesburg, having ridden over to try and see Bobby. He has gone away, however, for a few days. I saw Major Knight who is a staff officer and found out from him that I am to go to the Yorkshires 11th Coy, at Graaff Reinet. Am now going back to Elandsfontein.

Best love all round, dear people.
From yours affectionately
Allan

★★★

'There are strange rumours that Scheepers shoots all the officers he catches, so I'm thinking of resigning my commission at once.'

A town on the Sundays River, Graaff Reinet was garrisoned by the Coldstream Guards. For Allan it was 'the gem of the Karoo', an escape from sandstorms, Boers and extreme cold, a place for a hot bath for 'a bob' at the Drostdy Hotel, a game of tennis and snooker. No major battles were fought here and the Boer invasion of the Cape did not reach this far. Few Boers in the town rushed to join the commandos. The calm was threatened in December 1900 when Kritzinger crossed the Orange River with a Kommando of 400 men (another 300 having gone with other leaders) and occupied Nieuw Bethesda, north of the town. On 20 December 1900 martial law was declared in Graaff-Reinet and by the end of the first week in January there were 2000 troops protecting it. Families were brought in

*from the countryside so that they could not supply the kommandos who continued to move
about more or less at will. British forces eventually left Graaff-Reinet on 15 September 1902,
leaving 'a long legacy of bitterness in the town and district.' (A de V Minnaar (HSRC)). They
also left bullet holes in the bar of the Club, from firing their weapons on hearing the war
was over. The club remains open to serving and former Guards and the bullet holes are now
covered by glass.*

Graaff Reinet
2nd May

Dearest family,

At last, after many weary wanderings, I am appointed to a squadron, namely the 11th,
otherwise known as the Yorkshire Dragoons, and part of the famous 3rd Rgt. of I.Y. It
really seems an awfully good Regt., and the 11th about the best squadron thereof. It is
one of the only 3 first yeomanry regts. who were brigaded as a Yeomanry brigade and
went on trek as such. Hence the officers are exceedingly cavalry, so please address my
letters to 11th Squadron, 3rd Regt., not to 11th Coy., 3rd Battn. Savey?

Now who do you suppose is my C.O? None other than Major Edwards who used to
be Adjt. of the Montgomery. Y.C. There is a coincidence for you. Well, as to how I got
here. When my section was split up, but hold on a bit – I'd better explain that a bit first.

Most of my men, (about 90 of them), were for the Yorkshires, (11th, 9th & 66th),
but on board ship they were all full of great schemes for keeping together in a section
under yours humbly. When we got to E'fontein and the men were asked where they
wanted to go to, they said the same. But, on sending my Colour Sergt. next day to take
the names, I found that about 30 and the N.C.Os wished to stop. I didn't say anything
although it was a bit sudden, but I received a deputation that evening asking whether, if
they stayed together, they could have a new colour sergeant.

Secretly sympathising in my heart with them, I told them to go to 'ell, and next day
all but the men for the 66th were despatched. These were composed not really of men
enlisted for the 66th but of an old and faithful few, who I said had better go there, and
I'd try and do similar.

Then I borrowed a nag and rode over to Jo'burg to try and see Bobby Wynne but
he was not there. I then went to the I.Y.D.A.G. Major Knight, and stated my case. He
was very good and gave me all I wanted, except that, as the 66th were full up, he sent
me here. I found the 11th under Major Edwards in the train at Rosmead Junction and
I came on here with them. They were full up of men, and the first draft from E'fontein
have not yet arrived, being lost on the way somewhere.

So after all our fine efforts, my men were passed over to the 9th Sqdn., (Yorks Hussars),
and I was given a troop under Major Edwards. I'm satisfied very well as this seems quite
a crack lot. We are lying here now, waiting for horses, (ours were left at De Aar).

When we get 'em, we shall probably go on trek after Kritzinger, Hertzog or
Scheepers, all of whom are dodging round this district with kommandos. There are

strange rumours that Scheepers shoots all the officers he catches, so I'm thinking of resigning my commission at once.

This is a very pretty place and very hot for S.A. It is known by the flowery name of the Gem of the Desert, though it is not necessary to put that on your letters to find it. There is a club, hotels, library, Botanical Gardens and 'everything in the garden's lovely'. It would be the devil of a country to fight in since it is so hilly but, of course, it's as bad for our Brother Boer as it is for we.

Some of the hills are 4 & 5 thousand feet above the plain. The actual height of the tallest is 7600 or thereabouts. Of course they are fearfully steep and rocky. There is lots of scrub, cactus, prickly pear and suchlike about. I shall be glad to get on trek again, and expect I shall be 'fore long.

George will be glad to hear that my kit, saddlery etc. is an object of admiration and encomium from all beholders. I flatter myself we laid out our spondulicks well and I can pack everything necessary and a lot of luxuries in sufficient compass to be easily taken on trek. The superfluous I am leaving here, I think, at the Drostdy Hotel.

There are 5 officers in the squadron. Major Edwards, Hamilton (an Irishman, who has been out all along), Chichester, (a C.I.V. who has come out again), Cockell (an ex sharpshooter, who has also been out all along), and me. The men are principally the new lot, but the first of them, and have already been on trek and seen fighting. No more at present; too dark.

Saturday

The mail goes today so I am finishing this. There's not much fresh, except that the first draft from my section arrived last night, having been down to Worcester and back round again through De Aar.

I've also got a tent lately. Hitherto I've been living in what we call a caboosh, which means a sort of dog kennel contrived of blankets, waterproof sheets, corrugated iron, old oatsacks, or anything else that comes handy, and just holds one. I have also acquired a pony, and hope to get one or two more shortly.

I now have two servants, a body and a groom, and am a bit of a toff. They are both good fellows, especially Coates, my first servant, a big Yorkshireman, with an accent you could cut with a knife. He is half a horse-coper and half a hawker. He was a corporal but chucked up his stripes to stop with me. A grand chap. The other fellow has been in service as a groom since he was a boy.

Best love all round,
Allan

★★★

Graaff Reinet
17th May 1901

Dearest People,

Still here, but we got a lot of horses yesterday and I hope we shall soon be on the trek again. I managed to snaffle one of these horses and think he will make a good 'un. I have now two: one, an old grey pony about 15 hands, (country horse), an awfully good nag, rather thin. He can gallop like smoke, and turn round on a threepenny bit, and is as knowing as a Christian. The other is the one I got today. He is a slashing big bay, with white points and big head and feet. He is awfully poor and thin and in a filthy state but I think he'll soon come right. He is nearly 17 hands, I should say, an awfully big horse for this country. Very comfortable to ride and well broken, or seems to be.

We have a pretty good time here, if a bit slow. The worst is the sandstorms of which we have already had two, each lasting a day and a night. The whole of that 24 hours is a nightmare of stinging red sand which penetrates everywhere, even unto the cockles of your heart. No tent is proof against it and it spreads itself gently in a thick layer over everything, including your hair, clothes, eyelashes and person generally. Sunday was the last and about 10 a.m. I saddled me mine ass and fled on the wings of the wind to the town and hid myself in the hotel until nightfall, when the winds abated and gentle rains fell. I then returned to my tent and, burrowing under a young sand bank, I unearthed my flea bag and speedily fell asleep.

A learned man has given this definition of a subaltern of the 3rd Regt. I.Y: 'A species of wild ass which dwelleth in the desert and exists chiefly on sand'. A true word. We don't do many duties here except a chain of small pickets at night along a spur of a hill hereby. I've done it four times already but that's about the record. You can ride in for dinner, so it's not a very great hardship.

I've had three or four letters from you, and was glad to get them. The funny part is that one I received yesterday was posted the day after I sailed. I've also had Kitty's and suppose she will be home by the time you get this. If so, here's to her and I will come out to Mexico to see her some time, if necessary. In the meantime, the best of luck to the old bird and her young man, and the blessing of a pore soldier 'by Afric's sunny fountains'. I don't know who wrote these beautiful words but I think it must have been the Bible, because nobody else would have called a mud hole a sunny fountain; I suppose it's another of those miracles or parabolas, or whatever they are called. Anyway I expect I'm as near the mark as 'sunny fountains'. Wot oh, Chummy! I'm writing this in bed and am somewhat constrained. This is my last chance this week since the mail closes 8.30 tomorrow morn. I would have written this afternoon but I went down town and speculated a bob in a hot bath at the hotel.

I hope the family and all hangers on thereto are in good health. Personally I am going very strong and send everyone my very bestest love. I'll try and manage a bit of a budget next mail.

Best love once more from
Allan.

Remember I'm only a lieutenant now, please.

★★★

24th May

I'm writing this on Spur Redoubt Picket about 9 p.m. and very sleepy. Yesterday I turned out at 6.15 a.m. for early stables and at 8.45 went on reconnaissance until 2.30 p.m. without a dismount. I rode the big bay and he carried me well over damnably rough country. After stables, etc., in the evening, I couldn't sleep a wink for tooth ache. 6.15 next morn & Squadron Orderly Officer. Watered about 9, back about 9.45. Parade about 10. back about 12.45 and groom & feed. Lunch: 2.30p.m., riding class under Sq. Orderly Officer. 4 P.M., water, 5 p.m. night picket. So I've been on the trot pretty well, you see, and shall be glad to get to bed tomorrow night.

This is written in the 'Caboosh', a weird word meaning a shelter composed of a railway waggon, oil sheet and some sticks. Beside me sleeps the worthy Coates, the best Yorkshireman who ever came out of Yorkshire. Dear old Coates! He's just heard from the missus whom he left 'reet poorly' and is sleeping the sleep of the just in consequence. He's an awfully fine looking man and seems awfully fond of me. Just outside is old Paddy, my grey pony, who sticks his head in at times to inquire for bread which I haven't got any. He's a dear old chap and about the fastest horse in the Regt.

The bay has turned out very well although I had to provide him with a pair of fetlock boots as he brushes both feet, but that doesn't matter. I've taken another pony on trial, a little roan mare about 14 hands and never been handled before. I've ridden her twice and think she will come on all right. She's a regular picture as far as looks go, and only a four year old, so she ought to turn out well.

I think I will finish now since my candle is about done and also I have to inspect my sentries about 1.30, which is a two hours' job in the dark. We are having a fine time now breaking horses, etc., and old Teddy Edwards has once or twice complimented me on my troops' proficiency in the various branches. Our brother Boers collared a train about 10 miles from here the day before yesterday and we are going to go look-see tomorrow morning.

★★★

Graaff Reinet
May 30th, 1901

Dearest People,

We've not yet left here although daily expecting to do so. We were ordered off to Kendrew Siding last Sunday but the order was cancelled. We are now supposed to be ready to start any time. Henniker's Column [Colonel Henniker, who on 17 January 1902 at Church Square, Graaff Reinet, read the death sentence to Scheepers] came in the other day and are still here, mostly Bushmen. Some of them spotted my big horse and told my servant that they had left him here some months ago for dead. His rider was shot through the leg and the bullet smote the old nag in the side and practically killed him. It's in him still, but he's worth a good many dead horses yet; he improves every day and everybody says, 'By Jove, that's a fine horse you are riding'. He's a Waler, bred in Melbourne, and has been hunted. It's rather funny to see my groom, who's about 4 feet high, trying to get on to his back. He has to climb up.

I am in very good health, thank you, and couldn't be better. I had a tooth extracted last Saturday, as ever was. Being rather funky, I said I'd have gas. When I came round, the dentist was looking rather limp and done up and the old molar was reposing serenely in its old place, quite unshaken. However, after a few rather trying moments, he had another go and, in course of time, the bottom of one fang came off and the tooth out. '10/ please. Good morning and thank you'. I spat blood and oaths for a few minutes, and then went round to the club and had a couple of brandies and sodas, after which I felt better.

Next day being Whitsunday, I saddled me mine ass and went forth into the veldt and after hunting all day I slew a duiker bok. Likewise one monkey who made faces at me from a tree. I shot him in the throat with a bullet with the top cut off and blew most of his back off, so the skin wasn't worth taking although beautiful stuff. The buck's head I sent to Port Elizabeth to be stuffed and the boys have cured the skin for me. It's rather pretty. The little carbine is very good. I shot a hare from the saddle the other day and cut him neatly in half. The buck was lying down trying to hide and I shot him behind the shoulder. He never got up. I can't shoot at a target with it, though. I was trying at the range the other day and got six misses before I found the elevation. It was 400 yards and the sighting was about 310, but it's fine for sporting, and everyone wants to buy it.

I get on fine with Major Edwards. He's a fine old sportsman, and an awfully good sort. Cockell and I sleep together in one tent, and are very chummy. He's a very good sort, but rather one of the cock sure sort which we chip him about. He takes it very well. Chichester, or Chichy, is a dear, motherly sort of a body with specs. He's our mess president and is really a dear old sort.

Hamilton has gone buying horses long ago and may not come back for months. We have another sub. attached, called Dunlop, who has been out here some years. He is a decent sort but young for his age.

I enclose a photo taken up on a beastly picket we do, called the Spur Redoubt. We were up looking at the ground. Major Edwards on my right and Chichy on my left. The other two fellows belong to the 9th Squadn. (Yorkshire Hussars). You can't see much of me because I was riding a little Basuto pony called Punch, belonging to another fellow in the 9th, a grand little horse. I very nearly bought him as his owner is going home, but refrained. It's a mug's game buying horses when you can get them for nothing. I want another horse but haven't found one yet. I picked out a little roan mare the other day and snaffled her but I think I'll send her back to the lines. She's the picture of a little horse and only 4 years old, but she's not 'wick' enough, as Coates calls it. It means lively.

These mares are funny. The Boers never ride a mare and they seem stupid. She had never been handled before she came up and when I get on her, instead of playing up and bolting like an ordinary horse, she turns stupid and simply won't go out for a walk. We got a lot of beautiful unbroken mares the other day, but they are all the same. A baby could stick on them and they will not go, or else they go sideways towards the other horses. Mine developed a shocking cold the other day so her training is arrested, and I don't know whether I'll keep her or not. I might be able to swap her well as she is a perfect little thing to look at.

No more tonight as it's dinner time.

31st.

Another foul sand storm again today, so bad that we couldn't parade. It has just moderated somewhat, (4.30 p.m.), after lasting since about 12 o'clock last night. While it lasts you can't wash or shave or do anything but lurk in corners and gasp. We have a room now for our mess, which is a great thing. We have quite a decent mess, which costs us about £6 or £7 a month and £5 entrance. We live very comfortably. I'm afraid to go back to my tent as 1 know it will be one thick layer of rich brown dust over everything.

Yours affectionately,
Allan

With Doran's Flying Column

As a Lieutenant with 11th Squadron Allan was appointed to the flying column led by Lt. Colonel Doran of the Royal Irish, in pursuit of Boer kommandos in Cape Colony, south of Orange River. Here, Allan came into daily contact with the Boers. In August 1901 he was appointed temporary transport officer of the Column. Severely wounded in an engagement at Rheboksfontein he nonetheless was first into the enemy's camp with the detachment that came within a whisker of capturing Gideon Scheepers, Kritzinger's second-in-command. Scheepers was 16 when, in 1895, he joined the Transvaal State Artillery as a heliographer in the Veldt Telegraph. At 20 he was promoted to sergeant and at 23 he was in command of 150 men. In the face of rising absenteeism, Scheepers was an inspirational recruiter for the Boer cause.

In October 1901 Scheepers fell ill and separated from his kommando, was captured by British forces and detained at Graaff-Reinet. Charged with war crimes under martial law, (it was claimed he thrashed a pregnant black girl until she gave birth), he was sentenced to death and executed in 1902. Arthur Conan Doyle (in his Great Boer War) regretted his execution but said, seemingly without irony, 'our word was pledged to protect the natives, and if he whose hand had been so heavy upon them escaped, all confidence would have been lost in our promises and our justice.'

Aberdeen,
June 12, 1901

Dearest People,

We are now on trek once more. We are on a column commanded by Lt. Colonel Doran of the Royal Irish which consists of us, (11th Squadn.), Warren's Mounted Infantry, two guns of the R.H.A. and fifty of the Cape Colony Cyclist Corps. About 400 in all. Doran has this district to operate in. It is a fairly large one, with some most damnable mountains and rocks and plenty of Boers. The worthy Scheepers has the largest kommando, and Malan and one or two others have parties knocking about. They have a most sporting time since when they've had enough scrapping, they retire to these mountains and you can't worry them much there.

We left Graaff Reinet about 10 o'clock on Monday, the 3rd, with the guns and cyclists and got here on Tuesday night, where Warren joined us. His is a pretty new corps but formed almost entirely from 'time expireds' of other Colonial Corps, like Kitcheners, Brabants, Roberts, etc. They are pretty hot stuff and old Warren is a terror. He's a great big fat white-haired old chap with a red face; horribly vulgar, but simply revels in a scrap. He fairly beams when the ping pong begins. Doran has seen a lot of service, has a fine chest of medals and is a brevet but, so far, he seems too slow to catch worms.

We rested here on Wednesday and on Thursday went out north to a big valley between high hills where about 200 Boers had been having a fine time. They were there in force but we got there to find them gone. They went west, leading their horses over a pass in the mountains where you'd think a goat couldn't go. Well, we couldn't go over, so we went back to Aberdeen and trekked at 7 a.m. next morning round the mountains after them. They were reported at a place called Oorlogspoort, so on we went, Friday and Saturday. Saturday afternoon we saw several small parties afar off and at last spotted Mr Scheepers, near a farm, about 4 o'clock. They bunked off promptly and took up a fine position on a kopje in the mouth of a pass with high hills behind him and on his flanks. We left the convoy at the farm and went out to see him. I was escort to the guns. We advanced as far as a big donga about 3000 yards from his position and you couldn't see a Boer with a telescope. I just spotted one with my glasses and someone else saw one, too. We dropped a few shells on the kopje without drawing him at all and a couple of squadron of Warrens advanced and dismounted. They went up to about 500 yards without a shot being fired and then, all of a sudden, ping ping all over the kopje. General advance then and Cockell, who was doing left flankers, managed to get in with the others. Chichy and Dunlop were rear guard and didn't get up till the position was taken and I had to stop with the guns. I'd got my troop in the donga and while I was talking to Doran, Major Edwards, the gunner officer and the staff officer and watching the gun practice, old Warren rides up to my fellows and takes them into action and I had to ride in and fetch them out again. The Boers were just about clearing then.

We went back to the farm and camped for the night. Next day the black scouts found they had trekked past us in the night and offed it back to the hills near Aberdeen. Off we went, leaving the convoy to follow the road and sighted them about 2.30 in the afternoon. I and Dunlop were doing left flank and the Majaw was with us. We'd been going over shocking country all day without any water, so when Warrens hooked after them, we lay low and trotted quietly to cut them off from the pass. We'd got about half way when Doran appeared from nowhere in particular in a helluva stew. He'd lost the guns behind somewhere, he didn't know where the convoy was and Warrens were just disappearing in the dim and distant vista of the future in full cry. He wouldn't let us go on for fear of losing us. At last he spotted the convoy from the top of a ridge and sent me and two men back to find the guns and bring them in. I found them all right but we had to go a long way round to come to the convoy as the country was quite impossible for guns. When I'd found them, I offed it to a farm and watered my horse and got some chickens. Then I went on along the bottom of the hills until I came on Warrens at a farm where they were resting after having a warm ten minutes with Mr Scheepers about half an hour before. They'd bagged two and wounded two more, so the Boers had gone into the hills. It was the very farm that we were making for when old Doran stopped us, damn him.

Well, we went back to the convoy and found them camped on a beastly stony rise, with no water within 5 miles. Next morning we trekked early to get water and arrived at a farm with beastly bad water about 9.30. There we outspanned and waited information. We were about 4000 yards from the mountains. Opposite us there were two big kloofs and the Boers fired from the one marked A. in my sketch and some black scouts who went poking their noses in.

Dunlop had his troop out as a sort of picket on a little rise in the mouth of the other kloof, marked B, and, after having some breakfast, I went out to relieve him, telling my troop to follow when they had had their breakfast. Dunlop went in and his troop stopped till mine came out. In the meantime Doran advanced up 'A' kloof, without any result, so he came back again. I couldn't see them in the kloof but, just as they started to come out again, we spotted Boers leading their horses across the head of our kloof right up in the tops of the hills, among dam' great precipices, etc. They came from C and went behind the big ridge D. This is a huge precipice with a flat top, so high that you can only see a man on the top with a pair of strong field glasses. Presently I spotted them appear on the sky line and started potting at the column returning to camp from A. I was right under them so they didn't see me. Presently my troop came out and comes up to me at B. They left them alone, thinking they would come up the kloof but of course I dismounted them behind the kopje. Then I went out on my ridge to try and find some sort of position to fire from at these sweeps. They gave me and old Barton, my sergeant, a pretty hot time for a bit and, when I tried to get my men into position, some brutes at E, another huge hill, completely dominating me, started sniping into us. They were pretty close, (about 1000 yards), so we turned our attention to them and shut 'em up. On this, the D chaps disappeared and presently came out on the head of the kloof again with their horses, evidently to work round to join the few at E. I put some of my chaps to fire volleys at 2000 yards at them and turned them up a watercourse, so they had to go a long way round to get to E. In the meantime, E chaps woke up again and we had to shut 'em up again. There were only about 2 or 3, thank the Lord!

Then shortly, Teddy Edwards sends me the order to withdraw, which I did thankfully. By this time it was after 4 o'clock. We hadn't retired more than about 300 yards when the swines arrived at E and peppered us into camp. If we'd stopped three minutes longer they'd have had us on toast. Of course, when it was too late to do any good, Doran ran out a gun and dropped a few shells on the ridge. You could see them run like hares. They came back next morn and watched us trek into Aberdeen, where we landed yesterday, for what purpose, I know not, unless it's supplies.

13th.

We are off again tomorrow, I hear, so will post this. I think we are going back over the same ground as before.

This place is either the first, or the last, place God made. I should think it's a regular hotbed of disloyalists but they've got the right man for commandant, an old Major Sawyer. He plays the devil with them. At intervals he rings the alarm bell and every civilian who is not a known loyalist, and has a pass as such, has to remain indoors with doors and shutters closed until further orders. In the meantime the others repair to the sangars in the town and fire down the streets to encourage them. Then sometimes he parades the devils and drills them in the correct manner of taking off their hat to him, and saying 'Good morning, Commandant'. When we went out the other day, an old lawyer here, a very influential man, told somebody that the Boers had captured Willowmore, (a little place in this district), and that we had gone to try and recapture it. Old Sawyer promptly ran him and gave him 30 days hard for circulating false reports, paraded all the men in one line, women in another, kids in another, read out the sentence and made 'em all sing, 'God save the King'. They daren't call their souls their own.

I am very well indeed, thank you, and hope that all at home are the same. My great trouble is that I have lost dear old Coates, who had developed into the best servant in the regiment. He went into hospital the morning I left Graaff Reinet. He was ill off and on for a week before, mostly with a violent headache. This came to an awful state the night before we trekked and, during the night, he went clean bang off his head and had five fits. The doctor said epilepsy, though it was nothing like the symptoms of epilepsy you hear about. I thought he simply went off his head from pain. I never saw anyone have such awful agony. He was awfully keen to come out and slay Boers, too, poor devil. I've now got a dam' fool, who's practically no good to me at all. Old Coates used to look after me like a father, and see that my groom did his work too. Also, he was the most marvellous man at packing and could do anything. I hope I shall get him back but if what the doctor says is true, he will never get right again. He'd never been ill in his life before, was married and had a kid.

Well, goodbye, good people all. I suppose Kitty is at home and going strong. I wish I could see her.

Yours affectionately
Allan

Aberdeen
16th June, 1901

Dearest People,

We've had a silly sort of time since my last. The beastly Boers are back again, in the large valley north of the town where they bunked from the first time we went out from here. It's the devil of a place, surrounded by huge rocky mountains. All the kopjes in the valley are stone heaps and all the bottoms prickly pear and dongas. There are patches of solid prickly pear three or four miles square nearly. I don't know whether you ever came across the beautiful plant in your various peregrinations but, anyway, you have my solemn assurance it's the devil of a vegetable. The spikes grow over the flat sort of cactus leaf (rather like a hair brush) and are longer than pins and sharper than needles. There is no 'give' in the plant at all so when you run against the end of a few thorns it's not the pleasant homely old feel of a hawthorn bush when you sit in it, but a rasping jar as the prickles penetrate gently to the cockles of your heart and break off, leaving about three quarters of an inch in your knee cap, which is the favourite spot for attack as you ride through them. It's regular agony. You undress yourself and pull them out and, for two or three days, that knee is as sore as if you had hit it with a hammer.

In amongst this sort of stuff there are any amount of good farms and here our brother Boer frequents and has a good time. The day before yesterday Scheepers commandeered some stuff from one farm and gave 'em a cheque for about £150 on the Free State Government.

We are quite powerless to shift them with the troops we've got. Our fighting men aren't much over 300, if that, and they must be about 400, and they say Kritzinger is coming to join 'em. We simply sit tight here and wait for more troops. Their pickets are only about 4 or 5 miles from here.

Last Saturday we went out on reconnaissance to have a look at 'em and advanced about 12 or 13 miles up, to where they held us, opening the ball by firing on Warrens from the bush and wounding a few horses. We then took up a position, shelled a few harmless kopjes without any apparent result and, after an hour or so, retired. I was on the left flank and took up my position on a ridge running at right angles to the high mountains on my left. I rode up and dismounted just behind the sky line and, as I did so, I heard a few shots on my left from the mountains but, since I couldn't hear any bullets, thought they must be further on and firing at the main body. Well, there I stopped all the two hours and at last retired. No sooner were we mounted and moving off when the swines started sniping and wounded a horse of mine. They'd been there all the afternoon and afraid to fire, the rotters. When they did, they couldn't shoot for toffee.

We had a subaltern called Jansen, of Warrens, and 20 men cut off. He was a good little chap but rash as blazes. He goes chasing ahead not caring a dam if it snowed and he got cut off. He sent in a message which the ass of a man took in to Aberdeen instead of bringing it to the column. When we got nearly home, we met the garrison going out to relieve him but, for some reason, Doran wouldn't let them go and took no steps at all. Consequence was little Jansen held out till 7.30 next morning and was then brought in by his men with the top of his head blown off. When he and his sergeant were shot, the men surrendered to about 150 Boers under Scheeper. We buried them on Monday. Poor little chap! I was at a dance with him the night before. There were three Jansens. The eldest was killed early this year, poor Tommy last Sunday and the youngest wounded before that. Old Warren has made him go home to his mother.

Goodbye and best love all. No time for more. Five minutes to post.
Yours affectionately
Allan

★★★

Wheatlands Farm
Nr. Kendrew [30 km south of Graaff Reinet]
27th June, 1901

Dear People,

I'm sorry I had to wind up last week so abruptly, especially since I found out afterwards I was a day too soon.

I hope everyone at home is blooming as I am at present. We are on the Wallaby at present, (that's two at presents), but where we are going, I dunno for sure.

After Sunday, 16th, when little Jansen got shot, we stopped at Aberdeen until Saturday following, only going out once, (up the Valley of the Shadow as usual), and bringing in a farm during that week. On Saturday we left Aberdeen and Mr Scheepers to their own devices and made a two days trek to Kendrew Siding on the railway, where we took on supplies and trekked to this farm S.E. of Kendrew. This is the finest farm I've seen in South Africa. When you are in the homestead you might almost think you were in a big English farm. We stopped for the night and then went on 6 miles more, when we camped and went out and reconnaissanced without seeing anything much beyond any amount of game: buck, koorhan, hares, etc. By this time we found we were after Kritzinger, who was located about 20 miles from here, north. Three or four other columns were after him and we expected to have a royal scrap. This was Tuesday, 25th.

That night we were ordered to Pearston to await orders, and trekked next morning and, about two or three in the afternoon, having just sighted Pearston, where it was rumoured there were three pubs, Doran received a despatch ordering us back to Kendrew. So we had to turn round and cover the distance between three and sunset that it had taken us from 7.30 till 3 to do. We camped at last, and this morning came on here where we arrived about 10.30 a.m. and are resting the rest of the day.

In'no'more!

French has taken over the Colony and was last heard of at Graaff Reinet. Rumour says that we are going back to play 'ell with Scheepers. I hope so! Everyone hopes Kritzinger will join him and then we shall have 'em all together.

There's not much news of late. One day has been much like another. I hope you are having a good summer and that Kitty is having a good time. I should like to hear from her once more. All letters are thankfully received. I don't know when I shall post this, but goodbye for the present.

[According to the historian David Mcnaughton, whose grandparents farmed Wheatlands in the mid-twentieth century, the farm was said to be haunted by the ghost of a British soldier. Wheatlands is now a guest house.]

★ ★ ★

Kendrew Siding
Cape Colony
July 2nd, 1901

Dearest Kitty,

I got your letter a day or two ago, and rejoiced before the Lord on the lonely veldt. I wish you hadn't wound up so abruptly, since it was just getting interesting. Good thing you had such a fine voyage and interesting companions. [Allan's sister Kitty, now married, has emigrated to Mexico.] I suppose you rather put the lady bare back-rider in the shade after your experiences among gauchos and vaqueros, etc. Although you are not complimentary to New York, it is a place one ought to see, isn't it? And you can sling in a 'when I was in New York' into your conversation occasionally. How does Welshpool strike you after these weary years? It's a restful sort of little place, isn't it? Please write me a long letter and tell me all about it; the Vulchaws, Connie, Boeufs, and other local attractions.

Personally, we've been having a very quiet time the last few days, stopping here, and doing dam' all. In a short time, I think we and one or two other columns are going to visit the worthy Scheepers, near Aberdeen, where he has a mighty stronghold, and then there ought to be some fine fur flying. He's rather a sportsman, old Scheepers. He says funny little things or sends in cheeky messages. One was 'If the English would only stand: I'd sweep 'em into the sea in three months.' Then he rode into Murraysberg one day, and gave all the school children a holiday in honour of his arrival. He collars the farmers' stuff and gives them cheques on the Free State Government, bidding them cherish them carefully, and keeps his tail up all round.

I had a couple of days after buck here and got a fine springbok yesterday; a very sporting shot, 300 yards off and going! Broke both shoulders and grassed him in fine style. I'm sending the head down to Port Elizabeth to be stuffed and then to be sent home.

★ ★ ★

Petersburg,
July 6th

We moved up here, leaving Kendrew at sudden notice on the 3rd. This is about 35 miles from Kendrew and is a little hamlet right among the mountains. The mountains of South Africa must be seen to be believed; not so much for their height, (although that is pretty good), as for their ruggedness, bareness, stoniness, steepness and general sanguinariness. Their quantity, also, about here is dreadful. Our object here was to dislodge Kritzinger from the mountains east of this place but, as he doesn't seem to be there to be dislodged, I don't quite see whether it can be done or not. We got here, on Thursday and yesterday marched at 7 a.m. without guns or transport to play 'ell with Kritzinger who was supposed to be in a kloof the other side of the hills. We got to the foot about 3 or 4 miles from here and began to ascend what was known as a road or path. Talk about roads!! Can you imagine one of George's unbroken stone heaps with the stones varying in size from a loaf to the dining room, strung out to form a line ascending at a grade of about 1 in 4 for 5 or 6 miles, and winding in and out round little kloofs. That's our road! In places it was gone altogether and then we had to climb over ground a bit worse, though not much. Of course we were leading our horses, in single file. I was rear guard and, in addition to dragging my weary self from rock to rock, had to curse on all the poor stragglers from the column who lay in the dust and mopped themselves. Of course we all had our coats off and, when we got to the top, the breeze simply touched the marrow in your spine. Consequence as regards me, stiff neck and sore throat. When we reached the top there was a sort of Jack and the Beanstalk country all on its own, with its own little hills and valleys and rivers, and grass, my dear, actually grass! Some of it was quite green, too. The horses wired into it like billy ho. We reached the top about 12.30, and then went on about 8 miles, I should think, with several short halts for reconnoitring. The earth is black up there instead of the good old south African brick dust. We passed two Kaffir huts, I think, altogether till we got, (after another climb through the head of a kloof, knocking spots off the former experiences), to a farm. The people there didn't consider themselves near Petersburg at all but regarded Cradock, 36 miles further on, as their town, I believe they could get waggons up from Cradock. Well, we got to this farm about 5 p.m. after trekking all day, and off saddled and fed the poor horses and then settled down to a bad night of it, since we had not expected to remain out. The men had some biscuits and bully, I think, and we had nothing. But Chichy went to the farm and bought us some bread and chicken. It ran to about half a slice per man and a wing of a chicken between five. Also we had a bottle of milk and some chocolate. Then we turned in and slept in the poor horses' blankets until moon rise about 9 p.m. when we were kicked out and trekked back again by moonlight, arriving in camp about 5 a.m. the next morning, which was this morning. By Jove it was cold up above! The whole time we never saw a Boer. I think Graaff Reinet is now our objective, but don't think we shall get in till Tuesday.

★★★

Graaff Reinet
July 10th

I am winding this up now, since I may not get another chance of posting as we leave tomorrow morn for the trek again. We arrived here on Monday night, and were ordered to trek at 6.30 this morn, but the order was cancelled in the small hours, and now we have to go tomorrow. I dunno where we are going.

Write us again soon, a long letter and tell the family to send a *County Times* or any other paper sometimes. I have had two or three Expresses, for which much thanks.

Best love and luck, dear Kittens,
From your affectionate brer,
Allan

★ ★ ★

'I tried to cheer them up a bit, told them it didn't hurt much to be hung, etc.'

Richmond, C.C.
July 10th; July 23rd, 1901.

Dearest People,

It's a fearful long time since I wrote home last; in fact I can't quite remember when, but I think it must have been from Graaff Reinet, which was also the place where I had my last bath until yesternight, so you can see I've not been neglecting you unduly. I hope that everyone has been all right at home and blooming, as it leaves me at present. We haven't had any mails since I can't remember when, but I think I've had yours of 16th of June or thereabouts. I hope to get some soon, when we get to the line again, which should be the day after tomorrow.

We left Graaff Reinet at 6.30 on Thursday evening, the 11th inst., and trekked until 2 a.m. towards Aberdeen, when we reached Biggs Farm, (the one we camped at the first time we left Graaff Reinet on June 3rd). We stopped there until 5 a.m. and then trekked on to Pienars, (I am going to try and make a sketch). We got there about 9 and left the transport and went north about 8 miles to a little kopje close to Boissons farm. The big kloof running north is one of Scheepers' happy hunting grounds and he has a laager (or two) about 15 miles up. It was all prickly pear and bush as far as we could see and high mountains all round, of course. Just after we got behind the kopje, we espied some dust a coming down the kloof along a road. It turned out to be 7 Bohers bringing a waggon of mealies down to go round the mountains to the Happy Valley, (old Scheepers' great feeding ground). They rode right into us, with the result that one got it in the neck, so to speak, and we collared five and the other took to the Bush. We drew for him about an hour but couldn't get him. Eventually, Captain Saunders of the 24th Squadn, dropped on him, when he went out to bury the dead. I was told off to take the prisoners into camp with my troop. Since the bush was right up to the road most of the way, I wasn't taking any chances so, with the aid of half a dozen head ropes, we attached them gently but firmly by the neck to a trooper's saddle and went our way rejoicing. I also, with my own fair hands, made the devils fast for the night. They were a pretty mangy looking lot.

Next day, the 13th, we went round the Little Camdeboo and camped about 8 miles from Aberdeen, north of the road, about 10 a.m. Then the column split up and went out, our squadn. going up to hold the Nek at Freynsfontein farm. Some Boers having been reported as coming down that way to go round to the Happy Valley didn't come, however, and old Edwards sent me to the farm to bring in the farmer and his man. I'd been up there before, spending a pleasant half hour talking to the two daughters who were rather pretty and could speak English. So when I went up for the old bird, there was a helluva row. It seems the old swab had done two months in Graaff Reinet already and been let go again. Well, I couldn't wait, so I had to tear them apart and left the old woman, the two chicks and the hired man's wife howling grievously on the stoep. I tried to cheer them up a bit, told them it didn't hurt much to be hung, etc., but they wouldn't stop, except the youngest chick who seemed to appreciate my efforts more than the others and even waved a tearful farewell when I'd seen the old man started on his road to the mines, so to speak.

We stopped in camp that night and next day, on account of its being Sunday and the Colonel not having any information. By this time we had ascertained what the game was. We were part of a beautiful concerted movement to shift Scheepers, Hugo, and Malan out of the Camdeboo and herd them north. Wyndham was on our left, Lund beyond him, Scobel in the mountains, Carew God knows where, and God knows who somewhere else. Well, we shifted them, and they slid for Oorlogs Poort, where we fought them before. We went after them and they offed it up Murraysberg, way before we caught them, and slung off after them through the mountains. Oorlogs Poort is to the left of my sketch across the flat and the Murraysberg road runs up the left hand side of the Camdeboo. We got to Murraysberg on the 20th. It had been looted by the Bo-hers about 10 days before and the English stores burnt. It's such a beastly disloyal place that the Government won't garrison it or send any provisions in. Next day we left for Richmond and spied 9 Boers about 10 o'clock. My troop and Dunlop's, with old Teddy, chased them for about 12 miles but we had to chuck it at last since we were getting too far from the column. Coming back again we espied some mounted men driving horses, so I went in chase and Dunlop went to head them off. I lost sight of them for a bit crossing a river, but picked up their spoor and chased 'em about two miles. Suddenly I spotted a farmhouse with some saddled horses in the kraal. 'Form Troop. Out the ground Scouts. Open out. Gallop like 'ell.' I was making a most spirited attack, when suddenly I found I was chasing one of the Cossack posts of the column which was halted near the farm and outspanned. So we came on here, arriving yesterday midday. For the last few days we were on half rations and been doing anything from 20 to 28 miles per diem.

I think we are moving 6.30 a.m. tomorrow, for Hanover Road on the De Aar Naawpoort line, 2 days trek, I dunno what after.

I'm feeling very fit, thank you, and hope everyone at home is ditto. Write me as many letters and send me as many papers as you can. By the bye, if George puts any more of my letters in the papers as Betty says he does, I'll come and haunt him. Please, please don't!!! That's a good man.

I'm very pleased to hear about Kitty and Roney, etc., but don't think I shall get married before the spring. I hope that the Llanfair Railway [the narrow-gauge Llanfair railway opened in 1903, joining the rural communities along the line to Llanfair Caereinion with Welshpool] locos don't interfere with Comet's rest, and that the other excitements of W'pool aren't wearing my family away to a shadow.

Your affectionate
Allan

★★★

'I took in six prisoners the other day and on the way home they each gave their horses with their blessings to about three different Tommies.'

Richmond, C.C.
July 23rd, 1901.

Dearest Maude & Doy,
(also including John, the boy, and all London friends),

I have been waiting a long time for a decent chance of reminding you that I'm not dead or lost, and I hope that you will not think me more bone idle than necessary for not writing all this time.

As this seems to be in the nature of an apology, I will go on to remark that I am writing this on my knee with the end of a candle, (also on my knee), and that my fountain pen has just run out. Also the wind blows cold. Talking about cold, it's awful in the mornings. We generally trek about 6.30 a.m., which means turning out at 5, amidst frost and ice. When we watered this morning, three hours after sunrise, half the dam was covered with ice. Of course we are pretty high up here, and have been messing about these blooming mountains for the last month.

We don't have a very exciting time, though it's better than nothing. We do get some sort of scrap or something about once a week, and the rest of the time you are expecting it. This district is the Happy Hunting ground of our brother Boer. He selects a nice large kloof, (sort of valley between mountains), with about a dozen nice fat farms in it, and the rest prickly pear, mimosa, thorn, dongas, etc., and there takes up his quarters, about 200 strong, more or less. Presently a column comes along, Brother Boer waits in the prickly pear or on the tops of the hills, and laughs at them. Also shoots. The column laboriously goes round and climbs the hills, thirsting for blood. Brother Boer reported 50 miles away in another kloof in another range of mountains, worse than the first. We catch a few sometimes, and they are a pretty measly lot of swine when we do. They do get in a funk if you get close to them. An officer rode up to four the other day, and held them up without even a revolver. They dropped their rifles like hot potatoes, knelt down and prayed. I took in six prisoners the other day and on the way home they each gave their horses with their blessings to about three different Tommies, hoping to soften the hearts of the cows, so to speak. The blighters hadn't anything else to give.

★★★

Hanover Road, C.C.
July 27th

We've shifted on here now and have had two days rest, which we needed, or the horses did. We probably trek south again tomorrow, over the same ground. This place is on the De-Aar Naawpoort line, and consists of a station and a store. We came through Hanover on our way and outspanned an hour or so there.

At this point it occurs to me that perhaps you do not know that we are on Doran's Flying Column, which we joined on June 3rd, and have been pursuing after Scheepers, Hugo, Malan & Kritzinger ever since. The first three are generally together. I think that the Colony will see the last of the war, but not yet awhile. The Free State & Transvaal have been cleared of food, etc., and the country is more open. Down here they can get plenty of scoff, and the country is the devil. Very fine as regards scenery, but not adapted for successful Boer hunts. I don't think people at home can understand the extent, height, depth, steepness, thorniness, rockiness and general sanguinariness of these dam' mountains. If you sit down, you sit on a prickly pear bush, and if you stand up, you slip on a stone and fall down again. If you lie down, a mule comes and treads on your stomach and, when you hit him, it's generally on the teeth.

Dear, dear! What a grouser I am. I would much rather be here than the Free State, for it's much more interesting, and you can get nearer to Brother Boer. Up North, (you notice my pen has returned to duty), it's all flat and monotonous, but the Colonial mountains are really fine to look at and there is always the excitement of knowing the Boers may only be a quarter of a mile off, round the next corner.

I hope all the Sherriff Roadians are enjoying robust health. Personally, I am very fit, except for a few veldt sores which are unpleasant, though pretty harmless. If any of you can find time to drop a line, it will be found very acceptable since we don't get much literature here. We haven't had any mails for about three weeks now but have wired for them and expect them here tonight.

I will now bid you farewell, since my hands and feet are getting cold though it's only about two o'clock, but it's a beastly cold day. It was snowing this morning and it looks as if we are going to have a cold trek.

Best of love all round,
Your affectionate,
Allan

Cape Town
Aug 6 1901
To Hutchins, Welshpool.

Forearm nupta feralia domator
[Forearm was wounded slightly.]
Wound is healing rapidly invalid is now quite well and will write you, Allan.

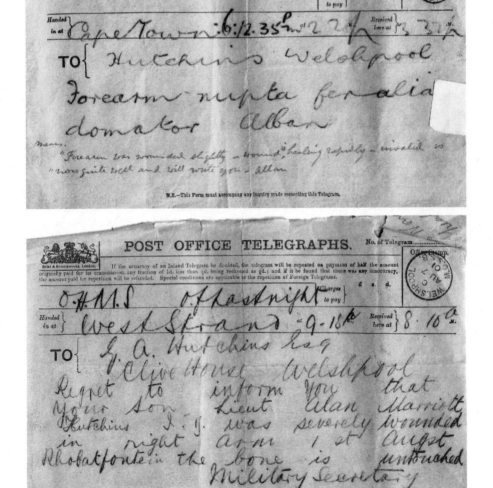

Announcing Allan's injury, 6 August 1901.

Cape Town Aug 7 1901
To: G.A. Hutchins, Esq.
Clive House, Welshpool

Regret to inform you that your son Lieut. Allan Marriott Hutchins, I.Y., was severely wounded in right arm, 1st August: Rhobatfontein. The bone is untouched. Military Secretary.

★★★

Ten Minutes from Capturing Schmidts

'I took his kaross, and his field glasses, whip, a lot of letters and several little things off his bed.'

Drostdy Hotel,
Graaff Reinet
Cape Colony
7th August, 1901

Dearest People,

I hope that you have received the wire I sent off about my terrible injury and haven't been in a state of anxiety about me. The man at the post office at Aberdeen, which was the first place I could wire from, looked at me suspiciously when he saw it was written in cypher and couldn't quite make up his mind whether I would shoot or not, evidently thinking I was a desperate character. I am all right now, as you can see by my being able to write with my bad arm.

Well, let me start at the beginning. I think I was at Richmond when I wrote last. We left Richmond 6.30 a.m. on Wednesday the 24th July, trekking north through Hanover, to Hanover Road on the Nauwpoort to DeAar main line, which we reached on Thursday afternoon, 'and there we rested a little while 'till Sunday the 28th. I think we were all sent up, (about eight columns I think), to stop De Wet and Delarey coming down. They didn't come anyhow, since Delarey couldn't feed his horses, and our Brother Boer has had enough De Wetting, and De Wet didn't like to come without followers, though I'm sure we'd have made him welcome. French came down to Hanover Road while we were there and there were great confabulations, without much result that I can see, so far. By the bye, did I tell you that French sent us, [Doran's Column], a congratulatory telegram one time? What for, God knows! That was some time ago.

Well, on Sunday we started south again. As far as I can make out the idea was this, (these ideas and schemes are nodam' good, as they never come off, but this is by the way), our eight columns were to trek south on a narrow front, then turn round, spread out, then drive right up again, pushing all the Boers out of the Colony with a loud pop. Crewe and Scobell were in the Camdeboo ever since we shifted Scheepers in the middle of July. Well, back south we started, leaving Richmond on our right and reached a farm called Hartebeeste Vlakte on the night of the 31st, rather late. All this time it was very cold. We hadn't seen any Boers for 10 days and things were getting a bit slow, so we sent out a couple of boys who belonged to that part, to see if they could hear of anything. They came back and reported Schmidt's kommando, (over a hundred), in a laager at a farm about 8 miles off in the mountains, so we started at 2 a.m. for a moonlight jaunt. At last we came to a farm with 7 beauties fast asleep in it, and we gathered them. The next farm was supposed to be the laager, so we went on and surrounded it about 4.30 and waited for daylight. When it came at last, we found we'd got the wrong farm. The laager was about 2 miles off in another farm, up a little kloof. It was too late to try and surround it, so about 7 a.m we got mounted and went for it, hell for leather. I was supporting the C.M.R. scouts on the right. When we got into the kloof they spotted us and offed it pretty smartly up the hills all round, where they let drive into us pretty hot. I've made a sketch. I was riding up the right of the kloof and the hill on my right was rocky and so steep, it was like a wall. The edge of a plateau, in fact so being close under it, we couldn't see what was on top. When they opened fire, the place was so rocky that it echoed all over the shop and we couldn't locate them at all. Suddenly, as we galloped along over the most damnable ground, expecting to break our necks before we got a chance of being shot, there came a most terrific banging, right in our ear'oles apparently. We jumped off and rushed the kopje waving revolvers about 6 foot long and were much relieved to find the Boers weren't anywhere near it.

We dismounted at A on my sketch and went straight up to the edge of the plateau about B. To make things a bit more lively and to stop us getting stiff, our rear guard let us have a few volleys at about 600 yards and we had a devil of a job to stop then. At the same time, the Boers were firing at us from God knows where. I was about there nearly a quarter of an hour, wandering up and down the place trying to find out where the swines were. Then we saw some Boers retreating over the uplands towards C and we advanced towards them. They at once took up position and opened fire, and it was hot, by Jove! They were kicking up all round and I saw a bullet drop a little way in front. I don't mean I saw the dust, (there was plenty of that), but I saw the sun on the bullet as it fell about 6 yards in front of me. Next instant I got it in the arm, and a few minutes later the Boers offed. I don't think it was this lot shot me but some swine away on the left of the kloof, since the bullet must have been spent or it would have gone through. As it is, it now resides somewhere between my elbow and my wrist. Well, when we had cleared them, I tied it up and went on about half a mile, when the bandage slipped and I had to do it up again. This lot turned me up a bit so I let my troop go on with Major Edwards and Dunlop's troop and sat down for a breather. This was about 8 o'clock, I should think, on the 1st of August.

Well, after a bit my servant came across me and, after walking up to see where the troop was and seeing it about two miles off on foot, trying to catch 30 Boers on horseback, we decided it wasn't good enough so we climbed down into the laager. We'd got right above it by then. By a bit of luck, we were the first into it so I got a bit of loot.

They'd scooted in a hurry, you know, and left all their blankets, food on the fires, and some horses and saddles, etc. It was just as they'd left it 10 minutes before. But the plum of the business was Schmidt's room in the house. He had been wounded in an attack on Richmond about a month before and was in a pretty bad way. How they got him off is a wonder, since they had to bring him there in a cart and he'd been in bed ever since. I took his kaross, and his field glasses, whip, a lot of letters and several little things off his bed and round it. Altogether I did rather well. I got another splendid sheepskin kaross off a horse in the kraal. When I was in the middle of it, up to my eyes in loot, old Doran comes up and sent me up the sluit [a dry gulch or channel] with two men to see if we could find anyone, but we only got some more loot.

Oh, I forgot. Before he sent me, some swines came back on to the hill at D and gave us a hot time in the farm. There were about 6 of the farmer's women in the house and they raised Cain. I never heard such a row in my life. They hung round my knees when I was trying to arrange the sweeps on the kopje, calling on me, the Almighty, and the devil, all in one voice, not to shoot or they would all be killed. When Doran came up, he sent a troop on to the kopje on the left of the farm and they cleared. Then I searched the sluit and came back to the farm and had a sandwich. Then Doran said we'd retire, so he and a sergeant of the C.M.Rs. hoisted me onto old Paddy and I went up the kloof to find Major Edwards and bring him in. I found him away up, about E, having worked right round. Then we went back and met our convoy at the farm which we surrounded by mistake, and camped there for about half an hour to feed the horses, bury the two poor fellows who were shot and then resumed our trek south about two days behind where we should have been for the scheme. Our casualties were: 1 officer wounded, 2 men killed, and 1 wounded. I got my wound dressed when I got to camp that afternoon and, next day, rode in a Cape cart, so I did the next and the next, which brought us to Oode Plaatz, the scene of the Battle of Hutchins Ridge, (June 10th), as it is now called all over the world. This was Sunday the 4th. By this time we'd used all our supplies and a day over, so the convoy started at 11 p.m. on Sunday night for Aberdeen to get supplies. I went with it in a Cape Cart, and got in about 5 next morning. Stayed at Aberdeen that day and came on here last night. They are sending me on to Deelfontein, I think, to be X-rayed, and have the tooth – I mean the bullet – out. I start from here 7 a.m. tomorrow morn. My arm doesn't give me any trouble, except that I have to do everything with my left hand.

I wish to thank the family for their last budget which I received. It was that of June 28th and was very newsy. I wish the dose to be repeated often. I wonder whether Mue is still there, I suppose she won't be when this comes anyhow but I hope it will catch old Kitty before she sails. Good luck and lots of fun to her, and to our next merry meeting. Hoch! Hoch!! as we used to say in Germany. Please congratulate Trow for me on his promotion and tell him not to be too hard on the poor privates, as the old lady told her son when she heard he had been made orderlyman.

Yes, Ma, Cockell is the man you refer to and is awfully pleased to find you know his people, since he is rather chummy with me. He says he is going to write to you, and is really an awfully nice sort of youth, about 7 feet long.

Podgie informs me that a person named Maurice has started cutting our hay. Can this be the one and only, fallen from his high estate, or is it a misspell of the humble but industrious John Morris?

I'm glad to hear Roney is all right and beginning to do a bit of work. You can tell him that the bullet has hit me on the inside of the fore-arm, half way between the elbow and wrist, and about the middle line of it, and then ask him where it has gone. It can't be felt, and I'm laying 6 to 4 against him, though I dunno myself.

It's got quite warm these last few days and spring is beginning. Oh, another bit of news for you. I'm a lootenant now, from the 5th May. Goodbye, now, dear people. I hope to be back on the column in a fortnight, so don't think I'm dying or anything. Best love, and hoping to get some mails soon

Yours affectionately,
Allan.

★★★

A military court sat in Graaff Reinet, at the Drostdy Hotel (where Allan often dined), often presided over by Doran. Prisoners were incarcerated in the town's jail and sentence passed in the square – Major Shute reading the judgment of the court and Col. Doran often being on the panel of judges. As a warning to would-be rebels, all townspeople were ordered to attend. Lotter, Kritzinger and Scheepers were all condemned here; Scheepers and eight others were executed here, at dawn outside town on the Murraysburg Road. To ensure his burial place was not made into a shrine and Scheepers a martyr, (as a Free Stater, he could not have been tried as a Cape Rebel and there were many objections to his execution on this basis), his body was buried in the river bed. His remains were later removed by the British and have never been found – his mother searched for them until her own death. A shrine has been erected, however, above the spot where it is believed he met his death.

Central Hotel
Middleburg C. C.
22nd August 1901

Dearest Family,

I think I wrote last from Graaff Reinet. I left that spot on the morning of the 8th, Thursday, at 7 a.m. But first let me tell you that I saw old Hamer of Tyn-yr-eithin at Graaff Reinet. He is now an ossifer in the Prince of Wales' Light Horse and is very fit. Charlie Elwell will be glad to hear of him; he is on Hunter Weston's column, and went up the Line with me next morning as far as Bethesda Road, and we had some long yarns. ['Hunter-Bunter' who, in Roberts's push to Pretoria, distinguished himself by blowing up the railway and capturing 28 locos and a 1000 tons of coal. Conversely, on 1 July 1916 on the Somme, his unit took the greatest casualties of any when he set off his mines early, thus warning the Germans of an advance.] We got hung up at Let's Kraal, from about 10 a.m. till 5 p.m. by Theron's kommando, who were waiting for us a little further on. The Armoured Train and a troop train went through and the sergeant in charge of the first got killed, a trooper wounded and a nigger killed. Eventually the armoured train came back and we went through and stopped at Bethesda Road that night.

I got to Naauwpoort about 10 p.m. next night and went up to hospital, and was sent on next night, reaching Deelfontein the following morning, Sunday, 11th. I was X-rayed that night and found that I hadn't got any bullet in me at all. Whatoh! What became of it is a mystery. I think it must have been a spent bullet which went through my sleeve into my arm, struck the bone bounced back and dropped down my sleeve. I'm all right now and healed up. I couldn't get any news of the column, so I left Deelfontein the following Thursday and went down to Graaff Reinet, which I reached about 7 p.m., Friday night. On Tuesday morning I was sent back again here.

The column had left here the morning before I arrived and, at present, I'm like Mr. Micawber, waiting what may turn up. This is French's Head Quarters, you know. Oh, I forget to tell you we were held up again at a place called Eland's Kloof, with the news that 200 Boers were at Let's Kraal again. This was while coming up here. The Armoured Train came down and fetched us through all right. There, I think that's all about me.

Now, how are you getting on? I've not had a mail of any sort since I was at Hanover Road, the 27th July. Oh, I got a *County Times* at Graaff Reinet which was very acceptable. I should like it every week, if convenient.

I think this should arrive about Podgie's birthday. Many Happy Returns, dear girl, and may you flourish exceedingly, like a young bayleaf, I mean bay tree! I hope that all the others are also in good form and fit and possessed, everyone of them, of a fixed and high resolve to write me long letters each mail.

Your affectionate,
Allan.

I forgot to tell you that they shot three rebels in Graaff Reinet the day I was last there, just to encourage them a bit. I went to see them sentenced, together with another batch who got Penal Servitude for Life. In this last lot, I recognised a couple I knew.

★★★

Garstland Kloof
In the veldt,
Somewhere between Cradock and Graaff Reinet
5th Septr., 1901

Dearest family,

Just a line to tell you the latest, since I have a little time. The convoy is going into Cradock to fetch supplies and will post this.

I stopped at Middleburg about 10 days altogether, and was just getting set, when I was ordered off to Cradock to rejoin. I was out all the morning that the order came, on patrol with Fuller's Scouts, and got back at 1 p.m. to find that I had to leave at two. It was rather a rush but all was well and I reached Cradock about midnight and found the Column. Next morning at 7 a.m. the 11th Squadron and C.M.R.s. were started on a three days' patrol in the mountains, so I was not long in getting on trek again. That evening we reached a farm where we stayed next day until midnight and then we started over devilish passes and mountains up among the clouds

The main part of the Squadron were making for the head of a kloof called Garstland's Kloof but I and Byrne of the C.M.Rs. took 30 men and went a long way round to search for 4 Boers and agreed to meet at a certain farm in Garstland's Kloof. Both parties had Dutch men for guides. Well, after a devil of a night's ride, about 8 o'clock next morning, made Garstland's Kloof and, looking down into it, we saw the rendezvous, with the Squadron apparently in it. We rode calmly down and approached it. When we got about 600 yards off they let rip a volley into us and we then had the unpleasant truth forced upon us that the Squadron hadn't arrived, while the Boers had. We scooted and shinned up a Kopje and just then the others came down the other way. The Boers then scooted, going over the top of the highest and steepest mountain they could select. From the top they threw things at us again.

Nothing of importance has occurred since, except a few shots this morning; we ensnared a Boer.

I got about five letters at Cradock and was 'much pleased' but can't reply to all now. Thanks all of you very much. I'm very well now, thanks, and hope you all are at home. I'm going to try and send Kitty a nice Kaross for a wedding present but can't find the opportunity just now.

Best love all round,
Yours affectionately,
Allan

★★★

Allan once wrote that his correspondents in Britain would know more about the war than he did. In the following letter, written from Molteno a few days after he and 30 men engaged a Boer Commando at Garstland's Kloof from which the 'Boers then scooted', he has learned that the commando was then 'collared' by Scobell's Column.

Major-General 'Harry' Scobell received information that 130 commandos, brilliantly led by Lotter, were laagered at Bouwershoek near Petersburg in the Tandjesburg mountains. Moving quickly, Scobell's column, consisting mainly of men from the 9th Lancers and the Cape Mounted Riflemen, surprised Lotter in a midnight raid. Surrounded, protected only by the low stone walls of a sheep kraal, the Boers lost about 19 men killed and 50 wounded; none escaped. One eyewitness described a sight that 'was horrible in the extreme … In fact the place was like a butcher's shop, some men making awful noises

groaning, clutching the ground and rolling in the dirt in their agony.' (Packenham) Lotter
was captured. About 200 horses, and a large supply of rifles and ammunition, together
with some dynamite, were taken, as well as all the vehicles and supplies. Lord Kitchener's
despatch of 8 September, 1901 describes the Battle of Groenkloof as a brilliant success
and, with other reverses, Boer activity moved away from the area around Graaff Reinet.
Lotter was condemned and executed at Middelburg on 11 October, 1901. The farm at
Bouwershoek is in ruins but the sheep kraal remains. A British cemetery is close-by; the
Boers are buried at Petersburg.

Molteno C.C.
Septr. 10th 1901

Dearest People,

We are now in fresh fields and pastures new, having trekked across here from Fish River
and instead of now being directly under French, have to report to Colonel Haig who
commands here.

Cole Hamilton, who was our senior Sub. you know, has now come back; he came
with me from Middleburg and is now a Captain and has taken over the Squadron from
Major Edwards, who stays on as O.C. Yeomanry to the Column. He is a very nice fellow.
We got up here last night and the rain, which had been threatening since we left Fish
River, started as we arrived and poured all night while today, it still threatens. We all
went down to the hotel for dinner and, afterwards, the Major and I, being the last to
leave, funked it, and surreptitiously ordered a bed room, and scored off the others like
blazes. The only drawback was that some swine sneaked my waterproof cape but since I
sneaked it also, I'm not much out of pocket over that lot.

The Transport Officer to the column has had an accident and has to go to Hospital
for a bit, so today I am to take over his job till he comes back. I don't like it at all, but I
suppose it will be good experience and, anyway, I can't get out of it.

We picked up two wounded 17th Lancers and two wounded niggers at a farm yesterday and heard about the scrap which took place the day previously.

It seems as though we should be here a day or two more though we don't know for
certain. There are some strong Kommandos where we are going, so there ought to be
some fun.

You remember me telling you about Garstland's Kloof? Well, Scobell's Column was
waiting for that little lot in the Kloof that they cleared to from us and chased them
Petersburg way and collared the lot, including Lotter, the Commandant, so our work
wasn't all in vain after all; though if Doran had carried out his programme of coming
up the Kloof, (Garstlands, I mean), to meet us, *we* should have had them. As it was, they
passed between him and the mountain, and Scobell got them. Just our luck.

11th

I think we move tomorrow morning and I have been busy today loading up the supplies, etc.

Later.

I don't think we shall now after all, since Doran hadn't had any orders about an hour ago.

How are things at home now? I suppose that you will get this about apple and pear time. The spring is setting in with us now, though it has been very cold the last day or two. The peach trees are all in blossom and make the farms look very pretty. Nearly all the decent Homesteads round the Colony have a few poplars and gum trees and an orchard, and a few acres of cultivated ground, (generally lucerne), which is most deliciously green; just like a field at home and such a contrast to the blooming old veldt.

Did I tell you I went to a dance at Middleburg when I was there? It was given by French's Staff and was quite enjoyable. I met three or four people that I knew before, or knew their relations.

The fellows are all chipping me now about my new job and call me the Mulester, the Waggoner, etc., and anxiously inquire what is the best stuff to feed mules on. The great perquisite of the job is that I am the only man who can wallop the niggers on the Column so they have to be sent to me for treatment. It's fine exercise. I hope things are going well with you, and that everyone is as well as I am at present.

Good luck to everyone, and best love,
Yours,
Allan

★★★

The Imperial Yeomanry hospital at Deelfontein – created out of nothing on a railway siding west of Richmond in the Northern Cape – became the biggest British medical facility in South Africa. 'The sick and wounded could be carried from the ambulance trains straight to the ward,' wrote Lieutenant-Colonel AT Sloggett, the officer in charge. On the night 50 nurses arrived from England their tents were blown away by a Karoo storm but Deelfontein was otherwise considered peaceful: 'Only the trains bringing hundreds of sick and wounded reminded us of what was happening up north,' wrote Charles Fry, an orderly in the X-ray unit. Today there remains only a hotel called The Yeomanry and a graveyard of British soldiers.

Phoenix Hotel,
Molteno,
September 11th, 1901
W. Gibson

Dearest Becky,

You have been a very faithful correspondent of your young brother's and I think that duty calls me to write you a few lines to thank you very kindly and to express my wishes for your great salubriousness. How goes the war in Bridgenorth? There was a Major Starkey commanding this Squadron, (Yorkshire Dragoons), in the old days before the new Yeomanry came out. I wonder whether he was any relation of the old firm?

The bullet that I caught the other day is a mystery. There is no doubt that a bullet went through my sleeve and hit me a shrewd blow on the arm, and that the doctor put a probe about three inches in after it but, when I came to be photographed, there was no sign of any furrin body at all, at all. Where it got out is unknown and unfathomable. I don't believe it did and that them X-rays are a fraud.

I've had a great and glorious appointment given me yesterday, which I intend to resign at the earliest opportunity. It was a case of having greatness thrust upon me. I am now Principal Transport Officer to Colonel Doran's Flying Column, which means I have to grease the wagons, whack the mules, and wallop the niggers of that fine body of men. Thank the Lord it's only temporary, during the enforced absence of the regular man, who walked over unseen precipice at Maraisberg while returning to camp after waking up the inhabitants of that sweet secluded spot.

I heard rather a good yarn the other day about the Yankee who was doing the Holy Land, which perhaps you haven't heard. He eventually arrived at the Sea of Galilee, and being much pleased with it, engaged a Holy-lander to row him across. On arriving at the other side, the holy one demanded a most exorbitant fee, and after much altercation, the Yankee found he had to pay. Reluctantly he counted out the spondulicks, and as he turned away, he remarked bitterly, 'No wonder Christ walked!!!!.'

How is the son-in-law? From what I hear the happy day approaches by leaps and bounds. 'Tis glad I am to congratulate the both of you, and by the time I see Merrie England again I hope to come and call on Dr. and Mrs [Dr and Mrs Roney Schofield, Becky, Allan's sister] in their own establishment. Mind, let me know as soon as anything definite is fixed. I didn't hear when Kitty was to depart again till she had almost gone. Why doesn't Schofe send me a line or two occasionally? Make him do so and tell me a few of the latest stories to while away the time. You can't believe what a treat home letters are in this God-accursed country, where every inhabitant is about half civilised and everything in the way of civilization reminds one of tinned meat. I can't explain the feeling properly but nothing seems properly finished, if you can understand me.

Well, old Sweetness I think I will tear myself away. We move from here tomorrow, so

Good Bye! Best love and lots of luck! Your affectionate Brer

★★★

Smuts led a Kommando of around 500 men in the Cape, harrassing the British and humiliating the 17th Lancers at Modderfontein. Kitchener respected Smuts as a soldier and so pursued him relentlessly. He escaped capture more than a dozen times. In May 1902 Smuts and Kitchener sat down together and drafted the peace treaty that ended the war. In 1906 Smuts became Colonial Secretary in the new South African government. He was a General in British uniform during the First World War and a Field Marshal in the Second.

At Modderfontein on 17 September 1901, in freezing, torrential rain and with little ammunition and few horses, in desperation Smuts led an attack on C Squadron, 17th Lancers (the Death or Glory Boys), camping at the pass above Elands River Valley. Smuts' vanguard, dressed in looted British uniforms, ran into a Lancer patrol. General Haig later described the incident in a letter to his sister:

> The officer in charge of it saw some men in khaki whom he took to be some of Gorringe's column which was expected north of the post. These men levelled their rifles at him when about 200 yards distant. He shouted to them 'Don't fire. We are the 17th Lancers.'

Meanwhile, Smuts led the remainder of his force in an attack on the British rear. The Lancers lost 29 killed and 41 wounded before surrendering. One of the commando wrote: 'We all had fresh horses, fresh rifles, clothing, saddlery, boots and more ammunition than we could carry away, as well as supplies for every man.' Haig raced to the scene of the disaster and renewed his order that all Boers caught wearing British uniforms should be shot. Today, there is a mass grave at the farm.

Mount Stewart
Cape Colony
October 1st., 1901

Dearest Kitty,

It's many long days since the last letter so I shall let rip now in the first person and get it over.

I left Molteno as chief principal transport officer extraordinary to Col. Doran's Flying Column, which proud position, I am glad to say, I have now vacated, the regular man having got over the effects of his drunken state and rejoined. During the time that I was on the Staff, however, I managed to hit some of the most awkward work in the transport line that I could have. When I took over, the wagons and mules were in a bad state and you may remember we had two or three day's rain at Molteno.

Well, we started off after Smuts on 12th. Sept. Dordrecht being our objective, but we never got there, wandering about after the wily Boer and passing close to Sterkstrom. On the 14th, my buffday, the rain began again and dam' cold, and just as we were moving off after the midday outspan, 15 brothers galloped right across our front about 4 miles distant, and up a kloof. It was a carefully laid trap but it didn't come off since we only chased them with a half squadron, which wasn't taking any kloof, (when I say 'we', I mean The Column; personally I stayed with the mules, hoisted the Red Cross on a wagon, got inside, and gave out I was the Doctor). In the meantime we moved into the hills up a different pass, sort of converging with the other, and hadn't gone 10 minutes before our Advanced Guard came into action; the swines were full the 'ouse, so to speak, and poor old Cockell's mare, (the same that gave me a rough ride once), put her foot in a hole, going at speed, and the old chap took a devil of a toss, with her on top of him. He was unconscious for three days and will probably have to go home. Concussion. Poor old Cockles! He was very Fed Up and won't be sorry, I don't think. When he began to come round and know things a bit, he couldn't remember anything about his toss but had a firmly rooted belief that he had rheumatism, 'and dam' bad rheumatism, too', as he told the Doctor. Well, Mr. Smuts had to run, and I had to beat the poor blooming miles after him somehow, and that night more rain, bucketsfull.

Leaving camp next morning, we had a shocking bad drift to cross and what with staff officers, niggers, mules, rain, mud, and general nuisances, I began to get fussed and presently it resulted in me and the chief staff officer standing on a high bank overlooking a roaring torrent, talking big at each other, while the supply officer, finding the situation becoming strained, (awful nice chap), pinched my Sjambok to create a diversion and let into a poor harmless nigger like fury. It really was very humorous and eventually everyone swore eternal friendship. But the poor bleeding nigger didn't know what the devil it was all about. This was the Sawbath, and it rained steady all day.

To obviate further meteorological observations, I will now remark that it rained all the night and next day. Well, on Sunday evening we were stopped by a river and, Boers or no Boers, we had to wait for it to go down. We crossed at 6 a.m. on Tuesday, and trekked right thro' to Tarkastadt, (18 miles), arriving about 3 p.m. You might think I'd have a rest then, but no! I had to go straight into town and load supplies and then I didn't get a rest but went right along 5 or 6 miles more and outspanned. By this time it was about 7.30 p.m. and, at 10.30 p.m., we went on again, on account of Smuts wiping out a Squadron of the 17th Lancers a few miles farther on.

We outspanned again about 3 p.m. and at 5a.m. we went on again, and camped for the day about 9 a.m., men, horses, and transport done to the world. Mind, with all the work in the dark on soft roads, we had wagons bogged up to the axles every half mile. It's awful cold country round there, too. Well, to cut it short, we trekked on again next day to Maraisburg, (where we loaded up again), and on the 21st, got to Cradock where the regular transport officer was waiting. I was so pleased at handing over the job to him, that I went and recklessly expended 5 bob in having some old teeth out, which had made an abscess, took about a pint of neat whiskey, then subsided from five in the afternoon till 10 at night. When I woke up, I went to bed.

Off again next morning at 6.30, but 'back to the army agen, seargent, thank Gawd!' After some desultory trekking, reached Cookhouse on the 28th. Oh, old Doran had me up and thanked me quite civilly for 'the way In which I had managed the transport during Chapman's absence.' I said it was all right and hoped he was pretty well, saluted with both hands, fell over my spurs and retired gracefully. Well, at Cookhouse, the Column entrained. Our squadron took the first train and we left on Sunday night, (29th), en route for Mount Stewart on the Port Elizabeth Graaff Reinet Line. We should have been switched off at Zwart Kops on to the said Line but, for some reason, we weren't. Consequence was that when in the early morn I raised my fair head from my luxurious couch, (I was sleeping on some coal dust under a Cape cart), and gazed over the side of our dining car or coal truck, I thought I was still dreaming, for there lay the sea with stately ships on its buzzum. By Jove, it was good to see it. We had come on by some mistake to Port Elizabeth, where we stopped till about eleven o'clock.

The good ladies of the town sent down and had all the men up to breakfast in the Feather Market. The inhabitants had, of course, had lots of troops through there but they had never struck a Column on the line of march before. As one lady remarked to me, 'They are a tough looking lot.' Since at this moment she was thoughtfully regarding a man who had no seat to the garments which should have had a seat, I agreed with her heartily. We went on again about eleven a.m,. and at last struck Mount Stewart about 11 p.m. and detrained the horses.

Next morning we had to get the wagons off and, since there was no loading dock, I was allowed to try my hand on building one, which I did out of a load of sleepers and some old rails, and have been highly complimented by all ranks. Here we have been since.

If we stop another day or so we may get some mails. I was very glad to hear of Carrie Elwell's engagement, and hope they will hit it off. Anybody ought to be able to get on with the old girl and be happy. Good luck to 'em. Everybody seems to be marrying or giving in marriage nowadays, I think something ought to be done to stop it.

I have stuck at this point of my letter for half a day and still I don't find the Muse kind. This place is quite Godforsaken, consisting of the station and three tin houses and a bar in a cow shed. The only thing exciting at all is a local officer, whose brother fell off a horse yesterday and is dying, who comes to our mess to see the doctor and to inquire 'whether that bl –y fool of a brother of mine can have a drink,' or a smoke, or something of that sort.

Octr. 3rd.
I have to day been again ordered to take over the Transport, since that swine Chapman has worked his ticket again in the most barefaced way I've ever seen. It's rather funny, though I don't feel much like laughing; He has false teeth and he simply went to the Colonel and said he had dropped them and a horse had trod on them. Of course, he had them in his pocket all the time. And D., who considers himself such a helluva smart chap, sucked it all down like milk and has given him leave to go to Port Elizabeth to get some more, without even asking the doctor, who had refused Chapman a certificate point blank. Then the fool sends to me that I must take over from Chapman again, and of course I kicked, and got the Major to go and beg off. When that being no good I went over, too, he simply got on his high horse and refused to listen. So I've got to go through it all again, doing another man's work.

We are having a decent rest here but I expect we shall have to pay for it when we get started again.

Now Kittens, I think I will finish up. I hope you will have, (or, rather, will have had a nice voyage out and that you will soon be safely and happily tied up. Your young man is a jolly lucky devil, anyhow, though I says it as shouldn't. Best love and lots of luck to both of you, and tell him I looks towards him and likewise bows.

Love to all the home birds as well, especially the old 'uns,
Yours affectionately,
Allan M

★★★

'I think I could have got a Cavalry commission the other day like winkin, since they sent round for applications, but its no good without at least £600 a year.'

To be read by the family A. M. H.
Somewhere near Pearston,
Cape Colony
October 15th 1901

Dearest People,

Nothing very much to relate since my last, except that I am all right and hope you are equally salubrious. Write and tell me about the County Ball. I suppose these must have been great do's. Also the Yeomanry presentation must have been just tremenjous, with such elite to send it ohf. Do you think they will save me a Cup and a medal? I think they ought to, don't you? I hope they won't treat me dirty.

They Valianteers must look noble in their khaki, too, though personally I like summat a bit gaudy-like for home uniform. Out here, the sight of a civilian rig out attracts more attention than any khaki.

Several inquiries have been made as to pronunciation, so I think I will give you a few. Firstly, Graaff Reinet is Graaf Renett. Scheepers is Skippers, to rhyme with her-rings. Bye the bye, we've just heard that the old swine has been caught sick in a farm down Willowmore way. What a chance for someone with a trusty revolver and a silent tongue! But I digress. Fouche' is Foo shee and Malan is Malon. Botha is Boata and Delary has the accent on the last syllable. I can't think of any more.

I was much interested to hear of Kitty's and Betty's doings and about the former's departure. Poor thing! As Mrs. Boulf would say, she couldn't get away at all, at all. Her list of presents is pretty extensive, isn't it? I must send her a little offering when I get a chance of getting hold of one. I wish George luck with his Rifle Range, and it looks like he is getting one, doesn't it? It will be a fine thing for W'pool if you do.

As to your inquiries about Capt. O'Shea, or whatever his name was, getting a D.S.O.

at Rhoboksfontein, (or Rhobatsfontein as the County Times hath it), I dunno, since there was certainly no one of that name there, or any Bushmen, so it must have been somewhere else.

Our Column consists now of the 11th, 23rd. & 24th I.Y., 50 C.M.Rs. and 2 Guns, (R.F.A. now Elliott with his R.H.A. left us near Cradock, en route for home. I escorted him to Mortimer Station and saw him off).

The other day Dunlop and I applied for Commissions in the S.A.C. and Rose-Johnson, the Staff Officer, tells us the old man, (Doran), has recommended us in a most rattling manner. So, as you were about what I said of him in my last. I don't think there is very much chance since they are very full up but you never know. Perhaps Pryce J. might do summat, eh? George needn't trouble about the provisional Squadron; I don't think they would be any good to anybody and just as expensive as the Line. I think I could have got a Cavalry commission the other day like winkin, since they sent round for applications, but its no good without at least £600 a year. Teddy says so too. Irwin of the 24th applied and got one in the Royals, but he's got lots of dibs. An awfully nice little chap. Old Teddy has been awfully good about these matters and I believe he would be awfully pleased if he could get Dunlop and me a start. He takes a great deal of interest in it. We are awfully lucky to have him in the Squadron, and the 11th is *the* Squadron on the column.

Now as to our wanderings of late. We have been on the Strategic line lately, instead of the Tactical, and the same is dam'rot and don't pay.

We left Mount Stewart at 6 a.m. on the 5th and had a long trek down the Line to Wolvefontein, where we camped that night, and went on next morning to Klein Poort, about 6 miles, and stopped that day. Next day we came back on our tracks through Wolverfontein and Salypans Nek and struck east towards Darlington, where we went on to next day. We left Darlington on the 10th and had another long trek, about 30 miles to Jansenville, where we camped that night, and remained till 4p.m. the next afternoon and then trekked on through the town to a place called Well-Gelegen, which we reached about 9 p.m. At 1 a.m. next morning we moved on towards Graaff Reinet and camped about 7 a.m. We were supposed to meet Smuts that morning, but he apparently had another engagement and was not forthcoming. Smuts is the particular Kommandant that all these mysterious operations were directed against. (I don't understand them, and therefore can't explain, but the idea seems to be to find out where the Boers are and then trek the other way like blazes.)

On Sunday, 13th, we moved again, (Reveille 4, move 5.30, which is the order of the day now the Summer has come on), and had another long trek reaching Pearston at 9 p.m. There was some news there. 180 District Mounted Troops, part of the Cape Colony defences, in position had surrendered to 200 Boers without hardly firing a shot, about 14 miles from Pearston. Of course, the stinkers were all dam' Dutchmen who had been allowed to enlist and that's the result. They simply refused, in a body to fight and handed over their rifles, saddles and ammunition to their pals, the brave Boers. What's left of them is wandering about the mountains about 6 miles from here, afraid to go down. They had better not come here, unless they want to get booted. I don't know what they are living on but I should think grass would be good enough for that stamp of cattle.

We left Pearston at 4 a.m. the morning after we got in and climbed up here, about 14 miles north-east, and have been here ever since, trying to get a few wagons up. What happens now, I dunno. I hope that we take pack mules and follow up the Boers. If we don't, all we can do is climb down again and go somewhere round, since wagons won't go along here.

That brings us up to date. I don't know when I can post this, so will leave it unfinished for the present.

★★★

22nd, Bethesda Road
Since writing the above we have moved on here but nothing interesting has occurred except that I have received yours and Betty's of the 20th. September also yours of 27th. From the last place I wrote which is called Mooifontein, and is a farm at the top of Buffel's Hoek Nek, we trekked along Buffel's Hoek towards Somerset East, but turned towards Cradock, going along the road over Brand Kloof Nek and down Brand Kloof, which is the road the Squadron took when I rejoined it at Cradock on the 1st. Septr., but we turned up to the right for Garstland's Kloof that time. We camped about 4 miles from Cradock when we got there and trekked through the town and straight on West again. Dam' shame to rush us through like that, and of course about four men deserted promptly and stopped in Cradock. Eventually we came here. Smuts, when we last heard of him, was about 2 days ahead of us and we are following up in case he breaks back again. The other Columns are waiting for him all right, and Lukin [Major General Sir Henry Timson Lukin, Commander of the Cape Mounted Riflemen] killed one and collared five yesterday or the day before. They are all pukka Boers, Transvaalers and Free Staters and are full of bukh [talk, from the Hindi *bak*, hence boasting] since they collared the D.M.Ts. and smashed up the 17th., which last fray I was not in but was not far off. I've told you about it before. I, at that time, was Mule whacking. (Oh, bye the bye, I didn't do the transport the second time after all. My remonstrances must have worked on the old man after all, and without saying owt to me he told off Burrwell, one of his Staff Officers to do it, much to B's disgust. I scored one there). Old Swettenham seems about as mad as ever, according to all accounts. Why isn't someone hired to kick him? I'd subscribe a quid if necessary.

We are having quite a nice rest here. I don't know what our future movements are to be.

I should rather like Cox's to send me a bank book, if that is the right term. Anyhow, I want to know how much I owe them. Could George ask them to do so, please?

I've no more to tell you, and think it is about time I posted this letter. It has been running on a long time now. I think I had better order some things I shall be wanting through you now, since otherwise I might leave it too late. On second thoughts I will leave 'em for mature consideration, since I'm not quite decided what to get, except a pair of moderately light shooting boots – size easy 7's – which you might despatch, together with the bill. As to George's enquiries about the clothing, that's just what I have left for consideration. Anyway don't do it without me.

Best love all round, dear people.
Yours affectionately,
Allan

★★★

Bethesda Road
26th October, 1901.

I am reopening this long epistle since I have just received your letters and papers of Oct. 4th and was much gratified thereby, also by the extremely military photo of George and the old lady, Nina and the house, etcetera. It's awfully pretty and I was glad to see it.

It's bad news about your leaving the old place. I wouldn't if you can possibly help it, really. What's it all about?

Thanks very much for the Medal ribbon and Maude's photo. Keep the Medal safe and dark. We might bag a brace as Teddy put it.

George is mistaken in thinking that our column is ever attached to any other, (Scobell's, etc.). We operate in conjunction but never hook on. As a rule we are directly under French but Haig has had charge of the 'Smuts' Columns', worse luck! Lukin of the C.M.Rs. has got Gorringe's Column now, and will probably make things hum a bit.

Since last evening we have had a dust storm, a thunder and a locust storm, which last is raging at present. They've been going over for hours.

The Major and I went out to try and get a buck last night, but didn't hit any. I happened to find an old dead buck all dried up, which someone had stuck up on its legs, and I went over to the Major and pretended to suddenly see it and kidded him on to shoot, and he bombarded it heavily for some time. I've not dared to tell him that I'd seen it before, or I think he'd shoot me; he was so mad when I suddenly found it was dead.

No more.

Yours
Allan

★★★

Letjes Bosch Siding,
Cape Colony
November 12th, 1901.

Dearest Famille,

I see with dismay that I have left another very large gap to bridge over with this letter but will now take to the job with all apologies for my remissness. Since my last, which I think was from Bethesda Road, I have received yours, Betty's and Billy's of October

11th. I think I will give my usual itinerary first and answer yours afterwards.

After lying at Bethesda Road for 6 days awaiting Orders, we moved at an hours notice at 4p.m. on the afternoon of the 28th. What we really had to do was to proceed to Graaff Reinet and entrain there for Willowmore but, mystery being dear to the hearts of French's Staff, his C.S.O. looked up the map, saw there was a station called Lets Kraal between us and Graaff Reinet and in a dark and secret manner ordered us there.

We started, as I said, at 4 p.m. and after wandering over the most horrible road down a beastly little Kloof, crossing and recrossing the Zondag's (Sunday's) River, we arrived about 8 p.m., at last, at a drift which was impossible and impassable. We stuck there (about 6 miles from Lets Kraal) until 10.30, it raining all the time, and then returned to a farm called Colonies Plaatz and camped for the night.

At 4 a.m. next morning we started again, repairing the drifts as we came to them. After the guns had crossed the one that stopped us the night before, I went back to relieve Dunlop who was rearguard behind the wagons, to manhandle them along the bad places. Chichy was at the drift in front. After abandoning two wagons altogether, and leaving 7 others in comparative safety along the road to be brought along next morning, (one in the middle of the River), we arrived in camp about 9 p.m. Six miles in 17 hours, with 6 drifts. Well, there we were at Lets Kraal as ordered, but there was no getting any farther. We were there fast, kept in by the mountains and bad roads and swollen rivers. We might have reached Graaff Reinet in one day from Bethesda if we had stuck to the main road! By this time we had been whistled off Smuts and were going to play with some more Boers who were trying to get over the Zwart Berg Mountains into the fat Oudtshoorn district where they would be in clover.

Well, we waited at Let's Kraal for orders 2½ days and eventually had to make platforms and entrain there, since we could not get away otherwise as the rains continued. We left about midnight on Novr. 1st. Our train was the first, with all the 11th. Squadron on it. The first half dozen trucks were long bogies with the Squadron wagons, our Cape carts and the Doctor's Ambulance, etc. The men were stowed between the wagon wheels, etc. Dunlop, Hamilton and I were under our Cape carts in the rear bogie. Behind us was a short truck with the 2nd Troop men in it. Behind that, 17 horse trucks, and the guards van with the Major, Chichy, and the Doctor in it. Coming into Graaff Reinet is a long curved incline running down on to the long railway bridge, about 40 feet above the dry river bed. Well, in the early morning I woke up with the consciousness that we were going at a devil of a rate and just then our truck seemed to spring forward and slow gradually down again. I turned over and off to sleep. Hamilton woke me up just as we ran into Graaff Reinet, saying, 'Hutchins! HUTCHINS! Half the train has gone!' I got up and saw that we were the last truck. We both laughed a bit, then some men in front shouted that they'd seen the rear of the train go over as we ran down to the bridge. That stopped the laughing pretty quick. Hamilton took nearly all the men and started back up the line. He wouldn't let me come since I was the only one who could be left with the train. Dunlop had jumped out, being awake when the train slowed up after the accident. Well, when they got back, they found the most awful scene. The short truck with the men had jumped. Mercifully, the couplings between us and them had snapped,

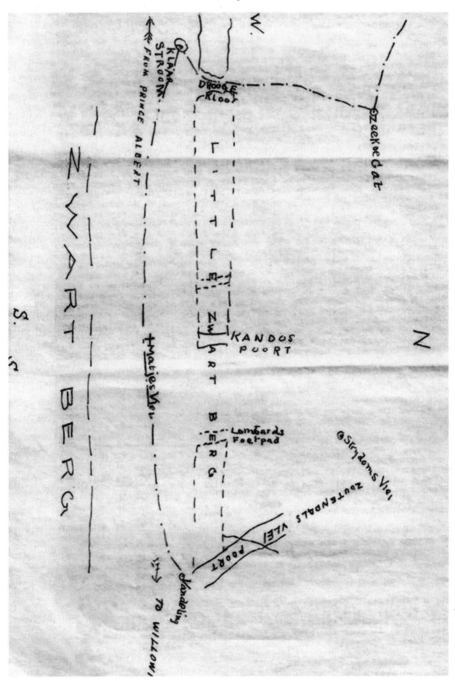

Sketch map accompanying letter of 12 November 1901.

or else I'm afraid the 11th Squadron would have ceased to exist as a fighting body but
would have made great holes in the rocks of the Zondags River. The truck with the
men, the one that jumped, ran into the sandbag redoubt at the head of the bridge, the
Sentry basely deserting his post when he saw us coming. Good for him!

Every truck between that and the guard's Van was telescoped, overturned and played the devil with. Out of 149 horses on the train, we reloaded 44 when we went on.

The guard's van was derailed but on the whole train not a man was scratched. But those poor horses! They were strewn in heaps with wreckage over, under and through them! It is an irreparable loss to us, since we had gradually got them fit. You see, perhaps we get 30 remounts at a time. Well, out of that lot, as a rule about 20 are lost the first month from exhaustion, sore backs, etc. The remainder, you couldn't kill with a crowbar. I had horses in my troop which came on the Column when I did, in June. Well, those we lost will take months to replace. They gave us a hundred remounts when we got to Willowmore, and very good ones too, but, of course, as soft as butter. We want more already.

Old Paddy, the apple of my eye, so to speak, was as near dead as dammit, and a great cut on his poor old nose. I got him hobbled down to the Remount Camp, (I suppose you know the Regimental Head Quarters are still at Graaff Reinet), and got Bouthwaite, our Regimental Vet, to look after him for me. I lost a grey stallion that I had just sneaked and a grey pony that I'd had ever since Warren's M.I. broke up. I managed to save my two bay ponies, though one is still a bit stiff. One I got at Aberdeen when we commandeered the town horses there, an awfully pretty blood looking little thing; the other one I got out of Cockell's Troop when I rejoined the Column from hospital. He's a Basuto, I think, a very thickset little devil, and tripples like blazes, if you know what 'trippling' is. It's a sort of run, a great pace out here since it's so comfortable. Then out of the remounts at Willowmore I got another useful sort of a bay pony who shapes well and a black mare which was very poor in condition and had to be shot yesterday when I was away. She wasn't bad but the heavy trekking we've been having killed her. So I've only three horses now to mount me and my two servants.

Well, to return to the train. It was pretty anxious times for a bit for both the guard's van lot and for us, since they, jumping out on hearing and feeling the shock and seeing the fore part of the train gone, thought we had gone into the river, while we, of course, thought *they* were in the wreckage. A most providential escape all round!

Well, we loaded up the survivors, and got agate again, as they say in Yorkshire, leaving Graaff Reinet about 2p.m. We stopped at Klippatz Junction for the night and got to Willowmore about 9 o'clock next morning, Sunday, and detrained. We left at 4a.m. on Tuesday morning and moved West along the Valley (Willowmore). This valley is separated from the Oudtshoorn Valley on the south, by a great range, called The Zwart Berg. On the north runs the little Zwart Berg, and this is the one we were holding, the Boers being north of it − and wanting to get to Oudtshoorn. When we got to Vandeling, at the bottom of Zoutendals Vleinpoort, the 11th remained with the convoy, the 24th went to hold Kandos Poort and the Colonel, with the 23rd and the C.M.Rs., went to Zoutendals Vlei Poort on reconnaissance. This was on the 5th. On the 6th we, under Major Edwards, moved on to Majes Vlei, while the Colonel went down to Strydoms Vlei and there ran into an ambush of about 40 Boers under Malan. Our old friend Hugo, Scheeper's pal, was also present, also Lategan, whom Scobell played the devil with in the Camdeboo. They promptly shot the Colonel and four men and hooked it. The Colonel was shot in the leg, but his horse was shot, too, and fell on him and damaged him badly. Ross Johnson, the Staff Officer, pursued for some time, but eventually came into Kandoss Poort that evening. The Major took over Command. That night, Hamilton and Chichy went out and held Zoutendals Vlei Poort, I held Lombards Voetpand, the 23rd. and C.M.Rs. held Kandos, and Dunlop the next path to the west. Drooge Kloof and adjoining paths were held by D.M.Ts.

Next morning the Major moved out through Kandos with the 24th and the 23rd and the convoy went on to Klaarstroom, about 18 miles. We followed after as we came fluttering down from our mountain eyries, so to speak, and landed at Klaarstroom about 9 p.m. On at 4 a.m. next morning, through Drooge Kloof to Zeekoe Gat, where we camped that night. We got a despatch in the night from Major Edwards. The Boers were north west at a farm called Rietfontein and he was at Sprewfontein. The Boers were coming south to try and cross again and he thought if we came on them in the early morning, they might run in to him. So we moved at 3.30 a.m., leaving the convoy, and got to Rietfontein about 7 o'clock.

The Boers had been there right enough, had seen us coming and had made an ambush. I was Advanced Screen with my troop and, of course, when they spotted what was coming, they offed it like blazes half an hour before we got there, going north, the swines. We pursued for two days, always about 45 minutes behind them, but at the end of that time they struck off east into the veldt and doubled back towards the south again. On the third day they had increased their start about 8 hours.

Here a despatch from Major Edwards caught us, (11th inst.), and he came up early that morning with the 24th and took up the chase, sending us to here with the convoy for a day off and to get provisions. We'd been living off the country since we left Zeekoe Gat. And here we are.

As I understand it, the situation is: Major Edwards is chasing these jokers towards the Zwart Berg again, the passes being held by the D.M.Ts. who are 'Devils for their Vittles, and Baa lambs to the foe'. I suppose we will soon be on the wing again, taking out supplies to the Major. The Colonel's brother Col. W. Doran is coming to take over the Column while the old man is away, so as to keep it in the family.

Thanks for the home letters. I am getting on very nicely, thank you, and hope you are the same. I am glad to hear the County Ball went off all right, and that you all had a good time. Toosie gets very excited over my not telling enough about myself. It seems to me that my letters don't do much else but talk about myself and as for telling her when, how, and where, things happen I simply smear pages with it. I'm not wasting my substance much, I don't think, if I get my rights. I about live on my seven and eight pence, I think, and allowances, etc., are to the good. Whether I will ever succeed in getting them, I dunno, but I hope for the best.

Well, good bye now. I hope everyone in Welshpool is well, and all friends and relations. Best Love to you Homebirds and the rest.

Yours affectionately,
Allan

Dreifontein,
Nr. Sutherland, CC
23rd Novr 1901

Dear People,

Only just a line by candle light to tell you that I am still serene and hope you all are, too. We left Letjesbosch the day after I wrote, trekked east again and rejoined Major Edwards and his party.

The new Colonel, W. Doran, joined us at Letjesbosch. We then, at Uitkyk Siding, split up, he Colonel taking a hundred men and chasing after the Kommando eastwards and the remainder following on with the convoy. Needless to say, the Boers got away easily and the Colonel abandoned the chase about 35 miles beyond Sutherland, a pretty good run from near Willowmore. The Colonel only just stopped in time, since there are about 700 Boers, (some say 1500) just where he was going, who made Colwell, with the 5th Lancers, run like hares a few days before. I'm very much disgusted with the way the chase of this, Malan's, lot has been conducted, but I'm sick of grousing about it, so no more. These 700 are fine pukka Boers, they say, all in khaki and sportsmen, so there should be some fun.

We have come out here, about 15 miles from Sutherland, to rest a bit, and stop the Boers coming south. How, I don't know. Sutherland is 100 miles from anywhere and the town, such as it is, is cleaned out of everything in the way of supplies, except military ones. We shall probably, from all appearances, be up here somewhere for months, so don't expect regular letters since we are quite out of the world, away from the Line.

This is a miserable country up here. We are about 6000 feet up and it is mostly cold. The seasons are far behind where we have come up from and we are getting a second winter. We've had a good deal of rain too. The Convoy is going into Sutherland in the morn for supplies and I shall send this in by it and hope it will catch the mail, if the postcart happens to run from there. I believe it does, once in a while.

I don't think there is much more to tell you and I'm afraid this letter is rather dull, but times haven't been exciting since the last. I hope that all you folks are having a good time and keep well. I suppose you are getting in form for dancing.

Good bye now and best love to all round, especially Toosie and George. I must be up at 4 to see the convoy off, so will now seek the downy. Bye bye.

Your affectionate,
Allan

★★★

DamsLaagte,
Nr. Matjesfontein
Cape Colony
Decr. 2nd 1901

Dearest People,

Just a line, again in a great hurry, to wish you a very happy Christmas and a similar, only more so, New Year. I feel a sort of 'the things we ought to have done' feeling about not sending everyone separate letters and cards and all sorts of things, but we are in most uncivilised parts of South Africa and continually on the run and somehow one can't do much. It's just as much as we can do to write a home letter occasionally and keep ourselves washed, clothed and shaven but all the same I do feel rotten, not being able to do more than scrawl this, which *may* get to you by Christmas, since the Sutherland Matjesfontein Post Cart is expected through here to night.

The beastly Boers went north just after I wrote last and so, not being able to follow them up by ourselves, besides there being very little supplies in these parts and not having anything better to do, we trekked south, nearly to Matjesfontein on the Cape Town line, and met a large convoy, (about 100 donkey wagons), coming out to Sutherland; we are now escorting them out. Since the outside pace for donkey wagons is 1¾ miles an hour, you can imagine it is not a very exhilarating job, and they straggle out for miles.

Our convoy went into Matjesfontein and came out again with supplies and we got our mails and mess stores which were like Balm Gilead, so to speak. Once more we smoke cigarettes and smell the cork of a whiskey bottle occasionally and have milk and sugar in our tea and a bit of bread for our stomach's sake.

I have just snaffled another mount, a terrible looking creature like a camel, but his paces are great. He is one of these tripplers, pacers, or amblers, whichever you like to call them, and he takes you along about 8 miles an hour while you sit in the saddle just as if you were walking.

There is not much of import to relate of our doings lately. We generally trek at 4.30 and with these verdomte donkeys it's sometimes 2 a.m. The new Doran is not beloved by the column. He seems to be a stinker and madder than the old man was before he got broken in to having a whole column to himself.

We expect to reach Sutherland in a few days and what we do then is unknown. We are under the directorship of Haig again and don't care much for the idea. Have you read Kipling's poem M.I. [*Mounted Infantry of the Line*]? It's a great thing and we all quote it but, to the uninitiated, it must seem rather obscure.

I wish my mother could see me now, with a fence-post under my arm,
And a knife and a spoon in my putties that I found on a Boer farm,
Atop of a sore-backed Argentine, with a thirst that you couldn't buy.
I used to be in the Yorkshires once
(Sussex, Lincolns, and Rifles once),

Hampshires, Glosters, and Scottish once! (ad lib.)
But now I am M. I.

But the old man is all there right enough.

I don't think I can write any more since it is after 10; we trek in the morn at 3, the post cart goes in the night sometime and I must go to bed.

I hope you are all well. Personally I remain most disgustingly fit, as all of us do on column. There are only two ways of it. If you are fit, all right. If you get sick at all, you jolly well have to go to hospital, as you can't hang on otherwise, so there is no need for anyone to worry.

Now, good people all, a very merry Xmas and a happy New Year, with lots of fun and oceans of beer, which is poetry, composed by me on the spot.

Yours affectionately,
Allan

★★★

16th December 1901
North of Sutherland C.C.

Dearest Family,

How are you all getting along down in Pool? When you get this I suppose you will be just working off the effects of the Christmas festivities. We are wondering where we shall hold ours, since no one quite knows what is going to happen. I think I wrote you last on the march from Matjesfontein Station to Sutherland with the ass wagons and hoped it would reach you in time for Christmas. Of course, I missed the post cart and had to gallop back about three miles after it and got my letter off.

This district is composed chiefly of Matjesfonteins so don't get confused. Among others, this farm is one. We got to Sutherland in due course and there we went straight away through the town on a burst north, being reinforced by the 5th Lancers under Colwell, and a few Prince of Wales Light Horse. We had to go 120 miles in 4 days to relieve a small garrison which some idiot had left at a farm called Tondelbosch Kalk, and which the Boers were giving snuff to, or which was giving the Boers snuff, as the case may be. They were anything from 500 to 1300 strong (the Boers) and we had about 800 and the garrison about 100. There are more of the enemy in this district than we've ever struck before. There's only ever been one column up this way, and the King's Law doesn't seem to run to any great extent. It's miles from anywhere, and isn't a bad sort of country, only absolutely treeless, except for a blue gum or two on a farm yard. It grows huge quantities of grain which is now standing and which we feed our horses on (also the Boers) and is full of Boers and Bush ticks which burrow into you and hold on like death across a dead nigger (the ticks, I mean, not the Boers). On our way north we fell over several lots of Boers and gathered in 8 or 9 and lots of their horses and mules. Captain Saunders of the 24th had a most exciting time one day. He captured a Boer and sent him into camp and then he and a corporal of his chased him and 5 more about 7 miles. Saunders took the devil of a toss, shot a Boer, captured another and came back covered with blood and glory. We had a sergeant shot that day, and have 3 men missing. We relieved Tondelbosch all right, the Boers having returned about 2 days before we got there, after besieging it for 6 days and giving it a hot time. The garrison had 2 men killed and 5 or 6 wounded and the Boers admitted to having 23 wounded, and our fellows found about 7 graves so they struck a wrong 'un there. There were 12 commandants there, of which 3 were wounded including Maritz, the big boss. This chap came down from the Free State with about 14 followers 6 months ago and has organised the whole of the rebellion in the Western provinces and has now the command of about a dozen commandos, about 1300 men. They have made a sort of depot up in Bushmansland and have great stores of grain, ammunition, etc. buried there. The garrison consists chiefly of the Bushmanland Borderers who are more or less coloured and are called Bastards. These people live in little colonies by themselves, quite distinct from Dutch or Natives. In appearance they are some of them just like Dutchmen and some just like niggers. They speak Dutch, are magnificent shots, can see as well as any field glasses, and hate the Dutch with a most poisonous hate. Vice versa.

We are now going south again and are nearing Sutherland. We have been picking up the remains of black despatch riders who have been trying to come through to us or vice versa, at some of the farms. There were 3 at this one. If the Boers catch an armed native he goes up.

I daresay we shall wait at Sutherland for some more columns and then come back north again and fight the good fight. But this is only supposition.

I find that if I can send this off at once per cyclist to Sutherland it may catch this mail, so I will finish up now.

With best love and a Happy New Year,
Yours affectly,
Allan

★★★

Brand Vlei (about 25 miles north of Matjesfontein Station)
Decr 22nd 1901

Dearest Ma, Pa and Podge,

I am trying to recollect where I last wrote to you from but can't quite do so. I think it must have been Sutherland on Jakhal's Valley, just this side. Nothing of note has occurred since except that we have slowly trekked down here and that I have received your letters of 16th, 22nd, and 29th of Nov., for which much thanks.

It looks as if we might have a day or two's rest here over Christmas but, of course, we may move at any minute, especially as we are in helio distance of Haig.

Now we have heard that old B. Doran has been given Hunter-Weston's column, it seems we shall be blessed by W's presence to all eternity, or 'til death do us part. There is nothing of excitement, except that 400 Boers have come down this way and are not far off. Is it true they have captured old Kritzinger? We have heard a rumour but don't know for sure. If so, it's good, because he's supposed to be the supreme Kommandant in the Colony.

I'm glad the two old birds had a good time in town. I want to see 'Sherlock Holmes' badly. No, George, I was not with the M.M.R. in Waterkloof when they turned Lotter. That was after our little 'do' in Garstlands Kloof, so I shan't get mentioned this time or any other, I don't suspect. So cheer up.

The *County Times* library must be the greatest acquisition and if ever I return to Welshpool I shall patronise it extensively. By the way, any odds and ends of literature such as 6d novels, etc., are all very acceptable after you have read them, of course. Not old ones I have read but new ones you see on the bookstalls and speculate 3d or 6d on. Don't send monthly magazines since we mostly see them when we strike a town.

I'm awfully relieved to hear that George has decided to keep Clive House on since it would be very rotten to leave it.

Has George got through those quarterly accounts yet? He is very smart at following our trekkings on the map. We have covered a bit of the Colony now, haven't we? Aren't they writing rot about harmoniums, kitchen ranges, etc., in the papers and doesn't it do your heart good to hear about the New Yeomanry, especially from letters written by S. African colonels? The new I.Y., when they first came out were all that was bad – or at least, the papers said so. Certainly they were pretty poor in most ways but they have two qualities that the S.A. born youth never has. The first is a sense of sacrifice and the second, pluck, or a certain amount of it. The free-born colonial, (mind, I'm only speaking of S.A.), has a fine, well-nourished funk of the Boer in his heart, which leads him to speak contemptuously and with much garnishment, (also a Dutch accent), of that enemy in bars and other safe places and to run like a hare when he gets near him. Did I tell you of the 25 Beaufort West D.M.T.s who saw us coming out in the veldt one day? We sent out one man to try to communicate with them but they didn't stop 'til his horse was beat so we sent in to Beaufort to let them know and thus rather spoilt the yarns they were pitching of bloody doings out on the veldt.

Affectionate greetings to all at Christmas,
Allan

★★★

Somewhere between Matjesfontein and Ceres,
C.C.
Christmas Day, 1901

Dear Schofe [Roney Schofield, Becky's husband-to-be],

Thanks very much for your kind letter which I had been anticipating for some time on account of my little sister, Becky, saying that she had been prodding you up. But, of course, I can see that the cares and worries of patients and preparing your abode and

– what must be the most difficult for you – looking respectable at the same time, have been taking up a lot of your time lately.

You seem to be going in great style in the new residence and from all accounts, it will be a jolly outfit. Your plan of the house was most excellent and instantly filled my trained eye with a vision of beauty.

Thank you very much for the cigarettes, old hoss. They haven't arrived yet but we are expecting a lot of parcels today or tomorrow. Baccy, as you know, is very acceptable at all times and I do shake your hand most hearty.

I was very pleased to hear of the Mexicans being so kind to our Kitty. It must have made the poor child feel quite homey. As Charley Elwell wrote to me, he thinks poor Kitty will be much better married. It's awfully funny to get Kitty's and Charlie's letters about the same incidents and compare them!

I greatly sympathise with you, my dear Schofe about the care one must take of one's footsteps nowadays with such nasty insinuating kind of folks around. I, too, have suffered, though I wasn't doing any harm at all, at all.

By Jove, who would be a doctor? If there was any doubt about the state of the young lady you mention when she came to you, I guess there's not much now! More power to ye, and after all, the poor girl ought to get a run for her money, oughtn't she?

I wonder what sort of a Christmas Day you are all having. From reports received, you must be having one of the old English sort: frost and snow. By the irony of fate, this is the hottest day we've had for ever so long. I'm writing this in the airy garb of a suit of pyjamas.

We moved at 4 p.m. last afternoon and trekked till 10 p.m. and came on here at 4.30 this morning. Our convoy should come out soon and we will then go on tomorrow towards Ceres, but not sure for what object. Hopefully, a rest!

The war that 'was practically over' when Kitchener replaced Roberts as Commander-in-Chief in November 1900 had become a monumental struggle between a limitless Empire and diminishing but determined guerrilla commands. Any pretence of it being a 'white man's war' was long forgotten with both sides deploying blacks in the hostilities. Predictably, blacks were treated as traitors by both sides and black villages suffered bloody reprisals. Black concentration camps were created near unoccupied Boer farms, intending that they become self-sufficient in food. Starvation, disease and poor medical care claimed 20,000 lives. In December 1901, Kitchener announced there would be no further civilian detentions, black or white – thus abandoning the populace to the veldt winter.

With a huge investment of men and money, Kitchener had turned the tide in the Transvaal and Orange Free State (or Orange River Colony as it was called after the British capture of Bloomfontein). Fortified blockhouses within shooting range of one another had slowed the rate of attrition. The Boers' best hope was to raise an Afrikaner rebellion in Cape Colony and Natal. Smuts penetrated the Cape and Botha humiliated Gough at Blood River Poort until, short of supplies, he retreated to the Transvaal. After de Wet raided a British camp at Tweefontein on Christmas Day 1901, Kitchener went after him with 20,000 men, including Boers now recruited to the British cause. Driven against the blockhouses of the Kroonstad-Lindley Line, De Wet escaped.

Jan 3rd 1902
Ceres District CC.

Dearest Family,

We left Brand Vallei (where I think I last wrote you from) on Christmas Eve about 4 p.m. and spent Christmas Day on the Veldt, arriving in camp about 10 a.m. so we had a nice long day to celebrate it. Nothing occurred of very great importance except that we had a gorgeous spread and that I was ill next day on account of a plum-pudding made by Cattley's sister. On Boxing Day we trekked on towards Ceres and eventually landed there about 9 a.m. on the following Saturday morning, which I think was the 28th. The inhabitants received us with open arms and, after a Sabbath of scheming and planning, on the Monday we opened the campaign by giving a gymkhana, which went off very successfully. There were three officers events; an orange catching competish (in which you charger down on a lady and she tries to hit you in the eye with a lemon), a charge race (sweepstake), a whistling race (in which you again charge a lady, get off, whistle a tune which she has to guess, and then race home). Major Edwards won the orange race in great style. We had a pretty good field for the charger race, and I think I was a bit unlucky in running fourth with one of my ponies (Bob) who is turning out very well. The Colonel was judge for the whistling race and just before we started he said to us that the first man who handed in his paper (with the tune written on,) was the winner. Well, after my fair lady (a Mrs Steyther) had guessed the tune I started back and found that as I came to round the turning post, Turner (the supply officer) was already almost home, while Hamilton, my skipper was a couple lengths ahead. But Turner's horse ran out and old Hamilton pulled out bang in front of the Colonel and reached out his paper straight over his horse's ears. The great man extended his hand, and as he did so, I came past 'with a song from the sea', so to speak, and got hold of it tight with my paper inside it. So when the old man had got over the fright we gave him he said I had won, which was most satisfactory. That night we gave a dance, and was one of the best little affairs possible. All the youth and beauty came, and there are some very pretty girls in Ceres. It went off beautifully. I danced 'most every dance and sweated profusely.

Next day was a quiet one, since we were sleeping off the dance, and nothing occurred of note except a cricket match in the day between the column and the Cape Police, and some polo in the evening. Punch, one of my ponies, plays very well. I've not tried Bob yet but I think he might do, if not too keen. I went to call on my lady love, Mrs. Steyther, that morning, to present her with the prize for the whistling race which was a gold bangle. She is a rummy little body, and as a mark of gratitude invited me to her picnic on the next day. I and Tabor went from ours and Turner and Hamilton turned up too, beside several others. The girls had been most judiciously selected and we had a very good time, the repast being excellent. We succeeded in setting the plantation on fire and had to turn out and extinguish it.

That evening there was another dance (private) to which Hamilton and Chichester went. I had not the pleasure of the lady's acquaintance so was not asked, but had an invitation to another house, the De Marillacs and went there instead. Since Chichy says the dance was deathly dull, and there are four really scrumptious De Marillac girls, I think like Mary, I chose the better part.

Next day we left 4.30 a.m. and are now about 45 miles from there on the Clan-William Road. They say we are going back in a few days but it seems a bit too good to be true. Trekking doesn't seem to be so exciting as Ceres, but we shall be alright again in a day or two.

I've had your letter of the 6th December with Cox's account and thank you very much. I see he hasn't yet issued my pay while I was a captain, normal my detention allowance, but I am writing him on the subject. Also thank you very much for the local news, which is all very interesting.

As to Cox's account, I think I am keeping pretty square and I haven't drawn any Field or Colonial allowances yet out here. Besides, I've had rather unusual expenses, what with my month knocking about between hospitals, for which the swines ought to give me compensation, as it cost me a lot – near £20 I should think. I don't expect I shall ever get anything though. Then I sent Coates my poor old servant a cheque for a fiver the other day, since I haven't paid him, and again Tilletson went sick at Ceres so I paid him up £8, and got some boots, shirts and clothes there too, so altogether I've not being doing so badly.

This is a very pretty district. Ceres is awfully pretty itself. There are so many trees that you can hardly see any houses from outside the town and the hills hang right over it, most unimaginably rocky and rugged. There is a very nice clear river too which we use to bathe. All the farms round here are much better class than the Karoo farms and mostly have fruit trees and oaks, and gardens. We are getting a good deal of fruit though it is only the beginning of the season.

I don't think I have much more of import to tell you. I hope you're all well at home and that you are not leaving Clive House. I'm expecting to hear soon of your Christmas celebrations, and hope you're getting some skating. I won't wind this up now since I don't expect I shall be able to send it for a bit.

★★★

14th Jan. 1902
Karoo Poort,
Nr. Ceres CC

Dearest People,

Nothing very much to say this time except that I am all serene and hope you are similar, only more so. We stopped at Ceres one day (and the day we got in) and the first night I had rather a nice little dinner party and the second we had a rippin' good little dance. I was on duty all the day or might have attended a ladies' cricket match. Since then we have had a dam' silly time. Simply trekked out 2 days into the Karoo and sat on a beastly sand hill. Then one days trek back again which brings us here. Our squadron went out on patrol eastwards the other day and we did nearly 60 miles starting at 5 a.m. and getting in 10.30 p.m. Oh, some of the column shot two Boers the day before.

Best love to all,
Allan

★★★

In the early days of February 1902, Smuts, Abram Malan and several other Boer leaders showed great activity in the country round Calvinia, 400km north of Cape Town. Their commandos included veteran Republicans from the north, who were more formidable fighting material than the raw Colonial rebels. Against them were British columns, including Doran's, which proved critically weak. Two clashes occurred on the same date, 5 February, and in each case the British were heavily outnumbered.

On the road from Beaufort West to Fraserburg a convoy led by Major Crofton comprising 60 Colonial Mounted Rifles and 100 West Yorkshire militia was attacked and overwhelmed by Malan's kommando. Crofton was killed and several men before Crabbe arrived with reinforcements. Meanwhile, Colonel Doran's column extricated itself with severe loss from 'a most perilous plight'. There is no better account than in The Great Boer War, *by Arthur Conan Doyle:*

The whole force under Doran consisted of 350 men with two guns, and this handful was divided by an expedition which he, with 150 men, undertook in order to search a distant farm. The remaining two hundred men, under Captain Saunders, were left upon February 5th with the guns and the convoy at a place called Middlepost, which lies about fifty miles south-west of Calvinia. These men were of the 11th, 23rd, and 24th Imperial Yeomanry, with a troop of Cape Police. The Boer Intelligence was excellent, as might be expected in a country which is dotted with farms. [Yet in Allan's account the British force had no reason to think there were Boers 'within a hundred miles'.] The weakened force at Middlepost was instantly attacked by Smuts's commando. Saunders evacuated the camp and abandoned the convoy, which was the only thing he could do, but he concentrated all his efforts upon preserving his guns. The night was illuminated by the blazing wagons, and made hideous by the whoops of the drunken rebels who caroused among the captured stores. With the first light of dawn the small British force was fiercely assailed on all sides, but held its own in a manner which would have done credit to any troops. The much criticised Yeomen fought like veterans. A considerable position had to be covered, and only a handful of men were available at the most important points. One ridge, from which the guns would be enfiladed, was committed to the charge of Lieutenants Tabor and Chichester with eleven men of the 11th Imperial Yeomanry, their instructions being 'to hold it to the death'. The order was obeyed with the utmost heroism. After a desperate defence the ridge was only taken by the

Boers when both officers had been killed and nine out of eleven men were on the ground. In spite of the loss of this position the fight was still sustained until shortly after midday, when Doran with the patrol returned. The position was still most dangerous, the losses had been severe, and the Boers were increasing in strength. An immediate retreat was ordered, and the small column, after ten days of hardship and anxiety, reached the railway line in safety. The wounded were left to the care of Smuts, who behaved with chivalry and humanity.

Elam's Hotel,
late Menzies' Sanatorioum,
Ceres
15th Febr. 1902

Dear Family,

It seems a terrible long time since my last but this is the first chance I have had really. I think the last was from Gansfontein in the Karoo. We left there on the night of the 31st and trekked north-east towards the Roggeveldt. The idea was to try and capture a small commandant named Geldenhuis (rebel) who lives at a pace called Waggon Drift about 30 or 40 miles from Gansfontein. After missing him at his house we kept on casting for him, until we ascended the Roggerveld by the Ganaga Pass on the night of the 3rd and 4th. The next evening (the 4th) Col. Doran, the Major, and about 120 of the column (picked for the best horses) left at midnight to go on to a farm called Matjesfontein where Geldenhuis was reported to be lying sick. We left the convoy and guns under Capt. Saunders with his squadron (the 24th) and C.M.Rs and what was left of the 23rd and 24th. Saunders would have about 80 of his squadron, 40 C.M.Rs and about 30 of the 24th and 11th. These numbers include sick and non-effectives, servants, wagon-men, orderlies etc. The camp was at Achter Kop and next morning he was to move to Middlepost, about 18 miles to the east from the place we were going to, and there we were to join him. Well, we (the patrol) moved off at midnight, and our information as usual being a bit out, we didn't get to the place in time to catch the commando, day having dawned before we got there, but we found them all ready for us. This was Abram Louw's little lot, to which Geldenhuis had attached himself. They shot Bingham of the 23rd through the head without killing him and then bolted as per usual. Hamilton and I with about 30 or 40 men found ourselves opposed to a similar force of Boers and spent a merry hour or two chasing them from kopje to kopje. Of course, they got away. Then we went down to a farm near at hand and camped while Dunlop went on to the next farm with a few men to fetch Geldenhuis who we learn was there. He got him and two others and brought them to De Hoop (our camp) a very nice farm with a loyal Dutchman named Vissasse, who was an awfully kind old Johnnie. We turned in that night and in the middle of it were woken up by a despatch rider, who had come through the Boer lines with the news that the convoy was surrounded and the wagons burning at Middlepost. We saddled up and reached Middlepost about 10 a.m. (we had to leave the prisoners). By the time we got there, we had given up all hope, since we met our mules and horses wandering about the veldt, and heard from adjacent farmers that the fighting had been renewed that morning at daylight, and had stopped suddenly at 8 a.m. I and Hamilton held the nek leading down to the farm to cover the retirement of the others who went on with the colonel (firing having been going on all the time since they got down), and then we knew for the first time that there hadn't been any surrender, and that the guns were safe.

It appears to have happened like this:

Saunders reached Middlepost on the morning of the 5th, as arrange, and camped, although he couldn't find an uncommanded position. Soon afterwards, the Boers began to appear. Mind, we had no knowledge of their being within 100 miles of Middlepost, and I don't know now whether the commandant was Malan, Van de Venter, or either. They certainly were not rebels or only a few of them. There were apparently about 250 of them and they began to occupy the high ground all round the camp and opened fire. Saunders made the best of a terribly bad position and eventually had to move out of the farm and occupy a hill. The Boers then came into the wagons but were driven out again, but when darkness came on they came in again and started firing them. In so doing they filled themselves up with our rum and whiskey, and fairly ran amok among the wagons, our men firing steadily into them and the Boers cheering every volley. Chichester and Tabor with the few men of the 11th held the most dangerous and important position in the lot. Once the Boers rushed at it and a voice called out in English, 'Stop firing, you damned fools, we're friends'. Thinking it must be us, Chichy ceased fire, but luckily found out his mistake in time. This was in the dark and he got a slight wound in the neck, that evening. Next morning the attack was renewed and poor Chichy got shot through the head. Then Tabor got it next, poor chap – the top of his head from his eyebrows clean gone. This was after he had shot five Boers himself. Then Ward of the 24th got hit in the stomach. There were five others (or six, I'm not sure which) were killed in that skirmish, all shot through the head. My troop sergeant, my servants and three of Dunlop's troop all got killed there. The total casualties were three officers and 7 men killed and about 19 wounded. Of these, 2 officers and five men killed belonged to the 11th, though I don't think we had 20 men in camp. We had half a dozen or so wounded too. The Boer loss is, of course, unknown, but must have been far greater than ours. One of my troop shot one swine about 4 yards range.

Well, eventually, we came and fetched them out but all the wheeled transport was burnt. Not a single thing saved. I left Middlepost as rear guard and we trekked straight off to De Hoop again in the dark and I reflected, as we went along, that A.M.H. and his fortune rested on four horseshoes. When we got to De Hoop about 2 a.m., we were glad of a snooze but went on again at 2 p.m. We had to clear for Ceres, for we were without food for men or horse, bedding or ammunition, and no one knew how soon the next attack would come. Since there are now about 1600 of the stinkers around the Western Province, we reflected that the sooner we got into Ceres and refitted, the better; and all the other columns were over at Fraserburg.

18th.

When we left De Hoop at 2 p.m. we trekked down an awful pass into the Karoo again and went on until 8 a.m. next morning, with only about one hour's halt, about 1 to 2. By Jove it was a trek. If we rode our horses, we were just on the point of falling off every minute with sleep, and if we walked, we wandered off the road and fell over bushes, and woke up that way. I don't believe there was a single man on the column who didn't fall asleep a dozen times during the night. We did 76 miles in 36 hours. After that we moved quietly on into Ceres, being met about three days out by wagons with supplies. Until then, of course, we had not a dam' thing, except a little wheat from the farms for the horses, goat flesh and anything in the way of meal we could steal. We got some mealies, roasted and ground them and kidded ourselves we were drinking coffee. It was fortunately pretty warm or else we should have been badly off, since some of the men hadn't even their jackets, much less blankets. The column is stopping at Ceres to refit.

We reached Ceres at last on the 14th and I got your letters of the 17th and 24th, also Roney's and Elsie's.

Isn't it awfully sad about poor Chichy, Tabor and Ward? Three of the most inoffensive, nicest fellows you could imagine, and all fought like tigers. They say Ward and old Tabor accounted for about 8 between them. Ward had one by the throat when he was shot, and finished him too. R.I.P.

Well, I 'm now down here in Cape Town on three days leave with four others, replacing some of our kit. I return to Ceres tomorrow night. I have got enough to go on with now, thanks, but will be glad to get the things I have already asked you for. Don't send anything else, since if you do we shall probably be duplicating orders. Many thanks for the boots you sent, they were very nice and I wore them once. I expect some greasy Boer finds them an improvement on his usual veldt-schoons. You might please order me another pair; not quite the same as they were a bit too high. What I want is an ordinary shooting boot, just over the ankles. Those came right up my calf and I was going to cut them down, but the Boers saved me the trouble.

Will you please get Smith of Shrewsbury to send me another pair of <u>saddlebags</u> like the last (not wallets, you know) and please let me have all these bills as soon as sent.

Three or four white <u>stocks</u> would also be acceptable – they make them with celluloid stiffening now – that's the sort.

If the field boots are not already despatched, please be careful re specification, since unless they are correct I may just as well get them out here. To recapitulate, I want them just like a jack boot but split over the instep for lacing, and according to the size that you will get from George Evans. 70/- does not appear too much if they are right.

½ doz. handkerchiefs, also, please; not too good since I lose them, and two suits of pyjamas. The things I ask for now, I am in no great hurry for, but the ones I asked for before I shall be glad to get at once. There, that's over.

I must apologise for writing all this selfishness, but it's been on my mind some time now.

I do hope you don't move from Clive House. It's such a nice old place, and I think it would be rather a mistake.

Now about this commission. I'm very comfortable out here and there isn't much chance of my getting the sack for another two years. By that time I shall probably have a squadron (I'm senior sub. in our squadron now) and that means about £400 a year. Then again, the army, I really, calmly and dispassionately, do not think is worth the candle. If I were to go into any line regiment, I should like to go to a decent one and that means more than we can possibly afford anyhow. Besides I've clean gone off infantry work and think that I'm beginning to understand a bit about cavalry work, and I'm positive there will always be a job to be got now in that line. Besides this work gives you an opportunity of seeing practical work and a much wider experience than you get at home and I think it will be better for me to go on comfortably out here, than to have to struggle to keep up appearances in a second rate marching regiment at home. As for the M.I. question of course, that is absolutely <u>en l'air</u> and at any rate I should have to do my 'square' some time.

So, I think, George, please, we had best shake it. And Sir Watkin [Herbert Lloyd Watkin Williams-Wynn, 7th Baronet, Lord Lieutenant of Montgomeryshire] is raising a Welsh Regt. is he? I hope he doesn't brutally assault more than half the recruits.

I'm sorry you missed the Salisbury Plain affair, but we can still scratch on in Welshpool, I suppose. Wouldn't you be sorry to leave it? I'm glad you have had some decent dances, and wish I could have been there.

Oh, Toosie, dear! Poor old Cockell had to go home. He was apparently still a good bit balmy, but we had a letter which I've not yet seen, from him the other day.

Thank you, Podgie, very much for the nice letter – you always were a good child. Now, good people, no more. I've spent a whole morning out of my miserable 2½ days' leave in writing letters, and am not half through yet. I must write soon to Kitty, Billy, Betty, Roney, Maude, Daisy E., and to the mothers of my poor sergeant and servant.

Good bye. Please let me hear often, although I don't ask enough questions.
Best love all round,
Yours affectionately,
Allan

★★★

12th March 1902
Victoria Road
C.C.

Dearest Family,

How is the 'ome curcle this long time? I trust everyone is like unto a young baytree. I'm trying to get your letters up to date answered; the last I received was Feb. 7th, but I am hoping against hope to get some today.

First, let me thank you kindly for the field boots, which I got at Beaufort West, and which are very satisfactory. Promptness and dispatch are strongly to the fore. I am now eagerly awaiting the breeches, when I shall be pretty well fitted out again. I have got most of my new kit and sent in a claim for the stuff that was burnt. Whether I get owt remains to be seen.

I see from the local press that there is great excitement about the Infantry training at Welshpool. I hope they pull it off, and that once more our one and only Podgie will be able to hang her little head out of the window as the gallant Cavalry go out forth to drill.

How did she enjoy being vaccinated by the dear charmer Notty? I suppose she sat behind a screen and put her arm through, in the Oriental manner.

As George observes, it is it is rather rough on these Boer kommandants when they are shot, since as a rule they are such gallant chaps, but I suppose they must stand by their actions the same as their followers or any other law breaker. And certainly it oughter encourager les autres!!

I am sorrier for Kritzinger than I was for Scheepers, for the latter was rather a swine, while K. is really a first rate chap. I believe he has murdered a lot of niggers though, so he will probably be for it.

As to the Indian Staff Corps., it sounds very tempting but I think I should have heard by now about the Commission if it was coming, and I told you a letter or two back that I was going on all right out here, so don't worry or be cast down at all, so to speak.

Thank William very kindly for the book she sent me. It was very welcome, and very amusing.

Allan is repeating a popular view of Kritzinger. Conan Doyle writes:

Kritzinger was wounded and captured by Doran while endeavouring to cross the line near Hanover Road upon December 15th. He was put upon his trial, and his fate turned upon how far he was responsible for the misdeeds of some of his subordinates. It was clearly shown that he had endeavoured to hold them within the bounds of civilised warfare, and with congratulations and handshakings he was acquitted by the military court.

In his Diary of the War *Davitt observes:*

The charge of shooting natives was even more hypocritical in its shameless effrontery. These natives had been armed and employed as spies and scouts by the English. They had been warned by Kritzinger and Scheepers, when Cape Colony was invaded, that they would be severely dealt with if they took up arms against the Republics, but would not be molested if they remained neutral. On the other hand, British Ministers in Parliament had declared, on the eve of the war, that no native people would be brought into the struggle by England. English officers, nevertheless, armed Kaffirs and employed them in that kind of work which is most dangerous and obnoxious to an enemy – spy work and scouting; and when these were caught in arms, and so engaged, they were rightly shot by the Boer Commandants. To an official at Murraysburg who denied that the natives in that locality had been so employed, Scheepers replied: 'You deny using natives against us! Why, I have shot them at 200 yards, and in the front line of fire, where your own men shrank from going.

★ ★ ★

Deelfontein C.C,
6th April 1902

Dearest Betty (in the first place)
and William (in the second)

Will you please allow me to make it a combined letter for the two little lovebuds, since I have so terrible many letters to write, and I am sure I shan't be able to find anything different to say in one from the other. (If you read this carefully you may be able to find some meaning in it. Wire me the result of your investigations).

I have before me two of the dear Betty's letters, one of Jan 17th from Aldenham and one of Feb. 21st from Eastbourne; and one of our William's of Feb. 4th from Kinloch. To go into these is the object of this essay. Talking of essays, did you see that one in the Pink 'un about cats – 'The pig is a natif of the Holy Land, and the dog is French, but the cat has been none from earliest times and can purr. Missis Bobbitwell, wich has got the 'leven children and comes to our house achavin, she said she coodent bear cats, and I heard Par spoke to Mar, and he said, Par did, 'that's a damm good thing for the mice, don't you think, mother?' Ha-ha!

What a gay time you must have had at Southport, Betty oh! With your festivities and celebrations I understand that the happy day is now fixed definitely and decidedly. It does seem rummy. Have you seen Carrie girl lately? Toosie describes her as 'radiant with happiness', which ain't bad for the old 'ooman. She'll be writing for the *County Times* soon.

I suppose our Bill is also somewhat radiant with happiness as the time approaches for her to cut her little stick from the north for good, and for her to have a royal campaign among frills and furbelows and chiffon gussets.

Thank you very much for the little verses. I enjoyed the first one very much, but I seem to have heard something like the young man of Bengal before, and if you will take a tip from the old firm, you will not repeat it to anyone.

I got Sara Jeanette's book from Billy and it was very amusing. Thank you. Have either of you read 'The Visits of Elizabeth'; and 'The Letters of her Mother to Elizabeth'? They are great fun; and Barry Pain's skit on 'An Englishwoman's Love Letters' is screaming.

I want William to send me the new book she refers to by David Kerr and G. Henty re my exploits as soon as it is published.

Have you, Bill, learnt to curl yet? What with the late post and your residence on the spot, you certainly should have acquired that gentle and alluring pastime. I note that the post has disappeared long ago at home.

As regards this column, there are all the signs of a long continuance and great rigour. Yes, my Becky, the papers were not very accurate in describing our little affair as a night-rush on a patrol. The johnnies on the patrol (I was one) were all right; it was the ones who stopped with the convoy who got socks. But we are all absolutely sick with the beastly unworthy lies which are being dished up to the people at home about the war. It's all bound to come out at last and then there will be a fine old flare-up. Of course, you don't want to be flourishing their opinions about, since I should probably get it in the neck if you did, but I'll tell you all about it when. I would now, but I have no ambition to be a Dreyfus as yet.

How is Charlie and the Hell-babe? I hope they and you two also continue to enjoy your convalesence. I'm alright as usual, and have been having a quiet time, also as usual. We still continue to carefully ascertain where our brother Boer lurks and then to trek in the other direction. Oh, lots of fun! Although we do not flourish our fighting capabilities much, we're open to trek any other column of our weight for a small purse.

The mess consists of Cole-Hamilton, our skipper, an Irishman; very nice chap indeed but not much headpiece; Cattley, the doctor, a rum old fish, who is a sort of mine of information and book of reference to the outfit; Douthwaite, our regimental vet, not very much class, but not a bad sort, surnamed Guids; or otherwise the Relic of the Old Fighting days, since he's always bukking on about the Old Third, and Methven's First Division; Sugden, our senior sub., a huge red-headed Yorkshireman; Dunlop from Jersey; a great favourite, and Chusty, the last-joined sub. All ripping good chaps bar the last, whom I can't stick. We all live quietly in peace with all the world.

Dunlop and I are now the only two officers on the column who have been with it since it was formed; which after all, does not seem to raise the feeling of respect for us among the others which we might expect.

Have you read 'Gal's Gossip'? In case you haven't, I will here relate the terrible railway accident which is reported therein. If you've read it, skip accordingly:

'A beautiful damsel, like as it might have been one of you, thank me – was cycling merrily along a road beside the railway. Suddenly she was horrified to perceive that a large slip of rock had fallen across the line. Like a flash she bowed her back to the work and tore along to reach the signal-box and avert a terrible disaster. Alas! But half-way there, and round the curve, dashed the evening mail. The brave girl sprang from her machine and tearing off the only red garment she happened to have on, a pair of scarlet bloomers, she waved them frantically before the approaching express. The engine rocked from side to side for a moment and then took a header down a steep bank, killing the fireman and fatally injuring the driver.'

Well now, my little dears, I must away. Cheer up both of you and haste to the wedding.

Best love all both of you,
Your affectionate brother,
Allan

★★★

28th April 1902
Goliadsfontein
Nr. Aberdeen,
C.C.

Dearest People,

Since my last from Deelfontein I have had one or two mail from you, and expect one or two more in a day or two. I got the third George Evans consignment all correct at Deelfontein with the stocks which I thought you had forgotten. Really my gratitude overwhelms me for the trouble you have taken, and the spurs and saddlebags were exactly what I wanted. Not that I mean the other things weren't but these two were replicas of the ones I chose myself. The things you choose for me are generally glorified editions of what I think I want.

Now in reply to yours of the 21st March. Thanks for Kitty's letter, and the various *County Times*. These last supply the cravings for news of two poor Montgomeryshire maroons on this column, namely me and a cyclist lad named Gregg from Newtown, who belongs to my company in the S.W.B.

I hope Nina agreed with the Vulchers over her fiddling and suppose that the charm of her music quite softened their stony bosoms. You ought to turn her on to Calabashie to get him to reduce the rent. Do you think that Connie would be sufficiently pre-served for me when I come home? I'm afraid she wouldn't do for a soldier's bride. (Dam' this pen, it goes on strike at times, and at others simply overflows with energy. It's the one Betty presented me with, and would be all right but I've had no ink for a long time and it has shrunk). I'm glad to hear that everyone is all right at home and that you have settled to stop on at Clive House. As George says, what an epidemic of weddings we are having. Spirit of competition, I suppose.

George makes a small error about our friend Geldenhuis. The one with Baden-horst is another. Our friend was run down a few weeks ago by some of the Bastards, near Calvinia, so he's all right.

Now comes my usual itinerary.

We were just getting set at Deelfontein, having been there over a week and gave a smoking concert one night. Usual sort of affair. Big bonfire, 'Take me home to Mother', 'Little Nelly's grave', doctors and nurses from the hospital, coffee and buns, etc. etc. We had a gymkhana arranged for the next day, too. We finished the concert about eleven, and about 12 I was setting the last doctor's legs on the perilous path home when we got orders to move at one. It appears that Malan has a young woman residing at a farm about 32 miles from Deelfontein and it suddenly occurred to old Stephenson to surround it on the off chance of his being there. Well, of course we couldn't get there before dawn, so we made two night marches of it and surrounded the farm OK. By Jove, wasn't it cold? We were just having a severe cold snap, and we nearly perished during the nights. Needless to say, the farm was drawn blank. Old Suggy and I thought we had dropped on a bit of all right though. We had to take up our position at the probable bolt hole, a narrow gap between the walls of the gorge in which the farm was and with the road and a stream running through. We dotted the men across the poort and old Suggy and I sat on each side of the road and froze in silence. Just as the sky began to brighten in the east, we spotted a head against it and down the road came a Johnny, tanning it worth the money. We could just make out he had a pot-hat on. I jumped out and stuck my carbine into his stomach, just in time to save his life, as Suggy is a bloodthirsty old devil and was drawing a beautiful sight on him with his revolver. A poor old nigger, going out to his sheep and finding it a bit parky, he was warming himself by a little gentle exercise. He was in the deuce of a funk and when we sent him down to the rear to be searched, he lay down flat on the road and said he'd rather be shot there.

Hamilton left us at Deelfontein to go into hospital to have his teeth and ears seen to. We don't really expect him back.

We trekked on from the farm (Wortelsfontein) to Blauwater on the Graaff-Reinet line and then on to Graaff-Reinet once more. At Blauwater I saw Harry Pryce-Jones who is stationed there and had a word with him. He looks all right. Graaff-Reinet was much as usual. We got there one morning and left the following evening having drawn a lot of remounts. Of course we made a night march to take part in a drive in the Camdeboo (we always do that). What Camdeboo means I've never been able to discover. [Nor modern researchers, who still can't agree on the meaning, some saying 'green hollow', others 'semi arid and mountainous'. Camdeboo now gives its name to the national park surrounding Graaff Reinet.] Skinner, the gunner, suggested that it might be the Hottentot name for Hell, but this is merely guesswork. We went out to Uitkompott and occupied the same kloof which we did when we caught the 7 stinkers there last July with good old Beauchamp Doran. (I saw the old cock in Graaff-Reinet, and he looked very well and was delighted to see us all. Riach the doctor, who used to be with us, and is now with him, says that he is now quite the society man, never curses wildly, and goes for the Boers instead of his poor ruddy officers. It's the other way about with us now). This time the enemy was Van Heerden [Carel van Heerden, a rebel from Aberdeen who had joined Scheepers early in 1901], who was up at the top with about 200 or rather less. He started down and we saw him about 8 miles off but he got the tip somehow and turned off to the right and went round the mountain towards what we used to call the Happy Valley, Scheepers old stronghold. We trekked round the other way, and next morning the convoy remained in camp with our squadron and the rest of the troops trekked off gaily into the prickly pear and into the usual ambush which occurs at a point about 16 miles north of Aberdeen. It is calculated that about 1100 men have been cut up there one time or another. They succeeded in getting the guns out, with a loss of three killed and seven wounded, but lost a lot of the remounts we had just drawn, by a stampede of led horses. Dunlop was there with some of our men and had one killed and one wounded. The remainder returned to camp late, stuck full of prickly pear thorns. Of course the column was very weak what with us in camp, and the 23rd squadron left at Uitkompott to block that kloof, so the Boers had a soft thing with the position and everything. We've remained here ever since.

The air has been full of rumours of peace, and from what I hear it probably will be peace in the Transvaal and Freestate in two or three weeks but Dunlop tells me it didn't look much like peace up the kloof the other day. What appears probable is just what we are hoping for; that is that peace will be proclaimed north of the Orange River, and that a few thousand troops will be chucked down here and blow the ruddy rebels to blazes. That would be a fine example to the Colonial Dutch.

★★★

Goliadsfontein,
Nr. Aberdeen C C
April 29th 1902

My Dear Roney,

I have been cherishing your last letter to my bosom for months, intending to answer it every mail, but alas! 'twas ever thus.

And the happy day is definitely fixed. Who is going to be best man at the ceremonial, old cock? That is one item that hasn't been sent me yet, so let me know.

Good luck to you, old man, and don't forget that if these combined worries should drive you to drink, there is always an opening for you in South Africa, since all the practitioners out here drink, except the Germans and lots of them do, too. So do not be downcast. Think what a royal time one could have chopping people's limbs off in the middle of a roistering drunk.

Reports about the house come to me from all quarters and the more I hear about it, the more desirable it seems. As an old married man myself, I am rejoiced to think of you two having such a comfortable abode, and some fine day I shall roll up in my Sunday best to call on you. I promise to behave myself in a becoming manner.

By-the-way, I feel it a paternal duty to point out to you, that if you take our Betty to any more at-homes or such like dissipations, you must ensure her leaving in such a state that she does not fall down the steps and sprain her ankles, and slosh the copper, etc, etc.

I got a letter a few weeks back from a mutual friend, with what I fancy to be your hand-writing on the envelope. I thank you very much for your kind attentions, but must really warn you, that if it comes to my ears again, that you take tea tete-a-tete with young women other than my sister, I shall lay the matter before a family council.

Have you ever made any particular study of veldt-sores? For the last month or so I have at intervals, been raising rather fine crops on my hands, but am otherwise sound in eyes, wind and limbs.

Our doings of late have lacked freshness or excitement. Our motto still is K.B.O. which means Keep Steadily Progressing, and has at last landed us, as we expected, back in the bleedin' old Camdeboo for the winter campaign. We ran into our usual Camdeboo ambush about four or five days ago, and since then have vegetated, and employed ourselves in picking out the prickly pear spikes therein derived. As usual, our next move is enveloped in mystery, but we are hoping it will be Graaff Reinet, 'the Gem of the Karoo', on land flowing with milk and whiskey (very good in the mornings). The air is full of peace and rumours of peace. I shouldn't be surprised, from what I hear, that by the time this reaches you, it will be almost an accomplished fact; at any rate, north of the Orange. In the meantime we still K.B.O. 'down where the red kopjes grow' as the poet [Shakespeare] observes:

Kopjes and Prickly Pear
And one clear call for me:
When all the ruddy Boers are dead
We'll hoof it off to sea.

Personally, if I can drop onto any kind of a billet to keep me in cigarettes and whiskey, or can find a Dutch vouw with sufficient needful to marry me and spare me the agony of work, I shall remain on for the present, and try to raise the tone of South African society. I find that I'm very comfortable in a way, and about as near being happy as any miserable traveller in this vale of tears can hope to be. My greater troubles are the days when I am on duty, or when my superior officers have a liver. So in the words of the great toast 'Let the war continue'.

I am expecting some mails in a day or two and hope that, if a letter from you is not amongst them, it will be among the next lot. There's a good many people at home who might drop me a line at intervals just to obviate 'auld acquaintance being forgot', and I keep worrying them for letters, but I daresay you will not mind, and send me one at an early date.

Now, old man, goodbye and good luck.

I hope that you are fit and well and will continue so indefinitely, so shake.

Yours as formerly,
Allan M. Hutchins

★★★

'I have just heard here that the stinker Van Heerden attacked Aberdeen last night, and was shot as a small tribute of esteem in return.'

On 18 May Van Heerden, Malan and Fouche attacked Aberdeen. 100 Boers entered the town and surprised the garrison, making off with horses. Van Heerden was killed. On 27 May Malan was severely wounded and captured near Sheldon station (only four days before the peace treaty was signed at Vereeniging). Fouche surrendered at the war's end.

Drostdy Hotel,
Graaff Reinet
May 19th 1902

Dearest Family,

Just my usual line to inquire after all your healths and to give the latest tidings re the Flying Column. I have about 5 letters from you on hand to answer but must leave them until I get back to the column and will then finish this up and despatch it by a swift horseman to the nearest P.O. At present I am escorting the convoy from a weird spot entitled Belthowwersfontein in the heart of the Camdeboo to Oudeberg (a post held by the 12th Squadron) about 12 miles north of Graaff Reinet. I set off yesterday from B——— fontein the day before yesterday (it takes too long to spell all that, and got to Ouderberg last night. Then old Henniker got the jumps and wired us to stop there until Doran sent us a bigger escort and I promptly got leave from Beauclerc (real live lord), 17th Lancers, to come in here, which I did this morn and write to you from the local pub (much to Toosie's disgust). Bailey's column is now to be broken up and the 17th Lancers and Bethane's M. I. are to join W. Doran with a Pom-pom while the rest go to old B. Doran. So now the Bohers are going to get 'ell and, in the words of the poet, 'Let the war continue'. I have just heard here that the stinker Van Heerden attacked Aberdeen last night, and was shot as a small tribute of esteem in return. May his bones be burnt over his grave! We had a long scrap with him the day before without any appreciable result, except that all hands got wised up as usual and one Boer shot, which comprises the total casualties, bar the 11th squadron, which experienced heavy losses (at poker) that evening.

★★★

26th May
Pearston

I have to finish this in the deuce of a hurry since it is now 10.35 and we have just been told that we can send letters off to Graaff Reinet up to 11. We haven't heard much about peace lately and it seems as if it had missed fire again. Never mind. We can stick it out if they can. I am very fit and well, and hope you are all the same.

As to your anxious enquiries about letters from me, I am afraid I have been very neglectful of late but time does fly so and one has such poor facilities for writing on trek. So please don't think I am dead or anything if I don't write. If I was, you would hear through the papers long before I could write and tell you.

Now, very best love to all, and keep your peckers up, and I will respond to your late favours next time.

Yours affectionately,
Allan

Peace: 'Othello's Occupation's Gone'

On 7 March 1902, Lord Methuen, with a column of inexperienced troops, engaged Koos de la Rey at Tweebosch on the Little Harts River in Transvaal where, for want of water, flying columns rather than blockhouses were still deployed. As well as losing six big guns, Methuen had 68 men killed, 121 wounded and 205 captured, and was himself taken prisoner. It is said that on hearing the news Kitchener retired to his bedroom for two days and declined to speak.

Despite such a defeat there was now an inevitability to the outcome of the war. The blockhouses were working, the Boers exhausted, the hoped-for Afrikaaner rebellion in the Cape and Natal had failed and burghers wanted peace to rebuild their farms, raise cattle and feed what remained of their families. Early in the war in a despatch to the Morning Post *Winston Churchill had written (as an exceptionally well-paid war correspondent): 'What men they were these Boers, thousands of independent riflemen, thinking for themselves, possessed of beautiful weapons, led with skill … moving like the wind.' But now the game was up.*

The civilian suffering was too great, the imperial resources too vast, for the Boers ever to win a final victory against a 'bottomless' enemy. Kitchener's scorched earth campaign had reduced the countryside to a wilderness in which Boer and Black alike saw their homes burned and their cattle slaughtered. A fifth of all Afrikaaners were now actively fighting on the British side. (including Piet De Wet, who led the hands-uppers in the Free State). Only Christiaan De Wet wanted to hold out for independence but, in face-to-face talks at Vereeniging, Botha (with Smuts and De la Rey at his elbow) persuaded De Wet that the best hope for a future self-governing volk was to concede that the war was unwinnable. There was a shortage of food and horses, the suffering of women and children was appalling and – horror of horrors – the blacks were mobilising against their weakened Boer overlords. Days before the Boer delegates sat down to talk in their marquee at Vereeniging, they heard news of Zulus killing 56 burghers in reprisal for a theft of cattle. After days of anguished debate De Wet, at the last moment, agreed to sign the peace terms at Pretoria on 31 May 1902 – 32 months after the war began.

The British claimed victory but, as Kruger had promised, the price of victory was staggering. 39,000 combatants died: 7,000 Boers, 22,000 British and colonial troops (of whom 16,000 from disease). 28,000 Afrikaaner non-combatants died in the concentration camps and an estimated 20,000 blacks. There are no figures for those blacks who died in combat or who were shot as collaborators.

Within 10 years South Africa was a self-governing dominion.

Cradock
9th June 1902

Dearest People,

Othello's occupation's gone, for as you will know now peace, perfect peace has been signed, proclaimed and generally obfuscated.

We heard about it on the 1st, when we were at Tarka Bridge, south of here, and received orders not to fire at any more Boers if they attacked us or anything else and the far-sighted General French wired us to send out two patrols of 20 men with those instructions; for what purpose it is not quite obvious. Poor old Spratt of the 25th and Sugden accordingly set off next morning in various directions and about 7 or 8 miles from camp, Spratt rode into 200 Boers who promptly told him to put his hands up. The poor old chap hesitated for a minute, since naturally he didn't like to trust himself and his horses and rifles to the tender mercies of the burgher and then gave the order to mount and gallop. He was promptly shot through the stomach, two of his men killed, one wounded, six or seven got away and the rest captured. Peace, perfect peace! The old boy died next day and we buried him the next at Tarka Bridge. You can't blame the Boers as they knew damn-all about peace and you can't blame old Spratt since he didn't know what the devil to do. He wasn't a peace negotiator and he wasn't a fighting party; the only thing against him was going into such a place without scouting it properly. But there you are. One of the best that ever stepped, and the best liked subaltern on the column. Never a grouse or grumble from the old man before or after the rotten affair. He was an Irishman and always had a joke for every one. That finishes all the C.I.Vs with our column. Old Chichy, Ward and now poor old Spratt. He was wounded when out with the C.I.V. before and invalided home.

Well, we've come on here. Fouchees command came in the day before we did and Colonel Copley who received their surrender, was so pleased about it that now you see stinking Boers riding about with field glasses and revolvers on, on horses bearing the Government band. It's sickening. Copley introduced Doran to Fouchee, and Fouchee wanted to shake hands. The old man stepped in the gap like a Briton and told the stinker off, alluding playfully to the ultimate fate of murderers. One up to old D.

There is some talk of us going to Graaff Reinet to mobilise but I dunno. We are sitting tight at present.

Under the Colonel's advice I have applied for the S.A.C. and sent in another application for general military employment, and have also written to the B.S.A. company. Anyway, I expect the third contingent of I.Y. will stop out a few months, so I don't think I shall starve at present. Nous verrons.

We had a thanksgiving service in the Market Square yesterday, and we've been having photos taken this morning. I must send you some. There was a dance the other night but I didn't go on account of veldt sores, which have been flourishing on my hands and feet of late and are rather unsightly. But they are improving and I think I shall make an effort for Wednesday night when we give a dance, or contemplate it. We are having a column dinner tomorrow; the old column that is: 22 of us.

Nina expresses mild disapproval of the new staff cap. We all wear 'em out here when we want to cut a dash and then they are rather handy things. I've had two already.

Well, dear people all, good-bye now; so long already, as the Dutch gentleman observed.

Best love all round and luck to the Coronation [Edward VII's coronation was planned for 26 June 1902 but Edward had to undergo an emergency appendectomy operation, so the coronation was postponed until 9 August 1902.]

Yours as ever,
Allan

★★★

Victoria Road Station,
July 2nd 1902

Dear Family,

We are now planted down here with several other contingents awaiting transport for home, 'We' means the 3rd Regt. I.Y., comprising 9th, 10th, 11th, 12th, 109th, 111th and 66th squadrons of that ilk, the colonel and the band, as the saying is; though Colonel Birkin having rushed home to take command of all the Yeomanry at the Coronation is not with us. We are under the care of Major Dawson now that Edwards has gone. The band, I regret to remark, is as yet invisible. It's a very dusty, beastly camp, and we are about 8 miles from Victoria West.

As to my footcher prospects, they are not doing much for us ossifers, but I have applied to transfer to Younghusband's Horse which will remain out some months. I have a reasonable chance since Major Younghusband as good as promised me the job through old Suggy. If it doesn't come off, I don't see why I shouldn't have a run home, since if you resign out here, you have to scratch for yourself to get a job and forfeit all claim to a passage home. Anyway, there's nothing to worry about nous verrons.

It's very sad about the King isn't it? We coronated him all right out here, having a big parade for the occasion, but it was almost authentically known then that it was off.

We trekked here all the way from Cradock via Middelburg. At Middelburg we parted company with the Colonel and staff, without much regret, and trekked on to Victoria Road as a yeomanry body entirely. Of course we gambolled all the way and from the amount of firing from the column at back at hares, hawks and all other sorts of wild fowl, a bystander might have imagined that a general engagement was progressing and might also have run a good chance of never imagining anything else in this world.

At Middelburg I bought another pony, a match for my stallion, and after clipping, hogging and generally bedevilling them, I sold the pair yesterday to a storekeeper here and made £25 on the deal, which considering as how they weren't a proper match, were both about 11 years old, had four broken knees between the two and were neither properly sound, was rather satisfactory to the old firm. All the same, they were a ripping good pair of ponies and if they had been young and sound, I wouldn't have taken £100 for them. As it was, I got £70, which is a very good price for 14 hand horses out here, where a Dutchman thinks £40 a very big price for a pair of horses 15 hands and over.

I have been searching around for your last letters to me but I regret to remark I can't find them. I think I have had two since I last wrote to you, and also some *County Times*. I am glad to see that all is still well in Welshpool, and that George is still as military as ever. I have had several letters from Kitty, via you, and she seems to have an exciting but at the same time a rather pleasant time.

News, as you may imagine, is now very rare. I will let you know as soon as I can about what I'm going to do.

I enclose a few photos. Two were taken by a signaller of ours on the kopjes at Middelport during the engagement. The other one was sent out yesterday by poor old Chichy's relatives, together with a lot of others, and was taken by him on trek near Ceres. We are all trying to get a lot of them and if we do, I'll send them home to you. The pony is my old Bob, whom I'm trying to buy from Remounts. He's a splendid old pony and ought to be worth a good bit. He'd make a fine boy's hunter as he's very fast and can leap like a hare. That's Hamilton in the background with his old English mare, Mary Anne. Oh, I forgot to tell you that Hamilton is back again with the squadron, his remount job being through. So it's like old times again.

Goodbye now all. I'm expecting a letter from you shortly. Best love all round from

Yours affectionately,
Allan

★ ★ ★

Grand Hotel,
Cape Town,
31st July 1902

Dearest Family,

I'm sorry to say that I shall just miss the wedding by a short head but hope to be home shortly after, D.V. The latest news is that the regiment leaves Victoria Road (where we have been stuck for the last month) on August the 2nd and comes down and embarks on a mail boat but I dunno for certain which way it is. Anyhow, please don't make any preparations or bother yourselves about it in any way but just let me stroll up casually, don't you know!

All the various things I have applied for have come to nothing and South Africa is at present crowded out with people searching for billets. So it's home, dearie, home, for Allan M. for a short period at all events, and the same will be very pleased if you won't put yourselves about on his account.

As you will perceive by the heading, old Suggy and I are 'shaking a loose leg', to quote the immortal Belk in Kaapstadt, and mean to stop here until the regiment comes down. Up to yesterday the town had been full up of Boer Generals, Botha, De Wet, Delaney and Co. but, thank God, they were safely loaded up on the *Saxon*, yesterday, and are going touring in Europe as interesting curiosities. So we breathe again, though I was very nearly being kidnapped and taken up to give tone to Delaney's daughter's wedding feast. But I succeeded in pushing the invitation off and am still at large.

Expect me when you see me. I've had several letters from you but am waiting till I get home to answer them.

Best love all round,
Yours affectly.
Allan

★ ★ ★

Home

'It's good sport to be alive, isn't it?'

Aldershot
August 22nd

Dearest People and Bec in particular,

I am very much afraid that it's all up as regards my attendance at the wedding, as I have received several rude rebuffs on approaching the powers that be on the subject. The orders are that no officer can leave here until every man of his squadron is paid up and settled with, put into the train and tucked up and kissed goodbye; at present we are wrestling with parchment certificates, attestation sheets and all that sort of rot. So all I can do is send all best wishes and congrats. to the happy pair. Long may they reign, Gawd bless 'em. I have a ickle karross by me to assist the celebrations but can't get at it until I arrive at home.

As to George's other question about the commission, I think it is now too late to do anything in the matter and at all events the old objection still holds good. I am awfully sorry if there has been any disappointment for the old blank seems to have been very keen on it. We must have a talk when I get home and settle it all up. You see, I had only George's first hint of the matter when I got here, since everything from August 2nd onwards was held till we got home. So even if we had decided to go for it, it must have been too late from sheer force of circs. Never mind; it's good sport to be alive, isn't it?

Best love to all and especially the love-birds.
Yours affectionately
Allan

Easter week-end of 1903 found Allan in 'a shocking place, Brittas, a pub on a steam-train line 10 miles from Dublin', based alongside three other 'miserables' to do a three week recruits' course of firing. He consoles himself by hearing that 'the fishing is good so we have all invested in rods, the countryside being all moors and mountains'. In June he sails for India.

4

India

We're marchin' on relief over Inja's coral strand,
Eight 'undred fighting Englishmen, the Colonel and the band.
Rudyard Kipling

India. It's said young men went there to guard, govern or make money. For the late Victorians – Allan's generation – the jewel in the crown offered both a chance for advancement (at a precociously young age) and a shot at doing good: bringing justice, railways and commerce, building canals to irrigate crops for when the rains failed and outlawing the excesses of suttee and caste. Winston Churchill famously said India was no more united than the equator and in a way he was right: at the end of the nineteenth century the subcontinent of more than 600 feudal, princely states remained a chimera, a creation of British empire-builders with the co-operation of Punjabis, Sinds, Bengalis and Tamils – who preferred doing business with the British than with one another. When Allan arrived in 1903, 300 million people in India, Burma and modern-day Pakistan and Bangladesh were ruled over by 65,000 British soldiers and little more than a thousand civil servants. Few Indians ever saw a white face. No wonder Stalin thought it was 'ridiculous' – there were more English in Hull. And yet the British were supreme and had been so – with minor French incursions – since Robert Clive's victory at Plassey (Bengal) in 1757. There, Clive had pushed open a vast window of opportunity for British commercial interests (in truth indivisible from political interests) in the shape of the East India Company. 'Company' is not quite the word for an organisation that raised its own militia, administered justice and made once powerful princes into toothless figureheads. In 1803 the riches of Delhi were diverted in its favour. Nawab Shah Alam Khan was bought off with £100,000 pa – a huge amount of money – and continued to live as 'king' in the Red Fort.

Bengal was secured (despite incursions by Nepalese Ghurkhas), then Gujarat and Bombay. In the Third Maratha War of 1818 the Maharaja of Nagpur was routed. The Company raised its eyes to Burma, Afghanistan, Sind (now Pakistan) and the Sikhs in

Punjab. Punjab was least likely to roll over for the British and had expansionist ideas of its own, in Kashmir and Peshawar. Even now, Kashmir remains disputed territory. Afghanistan was of no value save as a buffer against Russian designs on British India. In 1840, when Russia showed an interest in Afghan factionalism by backing a claimant to the vacant throne, the British supported their own candidate by garrisoning Kandahar. They stayed for two years until, overwhelmed by factional fighting (nothing is new), they retreated and with their wives and children were massacred on the Khyber Pass.

Thus the Company created the Raj by a combination of threat, flattery and incentive. In defeat princes looked to Britain for money and position to maintain 'authority' over their own people. Smaller states were acquired by lapse. Should a raja die without male heirs his land (and revenues) were taken over by the British. It was rule by consent but with 'bayonets fixed' (David Gilmour, The Ruling Caste), held together by a tiny adminis-tration and an army of sepoys ('warriors') who were fed, clothed and paid on time and so were mostly loyal. Mostly, but not always. The mutiny at Vellore in 1806 was one of many, now mostly forgotten, which reminded the British to pay the troops, treat them well and respect their faith. When *the* Mutiny broke out in 1857 it began with rumours of animal fat being used to grease cartridges used by native troops. Worse, in Bengal the British had failed to maintain the complexities of caste, throwing higher and lower castes together; 54 Bengali regiments mutinied.

The ensuing slaughter brought its own loyalties. Ten thousand men of Allan's future regiment, the 3rd Gurkhas, marched from Almora under Jung Bahadur to storm the rebel-held Kaswiri Gate at Delhi. The Madras regiments stayed faithful. After bitter fighting the Muntiny ended in violent reprisals and the ruination of Mughal rule. After 258 years the East India Company ceded authority over the presidencies and states and from the ramparts of Akbar's fort at Allahabad the first Viceroy of India, Lord Canning, read the proclamation of British rule.

Two-thirds of Canning's India was British; the rest held by dependent princes. The Ghurkhas and Sikhs were rewarded for their loyalty and the rajas honoured and made wealthy in an 'enlightened and beneficient despotism' based on a stable administration, equal-handed justice and religious tolerance. In the Mutiny the beast had bitten the master's hand and the master had learned caution and possibly respect.

Though she never travelled east, Victoria adored all things Indian. The Empress entertained even minor princes lavishly and, to the embarrassment of her government, demanded obeisance to and respect for Indian culture and religions. Salisbury was chas-tised for referring to her imperial subjects as 'black men'; she asked her last Viceroy, Curzon, not 'to trample on [her] dear Indian children'.

In 1903, when Allan joined his regiment in Madras the peculiar relationship between Britain and the Raj was at its peak. When Edward VIII visited he was honoured with a grand durbar. The Indian Civil Service, if not perfect, was a model of efficiency and restraint – 'ridiculous' perhaps, but how Stalin would have loved just one generation of British administrators for his Soviet Empire: in India, generations of the same British families made a virtue of serving the Empire honestly and well. After 1870, recruitment for the Indian Civil Service had been open to examination and competition. In 1904,

Army Regulations purported to promote officers according to their qualities rather than their family name.

Few late-Victorians doubted that Britain was a force for good in India. Curzon declared that destiny had brought the British to India 'for the lasting benefit of the human race'. Curzon was 40 years old, educated at Eton and Oxford, whose family seat at Keddlestone Hall in Derbyshire was the model for Government House in Calcutta. In his short time as Viceroy (before resigning after a row with Kitchener) he declared the British heart 'was no longer in India' and yet did everything to keep Indians from power in the Executive Council – 'there is not an Indian fit for the post,' he said. He set about restoring the Taj Mahal (which Allan would shortly visit) and created the archeological survey, but he could not trust educated babus with their own history and to their disgust and without consultation, he split Bengal to create a Muslim east. Curzon was a man of his time, a Victorian patriarch for whom the question was not 'do we have a right to be here?' but 'do we have a right to leave?' Without the District Officer, the fresh-faced Lieutenant and the dissolute but dynamic planters India would fail – unravel into factions of Muslims, Hindis, Sikhs and Bengalis. Even Indians thought the British held India together. Madhava Rao compared British withdrawl as akin to opening the cages at the zoo – creating 'a terrific fight' with the tiger 'walking proudly' over the rest. For Rao, like many, the feared tiger was the 'mahamoden in the north'.

Only on the north-west frontier and in the Punjab was the Pax Britannica frayed and it was here in the mountains, where 'the chances of service were the best', that Allan sought action with a Gurkha regiment. He would have to be patient. By writ of Lord Roberts, all newly arrived officers were required to serve time in training and learn Urdu, before there might be any hope of advancement. And, as Allan was to discover, in India progress and promotion were painfully slow and life in the forts and the hill stations was routine.

In the summer of 1903 Allan sailed to India as a decorated and experienced soldier, the first Yeomanry officer to pass into the regulars. The Indian Service had better pay and pension than the British Army and competition for places was tough. In times past an officer would join a British regiment and later apply for transfer to an Indian regiment. Now, men of Allan's generation were posted to India on the unattached list and attached temporarily to a British regiment. So it was that Allan joined the 1st Leicesters. After a year a soldier joined an Indian regiment as a probationer and hoped to be kept on.

Aboard the SS *City of Vienna* with six other officers and two passengers he reached Port Said on 1 July and shortly after made a 20-hour passage through the Suez Canal. (In 1875 Disraeli had put a penny on income tax to buy the canal for £4 million from the penurious Khedive Ismail. 'It is now the Canal and India' said Disraeli's chancellor, Cairns, 'There is is no such thing as India alone.') Allan slept on deck and beyond Aden, in the 'pretty bumby' waters of the Arabian Sea, amused himself by passing reports of seasickness back and forth between his fellow passengers – all of whom were ill. Landing in Bombay on Monday 13 July 1903, Allan lost his favoured carbine to the customs – 'you can't bring any 202 bores into the country' – and put up for a single night at Watson's Esplanade Hotel. Reporting to the DAG, he found himself attached to the 1st Leicestershire Regiment, stationed in Madras – the main port of the old East India Company. Here he acquired 'large' quarters behind the 20-foot thick walls of Fort St George.

July 17 Madras

We left Bombay on Tuesday night and got here at 6 o'clock this morning (Thursday). Saunderson and Chisholm left Sarbier, but Matthews, Marshall, Steele and we two came on the same train. Marshall and Steele left us at Wadi, to go to Secunderabad, and Matthews changed just outside here to go to Wellington.

I have achieved large army quarters in the fort and hired furniture. Also a bearer, chokidan, dressing boy, moonski and some other devils who don't count. Between thirty and forty rupees a month I think, for what I've got. Most people one meets require baksheesh and so far I have not learnt who ought to get it and who ought not.

I have ordered some things from the regimental tailor, who seems to understand all right what is wanted.

In Bombay I met a man named Walker who was in the Yeomany with me. There was a photo of the 3rd IT in 'The King' of June 20 with me in it. I got Mamma's letter of June 19 and the photos, at Bombay. Thank her very much for writing. I've not had anything else. I think I shall take on William Watson as permanent agent to me, and bank with him, but I'm not quite sure yet. However, he'll do for the present.

I suppose Bob is sold long ago. I'm counting on that. The customs people at Bombay pinched my carbine, as you can't bring any 202 bores into the country. If my CO will give me a certificate that it's for Govt purposes, I can get it on, if not, I'll get William Watson to send it back home. It's pretty hot here. The rains haven't started properly yet though in Bombay it was one continuous downpour; but it's the other monsoons there.

There are very few officers here as the regt., or rather wing, has only four companies over here. The others are at Bellamy. They say that fever is pretty bad here but we'll try to exist. I hope something will shift us out of this ever long.

How are you all at home? I hope that all goes well and smoothly. Shall be glad of a little information on the subject from time to time.

My best love all round, including Bec and Roney

From yours affectionately
Allan

PS My address will be
Attchd 1st Batton Leicestershires
Fort St George, Madras

Within days of Allan's arrival in the feverish summer heat, the OC fell sick and as a as a Second Lt. Allan was given temporary command of a company. Already anxious to escape a 'rotten old port' and find action in the north, in Bengal or Punjab, he sought the ear and approval of the Adjutant. The Adjutant, 'a ripper', recited familiar advice – use all the influence you may have, you'll need it – and so Allan wrote to his father for help: 'what about old Benyon?' Meanwhile, with an eye on joining an Indian regiment 'up front', Allan began learning Hindustani 'under the gentle guidance of the Regimental Munshi' (secretary or clerk, from the Urdu). 'It's rather unfortunate', he says, that in Madras 'the swines all speak Tamil.' If he passed the Sovereign Standard he could get to the Infantry in six months, a strong incentive.

By August Allan had settled into the routine of Parade at 6.30, dinner at 8 and not very much in between. He was now a member of the Chepauk Club, the Adjar Boat Club, the Gymkhana Club, and was playing various sports. The serious business of finding a pony for hire was occupying much of his time, as was serious drinking in the mess. 'I am trying to keep straight' he wrote to his worried mother, 'though its not considered good form in this regiment to go to bed sober, except on Thursdays.' One man, he wrote, made himself unpopular by falling drunk on the table 'and had to leave – a promising soldier too.'

Allan did not write home frequently enough for his parents' liking and a letter to his sister may explain why: 'Madras is full of skirt ... with a little careful selection one may yet manage to amuse oneself.' However, he noted occasionally and briefly events in Lett's Indian and Colonial Rough Diary (2s 6/d) – 'got into loud clothes after dinner and took a rickshaw down to MF' – featuring amongst other women the mysterious 'M' ('saw M but couldn't establish comms though gallant attempt').

There is almost no mention of duties (nor would there be until he takes a civilian appointment as 2nd Assistant Commandant to the Lakhimpur Military Police stationed at Sadiya in 1909). After morning parade and two hours in the office, his work was complete by lunchtime. Weekends and Thursdays were free and officers had two months' leave per annum (three months for those at the frontier). An officer with ambition was expected to use his free time hunting tiger, riding and playing games, expensive pastimes and difficult to sustain without private income: no wonder Allan seems pursued by debt. On joining the Gurkhas he complains 'I have to pay nearly £7 for my pouch-belt alone'. 'Poodle-faking' – chasing young women – counted against one's becoming an officer in a pukka regiment, and though Allan pursued sports and women with enthusiasm he kept a keen eye out for preferment and nurtured that most useful of qualities in the cantonment, discretion.

Fort St George
Madras
July 23 1903

Dearest Family

There is not much of note to record since my last. I'm beginning to settle down etc. and have been put in temporary command of a company, as the OC there is sick like most of the rest, I pray every night for his speedy recovery.

There are only four of us to do orderly officer, so there's always that. We have a parade, every morning at 6.30 except Thursdays and Saturdays, and that's all the drill.

The other fellows are all very nice etc especially the Adjutant, who is a ripper.

I wish I was going as I want to be out in the country, not in a rotten old port. There are lots of wild beasts round here too.

The Adjutant has been advising me to worry up what influence I can to get an Indian regiment up front in Bengal or Punjab. He says it can be done by a little influence and not without. What about old Beynon?

I have commenced Hindustani and am making fairly satisfactory progress under the gentle guidance of the Regimental Moonshi. Some folks tell me that if I pass the Sovern Standard I can get to the Higher Standard in <u>six</u> months, but I haven't yet found out for certain. It's rather unfortunate that I can't practise my linguistic abilities on the pious Hindoo here, but the swines all speak Tamil, as George is no doubt aware.

I've not done anything in the horse line yet, it's rather a bad place and time they tell me, for buying ponies and I want to get settled well before I branch out into anything of that sort. It will cost me about RS 30 per month to keep a pony. I don't think the mess is a very expensive one though more so than the old MX.

The Master-Tailor has made me some quite good stuff at very cheap rates. He charges vey little for a suit of white. My servants seem a success and all goes well. My best love to you all of you.

Yours affectionately
Allan
It's pretty hot here and the mosquitoes are doing well.

★★★

Fort St George
Madras
Aug 20 1903

Dear Mamma

I got your letter of July 10 this morning, for which much thanks. It's the first one I've had from home since yours of the day I sailed.

I hope that the tea at Aunt Batt's was a success, and that you were not assaulted or anything like that. What were the strawberries like? It reminds me of one day long ago, when the dear lady nearly got hysterical and I offended Nelly Elwell by pinching a photograph of her (Nelly, I mean not Aunt Batt).

Thank you, I am trying to keep straight, as you put it, though its not considered good form in this regiment to go to bed sober, except on Thursdays, Thursday, being as you are, no doubt aware, a general holiday in India. Of course, it is not absolutely insisted on, and of late years only one subaltern has had to send in his papers over it; and his was a very bad case. It is the time that he fell down on the dinner table, but as he was able to immediately rise again, and was foolish enough to attempt to explain that he always liked 'to lie down for a few moments after dinner' he became unpopular and had to leave. A promising soldier too, I believe, in lesser aspects.

I have not yet speculated in any horse as I wish to hear from my old pal Cox first and also because the dealers are pretty thick as regards price. I must try and get one 'by private treaty' as they say in the advts. I believe this means that the seller asks £100, you offer £5, he immediately closes, and you shortly pay on third party £10 to take the animal off your hands.

We get a fair amount of work here, as so many of the subs are doing courses in various parts of Hindustan.

I belong to the MCC (otherwise know as the Chepauk Club) and am joining the Adjar Boat Club and Gymkhana Club. Everyone belongs to three and some have two or three more. For amusement, I have Rugby and Soccer Football, Hockey, Cricket, Boating and am thinking of taking up squash.

My Hindestani is progressing nicely thank you. The old Moonshi is rather a good sort, a Muhammad. My servants, all seem pretty good and give no trouble.

I get on very well with the other fellows. The three brevet-majors we have here are awfully nice. We have no captains, but drop from Major to subaltern. I don't know whether I have told you but the Wing of the Battn is at Bellamy. The Colonel went out to Kuddah park the other day and shot a large tiger, much to his delight. I find myself in difficulties for further news.

Best love to all, particularly yourself and George.
From yours affectionately
A

Fort St George
Madras
Sept 10 1903

Dearest Ma and Pa

It's very nice of you to keep sending photos which I greatly appreciate.

Yes Mamma, perhaps my conscience ought to smite me some for not writing longer letters, but really you have no idea how time is filled up. This week for instance, I arise at 5.15am and never have a breather until lunch. To such a state has it come that I'm quite ashamed to look my poor old mooshi in the eyeball. The dear old creature comes and sits patiently for hours at a time awaiting my coming and he has a mild hazel eye like a sheep's which cuts me to the heart.

After lunch one really can't do anything (although I'm writing this before I get too sleepy just after lunch) so we go to bed until about half past four, when a cup of tea sets us up to take on daily exercise in whatever form one fancies. I play rugger on Tuesdays and Fridays and sail on Sundays and one or two days in the week and the other days go to the Chepauk or Gymkhana clubs. If I'm orderly bloke (as today) and have to stop in, I generally have more Hindoostani to do than I can find time to, or if not Hindustani, I have some lecture to ring up for the Colonel or Adjutant. We have two a week. When you reflect that I am again temporary OC company, and that my Coy. is doing its annual musketing course, and that there are only four subs to do duty and that I am one of the few bridge players in the mess and so am always occupied after dinner and am also trying hard to sweat up the Under you will see that I have a few slightly extenuating circs. All well I have a holiday next week. I've got leave to go to Calcutta, to play for this city of bliss and prosperity in the forthcoming Rugger tournament, so away with the case!

I am still pleasingly uncertain whether I am solvent or not, and write every cheque with fear trembling as to whether it will be honoured or not.

As regards my monetary position, I believe I ought to draw about RS 30 per mensem after paying mess bills, servants etc, one of the chief expenses. I enclose a copy of a rather amusing letter sent to the canteen sergeant (who is a very steady unmarried fellow) by a native he had sacked three months ago. No more news, but lots of love.

Yours affectionately
Allan

★★★

Canteen Sergeant
D Fowler
1st Leicestershire Regt
Fort St George

Honoured Sir

The punishment for three months has a very good lesson learnt – and I shall not for the future lie or misbehave myself. I beg your sympathy on me shown as a vacancy now exists in your giving I beg your being so very kind to entertain me in the Boon.

God bless you and your Family for this act of charity, and I shall pray for you, pray for your long life and prosperity.
I am also a man with a large family.

I am your obedient servant
J Cuppvosauwny

★★★

Fort St George
Madras
Sept 24 1903

Dearest Ma, Pa and Family

We went to Calcutta on Saturday the 12th to play in the Rugger tournament but got beaten by the West Ridings who eventually won the cup. I'll give you further particulars again. We got back here last Tuesday evening and our own Tournament is now on. The first game was yesterday when Madras and Bombay drew, and they have to play again this afternoon. I'm 16th man, and have to play today. I hope we win.

Thanks for the cheque. Every little helps, as the monkey said.

Please excuse further, as I really want a sleep before the match and have only an hour.

With many thanks for your kind attentions in the way of letters, photos and papers; assurances that my correspondence shall improve, and lastly the very best quality love to you all.

Yours affectionately
Allan

★★★

Fort St George
Madras
Sept 24 1903

Dearest Family

I regret that I missed last mail, but I've been away again; to the other side of India this time. I had to take a draft of time-expireds and invalids up to the depot at Devlali near Bombay. I left on the morning of the 30th and got back this morning after travelling nearly the whole time. It was a beastly nuisance, especially as they didn't give me enough allowance to pay my exes. I'm about 60 dibs out over the trip.

You seem to be quite gay now with your parties and what not? Is tonight the County Ball? Do try to make Billy behave. How did Sir Watkins launch taste?

There, I think that's all this week, thank you. I'll try to write a longer letter next time.

My very best love and wishes to all of you, 'and this slave will always pray' etc etc as the pious Hindoo writes in his letters 'What need of more?'

Yours affectionately
Allan

★★★

Fort St George
Madras
Oct 15 1903

Dearest Family

Things jog along quietly. I get a fair amount of work, and am having a pretty fair time with my Hindustani. I'm progressing favourably and go for the exam (SS) at the beginning of December.

The Moonshi says I should probably pass now, but there's no use chancing it, especially as I am going to continue straight on for the Higher Standard. If I get through. So all this work will be useful.

I wonder, whether I could get into the Ghoorkas. That is apparently the best and hardest to get into. Can you sound old Beynon as to his influence being sufficient to get me into the 1st, 2nd, 3rd or 4th Ghoorkas, not the 44th, or kindred numbers as they are not pukka Ghoorkas. If he could get someone in high places at the War Office (such as Tom Kelly or someone who knows the AG out here) to drop an unofficial note to the AG aforesaid, it might be done. The crowd I refer to are front of the Frontier force and get all the fun there is going.

In any case, there seems better prospects now than formerly as all these Madras Regiments are being reorganised and may be used more.

I don't think its much use my worrying about the cavalry as the kit is not expensive.

I was told the other day that in many regiments the living was no more expensive than the infantry, but the kit is heavy. Although you don't have to buy your chargers now.

I think the Ghoorkas is the best thing if I can get it which is very doubtful. Will you please send me a copy of my record of service which we made?

I'm probably buying either a bike or a pony trap in a week or two and should be overdrawn if Bob is not off the hooks by then.

To turn to pleasanter themes I suppose the County Ball is over and done with. I will not ask you questions about it as I am sure I shall hear all next Monday. I hope 'twas a success.

We had a guest night last night, a lot of officers from a warship which is here for a few days came. Toosie plaintively asks for details of my uninteresting existence. Well, I generally get up about quarter to six and go on parade from 6.30 to 7.30. Breakfast anytime until 9 at which hour is Coy Orderly. At 9.30 Batt. Orders, about which time I generally collect the canteen money. Between 10am and Tiffin at 1pm I have various odd jobs such as lectures, paying out, my Hindoostani lesson if there is time and so on. After Tiffin write or read till about 2.30 and then sleep until about 4 when I arise, and clothe myself and have tea. Then all the whirl of Madras amusements is open to me. I may go to the Chepauk (otherwise the MCC) and play squash, or bridge or listen to the band; or else to the Gymkhana, and play football or watch a gymkhana or listen to the band; or else down to the Adyan boat club and boat or loaf in the club house. I don't belong to the Madras Club, or to the Adyan Club (there's a club there too) and haven't made up my mind whether to do it or not yet as they are rather expensive.

Dinner 8.30; after which bridge or any show that may be given such as concerts, dances etc. I don't find I have too much time as I generally have a Moonshi in the evening too. There you can't complain that this letter says nothing about myself as it bristles with as many as the Argos, whatever he was.

Please receive my very hearty love etc.
Yours affectionately
Allan
Excuse this letter being as dull but I'm sleepy

★★★

Fort St George
Madras
Oct 27 1903

Dearest Family

Madras is a very great place for all sorts of games; very different to what it was in the old days, by all accounts. We are quite energetic. Association football is the order of the day now, but is somewhat marred by the monsoon, which is on us in its glory.

I am buying a bike from one of our fellows who is going home on sick leave. I find I can't get on without one.

I suppose I shall get a double budget of news next Monday, as you didn't write last mail. The reason my writing is so funny today is that I have a sprained thumb, acquired by boxing last night.

The rain is rather upsetting our work as the Colonel set us a sketch to make, about 10 days ago, to be handed in by 1st Nov. Of course we all left it until this week and now can't get out to make it. We get bags of work to do, one way and another.

I had a little excitement last night. I was just retiring to my virtuous couch about 12, when one of the henchman of Hamilton the Gamson Engineer (who messes with us and lives pretty close to me – I live under the mess, this is getting a bit complicated isn't it?) came to me in great excitement. I gathered that his master was very unwell. He couldn't tell me what it was but imitated the symptoms. This, owing to the fact that Hamilton had dislocated his jaw, had a somewhat startling effect and sent me dashing out into the rain in my pyjamas, expecting to find a ghastly corpse. However, I was soon relieved, and when we'd sorted out the doctor, so was he.

I have rather good quarters. They are really a sort of bomb-proof I think, and consist of one long room, with two arches and little separating doors in the middle. Total length 70 feet. Outside is the bathroom, and a sort of cubbyhole where master's chokia and waterboy live.

Waterboy ran away the other day because 'Batten beating him'. When he came back, master also beating him, so honour was satisfied. My chokia (or dressing boy) is rather a lazy mite and also a scoundrel in his way. I keep him because he can speak Hindoostani and because I hate changing. We usually have a struggle about once a week after which he improves for a day or two. I might mention that 'struggle' is a euphonious term originated by Barnet, of the Gammers, who weighs about 14 stone. He used it to describe a difference of opinion with his chokia, who weighs about two since then we always use it. Our mess is increasing a bit again now, thank goodness, so we sometimes get a day when it is not a continued sweat from dawn till dewy eve. For instance I didn't get up until 7 this morning.

I hope to hear from some of you soon. Lastly, know that this humblest one continually prays at the shrine of Benevolent God for the safety and welfare of all your friends and relatives. What need of more?

Your slave
Allan MH
You will observe that my studies in Hindoostani give me quite a flowery style

★★★

Fort St George
26 November 03

Dearest Podgie

The weather reports from England are terrible. I suppose that you are getting your share in Welshpool, and my buzzer throbs with sympathy for you. I know what the place is like in wet weather. For me, we have been very lucky here lately in that respect. Although it is still monsoon weather, the past week has been nipping. So fine, and so cold that I have a blanket over me at night and sometimes consume a meal without the aid of a punkah. The rain is starting again today so we shall probably have a week's downpour. The barber told me so in my slumbers this morning. (He comes and shaves me before I get up; generally before I wake) I'm getting quite proficient at Hindustani now, and bukh away like anything. I'm thinking of 'going' Mussalman.

Of late, we have had considerable work. We are short of subs again, so for the last week I have been in the butts from 6 to 9.30 every morning, and look like continuing the practice for sometime. Then the CO gives us beastly schemes to work out. I have two to do by Monday and can't quite see how it is to be done. However, it's as God wishes as my munshi piously remarks.

I play association football twice a week now, and most evenings I have a regimental pugilist in to box with. The rains have also filled the Long Tank (a sheet of water about one mile by three in size) and the Adyar Boat Club sailing boats have been sent up there; so about twice a week including Sunday afternoons, I make up my mind to sail away, sail away. Such are my simple pleasures.

I also attend all the sergts dances in Madras, and am much in request by ladies of all shades of colour from snowy white to dark coffee.

Since the cold has started I am feeling quite youthful again, and full of energy. I made about fifteen calls the day before yesterday, and as a reward of virtue, was promptly asked to the wedding of the daughter of one of the callees. They <u>won't</u> let me alone. Haw!

Well, goobye now, my Podglet.
Best love and wishes to all the home circle.
Yours affect brer
Allan

★★★

Fort St George
Madras
Dec 24 1903

Dearest Family

Just a line to thank you for your letters, papers and photos and to assure that I am well although leading a <u>fearful</u> life.

At this merry Christmas tide I really have a tremendous amount of dissipation to get through during the next fortnight. I went to a ball at Government House night pre last and was also out dancing until 3.30 this morning so I feel rather frail today.

The photies of Welshpool were most beautiful and very acceptable, as I am beautifying my quarters at present, and will get them framed.

Our theatricals are going strong.

Will George please write to Hobson about my medal? If he don't buck up and cough it up, I'll have to get Major Edwards' signature from Egypt and apply again.

With lots of love
Yours affectionately
Allan

★★★

Letts No 46 Rough Diary

Sunday 3 January 1904
Church parade 6.30 am.

Met M in afternoon at usual spot. Couldn't stop long so she said, but eventually left me at 9.15, I went home and sat on roof and drank beer with Creagh and Vernon. Lovely night, and what with the beer, tobacco, moonlight and my late interview, felt quite peaceful.

★★★

Fort. St. George
Madras
Jan 7 1904

Dearest Podgie

The only thing of any interest I can think about to tell you, is the dissipations which we have been undergoing. It is, now, the Season in Madras, and so we all feel rather cheap of a morning. I'm rather coming out in the social line; at least for such a stay-at-home little mouse as myself. The last time I wrote you, I think was New Year's Eve. We had a sort of Ceremonial Parade on New Year's Morning at 6:25 am, so I didn't get any bed at all that night but turned in after toying with some breakfast and slept the sleep of the just, only being interrupted by various coloured dependants of mine coming in to hang garlands of flowers round my neck, which is their artless way of cadging for seasonable gifts. A garland of yellow marigolds, or a lime wrapped in gold foil is expected to draw at least a rupee.

Well, New Year's Night, I went to a big reception at Government House (full uniform. Phew!) After that I think there was a lull until Monday when I went to the State Ball at the same place (also full uniform. Also Phew!) Tomorrow night is a fancy dress out at the Ayar, which I shall attend if I can get a costume, and on the next night a small dance also at the same place. On the 12th but I am looking too far ahead. I'll tell you about them when they're over. Yesterday afternoon I was detailed to attend the Garrison Christmas Tree, and rather incurred the ire of the Padre by retiring from the madding crowd's immediate neighbourhood at an early stage of the proceedings with a suitable partner; thereby depriving him of two valuable assistants. Howsomedever, I'm quite well, thank you, and hope that you are all equally salubrious.

Best love, all round, my dears, and hoping you will endeavour to lead a new life in the New Year.

Yours affectly,
Allan

★★★

Letts No 46 Rough Diary

16 Saturday January
Got into loud clothes after dinner and took a rickshaw down to Madras Fair, which I hadn't seen so far. Ran across C and also other people, none of whom I wanted to see, while dodging Leicester sergeants in beer garden (very drunk) and, coming out of disreputable house ran into General just coming in. Home about 12.

★★★

In the New Year Allan is despatched with his company to the old East India Company cantonment at Pallavarum in the hills to the south west of Madras – now a suburb of Chennai.

Allan Hutchins out of uniform, 1901.

Clive House,

Welshpool.

February 10th 1901.

My dear Colonel

        I see by the papers that the W. O. are sending out
10000 Yeomanry instead of 5000 as in first orders.
Do you think it would be any use asking the D.A.A.G. Imp. Yeo.
again about a commission for my son Allan in the Imp. Yeo.?
We have heard nothing of his application which you were kind
enough to recommend and hand in the last week in January and I
see by the papers that Mr. Marshall Dugdale's son - 2nd Lieut.
in the Mont. Yeomanry of last year - has already had his
commission and been ordered to Aldershot.
I send you a copy of the letters I had from his late Captain -
(Captain Robert Wynn 49 Cmy. Imp. Yeo.) - as to his recommendati-
ation for a direct commission in South Africa.
I was doubtful whether he ought to allude to it in any way in
his nomination paper,as the letters in which I had the
information are of course private ones. But there can be no harm
I should say in letting the D.A.A.G. have this information
verbally or in any other way than actually on the nomination
paper.
        If you can do anything for me in this I shall be awfully
obliged as he is so keen on going and I should like him to have
a little "show" after his bad luck last time in getting enteric
just as the fun was beginning.

                    yours sincerely

                    G.A.Hutchins

To
   Col. E.Pryce-Jones M.P.

'I should like him to have a little "show" after his bad luck last time in getting enteric.'
One of many letters from Allan's father George in pursuit of his son's interests. This one is
to Col E Pryce-Jones MP, written after hearing press reports that the Yeomanry force for
South Africa was to be doubled, to 10,000.

Mama and Papa.

George and Eliza on their golden wedding anniversary.

'Oily Doyly', George D'Oyly, Allan's only brother and 13 years his senior, who served in the War Office.

Above: Toosie and Kitty at Clive House, Welshpool.

Left: The girls. Rear, left to right: Nina Hutchins, Aida Sybil Hutchins; front, left to right: Marianna Emily Kate (Betty) Schofield (neé Hutchins), Elsie Adelaide (Kitty) Vandergoot (neé Hutchins). Babies, left to right: Margery Schofield, Derek Vandergoot.

Aida Sybil (Billy), Allan's much-loved, much-teased younger sister with her viola. Billy archived the letters and mementos.

'Oh, how my buzzum swelled with pride as I sat my noble steed,' from a letter of 11 June 1900. The Proclamation of the Annexing of the Free State as the Orange River Colony. 'Look for the flagstaff with the Governor under it and the mounted men close behind which are us. Count five from the left of the line (the men's proper left) and you have me; four you have Charlie; first or second from the other end, Jim.'

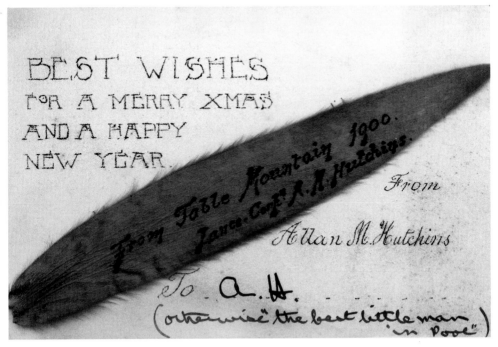

A home-made Christmas card from Allan as Lance-Corporal, 'otherwise known as the best little man in Pool', Table Mountain, December 1900. (See following page.)

Somewhere between
Matjesfontein Stn
and Ceres. C.C.

Christmas Day
1901.

Dear Schofe

Thanks very much for your
kind letter, which I had been anticipating for some time, on account of
my little sister Becky saying that
she had been prodding you up. But of
course, I can quite see that the cares
and worries of patients, and preparing
your abode, and what must be the
most difficult thing of all for you,
i.e. looking respectable at the same
time, have been taking up a lot
of your time lately.

You seem to be going in for great style
in the new residence, and from all
accounts it will be a jolly outfit.
Your plan of the house was most
excellent, and instantly filled

IN REPLY PLEASE
QUOTE LETTER.

B.

16, Charing Cross,
London, **12th April** *190* **1.**
S.W.

Sir,

In reply to your letter of yesterday we beg to say that a 2nd Lieutenant's pay in the Imperial Yeomanry is 6/8 a day, and his field allowance is 2/6, 91 days advance of which is issued by us. After the expiration of the 91 days, field allowance is issued in South Africa, as is the Colonial allowance of 3/- a day. We are, Sir,

Your obedient servants,

Coxle

G.A. Hutchins Esq.,
  Clive House,
    Welshpool.

Above: A second lieutenant's pay was 6/8d a day, 12 April 1901.

Left: the letter sent from Table Mountain, December 1900.

The worried father. A response to the Colonel's enquiry as to whether his son had arrived safely in South Africa.

G.W. Hutchins Esq.,

Clive House,

Welshpool.

Dear Sir,

With reference to your letter of yesterday, we beg to say the Mongolian arrived at Cape Town some days ago, and proceeded to Port Elizabeth.

Yours truly,

ALLAN BROTHERS & CO LPL & LDN LD.

per

On horseback – described in the letter of 30 May 1901.

'They are sending me to Deelfontein, I think, to be X-rayed.' A concert at Deelfontein Hospital, June 1900. It became the biggest military hospital in South Africa, built next to the railway on the Karoo. Today there is a Yeomanry Hotel and a military graveyard.

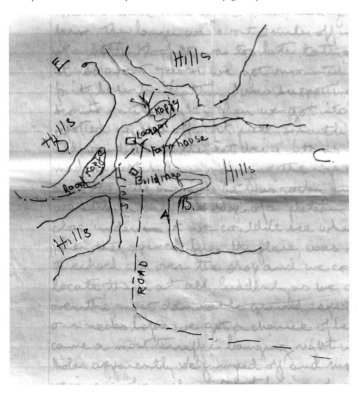

In pursuit of Schmidts, 7 August 1901. See page 69.

'I forgot to tell you that they shot three rebels in Graaff Reinet the day I was lost there, just to encourage them a bit. I went to see them sentenced.' Graaf Reinet, Cape Colony, 19 August 1901. The death sentence is passed on Fairie, van Rensburg and Pfeiffer. Like so many men in Cape Colony, they were treated as traitors for opposing British rule, and executed. Van Rensburg fought with Scheepers' kommando. He was 22 years old.

The Club at Graaf Reinet. When peace was declared, officers of the Coldstream Guards celebrated by firing weapons in the bar. The club, and the bullet holes, are still there.

Church Street, Graaf Reinet. The British left 'a long legacy of bitterness in the town and district'.

'The country we crossed was almost entirely the Great Karoo; an awful place.'

The letter recounting Allan's enteric fever addressed to Col Hutchins, his father: 'I expect they will all be shortly invalided home', 21 June 1901.

Fort St George, Madras, July 1903. Allan was attached to the 1st Leicestershire Regiment, stationed in Madras, the main port of the old East India Company. Here he acquired 'large' quarters (70 feet long) behind the 20-foot-thick walls of Fort St George, and for 40 rupees a month hired furniture, a bearer, chokidan, dressing boy, moonsi and 'some other devils who don't count'.

Government House, Madras. 'I went to a ball at Government House night pre last and was also out dancing until 3.30 this morning, so I feel rather frail today.'

Above: Allan in the uniform of the 3rd Gurkhas. 'My new uniform will cost a decent sum (it's dark green, with black facings, bye the bye, à la Rifle Brigade).'

Right: Allan as 'a dam' bobby' but with better pay and travelling allowances in a civil police appointment.

Lt. A. M. Hutchins I. A. _____ Dr.

DATES.	PARTICULARS.	Rs.	A.	P.	REMARKS
April	102 Drams of rum @/2/-	12	12	.	for recruits Camp.
	5 . Do.	-	10	.	for boat-men
	6. Pairs boot-Lace /1/3	-	4	6	Sepoys at Range.
	7. yds. white drill @/5/3	2	4	9	.
	4. Cotton balls ./1/3	-	7	"	
	Received Rs 16-3-3 Durjodhan Roi Hosp. 11-5-10				
	TOTAL Rs. ...	16,	3	3	

QUARTER MASTER,
L. M. P.

1|5

Dunbar
CAPT.,
Commandant,
L. M. P.

102 tots of rum, 12 rupees 12 anna: Lieutenant Hutchins' mess bill for the Lakhimpur Military Police canteen.

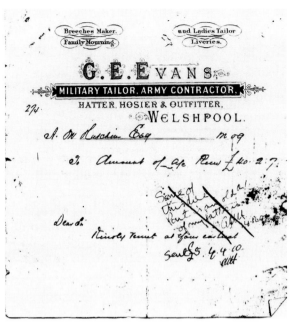

'Make Evans send a receipt.' From when he first left for South Africa and all through his service in India, Allan was indebted to George Evans, Military Tailor of Welshpool. Here he has paid £5 off the bill.

In January 1910 Allan relinquished his Civil Police posting and was appointed Assistant Commandant of the Lakhimpur Military Police Battalion stationed at Dibrugarh, where the District Club 'dispensed a generous hospitality somewhat stronger than the cup that cheers.'

Bill No. 101.   Month _October_ 1910

Capt. A. M. Hutchinson Dr

To Dibrugarh District Club Ld.

	Rs.	A.	P.
To Balance due from last month	122	6	6
„ Club Entrance fee			
„ „ Subscription for Nov 10	10	.	.
„ Tennis			
„ Billiards			
„ Liquor Oct 10	9	5	.
„ Card losing	5	12	.
„ „ Corner	.	4	.
„ Messing			
„ Rent			
„ 2 Coolies for Sending Liquor Tc With	3	8	.
„ 2 Bearer.			
	151	3	6

Credits.

By Card winning			
„ Cash & Notes	111	3	6
Total. Rs. ...	40	.	.

_E. & O. E._

Dated   1 . 11 . 1910   Secretary.

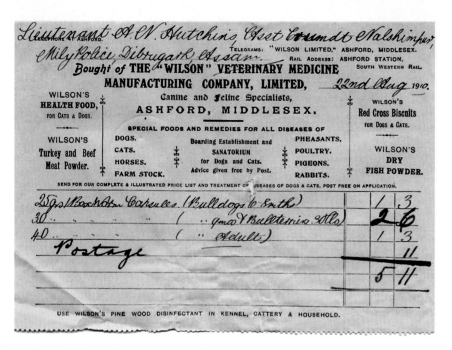

Bulldog medicine, 22 August 1910.

Bill for repairs to Allan Hutchins' uniform.

P. ORR & SONS,
MADRAS.

MADE AT
CALCUTTA, RANGOON,
AND LONDON.

Telegraphic Addresses:
MADRAS ... ORR.
RANGOON ... ORANSONS.
CALCUTTA ... JEWELRY.
London ... INDIARSL.

16, CHOWRINGHEE,

Calcutta, 16 DEC. 1910. 19

Capt. A. M. Hutchins,

Asst. Commandant,

L.M.P. B.G.

DIBRGARH.

ASSAM.

Dear Sir,

Inreply to your kind favor of the 4th. inst.,your last letter
appears to have been lost by one of our clerks, hence the reason that
no reply had been sent to you which we much regret. We recollect your
asking for wedding rings; & we now hasten to send to your goodself on
inspection, any of which can be altered to any size or shape, or we can
make one to your own design. The prices are marked in plain figures
on the tickets attached to them.

Re leather watch guard,we have not a copy of Marck's catalogue by
us so do not know the design you want,but if it is the ordinary silver
mounted guard we can send one in a few days from a new consignment expected
to arrive Monday.

Awaiting your reply and apologising

We remain

Yours faithfully,   rr Pr P. Orr

'I don't want to stop in Almora long or I shall be getting married or something.' Enquiries answered
about wedding rings, 16 December 1910. For whom the ring was intended is a mystery.

pay for February 1911

Rs 686 . 12 . 9

Deducted by I/o   2 . 10 0
_____

Net 684 . 2 . 9
_____

Deductions: —

Band Subs: 6 . 0 . 0
Charitable fund.   1 . 0 . 0
  Stamp   0 1 — 0
Canteen Adv.   36 . 2 . 0
Rai Amritlal Bahad.   — 15 —
Dr Marlie Jun.   8 . 0 . 0
_____

       52 . 2 . 0
_____

Balance   632 . 0 . 9
P⁴ into P.S.   634 . 10 . 9
_____
Differn   2 . 10 . 0

is due to the retrenchment made
by the I/o. which I shall cut
from Marli's pay. —
4/3/11   SB.

Pay and deductions for February 1911.

Abors at Sadiya.

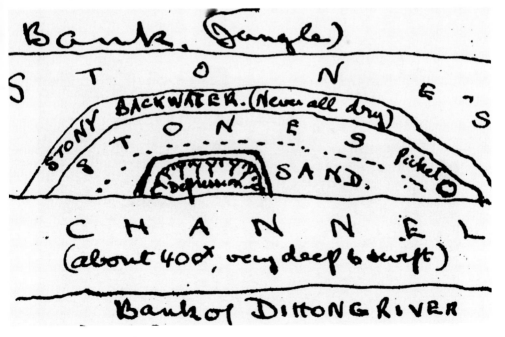

A sketch map of Allan's defensive camp.

Bliss and Dundas leaving Sadiya.

Steamers at Kobo.

At Kobo on the Brahmaputra River, the advance camp for the Abor expedition.

Drying out at Kobo.

Kobo base headquarters flooded.

Political officers with Mishmis.

GRIM EVIDENCE OF ABOR TREACHERY: A CAUSE OF THE EXPEDITION

AND SCENES OF THE BRITISH MARCH.

1. WHERE FOUR OF MR. NOEL WILLIAMSON'S PARTY WERE KILLED: THE BONES OF THE UNFORTUNATE MEN WHITENING NEAR RENGGING.
2. AS SEEN FROM THE 80-FOOT HIGH CROW'S NEST IN ITS CENTRE: THE BRITISH STOCKADE CAMP AT KOBO.
3. A GREAT LOSS TO THE EXPEDITION: THE LATE CAPTAIN A. M. HUTCHINS.
4. NICKNAMED "BUBBLE", ONE OF THE TWO SEVEN-POUNDER MUZZLE-LOADERS OF THE EXPEDITION.
5. NEWS BY HELIOGRAPH: L.M.P. SIGNALLERS IN COMMUNICATION WITH AN OUTPOST.

The officer who supplied the sketch for this drawing writes: "The party camped under big trees with buttress-shaped roots in the jungle. They evidently cooked their food here (for the black patch of the fire was visible in the foreground) and were surprised in their sleep. Two bodies were found near the fire, and the other two close by. A lot of Mr. Williamson's property, books, sketching-table, fishing-rod, rifle-case, etc., was thrown away in the jungle within a few yards after having been cut up." It will be remembered that the present punitive expedition against the Abors is a result of the murder of Mr. Noel Williamson and Dr Gregorson at the end of March last. Captain A. M. Hutchins, 3rd Q.A.O. (Queen Alexandra's Own) Gurkha Rifles and Assistant Commandant L.M.P., died on December 3 of pneumonia contracted at the front, above Mishing, between eight and ten miles south of Rotung

'Grim evidence of Abor treachery.' The *London Illustrated News* of 30 December 1911 records the death of Captain A.M. Hutchins – 'a great loss to the expedition'.

ON THE ROAD TO THE ENEMY'S STRONGHOLD: CARRIERS OF THE BRITISH EXPEDITION AGAINST THE ABORS.

THE ILLUSTRATED LONDON NEWS, DEC. 30, 1911.—1126

A REST DURING THE MARCH ON KEBANG: NAGAS OF THE TRANSPORT SERVICE ON THEIR ARRIVAL AT JANAKMUKH.

As we had occasion to note in our Issue of November 25 last, when dealing with other photographs of the Abor Expedition, some 3000 carriers were recruited for the British force from the tribes, generically known as Nagas, who live on the hills on the left, or south, bank of the Brahmaputra. Part of the Naga Hills is still under British control; in other parts the Nagas remain head-hunters; and head-hunting goes on within ten miles of many tea-gardens in Assam.——

[Continued below.]

WITH BASKETS ON THEIR BACKS AND WELL ARMED: TRANSPORT COOLIES OF THE ABOR EXPEDITION.

THE ILLUSTRATED LONDON NEWS, DEC. 30, 1911.—1127

CROSSING A MOUNTAIN STREAM IN THE DENSE JUNGLE: NAGAS OF THE BRITISH PUNITIVE FORCE NEAR JANAKMUKH, IN THE ABOR COUNTRY.

[Continued.]

——The Nagas are remarkable clearers of jungle, and can cut a road one mile long by twelve feet wide through thick jungle in two hours. They receive one shilling a day for their work with the Expedition. All those shown on this page and on the preceding page are armed with spears and dhaos, and carry their loads in conical baskets, which rest on the back and are slung by means of a band round the forehead. The Expedition passed through Janakmukh, on the Dihong River, on the way to Kebang, the stronghold of the Abors.

POST OFFICE TELEGRAPHS.

If the Receiver of an Inland Telegram doubts its accuracy, he may have it repeated on payment of half the amount originally paid for its transmission, any fraction of 1d. less than ½d. being reckoned as ½d. ; and if it be found that there was any inaccuracy, the amount paid for repetition will be refunded. Special conditions are applicable to the repetition of Foreign Telegrams.
Office of Origin and Service Instructions.

Charges to pay

Welshpool   Handed in at 12 47 pm   Received here at 1 - 9 pm

TO { Hutchins Acton Scott Hall marshbrook Ch Stretton

Dear Allan died yesterday dibrugart pneumonia

Hutchins

'Dear Allan died yesterday.'

The Colonel in mourning; Allan and his father shared a love of horses.

Pallavaram
Jan 27. 1904

Dearest Toosie,

I'm out in the desert, now so to speak, at an old cantonment whose glory has departed, and am field-firing duty with my coy. We're about twelve miles from the Fort; it is a very nice place as far as climate goes, quite cool and so on. The station society consists at present of us two, the commandant, (Major Ffrench, I.A. with whom we mess) and Lt.-Col. something something Chattergee, I.M.S – a full-blooded Bengali, much Anglicised. I've been to call on him this evening, as Ffrench said he would be annoyed if we didn't. We came here on 20th and go back about the end of the month.

I've got rheumatism at present, induced by the cold up here as compared to Madras. My Hindustani doesn't progress much I'm afraid. I was suddenly ordered to go in for (a) and (b) for promotion the other day with three others and had to sweat like hell to get it up in about 10 days. However, by the blessing of Allah, on being hauled into Madras last Monday, to meet the Inquisitors, I mean examiners, we all defeated them utterly and are through. But what has been stopping my work more than that, is the fearful-life, which means that most my spare time is put in wooing Morpheus.

Thank George very much for his trouble and for sending the various things. It's very rum that we should both have shaken a loose leg in Madras isn't it? I haven't yet found anyone who remembers him, but perhaps it's just as well. However I shall make cautious inquiries.

I think I wrote last on 14th. That evening I went to the Civil Service dance which was quite the best so far. It made the third one running for me. Next night I went to a musical 'At Home' at Government House. It was rather a bore. On Saturday night I shook a loose leg roundly Madras Fair. On Monday was the Sutherland-Ons dance; a sort of cotillian party. On Wednesday I came out here, and have lived a quite righteous and sober like life since except that last night the temptation of a Ball at Government House was too much for me, so I went in arriving back here about 4 this morning with racking rheumatism in my right leg. Tonight, the company give a dance to the local beauty, which I shall patronise (the dance, I mean).

I'm not sorry to be out here, because it's a very healthful spot, and Madras is really too-too now, as the races and polo-tournament are both on at present. Well, I must dress for dinner. My best love all round commencing with you and George.

Yours affectly
Allan

★★★

Fort St. George
Madras
February 22 04

Dearest Bettina,

From your remarks, I see you had an enjoyable season this Christmas time, or to quote your old Syriac expression, 'a very rorty time'; but I trust that this has not succeeded in disturbing that calm and dignified manner for which you are so justly celebrated, and which is so becoming in the help meet-mate-meat-you know what I mean – of a rising professional man. In this abode of tears out here, we also, in our quiet way, have been attempting to forget that life is but a curse, and that the rupee is but one and fourpence; and to a certain extent, success has crowned our efforts. Madras has its season in the cold weather, and begins about the middle of December, and begins to be gay. We had the last Ball of any consequence on the 15th last, to wit, the Bachelor's, and have now settled down to Lentin fare. There's going to be a fancy dress in the mid-Lent (I know the French name for this season but am gravelled as to how to spell it) which I think will definitely finish our dancing. I have not done so bad. In January I put in twelve dances and most other evenings had on something in the way of a dinner, reception, At Home or a theatre, and in fact at one time, was just about done, but being sent out into the wilds to field-fire for a fortnight just saved me from an untimely end. Quite the blarsy rooay, what?

Madras is full of skirt but, taken throughout, the standard of beauty is not high. Still you know, with a little careful selection, one may yet manage to amuse oneself. At the Bachelor's dance, driven to desperation by the idea that this was the last Ball, I quite excelled myself, and am afraid did a demned lot of execution, but no more of this. I can't help feeling a regretful sometimes. The latest thing is that we've been on Manoeuvres, starting on Wednesday morning last and returning home on Saturday night – three days of foot-slogging under a blazing blasted bloody sun, with fighting over a ruddy jungle in between. I don't mind telling you, that on Saturday morning yours respectfully was about as cooked as a toucher, but by the grace of God, and a seasonably timed halt for breakfast succeeded in finishing the march in style. There was only one other subaltern who did the same, fairly without having his rifle carried for him or something. As soon as our troubles were over, I succeeded in forgetting them by means of a judicious mixture of gin-and-soda, whisky-and-soda and the harmless necessary beer, and in consequence turned up at Church Parade next morning at half past six, as fresh as a lark without a trace of stiffness.

Apparently the old folks at home have been rather dissipated this year too; in fact the 'fearful life' seems quite the go everywhere.

Footer is over here now so I don't quite know what to do for exercise. I think I shall take up hockey and boxing. I have a most accommodating chap (a Tommy) who comes in and lets me bang him to my heart's content without getting stuffy and outing me. I keep him friendly by judicious beer, as he's the regimental fighting man and it wouldn't do to offend him.

Well, dear, I must away. I shall be awful pleased to hear from you and Schofe and hope it will be long. My best love to both of you and may your shadows increase. Goodbye.

Yours affectly
Allan

★ ★ ★

Fort St. George
Mar 9 1904

Dearest Pa,

I'm glad you are getting all right again after your tumble and hope you will be careful. I took a pretty good toss off my flat feet the other day, but only lost skin, though I managed to get rid of a considerable quantity of that. We had the regimental sports on 29 and I ran in the officers race. It was the last event and nearly dark, and they'd shifted the course, so that the tape was only about 10yds from the enclosure rope. In the excitement of a close finish (I ran second, starting scratch and giving the winner, who was the Q.M. 15yds) we, of course, never saw the rope, and the first four simply took unto themselves wings and hurtled about two horses lengths through the air alighting in a struggling heap on the hard and unsympathetic ground. It was most amusing – for the spectators. I'm nearly healed of my various contusions, now except a beastly cut on my shin where I struck the rope which won't heal.

Your inquiries re tents I may answer by saying that officers and men's are sort of square maloom. We have double roofs but T.A. only single. For further 'ticklers of the manoeuvre see former letters to the family. Each Co. has to go out again in turn to Pakawaram for two months to do Field Training and musketry. I don't know whether I shall catch it before my translation to other spheres, but hope so, as one can live much cheaper there; in fact about half as cheap. Now we are on the subject, I am banking with Binny and Co of here, and if you send my next quarter's allowance out direct to them by means of a draft, that will be best.

I've not struck the P.J. Reade or Reid yet; in fact I dunno whether he is in Madras or not, but if I run across him, I may call. I'm interested to hear about the J. D. Rees you know, in Montgomeryshire. Do you think he'd be useful in any way? As a 'little return, you know'.

I don't know why mother keeps bombarding me about Beynon. Surely I told you that he wrote me and I wrote him. My application is in, and he said he would get his C.O. to apply for me. I don't anticipate much chance of getting at K. [Kitchener] and working him.

Well, no more at present. We are starting beastly schemes again, and are pretty busy. The Hindustani progresses fairly.

With much love to all.
Yours affectly,
Allan

[The J.D. Rees Allan referred to was a Liberal MP 1906–1910 and a former Under-Secretary in the Madras Government. He was the author of *The Real India*, published in 1908 and still in print today.]

Later.

I wish [Rees] would turn his Parliamentary attention to showing up the scabby way this glorious Indian government treats its military officers. The latest economy is our baggage for service is cut down and we are to have the privilege of paying the mules that carry it, to make it square. Can you imagine having to pay your own transport and grub on active service? We have to. I wonder whether anyone at home when they were hearing of the military display at Agra for the Amir realised that the officers were heavily hit by having to go there?

★★★

March 24 04
Fort St George
Madras

Dearest Podgie,

Poor mamma seems very cross in her last letter about my 'mean, scrubby' epistles, but I greatly fear that this one will also excite her wrath. However, I wrote her a nice long one a little while back and hope her anger is assuaged somewhat.

We are that busy these days! Firstly, every morning at 6.15 we have to field train, at 9 Battn. Orderly room, 9.30 lectures, 11 musketry and so on for the rest of the morning. Incidentals such as boards, range duties, pay-days, Company rooms, rifle inspections, telling off prisoners, CO's lectures, canteen duty, etc, etc. don't count. To obviate the danger of us wasting our spare time we have about two 'schemes' (road reports, sketches etc) to do in the next fortnight, besides which, every officer is employed in tracing a series of maps in the Colonel's collection. This last was the last straw for me, so a babu is doing that lot at my expense. You can imagine that my chances of passing my Higher Standard on the 11th next are getting remoter. In fact, I doubt if I know as much as when I went up for Lower, although I endeavour to work with two munshis every day. As these gentlemen are in the habit of remarking 'that will show the result'.

K. [Kitchener] is coming down in the beginning of the month. They say he converses with every officer on principle. Give me half a chance and I'll ask him straight out for what I want. I hope he won't beat me afterwards.

We had the Mi-chalême dance at the Adyar Club a week last Saturday; quite a small affair, but what, ho! lots of fun. My only other dissipation lately was the St Patrick's dinner at the Madras Club, the most disgraceful orgie I have yet participated in.

Tell Ma that if I meet the Stacy Jones young man, I will remind him of our having played together as children. It might be good for a small loan.

Well no more at present, my love to all and sundry and keep on writing.
Yours affectly
Allan

★ ★ ★

Fort St. George
Madras
April 28 1904

Dearest Family,

My last week's promise to write a long letter today, has, I fear, come to nought as I really cannot find time. Thursday, as you know is a holiday, which today resolved itself into starting on the Range at 6 a.m. and finishing in the Canteen at 12.45. Since Tiffin I have been hanging around trying to get at the Adjutant, and am so fed up that I'm going to bed now (2.30) until it's cool enough to go out this evening.

There, I've been to bed now and feel much refreshed. I generally snatch a little repose in the afternoon as I'm mostly late to bed and early to rise.

Mamma's remarks about the son and heir's marriage makes me think of the Taming of the Shrew, only the other way round. He has a lot to be grateful to his wife for.

The new Army Order about influence etc. is another funny isn't it? What a dear old lot of hypocrites they are. George seems the sum up the situation very completely.

There's no news about my going beyond what I've already told you but I expect to be fired out of this at any moment; the sooner the better, since everyday means a loss of seniority and also of good hard rupees as well. Still, I shall be sorry to leave. The CO seems to have taken rather fancy to me lately and has been very nice to me; in fact at his monthly inspection of Coys he sort of insinuated in a few well chosen remarks that if all went on like this, Kitchener might be short of a job ere long. I couldn't quite make it out, as popularity with those set in authority is a new and pleasing attribute in yours 'umbly; the calm before the storm, p'rhaps.

We had rather a cheery guest-night the other evening, and Challenor, our only Captain, was had up by the dear old bird and informed that it must not occur again; what annoyed him apparently, was a billiard ball (we were playing fives in the billiard-room which adjoins the anteroom) flashing suddenly at intervals and with a crash into his staid rubber of bridge and being retrieved triumphantly by a subaltern officer arrayed principally in overalls, shirt, sweat and cheerful smiles.

So the S's fortune is still in the air is it? D'you know, I've struck a perfect counterpart of the old lady out here, the same old gush, the same old lies, the same old devotion to her family, and anxiety for her daughter's welfare, and the same old transparent insincerity. She has rather a nice girl, an ingenue, about 18, just out from school. I took her on the river last Tuesday and was overtaken by darkness, not arriving home till after dinner time. The old lady was awful arch about it, and asked me if I could live on my pay. Not there, my cheeild, not there!

Poor pa and his bike and horse accidents, stop me sleeping at night. He seems full of this point-to-point race and I'm only just surprised that he did not enter Comet and ride himself. I hope the knee is all right again.

I hope all are keeping well-an-'appy as it leaves me at present, except for prickly-heat of which I am devoured [prickly heat was described by one British officer as like 'sitting in a state of nudity on a horse-hair sofa'.]. It's deadly and my fair young body is an awful spectacle. Still I hope to survive.

The best of love and kisses to the family.
Yours affectly
Allan

★★★

Fort St. George
May 25 1904.

My dearest Podglet,

I do not hear from you very often dear. I'm not complaining but thought the fact might interest you. Mother's remarks re new-mown lamb and mint sauce made my mouth water. There really is no goose like Mrs Stevens [the family cook] in a manner of speaking. Tell pa he needn't be frightened that I'm unwell if he doesn't hear from me, 'cos my first symptoms will be frantic letters to say so. Also inform him that he is not to drink so much as the cause him to fall off his bike twice per week, and then blame the poor dumb thing. Dumb, I said. He is a very reckless old creature but I hope his legs are quite recovered ere this. If he rides poor Bob in the training, he should have his (Bob's) back stiffened somehow. A little buckram, or what not eh? Ask pa what he thinks of the new regulations, especially as regards India. The service is really going to the dogs.

The absurdity of the greater part of the new ideas is so patent, when one knows men, who have been tried and proved good soldiers, going to the wall to make way for the examination wallah. I am no orator, as Brutus is, but it does seem sanguinary rot. A man in this regiment, who received a brevet-majority in S.A. for his good work has just been passed over because he failed to qualify by 12 marks in one paper, although he obtained sufficient for a 'special' in all the others.

Don't forget that 'Efficiency' is the watch-word of the service. In old Madras, news is not particularly plentiful. I've been doing very little gadding for long time and live a very sensible, quite quiet existence. I get a fair amount of work in, in the mornings, and sleep most of the afternoon, in the evening I generally go to some club or other, usually to play bridge; from which gentle relaxation, I manage to add slightly to my income; very slightly. This week we have had the first rain this year. Monday it rained in the morning and all day today. I was on a court of inquiry this morning at the Arsenal and the officer in charge there showed us over. I was very interested. Did I ever tell you that Clive used to live in the Fort here, [Clive escaped the French attack on Madras to warn the British forces that the city had been taken. By coincidence Clive was a one-time resident of Welshpool, for which Allan's family home is named] they still pretend to know the house. Have I ever described my fellow messites to you. In case I have not, and news don't seem to come, I will do so. First the Colonel and as such, to be obeyed, as my friend Kipling says. A large, rather reserved very courtly man, about 46 I should think. A bit of a martinet, though, I should say, quite dispassionately, a bit subject to likes and dislikes. Thanks be, at present I'm in the first category.

The Adjutant, Major (Brevet) Wilkinson; a dark, good-looking, painfully thin and delicate fellow; the most difficult man to size up I've ever met: almost my idea of 'form' and beloved of most women; at the same time a thorough sportsman and a good soldier, though slightly slack. These are my impressions, but he is really most awfully difficult to really understand. A most interesting character. [Wilkinson had served under Colonel F. R. Wingate in the Expeditionary Force into Egypt against Dervish led by Emir Ahmed Fedil and the Khalifa Abdulla.] Then Capt. Challinor, who has not been here very long. He is an awfully good sort, an excellent bridge player, in fact rather a star at most sports and games. He's going home to be married shortly.

I have had to abandon this and have no time to go on with it. If I don't post now, I shall miss the mail.

Best love all-round
Alan M. Hutchins Esq.

A Commission with the 73rd Carnatics

Twelve months after stepping ashore Allan achieved the highest standard in Urdu, came fourth in his year for signalling and having served his apprenticeship with the 1st Leicesters, on 18 July 1904 was appointed to the 73rd Carnatic Infantry (formerly the 13th Madras Infantry).

He joined the 73rd CI in Singapore. Why Singapore? 'Because', he wrote, 'I had passed Higher. The 73rd wanted a subaltern and they won't send native officers on Colonial Service until they've passed Higher. Tha'ssall. I don't think it's with a view to making me Commander-in-Chief here, or anything like that.' The movement of mail is a logistical wonder with letters from home taking up to three weeks to arrive. 'We get our European mails by four different routes, i.e. P&O via Columbo; B.I. via Bombay, across India and via Negatapam; Messagerie and N. German Lloyd so we never know exactly when they will arrive.'

7 June 1904

Dear Mater,

Well, I've news for you: I've been appointed double-company officer, 73rd Carnatic Infantry. Although this sounds rather well, it is the usual appointment and to the regiment which, although I have nothing against it, is not one of those I wished for.

Composition is 4 Coys. Madras Mussulmans, 2 Coys. Tamils and 2 Coys. Pariahs and Christians. Pah!

The dear old authorities are a bit wearing, aren't they? Having delayed my appointment 3 months in order that I might apply for the regiment I wanted, and get the 't's crossed properly and the 'i's dotted in the correct place, they calmly drop the application into the nearest waste-paper basket and set about considering where this fellow ought to go to. The great compensation is that I shall see a little more of this goodly frame, the earth, before I settle down, as the regiment is at Singapore, whither I proceed at my earliest convenience.

This is not in the Indian command, you know. Whether this will make any difference to my pay or not, I can't tell. I wonder if I shall see old Jim Sweltenham.

At the end of the year the regiment is relieved and returns to India, to be stationed at Vizianagaram and Cuttack, so I shall have a nice six months change. I am hoping against hope that I shall not be compelled to remain at Vizianagaram very long but be translated to Gurkhas. When I get to my regiment I shall probably find out the best way to go to work. Major Wilkinson very kindly wrote about me to Heriez Smith who is the factotum of Sir Donald Stewart, commanding Madras district and now up at Ootycummund; he will probably be able to give me more advice.

I think I have rather acted the goat in not taking the offers of 10th Gurkhas and 64th Pioneers but I think that if things don't pan out right otherwise, I might still work one of them.

Now as to going. I'm thinking of leaving here on July 7th, three weeks today. I might go a week today as the boats run fortnightly but I am inclined to wait till the 7th. It only makes a fortnight's difference between British and Indian army pay which won't amount to very much and gives me time to pack up, say goodbye to my friends and admirers, without rushing things. Also, the great reason is that I am hoping that George will be able to wire me out my quarter's allowance to Binney by the beginning of the month, (July). This will enable me to get away alright and fixed into my new quarters. At present I am quite solvent but if I went away next Thursday, I doubt if I would have sufficient margin to pay freights, servants' passages, back-debts and so on and so forth. Of course, the trip is bound to cost me a certain amount, although nominally free. Could George, therefore, have my splosh wired out so as to reach me by the 3rd, say, or if this is inconvenient, wire me so that I can go to my friend, Binney, and arrange for what is known as 'a temporary accommodation'.

I am sorry to be always demanding money at the point of a bayonet but if they had been a bit more rapid in appointing me, I think I should not have required any further support. Anyway, I hope this will be the last instalment. With the native army I understand one gets about 100 rupees a month more pay and only about half the mess bill, 'a consummation most devoutly to be wished'.

I wonder what Singapore is like. Very much like the rest of the world, I expect; everone wanting to be somewhere else.

I've not had a bad time here and have made a lot of friends, so I shall be sorry to leave in a way. Still, it doesn't do to let your roots get too firmly embedded.

Letts No 46 Rough Diary

Thursday 30 June 1904
Met the Rose of Persia in evening. Got wet through by rain but not for nothing. Sent her home in a rick. which I had to go and fetch from inside the sentry's poot at Geogre's gate. He looked at me pretty hard.

★★★

Fort St. George
Madras
July 7 04

Dear Family,

Just a hurried line to thank you for the dibs which arrived all right, and to tell you I'm leaving this afternoon per S.S. *Zamania* (B.I.). I'm well unhappy and as happy as is consistent with leaving this regiment who have been very good to me and whom I'm very fond of, and also with leaving at least two feminine hearts much fluttered. Pooah little beasts!

Thasall.
Hope you're all well as it leaves me at present.

Thine in God's own hurry
Allan

PS some of our local shop keepers will also be sorry I've gone.

★★★

S.S.Z
July 10th 1904
Off Carical

Dear Family

I'm my road now for Singapore. We are lying off Canical or Kannible or some place like that, taking in cargo. We have called now at Pondichery, Cuddolore and here. We stop again seven miles on at Negapatam and have five days from there to Penang. Thence to Singapore. All goes well. I'm very fit and the only passenger aboard except some off-coloured blokes in the Third Class. She's not a bad ship but leisurely, decidedly leisurely. We get a rubber of bridge when in port.

I went ashore at Pondichery and bought some post-cards for Billy, Dizzie and Aunt Batt. It was the last place God made, and Cuddalore the first. I didn't go ashore at the latter, but shall do so at Negatapam, I think, and post this. I cleared Madras all right. They were all very kind when saying good-bye and came to see me off. Well, I can't think of anything to tell you. The officers of the MNI [Madras Native Infantry] now the 73rd say they'll be back in India about November, so I shan't see much of Singapore. This boat carries coolies from Negatapam to Penang. Also lots of cargo between these little coast towns.

I think that's all. Defend me from Toosie's wrath at my not writing.

Best love.
Yours affectionately
Alan

P. S. have arrived Negatapam and am going ashore this afternoon. The boat has been taking in bullocks all the morning. Phew! They go ashore in Penang. The decks nearly all covered with cargo as well.

★★★

Letts No 46 Rough Diary

Wednesday 13 July 1904
At sea. Good roll on all day and fresh breeze. Read the Octopus all day. Damn all else. Am getting fed up of the voyage as its shocking slow. No one to talk to. Ship's officers very decent, as is usual, but too busy to see much of. Skipper a rum old buster but a very worthy fellow. Better read than I am too, which is not surprising, is it? Played cut-throat after dinner. Lost. Slept in cabin.

Monday 18 July
Arrived at Singapore. Was met by Capt Anderson, the adjutant, who was very decent and drove me. Reported arrival. Barracks are temporary ataphuts and miles from town. About mid-day went down town with Broadbent and Mansfield (RE). Did some shopping and went to club. Dined in and played bridge.

Friday 29 July
While out today Chinamen gave me a) two coconuts, one green and one ripe, b) half a pineapple c) some pieces of sugar cane d) two mangosteens.

Saturday 20 August
Found I had organised a little dinner party in a moment of temporary aberration last nght, so dined two Germans and Hamilton at Raffles. After dinner took a little rickshaw exercise.

Sunday 11 September
Allenby drove me to Botanical Gardens. Back to dinner. Played piquet in my room after dinner.

Saturday 24 September
Went to club with Allenby; changed there and went to Raffles. Quite sufficient refreshment thank you, as far as I was concerned. Dined with Jim and M. After dinner M and I gave the major an innngs by going over to another party for a bit where I met an old 49-er. Then all four of us sat on a bench and drank brandies. 'She' was sitting between A and self. Don't quite know what happened but Jim apparently got rather fed up as he suddenly howled at us furiously. Some time during the evening I took her or she took me for a stroll around the gardens. I can't quite remember when, but believe that no harm was done. After sending them home blew round to the west end, couldn't find my particular so finished up at no. 9, rather defeated.

★★★

24th November 1904

Dearest Family,

Christmas greetings is my theme, Plum pies and mince puddings are my dream.

Hold up, horse! My Pegasus appears a bit out of hand at starting. I am sending my dear mamma a little pair of cloisonné vases (Japanese) and the two girls each a kimono (accent on the first syllable, please) to wear as a dressing gown. For papa, a Malacca cane which I selected for him in the rough. I regret this is the only absolute local curio but I can't think of any Malaysian artefact to send you. Everything pretty here comes from Japan or China. If the money market isn't quite so tight when I leave here, I will send you some more pretty things I have in my eye.

Well now, to confess. I looked at the sailing and mail list just now and found to my inexpressible annoyance that the parcel post closed at 12 today. As I drove down town yesterday to get these things for the mail which leaves tomorrow, it's a bit aggravating and now they won't go until the 30th. So there! So this is only to tell you to look out for these things and to convey my Christmas greetings in the meantime.

No news lately.

A very Merry Christmas, a happy New Year and lots of love from
Your affectionate
Allan

★★★

Singapore
14th Decr 1904

Dearest Podglet,

I think it's about time I unburdened myself to you for a change as I believe I have left many letters of yours unanswered. First let me begin with my usual apology for not writing oftener. Your mails from home have struck a sense of my shortcomings to the inmost cockles of my heart; but once again, let me assure my devoted parents and you that if any evil chance should befall me I will let you know. Hence, no news will be good news.

Talking about news, the latest is about our move. Some little time back we had a wire from the C-I-C that instead of going to Viz. And Cuttack, we were to go to Secunderabad. Hard on the heels of that, we got another saying 'stand by'. Then at last we had orders for Aurungabad, which is apparently final. It is up in the N.W. corner of the Nizam's dominions and has hitherto been a station exclusively for the Hyderabad contingent troops. But nous avons changés tout cela. Efficiency and Reform are the watchwords of the Service. Yes Sir! I'm told it's a good station in an interesting neighbourhood so we don't mind; though I should be very glad of another six months out here. I'm beginning to pick up a little Malay now (the language I mean, *not* what *you* think).

I'm glad Mamma's cough has turned out all right again and hope that she and Poah Pa will continue in the straight and narrow path of health. The news of Kitty is also more cheering; I am looking forward to hearing from her. I hope Pa gets his trip to London to give evidence in the 'Suit' [a contested will in relation to Penton Lodge, a family home in Penton Mewsey, Hampshire]. but let him remember the old adage about shaming the devil.

I like Mamma's warlike spirit and remarks anent the North Sea difficulty. She is quite bloodthirsty, a fitting mother for a warrior bold such as myself. I notice she imputes my long abstinence from correspondence to the influence of 'some girl or other again', coupled with the fact of my being an 'irresponsible idiot'. To both charges, I plead guilty. It is rather the climate of Singapore which is somewhat relaxing.

Is it true that Simpkin is now in the habit of giving garden parties on the dung-heap, at which entertainment blue-bottle hunting forms the great attraction? And that Coffie-Jones paraded the town on the day of his election in an emblematic car representing 'The rise of Teetotalism', the central figures being himself in his brother's well-known tall hat and D.P. as an awful example bound in the mayoral chain?

I don't know why mamma should have gathered the impression that I was overjoyed at going to Cuttack. What did I say?

In the matter of the saddle I do not know what is correct but if you send the old one I can have it fixed upright in India. If you insist on the old one, *make the makers responsible*. Either way, it had best be consigned to Messrs. Grindley Groom & Co., Bombay as that will be nearest for Aurungabad. As for wallets, I suppose I require them, of course; if you send the old saddle, the old ones will do.

Aren't you proud of William playing the violin-cello? She's the one to show who is the King of Glory, bless 'er 'art. There is a fetching little lady here who plays the big drum in a band at a sort of café or bier-haus place which is called the Tingle-Tangle for short; Union hotel is the correct title. Whenever I'm on the town of an evening, I go along there and have a dance with the big drummist. They are rather amusing shows, full of Germans and Austrians. There's generally some sort of a rout before the evening's out.

I have had a fair amount of amusement lately, including four very pleasant dinners on H.M.S. *Cressy*, who are a very nice lot of fellows. They gave an At Home here too before they left (they are on their way home to pay off), which was very successful. I was out to Tiffin yesterday and the day before; there's a bazaar this afternoon at which my presence is earnestly requested by certain fair ones but I'm not going though as I am suffering from a slight attack of the old family complaint known as 'cramp in the kick' or 'tightness of the pocket'. I shall go a little jaunt to the club instead with my rubber tyred turn-out. I'm exercising Major London's mare for him now, so I have two horses for nix. I've rather fallen in love with the little mare I got from the R.F. chap and am in negotiation for her purchase – not, as you might imagine, with her owner but with my old friends, Messrs. Binney & co., of Madras. I wrote 'em the other day, telling 'em to advance me seven hundred rupees or take the consequences and have not heard from them. I'm not very keen either way, though she is a good little hoss.

No news re Gurkhas yet. You are a bit impatient. Patience!

Well, goo-bye. Hope you received the kimonos, etc.
Best love to all of you and kisses and so on.
Yours affectionately,
Allan

★★★

Letts No 46 Rough Diary

Friday 13 January 1905
Good-bye to Singapore. Handed over barracks to a.s.c. Had breakfast with 95th then went down to town and afterwards to Clive. Then back up town to collect Colonel's stick from shop, and finally landed on Clive, with 13 dollars to take me to India. People saw us off and we sailed about 2.30

★★★

R.I.M.S. Clive
Gulf of Manar
19 Jan 1905

Dearest Family,

Another gap in my correspondence to be extenuated but you people seem to be so pleased and send such paeans of joy when I break one of my long silences that it almost tempts me not to write on purpose.

Well, we are now well on our way to Bombay. This is one of the Indian Marine troopships and more naval than the Navy. They <u>do</u> fancy themselves. She is rather an old tub, and this is her last trip, but we are fairly comfortable on board. There is no one beside the regiment except a fat old R.A.M.C. Lt. Col. from Singapore, and his wife. She is very nice, but he is – Scotch.

Literature and bridge are our two relaxations, and the journey so far has been calm and uneventful. We debark at Bombay, and train to Aurangabad, where we shall all mess in a Station mess with the other two regiments.

Papa has rather inflated ideas of the no. of officers in a native regiment. There are now no wing-commanders or second-in-command billets. There are one C.O., one adjt., one Q.M.S., one doctor (I.M.S.) 4 D.C. comds. and 4 D.C. officers. With men on leave, seconded, etc it is generally reduced about one half. <u>We</u> have a C.O., an adjt. two majors (D.C.C.) and four subalterns (two acting as D.C.C. one Qr.Ms. and one D.C.O. which is me) at present.

I am now pukka in the 73rd C.I.

Mamma's Christmas and new years letters just hit it off to a T. each arriving just a day or so beforehand. Thank you all very much for your good wishes etc. and for the photies. With all due deference, I think the latter are terrible.

I settled up everything in Singapore before leaving, but had to take an advance from the regt. much to my surprise. However, shall soon pull that up at Aurangabad, where I mean to do a bit of work for a change. You'll be surprised to hear that I've got another fit of teetotalism, and haven't had a drink for three weeks. Who says I can't do without it? I'm doing it for economy not so much for saving the price of the drink but to keep me quietly at home, as you can't go gadding about on the teetotal lay.

★★★

Letts No 46 Rough Diary

Monday 23 January 1905
Unloading baggage onto lighters from 6am until tiffin time. Regiment went ashore in the meantime. Eventually got started about 5.45 in first train [for Aurangabad].

★★★

Feb 1
Aurangabad [Maharastra]

Alas! I should have posted this in time for the last mail home, but in the hurry-scurry of moving up here the day eluded me as usual.

I have received two letters from you here, via Singapore. I don't know you are always so keen on putting the exact address on my letters and why people say they don't write to me because they don't know my address. If you've got my name and regiment you will probably reach me quicker by that address than any others.

I'm sorry my offerings didn't arrive for Xmas. The mysterious telegram is simplicity itself as Reuter's at Calcutta did it for me on my requesting them to do so. I myself have not been paying flying visits to that sweet spot. Thanks very much for your <u>kind</u> offer … dhobies of Hindustan and Far Cathay have worked their wicked will on mine, and my most respectable ones are some I bought at Singapore and $1 per dozen. Yes, I see that Beynon has been promoted. I may drop him a reminder later on but I can't keep pegging at him or he'll get fed up. Thank you very much for the news of the saddle. I think we had better say white dees if that's right for Gurkhas. The saddle can be sent here (Aurangabad). Will you order me a proper bridle, bit etc for which I will send you a cheque for in God's good time? It's awfully good of you to take so much trouble about it. I shall buy a horse soon now. I wish I had bought the little mare I had in Singapore. She was a topper, but I couldn't see how to raise the money Binney's were asking over it, so I left it alone. Now when it's too late, the old man says I can have about 700 when I like and pay back later. I shall get one as soon as I can; but every time I think of the mare I could cut my throat to think I could have had her for the asking. Damn sorry George couldn't get old Hutchinson not to be a swine, but these old blooders only do decent things for their pals, unless you're a bit 'fortiter in re' with them. If you are in town again, and should happen to call around and see him, as he said, you might mention that, having a certain amount of experience in the field, it is rather damn hard lines on me that I should be tucked snugly away in a Madrasi regiment, because some youths of irreproachable up-bringing and aristocratic connections must be put to the better regiments. I don't mind taking the ordinary chance where all start fair, but it stands to reason that <u>all</u> the appointments to the N.W. cannot at present go to men who have seen service. Why then, should I be buried? <u>All</u> the young officers coming to India aren't sent to Madras and of the remainder there must be one or two who can't claim my experience. But still, the Army Council will tell you that influence doesn't count in the service! What I said about the regt. being disbanded was not 'fun' as George suggests, but apparently it won't come yet for a little while, though certainly eventually [the 73rd CI was disbanded in 1922].

I had a letter and photo from Kitty today. She looks very nice.

Thank you for all the newsy talk about 'Pool and kind wishes etc. I think it was very good of you to write on Christmas day when you were so full. I drank your health on Xmas day, too. I'm glad you got lots of cards and presents etc. While as for turkeys, I wish that I'd been there. At the risk of making Toosie proud, I must say that no one, except

her, knows how to cook. I want her to send me some recepes, so that I can train my
Cook when I get one. The sort of things I want are like pickled herrings, stuffing for
geese, ducks, etc & liver sauce; not dishes. You write and tell me a few such things. At
least, tell me those three and I will think up some more to ask you.

I suppose I'd better tell you a bit about this 'ere spot. It is, as I have said, in the Nizam's
territory; and there is nothing outside the cantonment except the native city. No society,
I mean. There is a very nice mess for all three regts. and the members thereof all seem
quite of the best description. We have got a big bungalow where we all are pigging
together at present as there are no others available for a day or two. When they are, five of
us (or four) are going to stop on here. It is heaps big enough for six, and as they find difficulty in letting it, we get it for 100 dibs per month. The thing as worries us most is the
cold, which to our Singaporially and Madrasly enervated constitutions, is rather trying.
I have been very glad of my Jaegers once or twice. (The first time since leaving home.)

The sport round here, is I am told, excellent, but so far I have not shirked at all. I am
worrying on now for my retention exam. When I've done that, I may be able to get off
to a course or something. (there is a faint chance of my being Q M. during the absence
on leave of the present one Rs100.)

Then that course that you, Papa, are always telling me about, can't be undertaken for
a bit yet and as for the Tamil, I'm trying to dodge it altogether. It is used very little in
the regiment, sounds like the gibbering of apes, and is the language of a race I detest in
every way. I allude to the Southern Indian Hindoo. Mahomedans I can do with, but the
Hindoo – Pah!

Well, goodbye all until next time. Best love and kisses to all from
Yours desperately,
Allan

                                          ★★★

Letts No 46 Rough Diary

Monday 6 March 1905
Hamiliton and I took tonga and went and called on Syed Mohammed Belgrami the
Taluqdan of A-bad. Very affable old gent. Nice house. W and soda and cigarettes.

Thursday 9 March
Went to Rosa with Syed Mohammed. Started by tonga at 5, changed horses at –
Daulatabad and got to Rosa at sunset. Old man did us proud with outriders, guards of
honour, saddle horses to ascend hills etc etc.

**In the following letter Allan announces his transfer to the 3rd Ghurkha Rifles – 'one of the
crack regiments of the Indian Army' – and shortly afterwards his promotion to 'full-blown
Leuitentant – no more pay'.**

From Aurangabad he made the 1000-mile, four-day journey north to the 3rd Ghurkhas'

home at Almora in Assam, travelling by rail (there were 25,000 miles of Indian railways laid to 1905) and tonga dak *(a small two-wheel carriage pulled by a pair, pony or oxen) and arriving at Almora on 12 April 1905. Raised in 1815, with the consent of the Nepali Durbar Ghurkhas enlisted freely for British service (they still do). They stayed loyal in the Mutiny and had fought ferociously in the 2nd Afghan War and in the bloody skirmishes that defined British influence in the Punjab and the north-west frontier. The regimental history proudly describes what was, and perhaps remains, the highest ever campaign march, when a double company of soldiers climbed 18,000 ft over the Mirchauk Pass to investigate reports of Tibetan fortifications on Indian soil. The fort turned out to be a camp wall built to shelter travellers on the trade route. The 1st Battalion achieved fame for their part in an attack on the Dargai Heights, Khyber in October 1897 in which four men – from the Dorsets, the Derbyshires and the Gordons – won Victoria Crosses. (The 3rds were to win two VCs in the Great War). Major-General Nigel Woodyatt of the 3rd described the regimental talents thus: 1st for shooting, 2nd for polo and esprit de corps and 3rd for football and excellent training, the 4th for its dress and the 5th for mountaineering prowess and hill warfare. (Nigel Woodyatt:* Under Ten Viceroys*). In 1907 Edward VII conferred the title The Queen's Own' on the 3rds – changed in 1908 to the 3rd Queen Alexandra's Own Gurkha Rifles.*

Aurungabad,
Deccan
April 3 1905

Dearest Family,

In spite of the paucity of my last notes to you I have very little to inform you of, beyond the fact that I have been appointed D.C. Officer, 1st Batt. 3rd Gurkha Rifles. As I told you this was coming, in my last, you will have had time to grasp the splendour of my new billet. Of course, there are, as always two sides to the medal. For, the advantages may be summed up as follows. It is one of the crack regiments of the Indian Army; always stationed in the hills (at present at Almora, above Naini Tal) the chances of service are the very best; and the officers probably first rate (any way, one of them will be when I have joined.) On the other hand, promotion in the ordinary way will be slow. By promotion I mean to say to regimental billets, such as Comdt; Adjt; D.C. Comdr, etc. not promotion to a higher rank, which of course one is bound to get if one passes one's exams. Had I stayed on here [with the 73rds CI] I should probably have been officiating Qr. Ms. very shortly; and during absences of other people, probably have had a Do. Coy for a bit now and again. In the 3rd I see they have at present five captains who are D.C. officers. We haven't one.

Then I suppose my new uniform will cost a decent sum (it's dark green, with black facings, bye the bye, à la Rifle Brigade); and living in the North is more expensive than in Madras. However, the stations are quiet, so I hope to save money, once I get my uniform paid for. So, although I am very glad and proud etc. it's not <u>all</u> butter; and I wish it had come one year from now; still, one mustn't look at a gift-horse's age as the saying is.

I'm starting off at the end of this week to join; and then I suppose my wanderings in search of a regiment will have ceased for a period. It's not been bad so far, as one meets lots of nice fellows by knocking about from one crowd to another; and it stops one getting into a groove too soon. However, it's time I got a bit settled, and began to get through some courses (such as musketry etc) I have even once or twice allowed my ideas to linger on the subject of Staff College, but I don't know whether I shall ever really go up for it. We are getting one out here now, you know. I expect you have searched out Almora on the map by now. I get to my railway journey's end in about three days from here; after which there is a pony or tonga dak of about another day.

I hope to accomplish the journey without losing any money on it. I am taking my pony but I get a special allowance for her. Servants will be rather a nuisance as I don't expect either of them will stop up there with me, so I shall have to send them home again. It's jolly cold up there, you know. Probably snow at present.

I've been awfully distressed about poor Aunt Kitty and Uncle Jack. It is most dreadful; and those poor children! I hope that they have a long time to go yet; It's too awful to think of. I see that Charlie Elwell is married. Good for him! I haven't sent him a present as I'm too hard up at present but must see what can be done later.

Poor old Humph. got pushed downstairs by his missus you say? Good!

How's D.P.? Poor thing, it was too bad of 'em to fine him. If it wasn't for the likes of him it <u>would</u> be dull in Pool. I hope Toosie's and Podgie's snuffles are quite well, thank you and that George's neuralgia is quiescent. He asks me about 'retention' to 'vernacular' exams. Well, as I think I have stated, I floored the former, and dodged the latter. Tamil is a beastly language and Tamils are beasts; hence, I did not wish to speak their language or to them. So that's all right. I have to pass in Pavatia now, I believe, but only colloquial.

As to ma's adjunctions as to '<u>saving</u> a bit o' money' well, I would have done so had I been here for a bit but as it is, I'm afraid there won't be much saving for another year, though I will do as best I can. I think I shall do very well if I make both ends meet, and pay for my uniform and horse in that time. It's bad luck on the tin-box, but so it is.

6th. What about them recipes? Mamma is very dilatory about sending them; but never mind, I'll forgive her if she sends 'em soon.

I sent my pony off this morning, as they won't let me take her on the mail. I myself leave here on Saturday next as ever is and northwards ho! I shall be there (Almora) about Monday night which is pretty quick work for a thousand miles with a day's pony dak at the end.

All goes well, or as well as can be expected. It's a devil of a sweat moving. I think I must finish now. Best love and lots of luck from

Yours affectly
Allan

Some stamps for them as wants 'em. Don't forget Aunt Loo. They are Nizam of Hyderabad.

Almora and Kitchener's Test

'As you know, they are small, thickset, youth-full looking (as they grow very little hair on their faces) ugly, and blood-thirsty; but make excellent soldiers.'

The 3rd Gurkhas were raised in Kumaun, Garwhal and other mountain districts. Almora, the capital of Kumaun, was a Ghurkha stronghold before the East India Company claimed it in 1814. In Allan's time it was a route up to the Tibetan frontier and shooting grounds ('there are always people going up and coming down'). Situated in the foothills of the Himalayas in present-day Uttarakhand, it is remote: the nearest railway is at Kathgodam, 55 miles away on the plain – four painful hours by modern bus on mountain roads. Allan found it a tough journey from Aurangabad, 1000 miles over four days travelling by rail and tonga dak, arriving at Almora on 12 April 1905. (Two years later in a letter to his father we discover that the journey was made at his own expense and that he sold his 12-bore to pay for it). The Colonel put him up until quarters were arranged.

Later that same month Kitchener and his entourage arrived for inspection. As C-in-C of the Army in India Kitchener had decided that regimental bases should be located according to future needs, not historical precedence and thus regimental homes such as Almora for the 3rds, Dharmsala for the 1sts, Dehra Dun for the 2nds and so on, were potentially expendable.

K arrived at Almora on horseback from Ranikhet, 24 miles away, and according to Col. Nigel Woodyatt's History of the 3rd G's, *stood in front of the massive, two-storey stone barracks. For a better view, he took a step back, and another, until it seemed he might fall off the promontory upon which the buildings stood. 'Who on earth built them?' he asked. 'The men sir, with their own hands sir,' came the reply. 'What nonsense! Inconceivable.' K was impressed. The mess was deemed superb and the men, though 'awfully wild' were possessed of K's favoured qualities: modesty and courage. Interestingly, Almora was hithero known for the number of men suffering from venereal disease. The antidote – of bringing wives and children to live on base – was another reason why a move would be deeply unpopular and disruptive. K declared 'pride in the corps keeps men from this danger' of VD.*

April 12 1905
Almora

Dearest Family,

Although I finished my last letter in good time and put it in my pocket to post, I forgot to do so until too late so I had to bring it along up here with me.

Well, I have arrived, after a very dirty, hot and dusty journey with no end of changes and dikh. I got here too late to catch the regiment which went off for four days the morning I arrived (yesterday). They are out doing the final heat for the C-in-C's Cup. He gives one for the winners of an 'efficiency' test, you know. You've got to march fifteen miles in a given time, and then do an attack with ball ammunition, out-posts and rear-guards and all that; it's for the whole of India. There are five regiments left in now, of which this is one and means to win it. Well, I've only seen one officer so far (except me): the junior subaltern who was left behind to keep shop. He handed over to me and fled after the regiment; so here I am, monarch of all I survey. I am being taken in and done for by some of the ladies of the regiment, who are really most kind and give me food by turns. Mrs Woodyat fed me yesterday and Mrs. Hickley is doing so today.

So far I am enchanted with the station; it is in the most magnificent hills; right opposite one sees great ranges covered with snow. The snow here has gone, but I still feel a bit parky at times.

The bungalow and mess are all solid and substantial and more on the lines of English houses than the normal huge, open white washed rooms of the plains. By the way, the awful earthquake that smashed up Dharmsala and those places, cracked most of the houses here. [4 April 1905 – the deadliest earthquake in modern Indian history. Close to 19,800 people were killed and thousands were injured in the Kangra area.]

This is very different from most Indian stations. You see, the battalion is always here (though our friend, K. of K. is now thinking of altering that. I hope he doesn't) and has been for many years, and so sort of local associations exist which you don't find in the ordinary station where you are here today and gone tomorrow. So people take more trouble with their houses and so on, and there are one or two families of former officers of the regiment who make it their home. In fact, it is a home for the regiment, and not a temporary resting place.

It seems an awfully good regiment in all ways; the mess is good and cram-full of trophies, both of shikar and war; the men are by all accounts, wonderful; smart, and plucky and full of sport. They are always winning the Gurkha Brigade Football Cup, have had some wonderful men for the other great Gurkha event, the 'Khurd-race' in which men from all regiments scoot up and down a precipice about the height of Mont Blanc (more or less); and now look like winning this C-in-C's competition, which means being the best battalion in India. [The 3rds won the cup in 02, 03 and 04; Allan played a lot of football.]

You know what they look like I expect. I haven't seen many so far, except the recruits but they remind me awfully of Malays. As you know, they are small, thickset, youthful-looking (as they grow very little hair on their faces) ugly, and bloodthirsty; but make excellent soldiers, in fact the best, as they are so strong and keen; and are more amenable to drill and discipline than their great rivals for hill-work, the huge Pathans or the North-West hills. The latter although magnificent men and as brave as bedam'd, are such unutterable blackguards as to make their officers job decidedly difficult, in fact they won't have whole battalions of Pathans now but mix 'em up with other races. Kitchener is coming up here on the 25th to look at us. He will probably then decide the fate of the station; it's an awful shame if they take us away to Sandowne, where the 2nd Battalion is. By-the-way, Beynon is now acting as Asst. Mil. Secy. at Simla, during someone's absence, which perhaps may account for the milk in the cocoa-nut; in other words, my presence here. I have heard, unofficially, that it had been arranged for another man to come and take the vacancy but at the last moment, the C.O. heard something about him and wrote to say he wasn't wanted. Result – me. It seems as if someone had been doing me a good turn; anyway, it's a great bit of luck.

Well, I'll write and tell you more when I get a bit settled. At present, I'm all anyhow. Best love to you all, and lots of luck.

Yours affectly,
Allan.

I am a full-blown Lt. end of this month. No more pay, though.

★★★

April 26 05
Almora

Dearest Family.

I'm beginning to get settled down and so on, and am very delighted with the regiment and station etc. I'm moving my quarters today; the Colonel put me up when I came, and now I'm going in with two other subalterns.

The C-in-C's visit is over; he put up with our second-in-command, and dined in mess the night he was here, which by a coincidence, was the anniversary of Ahmed Khel. [Afghanistan, 19 April 1880, in which British and Indian troops defeated Afghan tribes on the road between Kandahar and Kabul.] So we had a big dinner. He was most affable and expressed himself highly delighted with everything. You know, we didn't win his cup which I told you about, (the general efficiency one.) We were second, the 130th Beluchis winning it. Much sickness all round, I can tell you; we shouldn't have minded so much if it had been Gurkhas, but Beluchis – there, one of the G. officers spat violently on the ground when the C.-in-C. mentioned 'em.

His Excellency was very complimentary and said it was a very close thing but the men were awfully wild. However, it can't be helped, I suppose. The fate of Almora as a station is still unknown; we live in hopes that after his visit, the heart of the cow (no disrespect intended) may be softened.

By-the-way, he rode my mare on parade when he inspected us, and also later on the same morning. I was nearly court-martialled as a large dog springing out, made her shy and nearly put him down. However, he sent me a message of thanks and approbation of his mount. I'll ask double for her now, if I sell her. He really did seem pleased both with the regiment and the station, though he wouldn't make up his mind as to whether he'd move us or not. He rather pulled our legs about it, too.

It's fairly warm here just now, though the last day or two have been a little cold. Our hot weather is coming on, during which I'm told it's quite warm all day and night.

How are you all? I haven't had a letter for some time, so I suppose you haven't yet heard of my move and are still writing to Aurangabad. I shall hear soon I expect.

Well, no more at present except best love to all of you, and hopes that all goes well.

Yours affectly,
Allan

Almora
10th May 1905

Dearest Mother

I have to express my thanks to you for your recipes, which you so kindly sent; for the ripping handkerchiefs marked and embroidered so nicely and to George for the saddle which I have now rescued from Messrs G. G. and Co. Herrings, I'm afraid, do not grow in India's coral strand but I've no doubt that your manner of dealing with them will appeal just as well to the ubiquitous 'pomflet' (generally inscribed on the menu as 'Fry Pamplet') as to the more succulent origin of the bloater, and kipper.

Yes, dear mamma, I've been pretty lucky as regards illness so far (I'm touching wood so do not fear to brag of it) and your kind inquiry re the behaviour of my horse (she's a mare, by-the-way) I am able to answer satisfactorily. She is a very nice mare; though it was rather a pity I bought her as it was a sweat and a certain expense bringing her up, and I shall have to sell her when I get a good chance and buy a black one, as all our chargers must be black to match our uniform, accoutrements, characters etc., and strike terror into the hearts of our enemies.

As regards how I spend my time, and what friends I have – to the former inquiry I reply that as you know 'lying 'roun' an' sufferin'' forms the greater part of all early exis-tence; as a rule I start by some sort of a parade at 7 am, breakfast about 8.30, some sort of mess work until orderly room at 11, which carries us on to tiffin about 1.30. After that the afternoon is available for study (ahem!), writing letters, a little repose, etc and about five or six we meet at the Club. A band twice a week, tennis, badminton, conversation, and a rubber or two, bring us on to dinner time. After dinner (at 8.30) generally two or three rubbers in the mess, and so another spasm of the agony of life is tided over.

Occasionally a little variety in the way of a field day, a game of hockey in the afternoon, a modest dinner party or something equally innocuous enlivens the daily round.

As regards friends, all here except the Col. and the other two subs. are married. They are all very nice, etc but I can't think of any particular distinctiveness to mention; the civil element consists of two correct sort of persons, and missionaries; the place is stiff with the latter, but I've only called on two so far. Personal friends I rather miss at present. Of the other two subs., the younger is rather young for me, though a very good little chap, and the other one, who is very clever etc. is rather puffed up, so to speak. He will be a Captain in a few months, and seems to want to anticipate a little of the honour and glory pertaining to that rank, and doesn't quite understand how he fails to inspire awe in a pup of two years service, like your 'umble 'umble. I expect we shall pull better when he grasps the fact that I'm not only just hatched.

(By-the-way, I've shaved off that heavy cavalry moustache of mine, and can pass for 22 anywhere.) So, I still miss mine own familiar friends of the Lunatics, Leicesters, Middlesex etc., though when the other unmarried fellows come back from leave, I shall have a larger selection to communicate ideas with. Of course, we all get on together very well, but what I mean is that so far there is not that familiarity which comes from parallel planes of thought, in a manner of putting it. For this great salt of life, I rely mainly on correspondence; although the average subaltern (as I dare say you have noticed) is not exactly strenuous as regards correspondence, we sometimes try to remind each other of our respective existences, and I've been getting rather a lot of letters (congratulations etc.) since I blew up here.

I have had your first letter since you heard about my (then) impending transfer and am deciding as to whether I will 'soar' as you so poetically put it, to C-in-C. I am not a soarer, you know; but I will let you know when I have decided. Yours and Billy's immoral suggestions as to employing 'undue influence' I reject with contempt. (I notice the 'undue influences' have a way of doing that, too, sometimes.) So my fascinations etc. must still go on wasting their sweetness on the desert air.

No, the pay is no more in the Gurkhas, and no less, but the living is more expensive. In a regiment like this, subscriptions are of course heavier than in the benighted Presidency (our pipes cost us a pretty penny for one thing), and in the North one has to keep more servants than below; and what with getting new kit and my 'ouse not yet paid for, it'll be a bit of a pinch for the next year or so; after which, I shan't have nothing to do but draw my pay until I'm a Capting; of course, one thing about being here is that there are no little temptations such as theatres and similar items which do make the nimble rupee prodigiously elusive. With care, I find I can just manage to carry on and save sufficient to pay off my present debt (for pony) and when that's done (about three months more) start to shed out shekels to the most accommodating military tailor I can find. By-the-way, I insured myself for 2000 rupee lets the other day (about £130) so as to make old Bremner (my late CO) moderately safe in regard to my loan from him. He didn't want me to, but I thought it as well, as a policy is always an asset.

When I spoke about a 'pinch' just now, I don't want you to think that it's anything out of the way – I live very well, of course, in the mess, and get lots to smoke, and drink, and wear, and all that; I only mean that my usual lordly ways have to be checked, and that I try to do without some of the more expensive luxuries that I generally rush at when I'm not thinking. I have a much better time than any of you do, so don't get wasting any superfluous pity on me.

As to the extravagance of the horse that you mention, it is and it isn't. I'm bound to have one, but it really is about as much use to me up here as a sick headache; still, as I say, I'm bound to have it and it only costs about five bob a week to keep.

The only news of any consequence is that we go to Delhi for manoeuvres at the end of the year when we shall do our tricks before the Heir apparent. If I catch his eye (there'll only be about 20,000 of us) I'll mention your names to him.

Well, I say good-bye for the present. I hope you are all well and happy, and that everything goes all right at home.

Bestest love to you, pa, and the two little homebirds, and also the rest of the family

From yours affectionately
Allan

* * *

May 30 1905
Almora

Dearest Mater and family

I have received your first letter addressed to me here and thank you kindly. I was surprised you'd seen photos of the place but you seem to find something out about me wherever I go.

I'll try not to get killed by a gymkhana or any other wild animal. The best opportunity of departing this life up here, is to fall over the khud (ask papa what a khud is). [A ravine, from the Hindi.] Poor little Tuck is always doing it, I don't know why he is singled out but he has had three narrow escapes lately and actually went over, horse and all, one time, but was stopped by some bushes.

I've just been loosed on to signalling as at present we are deficient of a qualified officer. Since I know damn all about it I have to go to the class at Kasali on Aug. 1st. I have to work at it a little bit. You're only allowed one shot, so it won't do to fail. I must do musketry sometime, and there's my c and d for captain. So I shan't be very idle for the next year or so.

Our principal excitement of late has been a garden party given by the mess to Almora, in honour of the General (Sir Alfred Gaselee) when he visited the other day. Poor little 'Bill' Hutchins, as is now known, was saturated with the arrangements and acquitted himself more or less with honour, except that he forgot to invite the General. Pip pip, to employ a vulgar expression, no 'arm done. A coffee-coloured collection of gents from Moredabad College came up and played us at hockey and cricket the other day. With these exceptions we pursue the even tenor of our way.

Best love and luck to all

From yours affectly
Allan

Letts No 46 Rough Diary

Thursday 14 September 1905
Twenty-six years of a mis-spent life finished today. Misere. Went off to unpronounce-able place about 15 miles off for 'scheme'. Got damped by about 9 pm.

★ ★ ★

Ladysmith
Kasouli
12 Oct 05

My dearest Family.

Very many thanks for all your kind birthday wishes; there seems to be some doubt about my age in the family circle. Kitty thinks I am 27 (I heard from her the other day) Mamma suggests 25. I make it 26. However, it is <u>really</u> about 21 in lightness of heart and general behaviour; and about 40 as regards the 'fearful life'. However, I'm getting much more respectable nowadays and shall probably get religion soon.

As regards the present you kindly ask me about, any little thing that you suggested would be most acceptable. Better not send collars, as they will be bad to pack, but such things as home-made socks or stockings, or hankies would be splendid. It's awfully good of you to think about it.

Your gaieties seem to be sufficiently numerous to supply spice to existence without prostrating you with their effects and frequency. There seems to have been lots doing in Pool and thereabouts of late.

What is papa going to do with his camera? Is he to develop into a 'snap-shot fiend' in his old age? I hope his new bridge turns out well; I should think it will be awful hand-some. Who is going to build it? I should think old Davy Davies the man.

Podgie is correct in her remark that getting new uniform is a nuisance; but as she says, it's a very nice one. None of your gaudy reds and blues and yellows, but a 'decent little' black with braiding galore. In spite of its affectation of modesty it costs rather more than red, with gold lace and all that. I have to pay nearly £7 for my pouch-belt alone. It's nearly finished now and when it's done you shall have a photie.

The signalling will be over in about a fortnight from now. We have started the exams already. Mama may well inquire what good it is when it's over. Well, not much except more work when one has passed. If one gets a special, one's name can be noted for employment or service which might be desirable in some cases; but that's all. Well, you know that lately (28th of last to 10th of this) we have been doing long distance works; which means that we were divided into parties and despatched to the four corners of the earth. For myself, I went to Simla, or rather Jutogh which is about 4 miles from the former. The great advantage was that I could run into Simla and confer with Messrs Phelps and Co. over my uniform, try it on etc.

However, there were other attractions. On the 5th I was bidden to the big Fancy Ball at Viceregal Lodge, the swellest function I think that I've ever seen. [On Observatory Hill, the extravagant work of Lord Dufferin, who inspected it twice daily in construction and thought it 'beautiful, comfortable and not too big'. Mary Curzon thought it 'vulgar and hideous'.] The costumes were magnifique. George Nathaniel looked very well in the costume of Lord Wellesley, when he was Viceroy, and Lady. C. as Berengaria was the finest woman in the room. She was all spangly and shiny with a 'wimple' if you know what that is.

On Monday (9th) their excellencies were entertained to a farewell ball at the Town Hall. This also was a bit of orlrite. The decorations were simply marvellous; you couldn't see a bit of the building anywhere. The L.G. for S.G. of the Punjab and George Nathaniel spoke at supper thereby boring such of the younger spirits who wanted to dance (such as myself) to distraction. Lady C. was again an easy first among the women. She seems very vivacious.

There were lots of Kasuli people up, and I filled my programmes both times and to spare. Did very well all round, in fact. A dinner at the Simla Club, a couple of tiffins, and teafights, and my visits to Phelps comprised the remainder of my Simla campaign. I met Major Woodyatt (of ours) at the Fancy Ball. He was there without Mrs. W. and looked rather guilty. We were both surprised to run into each other.

You ask me to tell you always about my friends etc. It's really very hard to talk of people you've never seen, but a brilliant idea has struck me. I will at intervals send you scraps of letters, and so on that I don't want, which will tell you a bit about people I know. Here is one from Tuck, in ours; an awful nice little chap, who is acting as my Almora agent and another from the Afghan Princess I think I told you about. I'll do this at intervals, but you must 'burn when read' mind. This will save a good deal of description etc. Of course I can't send you anything interesting, as I shall want to keep that myself but these scraps will sort of give you an inkling of how one exists.

A fellow I'm very intimate with here is a Capt. Wilkinson of No 8 Mountain Battery. He's a rum old bird, but we get on very well. Another great pal of mine is Rowan, in the Wilts. a sort of pocket Hercules about 5'6 high and 13½ stone in weight.

The fellows in our bungalow I have told you about. They are awful nice chaps and we get on splendidly. I enclose a few more typical specimens of my correspondence, and subscribe myself, with love to all.

Yours affectly.
Allan

★★★

Almora
31st Oct. 05

Dearest Family,

Many thanks for the photographs and newspapers as well as your recent letters. There is not a great deal of news this week. As you see, I am back again in good-old dead-alive Almora having arrived hither three days ago. The exams all went off well at Kasuli and to my great surprise, I succeeded in getting 4th place in the result, which is not bad out of 34. So *that's* alright. I shall be pretty busy for a bit now, working our signallers up for inspection and learning Gurkhali, which I am on the point of starting.

Everything here seems as usual. Our doctor and his wife have been transferred and we have a new and youthful medico. Edwardes has got a job in N. China and is off there immediately; his wife has gone home. Mrs. Hickley is also going home at once and Major Hickley in Feby. In place of these a subaltern Jackson, (Johnson's master), who has been on leave and Captain Dopping-Heppenstall (unmarried) are coming out this month. We have also just got a new sub., Stone, who is a decent chap. Shuttleworth is now a Captain and is away shooting.

We are all going out tomorrow to shoot the wily chikor, a species of partridge, it now being holidays on account of the men's religious festivals.
No more now.

Best love,
Yours in great haste,
Allan

* * *

Almora.
Boxing Day 05

Dearest Family

Very many thanks for your kind letters, cards and good wishes, which, owing to the prosaic fact that we get our mail on Mondays, were brought to me as I lay in bed on Christmas morning in quite the old fashioned way. It seemed to bring you all very near. Many thanks in anticipation of the kind socks which I am expecting daily. They will be extremely useful.

We had a most cheery Christmas here. We all agreed it was the best for many years. It was I think, though I says it as shouldn't, mainly due to my efforts in punch-making, which took me nearly a whole day. The result was something to dream about. We put away about a pint apiece after dinner (at which the only drink allowed was fizz) and as it consisted mainly of about 3 parts proof rum and brandy to one of less potent ingredients and we are all as fit as fleas this morning, (even the Major, who has a liver of the old school) I think, as all agree, that it was a success.

The day started badly, though fine and sharp. The Major about 3 pm remarked that it was more like Ash Wednesday than Christmas (see remarks re liver) and most of his hearers concurred. I was too busy with the punch and decorations and dinner to bother about him. We had a couple of rubbers at the Club, and the gloom did not lighten much, and then we repaired to Dinner which everyone in the station, bar one old lady who wouldn't be drawn, partook of in the mess. Practically all <u>our</u> people are out shooting; only the poverty-stricken are left; so we thought it would be very funereal. However, we mustered as follows Capt. and Mrs Eastmead, the only lady left in. Major Hickley who is in command at present, and as stated above, possesses a liver; also a gramophone and musical temperament. Me, cheery. The doctor, also cheery. Flowers, our Asst. commissioner, just about to be transferred; young, intellectual, decent voice. Cassels, who replaces him; large, quiet Scotchman with an excellent voice; Cantin, the district engineer. As soon as Dinner began, the fizz and the band started our tongues wagging, and by the time the punch had circled once or twice in the next room, we'd had a couple of songs; and the gramophone had been called on, we were as merry as grigs, whatever they may be, and wouldn't have called the King our aunt. Mrs Eastmead left about 12, and when we had had a few rubbers, and finished the punch, we adjourned to the Dining room, and finished up with black beer, grilled bones, prairie oysters (also manufactured by my fair hands) and general rejoicings. And so to bed.

Today the chief topic of conversation has been the punch. The major, whom I hardly expected to see at all today, beams all over when it is mentioned. I hope that you enjoyed yourselves as per usual. I insisted on them all drinking 'absent friends' as per our custom, and a silent minute after it. I see from your former letters that mamma is exercised in her mind as to what the 'pan' is that has been presented to the Prince. It's only betel, always offered as a signal that an audience is over and is, I suppose, called 'pan' because you'd want one to be sick into if you tasted it.

Thanks for kind inquiries after John. On his master's return he thought he had struck a good thing and used to play us off, one against the other. Having seen his real master safely through his Chota Hazri [early morning tea or light breakfast – still served without fail at St Paul's School, Darjeeling], he would trot off to me, and have a snack there. I would then go to work, and he would return to his master whom he would accompany to office about 11. His master, being in office till about 1.30, and me generally leaving about 12, he used to then accompany me to the mess. After tiffin he would attach himself to the one who came out first, and having seen that he had his afternoon tea, would look the other up, to see that the khitmagar was not neglecting his duties. After that his own dinner, and bed. Not a dull moment the whole day.

He has now been handed over to me, and his manners curbed.

I'm very sorry to hear poor little Vi has corpsed. She was a rum little thing. Yes, mamma, my chief is Col. Rose. He is a tip-top C.O. and anyone can get on with him if they are worth it. I don't know how he will take my latest development, when he returns from leave. It is this. The other day Hickley showed me a telegram just come, asking for officers for the Malay States Guides. I thought it over and decided to shove my name in, and Hickley (generally known as 'Koun Hy' meaning Who is he? from a cry in the Pathans used to have up in Wazirstan, during night attacks. Hickley was adjutant at the time, and as soon as the firing commenced, the Col. would be shouting Hickley, Hickley! The Wazirs got the idea it was a species of war cry and used to howl in return 'Koun hy Ikley'; hence the name. To resume, Hickley recommended me. I have a good chance I think. The reasons I sent my name in were brief, that it offers a chance of solvency in a shorter time than here. If I get it, I shall be seconded for 3 years, and go to the Malay States, where I shall receive pounds one per diem; free quarters and uniform; rising to 420 a year at the end. Roughly 30 pounds a month as against 22 or 23 which I get now, without quarters, which means about another pound or two pounds a month. As to whether I shall be better off depends, I suppose on where I go to. I think I might go to some place where I might, willy nilly, have to live cheap and save. The great drawback is that I may miss a campaign up here, but I shall try and watch that. If all goes well, I might in two or three years time, return home, via Mexico, as it would not be much out of my way. Rather a long time to look forward, though.

As for the Malay Street Guides, as we used to call them, after a not very reputable quarter of Singapore, they are, I believe quasi-military, and call 'emselves Sikhs. From what I've seen of them, I don't think the Sikh nation would be flattered, but still, it's not for ever, and the harmless necessary rupee is very elusive in Hindustan. I certainly shan't get 30 pounds a month here for another six years.

Of course, it's not nice to leave the regt. but Almora one can have enough of in a moderately short time, especially, when, as at present the stn consists of eight people; and I find that I don't like settling down. Been rolling around too long I suppose.

George asks whether 'any of us got a special' in the signalling. Most of us did. I thought I told you. Many thanks for his hints on rifle shooting. They came rather opportunely as Maj 'Nigel' our second in command is going to make Bisley shots of the young officers, whether they like it or no. I have already gone so far as to obtain a scoring book, a box of paints, and a bottle of cordite cleanser, so it looks as if I were getting on.

Yes, I <u>have</u> seen a heron. In fact, several. Thanks in anticipation of your kind pin. You're a dear. The same to Billiam for her photies, and I trust that with or without the Malay Streeters, I shall next Xmas be able to send you all little gifts.

Thine Allan.

27th
Parcel received this morning. Very many thanks. The socks are rippers, the pin sweet and the photos delightful.

★★★

In January 1906 Allan was at camp in Agra with 8 battalions of Gurkhas. There, 30,000 soldiers marched past Kitchener, Viceroy Minto ('pepperminto') and the Amir of Afghanistan. 'The ends of the line' wrote Allan, 'when we were drawn up for him, could not be seen from the saluting point, but faded away in the distance. I bet he trembholed.'

Agra
15th January 06

Dearest Family

Having been unable to catch a mail with my letter of 1st inst I have now to write another and send 'em both together. In the interim I have received your mildly reproachful letters of 20th Decr with accounts of your Christmas preparations.

We got in here all right on the 9th when it was raining like billyho, and are camped about 5 miles from Agra. This camp consists of the 20th and 21st Infy Bdes and the 1st Sappers and Miners. The 20th Bde is 2/10th GR, 1st and 2nd/3rd GR, and 7th GR, while the 21st is 1st and 2nd, 9th, and 1st and 2nd GR.

So we have 8 battns of Gurkhas all camped in one like along a straight road; the first time for so many to be together on record.

Our being so far away rather spoils our fun, as it is very difficult to get back to camp at night, if one goes gadding to functions etc; to hire a vehicle of any sort is beyond the resources of any but a millionaire, so we are reduced to bikes and ponies.

We have some mild amusements of our own; for instance Gaselee presented a prize for a tug-of-way tournament for 8 battns of Gurkhas (which we won all right yesterday) and another for a footer tournament, of which we contest the final with the 2/10th tomorrow. They have got a pretty good team, including a regular flyer of a British Officer who plays centre, so your poor son has his work cut out for tomorrow, if we aren't going to be defeated. We could certainly beat them all right if it wasn't for this chap, who is through your goal before you can turn round. Ah well! We shall know all about it tomorrow. We have had no time to play off any ties for the Gurkha Brigade Cup or the Garhwal do but are in hopes of keeping them both.

The camps in the town are very fine, particularly old K's, who always does himself well. It's all laid out with turf, and palms and what not.

The only function I have been to was the Chapter of Investiture held in Agra Fort where all the bugs had things hung round their necks by old Pepperminto [Viceroy Minto]. Rumour hath it that the Amir kicked at having to kneel to Minto in order to get his, but was eventually persuaded. I suppose it really was a very fine sight, but not easily describable. It was held in a place called the Dewani-am; sort of Oriental hall with shaded lights above, and simply blazing with the robes of the two Orders (Indian Empire, and Star of India), the dresses of the native chiefs, and the various uniforms of all concerned. I myself was at my best, in full war paint. The Amir generally wears the ordinary sort of red uniform that these Kingly blokes usually fill with their chests, with the Afghan fur cap on top. He is very fair, like most Afghans, and looks plump and good-tempered. His hair is dark, of course, but I think he might pass as a moderately white man. He came yesterday to see us in our camps, and wore the most extraordinary sort of European field-service kit, as did all his staff. The hat, thereof, is the worst line I have ever heard in modern times.

Imagine this in the most vile shade of khaki procurable on top of this Majesty the Amir of Afghanistan and its dependencies.

At the review, of course, he was in his nice kit, and looked very nice and animated. They say he stammers a good deal but takes notice most beautifully, and is very interested in everything.

The review was a magnificent sight. I, myself, was again, at my best. The ends of the line, when we were drawn up for him, could not be seen from the saluting point, but faded away in the distance. 30,000 of sorts. It took us nearly two hours to get past him, in the first march-past. Then we came back in brigades in line of Quarter columns, marching as Two Divisions. Including our eight battalions of Gurkhas, a solid mass of 12 battalions in rifle green went past at one swoop, which I suppose must be a record. I bet he trembholed – the Amir, I mean.

I went to a dance last night at the club; mufti. It was rather enjoyable, though I didn't know many people. However, that didn't matter, as I went with a party. No very big bugs there except the Misses Minto. I want to go and see the Taj Mahal, and the fort soon. I will let you know about them again.

There was an Open Cross County race for Native Troops yesterday, and to the intense consternation of all the Sikh and Punjabi flyers, who had got one or two champions amongst them, it was won by a rifleman of the 2nd Gurkhas, a man of ours being 5th, and 13 out of the first 20 places being taken by Gurkhas. Rather astonishing, wasn't it, when you remember that the country round here is flat as a pan-cake, and the respective length of stride of a 5'2 Gurkha and a 6'2 Sikh?

17th Jan

I leave today for Almora (by train) as the signallers and self are going to work up for the annual inspection.

I am very sorry to say that the 10th biffed us yesterday, 1–0. However, one can't always win, and since I have played for the team, we have had ten consecutive wins. We unfortunately had a man disabled before they scored, so we were not disgraced.

I went out and saw the Taj yesterday; it was very fine, and I admired it very much. I shall not be able to do Fatehpur-Sikri as time does not admit. I met Beynon and his boss, Genl Spens, in the Taj, by the way. Of course I have seen him several times here, as he often comes out to camp. He is now the father of another girl.

The Amir left yesterday and according to all accounts enjoyed hisself very much here, particularly his dinner with the chief (old K, I mean). It was quite hilarious, I hear, and all the sardars were full of beans and high living. Old Habibullah himself consumed eight pomfrets (a species of fish) according to an eye-witness. He inquired first whether they were river or sea fish, and on being told 'sea' he assuming a sort of 'that's all-right' air, proceeded to solemnly spear eight of them on his fork, and pile them on his plate. So no-one else got any fish at that table. He also made a very punishing attack on a fruit salad, simply swimming in maraschino, so his Mahomedy prejudices are apparently in abeyance.

One of his leading sardars tried to commit suicide yesterday by throwing himself off the fort wall. Reason unknown, except that it has been consistently rumoured that old Habbi means to have a few of their heads off when he gets back over the border for telling him that his army was as good as ours.

The footer-boots are top hole. I don't know whether they have been paid for yet, but will find out in Almora. No room or time for more.

Yours affectionately with best love to all
Allan

★★★

In March Allan wrote about the 3rd Gurkhas being made QO, Queen's Own. 'General Hutchinson' he wrote, 'with Col Ommaney and Col Rose will 'pay their respects to her Majesty [Queen Alexandra], and present her with some mementoes, such as an elaborate kukri (which she will find it hard to make use of), photographs, a history of the regiment, and what not.'

At Lansdowne for GOC inspection and exams, he completed his tactical aspect of (c) examination (Allan explains it in his letter dated 22 May 1907) scoring 78 per cent and so missing 'distinguished' by 2 per cent. 'The board said they were very sorry, as they thought from the first two day's work I should do well; the third day (tactics) we differed over an important point, and they fell on me.' Despite setbacks he wrote that 'we are again top of the Brigade in the GOCs inspection (Kitchener Test). Our 2nd Batt are second and the rest (including the 2nd) nowhere. Ha-ha!'

Allan returned to Almora as Station Staff Officer, (3rd class) with a SSO job at 'a clear 50 dibs a month extra', He studied Gurkhali, 'slacked the whole day and did a little poodle-faking'. On 4 April he was at Abbottabad on the NW Frontier for the 'khud race' and Brigade football. Khud, or hill, racing was begun by CG Bruce of the 5th to enable the slight but swift Gurkhas to compete at games with the Sikhs and Punjabi Muslims. They excelled at hill running. Bruce retired a Brigadier-General in 1920 and later led two expeditions to Everest. His journey to Abbottabad was extraordinary:

(a) walking seven miles, including a descent of over 3000 feet (b) a tonga ride of 12 miles (c) a short railway journey to the main line (d) a long railway ride on the Punjab Mail, entering the train at midnight one day and leaving it at midnight the next (e) another tonga ride of 44 miles including a midnight start and crossing a flooded river about one in the morning, with the water halfway up the seat (we nearly went one time).

The 5th won the race ('we are heartbroken') but the 3rds won the football. In May, he was in pursuit of a tiger. Tigers were considered a menace and a District Officer would pay a bounty for the carcass.

Almora
9th May 06

Dearest Family

Just a few lines to assure you of my health and happiness. The beastly panther (or tiger, as I now believe it is) did not fall prey, being too cunning for poor Bill. It killed the night before I had to start for Almora. I sat up over the corpse (a luckless bullock) from 3pm until 5am the next morning. As my damn bearer did not turn up as ordered in the afternoon, I had no bite nor sup from 8.30 one morning until 10 the next, nor any blankets. The animal came during the night, (though I didn't hear him) but as there were no trees about to sit in, and he being a wily 'un, he smelt me and after lying down for a long time about 30 yards off eventually retired. The only score to me was that he went hungry too.

We are going out to camp for a month in about 10 days; it ought to be very jolly.

We have just received a copy of the Stn General's (Eastern Command) annual training report to the C in C. Only one British, and one Native regiment are mentioned in it. Need I say that the latter is the 1st Battn 3rd Gurkhas, whose name occurs <u>three</u> times in connection with efficiency in scouting, <u>signalling</u>, and physical training.

Gen Henry, in the last 7th (Meernt) Divn Orders draws the attention of the powers that be to the high state of efficiency of the 1/3rd Gurkh Rifles. We shall be getting unpopular in this goes on. 'Who's like us? Damn few!'

I hope the spring cleaning is now over, and that the house is looking well. I am just moving into a new house; this one is too big as you must have 3 fellows in it, or the rent comes too heavy; and as fellows are always moving about, it's impossible to always keep it 'up to strength'.

I congratulate Montgomeyshire on its parliamentary representatives. The Government have one gentleman on their side anyhow, in Mr J D Rees. I send George his kukris this mail, and am sorry not to have done so before. Never mind the price; it is only a 'matter of a few rupees' and not worth talking about. When drawing and sheathing a kukri hold the scabbard by the <u>back.</u>

Best love
Allan

★★★

Almora, U.P.
16/5/6

Dear Family

I'm getting quite a regular correspondent, aren't I (Anglicé: Am I not)? This is partly the result of mamma's and the rest of your 'jippings' and partly of a little more leisure than formerly. Perhaps you'd like to know what my duties are at present. Well, firstly the signalling fate of the Battn. still rests in my hands and my duties in that respect include the elevating of the minds of the regtl. signallers to the higher walks of their profesh; the training of 'line' boys (Almora-bred Gurkhas) [soldiers' sons born in the regimental lines] with a view to their eventually becoming signallers; do three or four young officers; instructing the clerical staff in the theory; and instructing all officers and some Gurkha officers in semaphore signalling. I am also now doing my regular duty of double-coy officers, my boss being the very nice and able ossifer, Maj. Woodyatt, our 2nd in command. He is off on a staff billet (temporary) to Naini on the 25th and I shall have the double-coy till he returns, I shall have to put them thro their annual musketry course, which is no joke nowadays, especially in such a battn. as the 1/3rd. (George will be interested to know that the Native Army course is miles stiffer than the British.)

These duties, combined with biweekly lectures, schemes etc. and a (prospective) study of the beauties of the Gurkhali tongue, still give me enough to do to prevent what the French call ongwee, though I'm not nearly so busy as at the end of year. I have only the Soda-Water Fund & Factory to look after besides. I expect I've told you that we have our own Soda-Water (most regts. have out here) Dairy, Bakery, etc.

We go out to camp on 25th for a month, about 20 miles from here and some 3000 feet higher, to get some change of air. Its pretty warm here now (about 80°). Half the time we shall be flying about and carrying on 'Modern warfare under varying conditions' as we replied to a colonel man in the 2nd Gurkhas, who is acting temporarily as Brigadier, and who had the cheek to wire for our programme. (N.B. I need hardly state these remarks are not intended for publication). The other half we shall be in camp, and practising hand-to-hand jungle fighting, as it is all oak and rhododendron forest where we are going.

I was sorry to hear about poor Uncle Edward. George has told us so much about his inventions, etc. that one almost knew him. Your spring-cleaning reminds me of my present state in the new bungalow. I am having my sitting-room papered (sharing expense with the landlord) and the bedroom whitewashed blue as the saying is. It's lavender really, but blue is near enough. I mean to furnish my rooms rather gorgeously, as a change after the windsor chair and upturned packing case of the last few years; and as you kind people insist on sending me gifts at intervals, you might remember that little knicknacks (such as photo-frames etc) of an inexpensive description, will be accepted in future. Please don't think this is a hint, but you are always asking me to 'give it a name' so to speak.

I sunk a whole 10 rupees the other day in a mantel-border that's enough to take your breath away. I must send mamma one like it some day; native gold embroidery, of a paralysingly ornamental description.

I am enclosing a copy of a 'chit' received from our Subadan-Major the other night at the club, as a rather amusing specimen of English. (He wrote it himself, as he speaks rather well.) His name is Chamu Sing Burathoki, Sardar Baradur, Order of British India, and Indian Order of Merit. He is the third generation of a family who have been Subadan Major of this battn, his grandfather being in the Fort here when it was taken by the British from the Gurkhas. The 'chit' came as follows. Chamu had asked for permission for the regt. to have a tamasha and beat tom-toms etc., at night on account of one of their inummerable gods having selected this particular day as his festival. Permission was granted until 10 pm. on which the enclosed pathetic appeal appeared while we were playing bridge. He got his leave all right. We have two G.O.s that speak English; Chamu and his brother (who are deadly enemies).

Well no more at present. I've gassed an awful lot this letter. Many thanks for your kind letters etc of late. Aunt Loo has just sent me some hankies.

Best love to all
Yours affectly
Allan

[The 'Uncle Edward' mentioned was George's brother, a man without a full-time career but who invented the most ingenious, often intricate, machinery, generally too cumbersome to be of use to any manufacturing company. Many of his designs and blueprints are also part of the archive held in the trunks. Always short of money, his brothers Richard and George were often asked to fund his work. Edward lived with his parents, Rev. Richard and Eliza until their deaths.]

★★★

In a letter written on 19 June from Camp Ajar, Allan expresses concern that his sister, Betty, had been unwell and disappointment that he would not be at home to see Kitty with her with her firstborn son and his first nephew during their visit to Clive House. He described the camp and the activities, experiencing another close encounter with a big cat.

Camp Ajár
19th June 1906

We are some eighteen miles from Almora on a higher range (about 7100). It is all forest here; rhododendrons and oak and quite cool. Sometimes it's a bit cold, especially lately as we have had a good deal of rain. We are waiting till the rains break when we shall return to cantonments. I rather think they have already broken but only fitfully. It's a very pretty camp, scattered about in a little dell (good word, dell) and we have made most elaborate roads, etc. We went off on a week's expedition after the first week out. Service conditions and a double company representing a 'savage' enemy. It was rather fun though the country, of course, is rather difficult owing to the forest which is practically continuous for miles. This, together with the usual difficulty of manoeuvring in a country in which a bit of flat ground is a rare and wonderful sight, kept me alive.

It was on this 'dowr' as the men call it that, being out shooting one evening under a flag of truce, I met a leopard walking by his lone in the wild wet woods. It was a great bit of luck as it is almost unknown to walk into one like that. However, there he was and although I could only see about six inches of his shoulder between two trees, he met with injuries which terminated fatally. There is any amount of game in these woods: khakur (barking deer), gooral, serow, jerow (sambhar) and pig, as well as leopards. However, that is the only shot I have had so far.

We don't have too strenuous a time in between. We do a certain amount of field days, etc., and the rest of the time sit quiet and do quiet parades and so on.

Almora
UP
11/7/06
Messrs Lawn and Alder

Gentlemen

I shall be much obliged by your kindly arranging for the supply of football boots as per sample forwarded by G A Hutchins, Esq of Welshpool, if you can do so at a favourable rate. I purchased the sample some years ago at 6/8d per pair in England, and if you are able to supply at that (or a more favourable) rate (less freight) you can register the order for thirty (30) pairs without further correspondence, and deliver as soon as possible.

The boots, however, must in this case, be as per sample, and should you be unable to supply without some alteration in make or quality, samples and quotations, must be submitted for approval. In order to obviate this, if possible, I authorise you to take the order for the exact pattern and quality, at any rate up to a limit of eight rupees (RS 8/-/-/) free at Almora; but I trust you will be able to supply at a lower figure than that.

Size list for 30 pairs below.

Yours faithfully

Allan M Hutchins
Officer i/c Games
1/3rd Gurkha Rifles

PS Will forward size list per next mail.

★ ★ ★

Almora
25th July 1906

Dearest Family

How are you all? From mother's last letter I understand you have had an earthquake over there. Well, we get about one a month, though I've never felt one yet, as they occur when I am asleep, the last one cracked the band barrack and one of the bells of aims [see letter dated 12 April 1905].

I'm still quarter mastering for my sins. It's not the ordinary work that one minds, but the CO is such a devil for 'experimental works'. He loves playing about with anything new and as the QM has to do sort of scene shifter and stage manager for these, one gets fed up to a certain extent, and one's boots get worn out. At present it's new butts for 'fancy' practices, such as running man, and vanishing heads, etc and as I already have made about a dozen new dodges for these, I'm not so keen on them as I was. I've stuck my name down for (c) and (d) for promotion in October, too, so shall be glad when our Mr Jackson tears himself away from the gaieties of Naini Tal and returns to duty.

I send herewith a size roll for the football boots; I should have sent it last week but could not get it out of my writer. Please forward it to Lawn & Alder if you have placed the matter in his hands; if not, to 'Brown'.

There is some small and remote chance of my getting back my SA service, both for promotion and pension; I sent in an application several yards in length today. Time will show.

The Malay Staters sent round for more officers yesterday but I did not put my name down this time, as I don't think the pay good enough to tempt one away when one has so many exams left to get through.

Well, no more news, except that a badminton tournament is in progress at the club, and that our little dance the other night was a howling success.

Best love to all.
Thine as B4.
Allan

★★★

Almora
22nd August 1906

Dearest Family,

Today being mail day, and me being hung up in my office through the non-arrival of various satellites, I seize the tunniopporty of writing you a few lines on my best cream-laid wire-wove demi-official notepaper. Satan, as usual, is strong here, and each day is more strenuous than its predecessor. The vile Jackson continues to take months' extensions of leave at odd intervals and I continue to labour in the Quartermastering Dept. As this includes the erection of two new monorail galleries on the range for running target practice and two windmill target butts (all home manufactured) in addition to the ordinary work of the luckless QM., I'm awaiting Jackson's return with an eagerness that would be flattering if entailed by the desire of his company only.

In October I have to be examined in subject 'd' for promotion (having been foolish enough to put my name down for it) and regret to say that I don't see the remotest chance of passing it. As for Gurkhali, it's a back number completely.

The rain it raineth every day and the hills sprout like a garden of Eden [Allan's father was county engineer responsible for the construction]. It is very pretty now. The part as far as the above was written last week, in an odd moment in my daftar [office, from Hindi] but, as the critical moment as above indicated, I was called away and never got a breathing space until dinner.

So, again, the long deferred day of writing was postponed. I am sending you this mail a book called 'Almoriana', a series of sketches made by Major Ormsby (now of the 6th Gurkhas to his intense disgust). He is an awfully nice chap. I met him at Abbottabad. He hopes to get back here some day. I hope the book will be assistful in bringing to your minds some idea of the country round here.

My very hearty congratulations to papa on his so wonderful success in the Duke of York's cup. Verily he seems evergreen. Shabash jarvan! – which being interpreted means 'Good for you! I've hardly fired a shot since I left Singapore.

Sorry to hear that the tent got damaged. Conway is a stormy spot, as I remember from my camp there. We were nearly blown away, too.

I was awfully pleased to get the photo of the new nevvy. A lusty rogue he appears and does our Kittens credit.

Yours affecty
Allan A M. Hutchins

P.S. Great excitement here now, getting ready for chikor shooting on the 1st.

A Hindu Holiday

'They festivate for days, and sacrifice goats and buffaloes.'

Almora
19 Septr. 1906

Many thanks for your recent letters and *County Times*, etc. The last one I have received is the one with Aunt Loo's white heather.

I suppose dear Kitty has now sailed and am glad that she and her dear boy benefited by the run home. I wonder when they will come again.

Is Nottie really going to be married to a Humphriss? I think it was one of those we used to call 'Crazy Jane', isn't it? If so, it seems a suitable match, what?

Myfanwy, it seems, has also done the irrevocable; she ought to prove rather good selection, provided she hasn't got too pussy-pussy from constant intercourse from her ma. Where are they coming to out here?

Many thanks for the photo and good wishes. It's a good group but didn't do justice to our Podgelet. Talking about good wishes, I clean forgot about my birthday this year until the following day when I was at a wedding (the sister of one of our Majors, to an Engineer bloke) and I remembered by the time the fizz was opened, so it really was a rather economical lapse of memory, as I punished the Major's champagne rather severely.

This wedding is one of the small excitements that we have had of late. The 3 poor wretches had to go off in *pouring* rain and travel about 9 miles (over a bridle – not bridal

– path) to their first stop. We have had a second edition of the rains lately, only more so. However, they seem to be broken now and the best season of the year now opens.

Many thanks for all your trouble about the boots. I don't think the difference between the '3' and '4' makes any difference. In reply to your query, please tell Brown to send in his bill to O.C.1/3rdG.R. etc., and he will get his dibs all right.

Is the Llanfair bridge quite well, thank you? It was nearly finished when you wrote last.

Jackson returned a few days ago, so I am out of the quarter-mongering again, except the one job I desired to lose above all others, to wit, foreman navvy on the new range works. However, to oblige my pal, the Colonel, I am carrying on with this branch of knightly training, especially as the old man was rather civil and told me I was a devil of a fine chap, etc., etc., when I handed over to Jackson.

We have a strenuous time before us shortly.

At present it is ten days holiday for the Desehra (which you can refer to in 'Almoriana') but after that, oh dear! [More commonly transliterated as Dussehra, an important Hindu festival celebrated in September/October.] There is a long- haired sweep of the 2nd (King's Own or God's Own, or Somebody's Own) Gurkhas officiating in command of the Brigade while the General is away; and to show his authority he has signified his intention of carrying out our 'Kitchener's test' on 9th, 10th and 11th approx. Of course, the 2nd long to get their knife into us as they are by way of being the flash, polo play-ing, who-the-devil-are-you,-sir, Gurkha regiment and we have swamped 'em all round the last few years so we are not keen that this blighter should come messing us about 'clothed in a little brief authority', especially as we have had a few wordy wars with him already and as he is more like a musician than a Brigadier.

Then on 15th or thereabouts, it's hill manoeuvres with the only 'spin' [spinster] in the station. Although she is not a beauty, I found myself getting quite affectionate so thought it best to leave before dinner was over. Such is the effect of never seeing a decent looking woman in these God-forsaken parts. One would probably offer mar-riage to Mary Oney if the poor old creature were here and and made up to one.

By the way, one of our mild amusements at present is the observation of the 'affaire-de-coeur' of one of our subs., with the young lady above mentioned (not Mary, the other one). We are afraid it cannot come to anything as the poor fellow hasn't even passed his Higher Standard yet, and his only viable means of support are his pay and a large bulldog.

★★★

Almora
25th Sept 1906

My Dear Aunt Loo

Very many thanks for your white heather and letter which duly arrived last week. It is most kind of you to remember a graceless nephew, and I do like to see something that has grown and flourished in a Christian country. Our Captain Tilland rejoined yesterday after thrice and a half years in England, and we simply devour him with our eyes; he looks the picture of ruddy health. In a climate like ours, of course, we don't have much to complain of; we are all brown and hard and fit; but there is something in British beef and air that makes anyone just out from home look like a 'jovial monk' when compared to us poor sojourners in India.

It's very busy and troublous times with me, as usual. My exam, for promotion begins on Tuesday next and as I have hither to been so full up of regimental work, I have now to take advantage of the ten days' holiday we are having, to ring up a few of the broad outlines of the subjects. The holidays are for the 'Dasehra' a sort of Hindu Christmas-time, when they festivate for days, and sacrifice goats and buffaloes, and generally get full up of good fellowship, rum and goats-flesh. I was dragged away from writing this letter just now, by an emissary of the adjutants, to go and see a big sacrifice. I found about fifty goats in an enclosure, all surrounded by piles of rifles, with marigold garlands all over them and a lot of beastly old Brahamans from the city bazaar going through their tricks. Some other officers and myself being received by the subadan major, and the Gurkha officers, the proceedings commenced by the regimental pipes sticking up the march-past and a lot of blank-firing. The wretched goats being thus livened up, about ten of the Gurkhas then went in with their Kukris and grabbing hold of the nearest goats, chopped off their heads with one smack each. Others were employed picking up the pieces and piling them in front of the spot near the Brahmans where the goddess (Kali, Goddess of Death, Destruction etc etc was supposed to be stationed. It was all blood, and kicks, and rather unpleasant, especially if a foolish goat didn't stand still at the critical moment.

The proceedings terminated with cherry-whiskey, out of tumblers (at 10 in the morning!) cigarettes, and compliments. We had garlands hung round our necks, and looked most fearful idiots. A marigold necklace doesn't go well with a Norfolk coat and a sun helmet, however appropriate it may look on the 'mild Hundu'.

This afternoon, we all have to attend <u>the</u> sacrifice when there are two buffaloes to be 'put through it'. The first, and biggest buffalo is a most important animal; the idea being, that if the carefully selected smiter gets the head right off with one smack, we are certain to go on service during the forthcoming year. If not, the outlook is rather black; deadly peace will blast our lives unless some other performance is gone through to propitiate the goddess (and incidentally, the Brahmans).

After the performance, more marigolds and strong liquors. We have to take them, or the feelings of our hosts would be injured. As it is, only our interior economy is upset.

I am very well, happy, and broke as usual. I trust you, and the Welshpoolites are well, and with best love subscribe myself.

Your affectionate nephew
Allan

In October 1906 the 3rds were despatched to Kumeria to 'attack the [60th] Rifle Brigade from Ranikhet' who were undergoing their GOC's inspection. 'We didn't wish them any harm' wrote Allan

… but unfortunately, they have us no option but to mop them up. It was a pretty rotten show, and they were awful sick about it. Not unnaturally, the poor blokes got no sleep for three days. The first night they had night operations; the second at dawn was the eve of our attack during which night their camp was full of half naked Gurkhas, blazing off their rifles and having a good time generally (which the Ghurkhas officers slept peacefully at Hawalbagh dak bungalow); and the third they had to attack the 60th Rifles towards Ranikhet. The 60th have been a long time in the hills, and are a very fine crowd. Their scouts have been attached to us, etc, so the poor old Rifle Bde again found that sleep was difficult to obtain. It was bad luck, but the general insisted on their being 'harassed' and I'm afraid they were.

Beaten but not dismayed, the 60th challenged the 3rds to some khud-running, racing 'a 100 men of ours against a 100 of theirs'. Competitions between British and 'Native' troops were against regulations but the 60th found a way round them:

They invited 100 of the 3rd Gurkhas, and put up handsome prizes for them to compete for. The entertainment consisted of (a) 50 Gurkhas running over a course (b) 50 Tommies running over the same (c) 50 Gurkhas again (d) 50 Tommies. They were all time races. On the resulting times our fastest man did it in 25 mins, our slowest in 29.15. They had 4 men who beat the <u>latter</u> time, the quickest being 28.41 which put him after our 86th man. I don't know what their slowest time was, but it was about 40 I think. I don't think they will challenge us again. It was very decent of them to give our chaps such good prizes, and they did the men and us officers awfully well in the entertainment line.

*In December, with Major Kingston – 'a most amusing "raconteur", and has the largest fund of interesting lies of any man I've ever met' – Allan was in the Kosi River valley, 'A fertile river-bed, with bamboos, and all that sort of rot, and great dark-green hills all round, covered with trees, principally oak and rhododendron, in which wander all sorts of game (at least, I suppose they wander) from elephants and tigers, down to 'murghis', and monkeys.' 'We are marching on relief over India's sunny plains' he wrote, quoting Kipling, 'though it's not really on relief, and the plains have so far consisted of fierce hills and mountings.' Allan knew his Kipling and says 'There is no difficulty about books etc in India, we get everything just as regularly as at home, though not so soon.'
Contriving two days' rest, the officers' plans for sport were spoiled by there being no licences left for hunting in what was a Forest Reserve. The men were allowed to roam:*

There is some unreserved about three miles away but we have to leave that to the men, who have done pretty well, though we have our suspicions that some of the 'reserve' may have suffered. Three sambhar, two pig, and small game galore came in first day. One of the pig got up near camp and was pursued by the entire battalion with screams and howls, until at length it was 'beaten with sticks' (as they put it), and became 'without sense' (ibid) and brought triumphantly into camp, where it immediately returned to life, and had to be sat on till its throat was cut, my knife being borrowed for the purpose.

They invariably get anything that gets up close to, like that, when they are in force, principally on account of the noise they make, I believe. Even a chakor flying over camp has been known to fall in the midst, simply bewildered by the howls, and flying mass of firewood, cooking pots, etc. with which it was greeted.

The thing which arouses most enthusiasm is a 'mwighi', which means hen, and is applied to a species of pheasant, that looks rather like a common barndoor. For some reason this miserable creature arouses their violent passions, and the noise is indescribable, and the delight unbounded when at length it is captured.

The dense jungle held hidden horrors:

I have been out fishing, with Hepenstal, and Tilland, and caught a small (very) mahseen with the latter's rod. I was watching the latter fish, when I got a terrible fright. I heard something moving in the jungle behind me, but seeing nothing, I went to investigate. Coming round a bush, I suddenly observed an enormous 'oont' of severe and menacing aspect who was chewing large thorns out of the top of a tree. I ran like a hare. Afterwards, a measly looking native came and complained that I had frightened his oont, which I thought very insulting.

An 'oont' was a camel, as in Kipling's poem:

Wot makes the soldier's 'eart to penk, wot makes 'im to perspire?
It isn't standin' up to charge nor lyin' down to fire;
But it's everlastin' waitin' on a everlastin' road
For the commissariat camel an' 'is commissariat load.
O the oont, O the oont, O the commissariat oont!
With 'is silly neck a-bobbin' like a basket full o' snakes;

In the same letter, dated December 16 1906, Allan wrote about the 2nd Gurkhas:

Dehra is quite close, comparatively and is our Brigade Headquarters. I have been there twice. The 2nd Gurkhas are there; our great friends and rivals. They have the reputation, and 'tone', while we think we can whack their heads off at anything except polo, which they go in for largely, Dehra being practically a plains station, though you are not allowed to say so in Dehra. They are undoubtedly a fine regiment, but are a bit inclined to rest on their laurels, and go on the 'We are the Second' tack … the 2nd are very unkind to strangers, as a rule, which is rather a cheap form of side, don't you think? However, they have been at Dehra a long time and I suppose rather thinks it belongs to them, just as we do, in a small way, at Almora.'

★★★

In January 1907 Allan was back at Agra 'for a fine show for the Amir' and thence by train to Almora, 'to put a polish on the signallers for the imminent inspection.' At Agra he wrote to thank his 'Dear Aunt' for her present of hankies, Pear's soap and money: 'My bearer carries your good money about tied up in a hand-kerchief but I have failed to spend it so far.' He also wrote to his father asking for a loan of £20 which 'I hope to pay back in about 6 months'. (His father sent him £10).

In Almora he acquired a young Irish Setter, Mick, arrived from England ahead of his master Col Rose, and prepared for both the signalling inspection and the next part of his (c) examination at Roorke on 22 March.

Dehra Dun,
April 7th 1907

Dearest Family,

All goes well. I have been here two days and am off home tonight. I looked up Myfanwy and have been stopping with her ever since. She goes up to Mussoorie for the hot weather next Wednesday; it won't be very far for her husband to get up from his work to see her occasionally. They are, of course, devoted, and do not like the idea of being separated, even by so short a distance; but as Dehra is hotting up like one o'clock and she very delicate, the sooner she goes the better. As I dare say you know, she is in a very 'interesting condition' but she has been most awfully seedy since she came out. She has bucked up a little of late, though, and seems fairly fit at present so there is no need for alarming her people, in case they do not know.

We were most awfully pleased to see each other. She knew me before she saw my card and as for her – it's simply miraculous – if she let her hair down she would be exactly the same little girl I remember in Welshpool. We have had some tremendous chats about 'Pool and 'what not' and from what she tells me, they are very comfortably off. They haven't much of a bungalow here, as you can't get one but she has very nice things and good bundobast all round. She seems to be an excellent 'hussif' and does things well.

He seems an excellent chap; very hard-worked at present, I'm afraid, and doesn't get as much time at home as he would like. He is building the new lines for the 9th Gurkhas.

★★★

Almora
April 10th

Back again. I started this letter in the 2nd Mess at Dehra but did not finish as I catch the same mail today. All is much as usual here; the Colonel is off tomorrow for Merrie England and we are a bit short-handed but there is no exciting news. It's getting a little warm but nothing to hurt.

I have a number of letters of yours, including the one of March 21st. Father's staff ride without a horse is quite humorous; I hope he enjoyed it. Many thanks for the tenner but I do wish you would say whether it's *convenient* or *not*. As I explained before, it is not a life or death matter.

The photos have come (proofs) and are very bad. However, I will send copies of the best when I can get hold of them.

I was sorry to leave Myfanwy and her husband but thought it best not to stop too long as they are busy packing and she is far from well. She told me lots of gossip and scandal about local celebrities which you never mentioned. I enjoyed my stay very much.

The signalling result has come and is satisfactory. We are best in the Brigade and, indeed, of any Gurkha Battn. except the 4th whom, I hear, have made enormous scores. I don't quite understand it because they were not up to much before. The Colonel is rather pleased, as per enclosure, forwarded for information.

I hope the grasses were moderately satisfactory. I didn't think much of them but couldn't do better.

In haste and with much love
Affectionately
Allan

★★★

Allan keeps a letter from the now-married Myfanwy.

Artaigne
Happy Valley
Mussoorie
May 11th 1907

Dear Allan,

Many thanks for your nice letter which I meant to have answered some time ago but what with settling down, etc., I seem to have had little time!

I am charmed with the lilies; they certainly come up to your description of them.

The air is so beautiful and is doing me lots of good, although last week I had to go to Dr. Vaughan's home for seven days. They kept me in bed and I must say the rest did me good. Now I trust I shall keep fit. Lester comes up on Saturdays and goes back on Monday morning, 7 o'clock. I do wish I could have him up here always, then I should be perfectly happy!

The place is getting very full and calling seems to be the order of the day!!

It was so nice seeing you again and you must promise to come and see us next cold weather. I expect we shall come down about the middle of October.

Kindest remembrances,
Myfanwy Lewiss

★ ★ ★

Almora
22 May 07
(and d—med hot)

Dearest Family

Another mail-day came round without a due proportion of news to impart.

I'm still sorry to be unable to agree with papa as to the meaning of 'c'. The copy of King's Regulations to which I referred is dated 1904, so he must consider himself severely censured for not being up-to-date. However I will explain. Nowadays the fiendish regulations ordain that before promotion to the rank of captain, a sub must pass a professional exam (consisting of Topography, Fortification, Organisation, Law, History and Tactics) which is divided into two parts 'c', and 'd'; 'c' is practical, 'd' theoretical. Of course, it would not be in accordance with the best traditions of the service for 'c' to come before 'd', so you have to pass 'd' before you are allowed to go up for 'c'.

When you become a captain you have the pleasure of passing the two exams <u>again</u>, for major.

'Flying with the hare' certainly sounds a more interesting form of amusement than 'walking with the tortoise', and I congratulate my dear ma of having thought it out. All the same, I hope my respected sire is not developing into what Mary Ovey, of early fame, would have described as 'a b-------y ould Radical'.

We had a game of footer yestreen. Some of the 60th Rifle Scouts, 40 in number, are up here, learning how the Queen's Own do things. (We had them last year, too, you know, when the regt was at Ranikhet. Our battn and there's are great pals) and they challenged us. We defeated them 2-love, but expect they will do better next time.

Being a 'charming fellow' has received independent corroboration from Capt Lewis (read mamma's letter date 2nd inst) and so it's no use her trying to argue any more.

Glad to see Aunt Loo is settled down. I really must buck up and send her some little gift, as well as executing a commission she gave me. But this weather is making me as slack, though I do a little Gurkhali daily. [Allan studied 'the science and practice of the Ghukhali tongue' under the 'worthy Shukdeo, our regtl schoolmaster'.]

There's no news of any consequence, except that there's a fascinating wider [widow] stopping here. A little diversion of this kind makes a most pleasing change to the monotony of meeting the same (and rather uninteresting) regimental ladies every day.

Well, no more at present. Feel so lazy that I am going to sleep.

Best love to all of you from
Yours affectionately
Allan

In the spring 1907 the 'Unrest in India' was reported almost daily in the British press and debated in Parliament. The unrest was confined to Bengal where, following partition and the creation of an Islamic East Bengal in 1905, educated Hindus were protesting against a perceived (and probably real) loss of job opportunities in a shrunken beaurocracy and political isolationism. The British responded to the unrest by arresting recognised ringleaders, including five barristers accused of provoking riots in Rawalpindi. In June Allan wrote:

The 'Unrest in India' does not affect us up here very much. In fact not at all, unless they send us down to some disaffected spot to show 'em how much better it is to be good; but since the Govt had the sense to jump on the Babu spouters, I don't think there will be much more 'unrest'.

As regards Bengal, I don't think much harm is being done, as they are only fighting each other; and they have been drafting down a lot of Gurkha police lately, whom the Bengalis fear more than the devil.

In the same letter he describes the extraordinary matrimonial arrangements of his fellow officers:

There is (or was, as she had gone on a flying trip to Landsdowne) a fascinating lady here, who knows the P J Reids very well. She is the widow of a fellow called West, who was in this battn and was killed in the Bara Valley. She is one of three sisters (née Gibson) one of whom married our Major Hickley, one our Capt Edwardes, and the third our Captain West. As a consequence the battn is frequently known (in other stations) as 'Gibson's Own'. The old papa is still going, and is busy raising a second crop of daughters, having committed matrimony a second time (with a young niece of his) a few years ago. A wonderful old man; about 70 years old, and the youngest daughter not a year old yet!

In July Allan's hopes of an Adjutantcy were dashed – at least temporarily – and rather than wait in hope of getting the billet he decided to apply for a posting to Burma, a move that he knew needed some explaining to his father:

Of course, the pay of it is not extravagant, but it's a good thing from a professional point of view. So it's Burma for me, for two years, and myriads of rupees.

If I go to Burma now I shall get square and comfy in two years, and might

possibly get the Adjtcy. afterwards (this isn't likely as I shall be near my Captaincy).
If I don't, there is about eighteen months of hard work and no pay in front of me,
and after that the <u>chance</u> of the Adjtcy; and even if I got it there would certainly
be three or four years before I could save any money.

Don't think I haven't considered the question. (I'm writing all this because I'm
afraid papa will be sick about it). Being here on the spot, I can see better what the
best line is, so don't go and think I'm heaving chances away.

★★★

*In his next letter written from musketry training at Pachmari, Allan gave another reason
for not lingering in his present post: 'I don't want to stop in Almora long, before I go to
Burma, or I shall be getting married, or something.'*

Almora
July 31st 1907

Dearest Family,

I'm returning papa's most excellent orders, with many thanks. I remember having to
finish up my last letter in a devil of a hurry because old Colonel Molesworth was honking me forth with him to the post, and can't for the life of me remember what I told, or
didn't tell you. I left Binsar on Thursday and had a beastly wet journey over the twelve
miles to Almora but got in in time to attend a very cheery evening's entertainment
some enterprising spirit had arranged at the Club. Sort of concert with a short kind
of amateur dramatics and a kick-up at the end. After the austerities of tiger hunting at
Binsar (I told you the brute didn't show up, didn't I?) I was so khoosh and happy that
our leading spin thought it a good opportunity to induce me to proffer marriage. Her
mistake! However, it was a glorious evening.

Can't remember whether I told you of our other gaieties. Did I mention that I got
up a dance at the Club, and myself heartily disliked by a young lady to whom, Mrs.
Channer insists, I had been paying marked attentions? Men were short, she came late,
never got many dances, and blamed the wretched organiser, me.

Then we had a regimental dance, when the L. G. came. Huge fun and everyone
pleased. Had rather bad luck myself, though, because at the second dance, a wretched
cipher telegram turned up and the wretched S.S.O. had to slog off to office (raining cats
and dogs, too) to decipher it. I didn't get back until after supper too, but everyone was
so sympathetic, I had a great and glorious time to wind up.

I think I must try to get up something for next week. Beastly busy at present, what with
one thing and another, preparing a lecture to be delivered on Friday, among other things.

Mick has come back; such a funny sight with all his beautiful coat chopped off except
his poor face and tail feather (which hangs about 7 inches). He's awfully thin but very
chirpy and I thought he'd tear lumps out of me when we met. His idea of showing affec-

tion is to bite you as hard as he can whilst at the same time to yell the roof off. He is now asleep behind me, looking like a cross between a pointer and a bloodhound.

Hope you are all well and that the many and various visits that are being interchanged have been a success.

Not much on here at present, except work; two dinners and three bunworries for me this week, though. There's a new bit of skirt, too, by the way. Rather saucy, I should imagine.

The rains are with us though very light, considering. As one of our gallant field officers complained to me yesterday, they don't yet interfere with parades.

Well, I must away. Toodle-oo, (which I understand is the fashionable method of greeting now in vogue in the metropolis).

Best love,
Yours affectly,
Allan

To Pachmari for Six Weeks' Musketry; Pachmari in the Satpura Hills was founded as a hill station and cantonment in the 1840s by James Forsyth of the Bengal Lancers and was the summer home of the Central Province secretariat. Allan found it dull but a timely escape from Almora and especially a girl he was 'a bit frightened of'.

★★★

Almora
Aug 14th 1907

Dearest Family,

Am in a hurry so only have time to send a 'scrap' and give you the news. Papa will be pleased to hear that I flattened the Gurkhali this morning. The reason for this haste was that I am off to Pachmari on Saturday for a musketry course: two and a half months. They only gave me five days warning, the brutes, and so there's a good deal to be seen to. So will you 'please excuse' as the babus say?

Best love to you all and hopes that your enjoyments may continue. (I've been extraordinarily popular lately, by the way, and have been fairly gadding, too).

Yours affectionately,
Allan

★★★

Pachmarhi
CP
24th August 07

Dearest Family

Here I am you see, arrived and ready to commence the study of the theory and practice of Musketry. The course does not begin until 26th so there's not much doing at present. The gallant students are assembling day by day, while it rains with vigour, continuity, and despatch.

I'm not deeply impressed by the place, so far. The few people who are living here at present, do not seem particularly exciting, though Pachmarhi has a reputation as a gay place. It is certainly very pretty, or would be if the rain allowed one to see it. A sort of upland down; very green, and lots of trees; elevation about 3500. In case you don't know where it is, I may mention it is in the Central Provinces, about 32 miles south of the railway connecting Jabalpore and Itarsi, which places should appear on your maps.

There will be about 24 of us for the course. I'm living with Bayley (S Lancs) who accompanied me down (they are at Ranikhet); Mannering, 39th Garhwalis, from Lansdown, Mallock, 9th Bhopals, the junior instructor; and another bloke who hasn't turned up yet. Mick has also come along, and seems very fit, considering. He's a terrible dog to look after, and I spend a large proportion of my time dosing him, etc. I've not received any letter from you by last mail, but perhaps it has not been forwarded from Almora yet. I shall leave here about 26th October, so you can address direct to 'School of Musketry, Pachmari, CP' until about 10th Oct.

I was rather sad leaving Almora just when I did, as it was just about the one time of year when there is anything doing there. It was full of people (for Almora) and, as an eligible bachelor, yours humbly was in great request and quite a popular character. However I daresay thee will be something to do here, and it does not do to be too popular for long.

Well, I suppose I shall pass this class all right. After that, I don't quite know what will happen. I hope Burma will come soon; that will give me something to do, getting alway etc and once there, I might try to work for staff college, though this is only a vague idea so far. There is not much else left for me to do, until I get my stop, unless I do a transport or MI course. I don't want to stop in Almora long, before I go to Burma, or I shall be getting married, or something.

I feel that I'm not imparting much news, though there is not much to impart. Shall I describe my journey down?

I left Almora on Saturday after lunch, riding Tillard's mare. At Peora (9 miles) I changed to Maj Kingston's mare, meeting a planter, name of Nash, and having a drink with him at the dak-bungalow. Then to Ramgarh, 10 miles, and put up for the night at the dak-bungalow, with Nash. All this ride to K'godam, you know, is on a bridle road, over respectable sized hills, and down into deep valleys etc etc. From Rangach, next morning, on a hired pony to Bhim Tal, passing over the Gazar pass, 7,500 feet. Breakfast at Bhim Tal, a very pretty place with a lake. Then on, in pouring rain, to K'godam at the foot of the hills, 40 miles from Almora. Beastly, muddy K'godam, after dropping straight down four or five thousand feet. Bathed, and had a drink at the station. Then began to look about for Bayley, who should have met me there. In the meantime, my bearer got into a row with the local roughs and having severely assaulted one of them, is pinched by a swine of a policeman. Costs me three dibs to rescue him. Eventually Bayley turns up, and we leave at 7 pm. Dine on train, and change at Bareilly, at mid-night. Get on to another train, which lands us at Allahabad at 10 next morning. Breakfast, and a short run to a small station, where we board the Calcutta-Bombay rail. We dine on this and reach Piparia (our station) about 10.30 pm to the dak-bungalow, and to bed. By tonga next day to Pachmari arriving about 4 pm.

There! Bayley is worrying me to come out calling, so I must away. Love to all of you.

Yours affectionately
Allan

★★★

Pachmari
CP
19th September 07

Dearest Family

Very many thanks to you all for your kind birthday wishes, and the gifts, which latter I received on the very day itself. The stockings are beautiful, and I don't know why mamma expressed doubts as to whether I could wear them. I expected to see something very vivid indeed, but these are most decorous, and very grateful and comforting. Together with the saucy-tie, and the exceedingly neat pin deftly inserted in the front, I expect them to give the girls one of the greatest treats of modern times. It really is most kind and thoughtful of you all to send them; and graceless brute that I am, I forgot to send our Podge even my good wishes in time for her natal day. You inquire about Burma. I haven't heard anything except that they have put me down for it. It may be some time before I get it, as it depends on the number of applicants ahead of me. Perhaps I shall take leave after this course, but haven't any plans yet, though I don't feel too keen on spending all next winter in Almora. There's a girl there I'm a bit frightened of, for one thing.

How I should have liked to accompany ma and pa to the Shrewsbury show, and hear that splendid band, or rather bands! I'm very fond of music now, though am ignorant as ever, and not very classical in my tastes. Good news about the hay being so fine. You were very lucky to get it in.

Life here is not too exciting, the course takes up a good deal of one's time, naturally and we get footer and hockey. The weather is good now, and the country looking charming. Still, it's very dull. There is a small amount of society, but I haven't come across anyone very interesting yet. We had a picnic up to a hill-top the other day, and a mild sort of dance at the club on Saturday. A few very dull dinners, and rumours of forthcoming dances comprise the greater part of our social affairs.

Mick is fairly chirpy, and much admired. I hear his master (Col Rose) returns in a month's time, which will be a sad blow to both of us.

Major Woddyat has gone, or is just going. The 2/10th have been formed into two new battalions, and he has taken the command of one of them. They will be at Quattar. He is a loss to the regiment, as he is not only a very keen soldier, but one of the most 'charming' fellows to meet you could imagine, and in consequence has a good deal of influence in high succles. She was an undeniably clever and distinguished sort of woman too, though I didn't like her altogether. The feeling was mutual, and I think originally sprang from our having different views as to what the sphere of the senior lady in the regiment was. She certainly tried to run things too much, and she used to see that I revolted.

Well, no more this time, except to repeat my thanks for your loving kindnesses.

Yours affectionately
Allan

★★★

Pachmari
CP
10th October 07

Dearest Family

You will get this on about County Ball day. I hope those attending have a good time and uphold the prestige of the clan.

'The Birds of Passage' gave a dance at the club last night. We are not allowed to entertain at the Mess, as the commandant is a cranky old fool, and tries to lay down the way we part our hair and so on. So we had this show at the club. It went all right and there were crowds of people, though few of them were interesting. This place is deadly dull at present, though it has a tremendous reputation.

Yours
A

★★★

Almora
UP
6th November 07

Dearest Family

Back again as you see. Its a long time since I wrote, but not much of interest has occurred in the interim. The final exams at Pachmari went off all right; I expect I did all right, though we don't hear for two or three months. We didn't burden Pachmarhi with our presence long after the exams were over; most of us being at Piparia the same evening as we did the last paper. I stopped at the latter place next day and went forth and slew two black-buck. Got back here last Wednesday evening and found all much as usual, though the place is getting very empty after the hot weather people have gone down. The Colonel was just back, and Mick (the dog) and self were parted, to our mutual disgust. Mick can't get over it at all, but is always coming down to see me, and has to be chased back by the sweeper. Major and Mrs Woodyatt have gone for good; and Mrs Channer has gone home on leave. So barring the missionaries, who don't count, the society here consists of Mrs Kingston, Beasley, Eastmead, Hicklers and an old civilian bloke with a wife and daughter (very pretty). The latter collection have their eye on poor Bill [ie Allan], so he is off on leave on 11th for a month's shoot in the district. Can't get off before, as several subs are away on short leave, so I'm again combining most of the appointments in the station in my own sweet self. Adjt Quith, 1st DC Crush, TO Mess Presdt, canteen do, SSO etc etc.

The battalion is going down to Bareilly for the cold weather, as we have now been put back into the Bareilly Brigade. It will be rather jolly at Bareilly as it's a good big station. No news of any consequence about Burma though I'm pulling strings. Sent my name in for Burma <u>Civil</u> Police the other day, as they were inquiring for officers. Afraid it did not go in in time though. Seems a pretty good job. 500 a month to start on, exclusive of travelling allowance, and local allowance. Think I should prefer Military, but don't much mind, as it's only a means to an end, either way.

Got a new sub attached to us, and living in my bungalow. Ass, but may improve. Trying to palm him off on the local spin [spinster].

So sorry to hear that poor mamma has had rheumatics and cold, but trust she is now hale again.

Yours affectionately
Allan

★★★

Almora
Novr 12 1907

Dearest Family,

I'm off for a few week's shooting tomorrow, so take this opportunity of inditing a line in comfort. I'm going out in the district and shall not be very far from here most of the time. I may get bear, panther, serow, gural, khahar, chakore, pheasant or even a sambhar, but of this list, two or three items will satisfy me. A bear and a serow would be particularly acceptable.

Shan't get much leave after all. I've been granted 3 months but the Colonel says I have got to come back to Bareilly with the regt. We march on 7 Decr.

Your kind letter of 24 Octr with the programme of Church House show to hand. 'Turn him Out' was the one theatrical venture I was ever connected with. I expect I told you about it. When we were in Madras we got it up. (Poor Bill – me – as Nicodemus Nobbs and the padré's daughter as Susie) but just as we were ready to give it, the 'exigiencies of the service' broke up the company, both the Glossops and old Grant being ordered away at short notice. It was great fun, and Susie and Nicodemus, in particular, were much pleased with it. She is married now, to an awful idiot in the gunners.

Since I came back we have had a couple of afternoon hops at the Club, on band night. One yesterday, at which it required all my strength of will to save me from the vortex. However, tomorrow morning I take to the mountains. Almora will be very Tissy after Decr. 7th. Mrs. Kingston will remain up and the Woods (P.W.D. Engineer) will be in now and again, as will the Depty. Commissioner. Old Mrs. Govern will complete the party. All the rest are winging their flight to the plains.

Famine is imminent in the U.P. and Campbell, our Commissioner, has been put in charge; so I have indited him a politely impertinent chit asking him to give me a job if he can. I don't know whether it's any use asking him, but it's a chance. Channer has just been put on plague duty but they won't take subalterns for it.

It's getting a bit parky now in the morning and evening, but quite delightful. Can't think of anything more.

Best love to you all, from
Yours affectionately,
Allan

★★★

About 5 marches from Almora
Novr 27 1907

Dearest Family

It's a fearful time since I wrote, but though I have been on leave, little time has been available for correspondence. Luck has been so bad, and my shooting so poor, that we have done nothing but scour the mountains in the vain hope of slaying 'something worthwhile' and I am worn to a shadow. Yesterday, for instance, I got within 100 yds of two khakur, two bears and a sambhur, and never got a practical shot at anything except a khakur. This morning I met a lovely old bear promenading and the dam' shikari *wouldn't* see my signals for the rifle until he was gone. I've only got three days more, but we live in hopes. There's heaps of game all round me but the lack of rain has made the jungles so dry that it's awfully hard to get near anything on account of the noise one makes. All I've got so far is small game: a gural and a khakur. This in spite of endless hunting and sacrifice of goats to the jungle deities at the instigation of my orderlies.

I do wish I could take the three months which have been granted me but the Colonel wants me back for Bareilly, as we shall be short-handed. Such is life.

It's fine and cold out in camp nowadays and the morning and evening fires most acceptable.

I have no news to give you, being out here, away from everything. Major Brakespeare has rejoined but I haven't seen him; they say he is very cheery. Even the girl I love has parted from me irretrievably, alas! So Bareilly will be a welcome change to our Almora cold weather.

★★★

Kathgodam Railway Station
Decr 10th

What a chap I am! Mails may come and mails may go but I don't go on, never. Since writing the above I have marched into Almora, packed my household goods and marched down here with the regiment.

Good old Lil. She has brought it off at last. It is very hard to believe that Alfred really capitulated after so prolonged a siege, 'constant dripping', etc. Well, she used to be a d——mmed fine girl and I daresay he could have done worse … She was free from guile, anyway. It's quite a good precedent to establish that the bridegroom should be 'taken in' at the bride's while he is recuperating from the financial loss entailed by the purchase of the wedding ring. This should tend to popularise matrimony among the unmarried orders. I had forgotten that Edgar Hickman had married Hester Powell. In fact, I don't believe you ever told me. They were both old friends of mine (I broke his nose once in a row at the Royal Oak and my 'affaire' with her sister Sue was too notorious to be forgotten). Everone seems to be marrying. No less than two of our Almora belles have become engaged recently and 'She', the chiefest of them all, having furnished me with a touching letter of farewell and a remarkably fetching photograph, has departed to try her luck in a larger and more promising field on the Bombay side. I hope she brings it off.

Well, I hope this catches you before Christmas; it should come near it. Anyway, here are the very best wishes for a Happy Christmas and a great old New Year. I have failed to secure any Christmas cards as I was out on leave and the usual desirability attaches to Christmas presents. I feel an awful rotter over it, especially as you kind people are always so good, but it's impossible to raise anything of the sort in Almora and cash is slightly tight.

By the way, Burma *Civil* Police is off for the present as the swines have filled in the vacancies from the *Military* Police, after agitating all the regts. in India about it. I'm getting rather fed up, waiting for a job. They have put me in as officiating D.C.C. now, as we are short, but I don't suppose I shall get any pay for it. Still, it's a mark of confidence and gives one something to think about. There are wigs on the green here as they are going to bring in somebody (probably V. of Almoriana) as 2nd in command and our seniors are playing 'ell. Heigh-ho!

No more at present. I have been loading mules into trains all this afternoon and am tired. We reach Bareilly tomorrow. Best love to you all and renewed Christmas and New Year greetings and wishes.

Yours affectionately,
Allan

★★★

Bareilly
27th February 1908

Dearest Family

Your kind letter of Jan 30th duly received, and appreciated. You 'tell me off' for not writing oftener, and I suppose you really are justified, for I'm shocking bad at answering letters. However, I generally give good measure when I do write. Fact is, I can't write short letters, so restrain myself until news has accumulated a bit.

Well, the battalion left here yesterday morning for Almora whilst I stopped on here, living with the Scots Fusiliers, who are great pals of mine. The reason of this involves some explanation. To cut it short, I have got eight months leave home, and am coming as soon as I can. I didn't tell you before, for reasons. It happened thus. When I heard, about Christmas, that my name wouldn't come up for Burma until next year, I began to cast about for means to keep the wolf from the door, because as I have already told you I'm quite unable to give anything towards my few debts, in Almora. Two or three billets escaped me, and suddenly it occurred to me that if I could get a troopship home, and live quietly there a bit, I might straighten things out to some extent. So I stuffed in for leave and got it; and also applied for two troopers 'as per regulation'. Well, the first has already gone, and the next, [the *Plassey*] goes on the 6th. I'm afraid there's no chance of getting her, as they say she's very full and it goes by juniority. However I'm going down to Bombay on the off-chance, and having set my hand to the plough, don't intend to turn back. I hope not to have to book by P&O as I'm on the cheap; but mean to beat around the docks and try to make pals with the skipper of some tramp. So there you are! I'll let you know what happens, though it may be some time before I arrive in merry England. I didn't say anything before, as I thought I might have to cancel my leave, if I didn't get a trooper; but having allowed my thoughts to dwell on it so long, have finally determined to get home somehow.

I am assuming that you won't mind having me on the premises for a bit; and calculate that by living quietly, and getting a trooper back, I may be able to just about pay off my creditors, which will be satisfactory. I shall probably get an extension to a year, as well, by which time, my name will come up for Burma.

I hope you won't object to the plonking down of a fat soldier, somewhat poverty-stricken; I had hoped to have made a bit of a splash on my first trip home, but circumstances alter cases. There's one thing I've forgotten; that is this Zakka Khel business. If it develops into anything big I may cancel my leave yet. There's still a small chance of our going. [British punitive operations – or 'Willcock's weekend war' according to the press – against Zakka Khel Afridis in Afghanistan. It was short and severe. In the House questions were asked about the conduct of the expedition, specifically the destruction of homes and food.]

Well, I'm seeing my last of Bareilly for the present. I'm sorry, as it has been a pleasant time here, though rather inducive to extravagance (which you may have guessed, is my pet vice). The people here are very nice, and it's been gay lately. Last week was the 'Week' and Bareilly was full of 'fair women and brave men'. Let me give you a programme of my doings –

Feb 16th	Dined with Mrs S and party including a widowed sister, whom I think has her eye on Bill. [ie Allan]
Feb 17th	1st round of Inf Polo Tournament in morning. Same in afternoon. Scots Fusiliers at Home Place. Dinner at club, with lotteries after (I don't lott).
18th	1st Day Bareilly Races. 14th BL and 3rd Goorks ar Home. Dined with Mrs F and went to Naini Tal Volunteers Ball, with her son-in-law and younger daughter, the best dance here, to my mind.
19th	Inf Polo Tournament. 2nd Round. 48th Pioneers and 3rd Goorks at Home. Our Guest night. I dined Thornton (Scots F) and Mallet (14th BL). Went to lotteries at the club, after.
20th	2nd Day Bareilly Races. S Lancs at Home. Dined with Lambert (manager of the Railway here, an awfully nice chap). Bareilly Bachelors' Ball. Great evening.
21st	Final, Infy Polo Tournament General Spews at Home. Dined quietly in mess.
22nd	Bareilly Gymkhana Races. S Lancs at Home. Dined with General, and went on with them to concert and amateur Theatricals.
23rd Sunday	Took fairy for a ride in morning. Dined with Benyan in evening.
24th	Dance at club. One of the best
25th	14th BL and S Lancs Point-to-Point. Very cheery.

Today is 48th Pioneers sports; tomorrow Scots Fusilier's Point-to-Point and Saturday, 14 the BL sports. So you see we have been keeping our spirits up, and there are lots of social gatherings.

Well, that's about all the news. I'll let you know about my movements later. In the meantime, best love to you all.

Yours affectionately
Allan

★★★

Bombay
9th March 1908

Dearest Family

As usual, I missed the last mail by a day, but as you will get this long before you see me, it doesn't matter so much. Well, to get to the point, I sail from here on 14th per SS *Magdala*, for <u>Hull</u>, of all places; and probably won't get there for a month. She's not a bad boat, but slow. A tramp, needless to remark. The *Plassey* was full to overflowing, and I had not the smallest chance of getting her. I shall arrive home pretty poor, so don't make a fuss about it, but let me cream in, quietly and unostentatiously.

Came down here, leaving Bareilly on night of 1st with three fellows in the Scots Fusiliers. One, an invalid, went on the *Plassey*, and two went on Friday by the mail. All the world and his wife seem to be going home this year. Channer went on the mail on Friday, too, and Jackson is coming along soon.

Am living at Watson's Hotel; not much of a place, though the best here, bar the Taj Mahal, which is a bit too classy for one so poor as me. I got your kind letter of 6th Feb abusing me for not writing and I agree with you entirely. The only thing I get any satisfaction out of it is that by the time I get your telling off, you have got my next letter, which always makes me chuckle. Don't know what Maudie wants my address for. Sounds as if she were going to write, but I haven't heard anything.

All goes well. It's rather dull waiting for the boat, but all in the days work. Bombay is pretty hot, and there's not much to do. Shall be glad to get off.

The Colonel leaves Almora for his new billet the day after tomorrow. We are all very sad at his going.

11th
Your letter of 14th Feb has turned up all correct. It caught the mail all right, as the Kathgodam (station for Almora) post-mark is March 3rd. Father has done this before, so you can always depend on it. Yes, it must be rather empty at Clive House with only you two there. However, that will soon be altered now, as I shall roll up a fortnight after you get this if I'm lucky, and you will have me. Anyway, its too late for you to stop me now. And if Miss Nunn turns up too, you will be full up.

I didn't know that father was going to retire just now; however, I think he has had a pretty good whack at it, and it's time he had a look on, and let the younger bloods wrestle with the question of National Defence. If they all do as much and as well as he had done, there need by no anxiety about the matter.

No doubt it's a depressing matter, this casting out of the old hands when they have had a turn, but it has got to be. I was awfully sick when we pensioned off old Chamer, our Subadar-Major, this year. He was such a fine chap, and as active as could be. But he had had his turn, and was blocking the way for others, and there was no course but to shunt him. Just fancy your having the telephone. Splendid! All I want to do now, if I want seats for the theatre or anything like that, is to go into pa's office and ring 'em up.

Well, au reservoir! About a fortnight after this you ought to see me.

Best love to you all.
Yours expectantly
Allan

PS. Sail tomorrow, 13th. Get to Hull about 11th. We call at Port Said and Algiers.

★★★

SS Magdala
Red Sea
Suez
25th March 08

Dearest People

Fairly on the way home at last! We shall get to Suez the day after tomorrow, and I can post this. There is not much of consequence to tell you. This is a quiet old Hooker, and we have had tophole weather so far; so life has not been eventful. I get on very well with the ship's officers, as usually, and sit up on the bridge, as a rule until a late hour, swapping lies with the officer on watch. There are one or two other people on board, to wit, a young Norwegian captain and his wife; another captain (this is a bit involved, ain't it), an old retired civilian and his wife make up the rest. They are all family uninteresting and we don't bother each other much.

I told you that we should call at Port Said and Algiers; and can't think of anything else to impart. I'm fit as ever, and keenly anticipating the delight of home, and the flesh-pots of Clive House. Mamma will have to prepare all sorts of delicacies when I'm home. After all, there's no goose like Mrs Stephens'.

It was a coincidence my meeting Arthur Powell at Watson's; he looked just as I remembered him; have you heard that he has become a Buddhist, or something of the sort? We didn't have much time to compare notes, but this report seemed to be confirmed by what he told me.

You will find me with a broad Scotch accent when you see me. All the ship's officers are from Glasgow, and two of them have asked me whether I don't hail from the spot too. The skipper is a dear.

The evening before I left Bombay I ran into Major Kingston in Watson's. I'm always meeting someone there. He had brought his wife down, to send her home, and Major and Mrs Eastmead rolled up the same evening, as they are on the same boat. All India and his wife are coming home this year.

Its getting nice and cool now, after the heat of the Indian Ocean. Of course, the breeze accounts for it. We passed close to Aden and saw a lot of the Arabian shore. Ghastly place!

★★★

March 27th
Suez Canal

We entered it this morning and get to Port Said at about 11 tonight, so I must now close. We shan't stop there more than about 2 hours, and then on to Algiers, or possibly Gibraltar. It's very cold after the plains of Ind.

Well no more. Probably get to Hull about 11th.

Best love to you all.
Yours anticipatingly
Allan

★★★

There follows a gap in the correspondence and there are no diary entries until the New Year, 1909.

At Home in Welshpool

Letts No 46 Rough Diary

1 January 1909 Friday
Dispensary Ball. Took Billy. Pa and ma likewise. Pretty good. Cecily troublesome; is firmly convinced that I long to cuddle her!

2 January 1909 Saturday
United met at 'Pool. Proceeded up to Leighton and drew the 'Stubbs' Plantation. Got a fox there, and ran along old road, and across Walton Common. Huge field, but not many of 'em left after Walton. Straight on with hardly a check to Wallop Hall, and killed in lodge garden. Great run. Barney carried me wonderfully well. Also present: Vaughan Thomas

(master) Fred (huntsman) young Vernon, Sweeting, Miss (Pussy) Harrison, Charlie Jones, Tom Green, young (gunner) Harrison. Barney having had enough I went home.

3 January 1909 Sunday
Went to see young Blair in hospital. On way back, by Llanfair Ry Bridge, came on Her in bad company. Damn sick.

9 January 1909 Saturday
Got rather pathetic letter from Her, asking me to go and see her before I went away. Put my pride in my pocket and said I woud as soon as I could get back from town.

11 January 1909 Monday
Went to India Office and Cox's without getting much satisfaction. Say no chance by trooper! Went to 'Peter Pan' in after noon and was much taken. Top-hole scenery etc. Didn't care much for Pauline Chase but Capt Hook was a flyer.

13 January 1909 Wed
Heard (via W'pool) that I was to sail in *Dongola* on 20th. Good egg, but wish they had told me on Monday at India office. Went to 'The Bridge Builder' or Builder of Bridges or whatever it's called. Play poor, but acting good, particularly Vanburgh, who took me by storm.

15 January 1909 Friday
She came; it was rather a fight but we made it up at last. I was rather a swine I suppose. Damnable evening; raining like deuce. What with the rain and her tears my collar and coat shoulder were soaked through. Broke the news of my imminent departure.

9 February 1909 Tuesday
'Come back to Bom-Bom-bay' Got in early. Went ashore with Cochranes. Went to Taj and took room with Mitchell as Sussex Hotel very full.

25 Thursday
About Bombay. Left about 3pm for the North. Very comfy carriage and train.

In February 1909 Allan is back at the regimental home of Almora. But not for long.

15 Monday Feb
After much cogitation refused the police-billet; when the chit was written out, changed my mind and took it on. Everyone seemed rather sick, and told me not to be a fool. But there you are. I felt it was time to start something.

After four busy, mostly impoverished years of training, football, multiple duties, Gurkhali, gymkhanas and 'little subscription dances at the club' – and always hoping for promotion or more money – on 15 March 1909, Allan accepted a civilian appointment as Second Assistant Commandant to the Lakhimpur Military Police, stationed at Sadiya in Assam.

Almora
U.P.
Feb 16th, 1909

Dearest Family,

Was the Yeomanry Ball a success? And was she there?

I must give you my important news first. On arrival here I found that they had just offered me by wire, a job as Asst. Supdt. in the Eastern Bengal and Assam Civil Police, which after much cogitation and some reluctance, I accepted on condition they would let me go after two years. I have not had their reply, but expect it soon, and am pretty sure they will appoint me. I start on about Rs.550 a month which is not excessive, but a bit better than here, (we get 400 now, since the increase) I expect that I shall live much cheaper than at present (I get out of all subscriptions etc.) and as I shall be under the Civil department, I hope to make a good thing out of travelling and other allowances. I did not like to let the chance slip, but the drawback is that nobody knows anything about it, and there was no time to find out, as I had to reply by wire. The others all wanted me to refuse, but, chiefly on guess-work, I thought it might be just as good as Vonima and as it is offered at once, I'm going to try it, and let you know how it works out. Civil employment is generally a good paying job. I expect (guess) that I shall be upon the Assamese border, and have a lot of little posts to look after, which means big travelling! I see from the Army List that 3 other fellows in the Service are already on the job. Of course, Jackson says I shall be a 'dam' bobby', but I fancy it will be more of a military than a civil job. Else why take soldiers? However, the die is cast; if I don't like it, I can get out in two years at latest; and hope to do it sooner, if necessary, and get to Burma. I made a couple of friends on the boat coming out, who have promised to pull strings for me at Simla, where they live. One is a Colonel doctor, and the other is the wife of a sapper Colonel. And I don't mean to do any more waiting for things; this Burma biz. has taught me that; when I want anything again, I mean to wire-pull for all I'm worth.

It's quite possible that Assam may be a little gold-mine, of course. So hope for the best. Now for a little news of lighter vein. The usual journey up from Bombay, where I spent a couple of days waiting for my kit. Then I met Broadbent [J.T.C. Broadbent] the adjt. of the old 73rd, Carnatics, and also old Bremner, the Colonel. We had great confabs. At Lucknow I fell in at dead of night with two ladies of the Royal Scots (who came out with me, and are going to Ranikhet) and as they were new to India and frightfully fed up, and tired, and helpless, I convoyed them up, and sent 'em to Ranikhet from Kathgodam [the terminus of the broad gauge line from Bareilly]. It was a beastly shame they were not allowed on the troop-train with their husbands. However, they were well looked after from Lucknow, and seemed grateful. One of them was rather pleasing. She is recently married, and the sister of the latest Lady Rosslyn. In my anxiety for their welfare, I lost my train when changing at Bareilly Junction, but stopped the train by wire at Bareilly City while I drove furiously in two cabs to catch it up, which I did all correct.

I got in here on Sunday evening all correct, and it really was rather homely turning up again. They had ponies out for me, and my room all ready, and they seem so pleased to see me that I was quite surprised. But there was one horrid shock. That little knave, Friar Tuck, has gone and got engaged, and is to be married this year.

[sheet missing]

Writing home on 9 March from 'Bunglo', Ramgash Dak,' Allan explained he was being sent to Dacca for preliminary training:

I have sent off a parcel to you today, which is <u>not</u> valuable. It is a few old bits of Chinese silk which I came across packing, and which *might* be some good; and a Malay 'sarong' to be worn around the waist like a skirt, with the diamond patterns down the right leg. It's no good, but a curiosity. You get into it, and pull it out as far as it will go to the left; then fold back in front as much as is not required, and tuck the top corner into the edge in front of your tummy. Damn! Can't explain. Too sleepy.

12 March 1909 Friday
Arrived at Dacca. Went to IG's office Saw him (Bonham-Carter) and Hughes-Buller. Very nice, but made that I was to go forthwith to Chittagong. Back to club, picked up Miss Tucker and papa and to their house. Very low all this day. Shall not stay long in EA; can't say I fancy this job so far. However, nous verons.

Why did I leave my little back-room?

***

Chittagong
18.5.09

Dearest Family

No news to tell you, I don't think. I'm keeping pretty busy, but am fit as can be, in spite of the heat, and fever. It's pretty hot here now and I sweat like the devil.

Am feeling very undecided about what I shall do as regards stopping on here; the battn. expect to go to Chitral after all, and are telling me not to be a b.f and come back. At present I have the following choices –

Stopping on here three or 4 months saving a little money, month by month, and then taking on a Superintendent-ship in a beastly jungly East Bengal District for the rest of my two years. Trying to work an exchange up to Assam as Asst. Supdt. I think I could manage this; it wouldn't be so paying as the Superintendentcy, but would suit me better.

Trying to exchange to Mily. Police; the same remarks apply.

Going back to the pattan by Septr; doing Chital, and trying for Burma again. This is very tempting; and I could very likely get about square before we came down again; we get an extra 100 which would bring me up to what I'm getting now.

Between so many alternatives, I'm rather puzzled; but hope to come to a conclusion soon. Haven't been doing anything exciting lately; except on Sunday Mrs. Neilson took a bevy of us on the river in a steam-launch. Of course, when we'd started it rained like Billy-ho and we were confined in a tiny cabin, and stuffed ourselves with tea; and then played Up Jenkins, of all things, until it was fine enough for us to tootle up to the Club, about 7. There were nine of us, altogether.

How goes it in Pool, in this merry month of May? If Kittens is there, what a time you must be having. What's the boy like now? I wish I were there to see. Well, no more except best love to you all

Yours affectly
Allan

★★★

Chasing Opium Smugglers.

Chittagong
8.6.09

Dearest Family

All goes on as usual, except that we've having rather heavier rain than is customary at this time; its a bit early for it to be the real rains, but it looks like 'em.

I had rather an interesting job trying to catch some opium-smugglers at their little games, yesterday, but they were too wily, or our information was wrong, or something. As both the Excise people and our port-police are supposed to be implicated, you can imagine that it's a bit difficult to compete with 'em. However, it was rather interesting.

Opium-smuggling is a great business here; there are villages that practically derive their living from it; and it is worked by wealthy and influential men of the town. The idea is to get it into Burma, over the frontier at the south of this district. There's a huge profit in doing this, so they can afford to pay the preventive departments well. One big man, in fact, the biggest – called Jakub Ali, is at present under trial in a case, and is giving away the people he used to pay not to see things for giving evidence against him. He has enormous influence among the riverine population, so it becomes very compli- cated. There is a large riverine population all about this province; in fact you can hardly go anywhere except by boat, or steamer.

Very few people at home can have much idea of what police-work is like out here compared to there. The two great difficulties are that, in the first place, the chances are that the police are bigger scoundrels and liars than the accused in any particular case, and secondly, that there is no such thing as public spirit in this country, so that the only chance of getting evidence against anyone is from his enemies, in which case it is probably false. Again, even witnesses who do happen to mean to speak the truth, can be made to give most incredible evidence owing to the vagueness of the Oriental mind, and the lack of importance it attaches to precision.

And to these people we keep on giving law and more law, and complicating the procedure continuously; till really it seems to be the curse of the country in places like this. The litigation and crime is enormous. From the sedition point of view, this place is wonderful for E. Bengal; there are lots of babus, of course, but they seem an exceptionally well affected lot, and give no trouble. The Boxwell case, a few days ago, was not really a swadeshi crime. The young babu who did it only selected a European for his victim because he wanted to create a bigger splash over his exit from this world than if he slugged a native; a form of notoriety-craving which is not unknown in the West. And it was a babu who saved Boxwell, and captured the assailant; so that about balances things.

Well, this seems a dull sort of letter; but I must away. My munshi awaits me to teach me that beastly tongue.

How are you all? I keep very fit. I'm looking forward to hearing from you about Kitty and her family.

Excuse haste; best love all round
Yours affectionately
Allan

★★★

Letts No. 46 Rough Diary

Monday 21 June 1909
Was rung up twice and apologies offered. Bengali report of tiger at Tailandip.

Tuesday 22 June 1909
Left about 5.30 on bikes for Tailandip. Got there about 7 and found that the tiger (which was a panther) had been shot the day before.

★★★

Chittagong
28.6.09

Dearest Family

Your 'steemed favour of 10th inst. to hand this morning. It was a slightly sketchy epistle, owing, no doubt, to the excitement engendered by the arrival of the Van der Goot 'push' (as we say in America) and by the reminiscences of pa's and ma's recent splash in goodole London town. Well, I specs I shall have to 'scuse you this time, but when opportunity affords, should very much like to have more detailed accounts of the advent of the collateral branch in the ancestral home.

Doy wrote and told me that he was well over his operation which is good hearing; it's just like the old beast, isn't it, that he never told me, until now, that he had anything of the sort the matter with him? His mem-sahib also wrote and gave the news.

Am much pleased to hear that the revered parents enjoyed their little trip, and am sure it did 'em good.

Here all goes as well as is deserved, anyway. As usual, I'm writing this at 11 pm as I never seem to find opportunity during the day. I rise with the lark, and from daylight to dark, I do what, and whom, I have to do. It's by no means all work, though there's a fair quantity of that; but other matters take up a good deal of time, and the slackness induced by the climate prevents my snatching odd 10 minuteses for correspondence etc. We've not had any very striking gaieties lately; Tuesday last, the judge self-entertained a small dinner-party of eight (two women, six men); Wednesday there was the usual small afternoon dance at the Club; Thursday I dined out at a small party consisting principally of Mrs. Neilson, and her various attachés, whose name is legion; (I had the honour of driving her there, to the intense disgust of the remainder); Friday was the King's Birthday Parade; I'm rather chummy with Berkeley who commands the Valianteers, and Montague, a chap in the 5th Fusiliers, who is the Adjutant; so they inveigled me into being a galloper. Here, I find I've got twisted in my accounts. It was this night that we had the skirt-party; on Tuesday it was a bachelor-party. On Saturday we had a holiday; in the afternoon, the Neilson's took a girl who's staying there, and me, on expedition in tikka-gharris (if you don't know what they are, refer to Kipling) [Kipling's *The God from the Machine*] to a place called the Turtle-Tank. In the evening, the volunteers gave a King's Birthday dinner at the Club; Berkeley dined me and Chotznen and we had a very cheery evening till about 3am. Sunday, C. & I went to breakfast at old Cravens (where I used to live) and out for a rapid dash on the police-launch afterwards, to clear our heads. Then we had tea and tennis at Berkeley's. I forgot to tell you that on Monday (week-today) a report was sent in from a police-station about 14 miles off, that a tiger was in a village eating the inhabitants, and Help! please! So I biffed off at 12 midnight in a country boat; got on a bike next morning about 5 am and rode to the place; found the beast was a wretched panther, which had been shot by a native the previous evening; and so came back. Disappointed in my tiger, I turned on one side on the way back and tried to arrest some absconders, who were playing the bear with the local pl'eece, but they were far too nippy for yours tikka-gharris 'umbly and I lost about 4 quarts of perspi. for nothing. However, did some good, as I went and called the local thug or Zamindar [landlord, from the Persian], who was harbouring the brutes, and employing them as his standing army (a long-established custom in these parts. Every big landowner has a gang of badmashes or bad hats, whom he uses to oppress his tenants) and put the fear of God into him. He is now producing them rapidly to their intense disgust. Law is a funny thing out here. Two of the men I wanted lived in the next hut to the local choukidans (or village policemen) who daren't touch 'em! The choukidans are the Zamindar's men, too, and if they tried to arrest these badmashes, the Zamindar would turn the rest on to 'em for interfering with his 'lathials' (club-men). Don't you find it hard to understand? It's not as if these malefactors, as in Ireland, or Italy, were local heroes; the ordinary people hate 'em and are their victims, but they're too selfish to chance a row, in opposing them. When you get the issue complicated by the local pl'eece being in the pay of the Zamindar, and so on, you can see that the policeman's lot is a bit bewildering, even if moderately happy, in Eastern Bengal.

The rains are fairly on us now. Got a devil of a ducking this morning, out riding. I've got two horses to ride. Berkeley's mare, Vanity, the best horse in the station, and Montague's Sammy, a great old nag, who I'm going to drive when I can raise the wind to buy a tum-tum.

Thank God for good pals, who don't use horseflesh much, but keep it.

Best love to all.
Yours
Allan

                          ★★★

Chittagong
21.7.09

Dearest Family

Yes, mamma, I'm not having a bad time here, on the whole; though saving so far has been conspicuous by its absence. But I'm just finishing paying off my advance that I took to come out here. And you think I'm losing 'tone', do you? Well, well. Perhaps it will interest you to learn that in Chittagong I'm by way of being considered a bit of a blood; a Beau Kummel (or whatever the name is). An old lady besought me, not long ago, to be careful in this place that I did not lose my 'nice manners'. Aha! What price the 'charming fellow' now? And a (younger) lady who went home soon after I got here, wrote to Mrs. Campbell (my boss's wife) and asked to be remembered to Mr. Hutchins 'he's the nicest man I ever met'. But I mustn't tell you any more, or Billy will be too green-eyed for ordinary consumption.

The rains are upon us in their vigour; it's been the limit since Tuesday night (a week ago). Practically continuous and everything is damp and mildewy. It makes it very hard to get exercise.

I had a rather a hairy time for a few days last week. The judge, my stable-companion, had been seedy for a few days, but I didn't think there was much the matter with him. I went to a dinner given by a pal at the club a week last Monday, and there was a dance afterwards; which I enjoyed it all very much, the right person being present and correct, you understand. On Tuesday, I didn't get up till about ½ past 8 and then loafed around to see how the Judge was. He was very nearly snuffing out apparently; I telephoned the doctor, and rendered first aid etc. and to cut a long story short, he was dam' ill, and on the Wednesday night there was a consultation and they didn't know whether he would get over it or not. However, he's going on splendidly now, and is off to Darjeeling for a month as soon as he is strong enough for the journey. So I shall be a widow.

Well, I had to nurse him, and am rather a skilful attendant now. From the time I found him on Tuesday until Friday night I didn't go to bed; had 9 hours sleep in short snatches during that time. Fellows was very good and came and sat up, but I didn't like to leave him when he was bad, as I was more in touch with the circs. And he was a bit awkward, and wanted 'managing', which I've rather got to understand now in his case. So I got rather tucked up before I finished, but it was rather interesting; and people were awfully nice. I got ladies to make him things and people were always coming round to inquire. And from the Thursday morning he got steadily better and better.

Well, no more now. I must breakfast and send things off. I went out to tea yesterday, and for a little drive, but the weather is too damnable for anything. It's coming down in sheets now.

Best love
Yours affectly
Allan

Though grateful for the pay, 550 rupees per month, and the travelling allowance of his civil posting, Allan was keen to ensure his name was not forgotten at regimental headquarters in Almora when posts were being filled for frontline (ie frontier) service. By letter and by wire he made sure the regiment, and the police, knew what he wanted: active service, not training and tea dances, with the Gurkhas. Such self-promotion was a part of the game that all ambitious officers were called upon to play, especially in the Indian regiments and even more so in the Gurkhas where, as Allan had long since discovered, this strategy required both talent and patience. Knowing his own worth Allan played the game with gusto. In August 1909, he asked the Inspector General of Police if he had 'got him ear-marked for some fat job or another' or he would be returning (though he did not explicitly say so) 'C.O.D. to Almora.' Writing home on 3 August Allan continues:

> The I.G. in his reply, offered me a chance of the Mily. Police in this province; and the pickings of Mily Police depend very much on what station you get. The pay in the worst stations is a little less that I get here, and in the best a good deal better; so selecting the best I could find in the Civil List, I put a tremendous bluff, and I wrote back to the old bird saying that if he'd give me that I might find it worth my while not to revert; which is how the matter stands at present. I can't hear for a day or two. So he may give it me, or not.

In fact the IG offered Allan something rather different: promotion to acting superintendent for the District. Though only a temporary appointment for six weeks, replacing Allan's superior while he took leave, it was an irresistible opportunity for a 28-year-old and a problem solved for the older man. On 21 September Allan wrote home:

Campbell goes away this afternoon, so for a brief six weeks I shine resplendent in the capacity of Jack in-Office as the Babu said. I was gazetted the other day.

No, I'm not getting rich yet, mamma.

As the weather turned and the nights began to grow cooler, Allan celebrated his thirtieth birthday on 14 September:

My baldness advances apace, so you will be able to give up being anxious about me soon. [The day] passed off quietly, as the journalistic phrase hath it. For a birthday treat, I took the Neilsons and Barker out to tea on the river in the police-launch; being wily, I didn't tell em it was my birthday until all was over; but to no avail, as Mrs N is off to the bazaar this morning to buy me the fiercest tie she can find. Afterwards we went to their house and played bridge; they wanted me to stay to dine, but I wouldn't leave my poor ole stable-companion, who is rather bad these days. So had a quiet evening at home.

I had rather a good birthday present, as my bull-terrier (she cost me 50 dibs when she was 6 weeks old) which has been lost a fortnight was found by a pleece-man, and returned to me, very thin, but otherwise unimpaired.

Isn't it sad about my poor old pal, Ralph Jackson? He'd had his captaincy just a month and, you know, when he got the Adjutancy, he was awfully keen on it. I had a long letter from him on 6 and he died on 11. He was in love with Miss Savage, the Colonel's daughter, but thought she was too young so was waiting to come back from Chital before he said anything. She's an awfully pretty girl. I don't know what he died of but he was an awful chap for getting ill and has been in bed with a bad knee most of the time I've been here.

★★★

Chittagong

12.10.09

Dearest Family

It was very sweet of you to send the socks; with whom the kind thought originated, 'I shall not assume the province of determining' as my friend Lord Chatham puts it, as there is a confliction of evidence; but to all concerned I tender my kindest thanks; they are very tender indeed, and are to be worn next Friday afternoon, when I take my ladylove for a drive; if *they* don't do it, my last hope is gone.

You must really excuse me for being so ill a correspondent these days; really I mean well, but there are sheaves and sheaves of correspondence on my desk unattended to. The climate is so dam' slack; and I've an awful lot of work now that Campbell is away. However, the Puja holidays are at hand, during which time the offices are closed, so I shall have more time & be able to get out into the district a bit. They last until the end of the month, and after that it won't be long till Campbell returns. And then my Chittagong career is over, I've been informed that I'm to be transferred to the Bakanganj district, which the same is hell; all babus and beastliness. However, I can't grouse, as if I hadn't asked for it, they'd have left me alone.

It's dam' hot just now; but will cool off in a few days. The station is very empty, and will be emptier when the Pujas commence. There's a cricket team coming over from Calcutta, tho', during that time, which should liven us up a bit. There's no news; we've never anything to talk about here, except the latest scandals; it's no good telling you them, as you don't know the parties. All's well, and I'm very fit, save for an occasional boil, due to the climate, or else to a wave of blue ribbonism which I've been affecting the last few months.

On with the dance. Best love to all and more thanks for the socks.

Yours affectly,
Allan

Return of the 'Hopeless Ass'; Superintendent Campbell returned from leave on 1 November and Allan stepped down from his acting, temporary post. After a trip to Dacca 'They made me go there to appear in an exam which I refused to sit for' – he heard that his request for transfer to the military police 'was on the tapis, and as a transfer from Civil Police to Military has to go before the Govt. of India, the question was being delayed at Simla.' Frustrated and unsettled, Allan wrote: 'Campbell and I have rather been running up against each other lately, so I shall be glad to get away. He's a hopeless ass, and waster.'

In fact, Allan was offered and refused a post with the Dacca Military Police because he was holding out for a livelier time in the hills, where inter-tribal fighting, Chinese incursions and a wild frontier made law enforcement a more difficult and exciting task. Meanwhile there was no point, as he saw it, in taking exams for the Civil Police:

My trip to Dacca was quite a flying one; I was not prepared to take the exam as I told 'em when they asked me some two months ago. However someone produced a circular suddenly, saying that everyone liable to exams must appear, and they showed me in orders in the Police Gazette as one of those to do so. As a little trip to Dacca suited my book, I didn't argue, but went; bearded the examiners in my best 'charming-fellow' style and returned home at my convenience. It really was rather funny on the morning of the exam; all the other luckless weights turning up in fear and trembling; and yours humbly sauntering into the room, shaking hands warmly with the board, saying good-bye with profuse regrets, and sauntering out again, amid the curses of my mates.

★★★

Chittagong
30.11.09

Dearest Family

There is a chance that my next week's mail may arrive too late to wish you many happy returns, so to be quite sure, I am now going to tell you that I hope you all have a very Merry Christmas and a Happy New Year. I don't know whether it has come round quickly or not; in some ways it seems only yesterday that I was rapidly becoming stentorous and turkey-stricken at the ancestral board; and in others that it occurred centuries ago. Other surroundings make such a difference, of course. I suppose that to you, it doesn't seem very long. Well, we must remember to drink 'Absent Friends', mustn't we? I know you will, and so shall I, but where it will be is still unknown. As things go at present, it may very well be here; the powers that be maintain their sphinx-like silence, and I feel very much at a loose end. My raison d'être, as far as Chittagong is concerned, ceased on the 1st of this month, when Campbell returned from leave. This is rather unsettling, and I'm rather like the gent. in the Scriptures, who had not where to lay his head. My late landlord, Berkeley, has thrust me forth of his house, as he leaves for Calcutta tonight to meet his wife, children, sister-in-law, nurse, etc etc and has had to sweep and garnish his house for their reception; so the Club affords me a temporary, and not very enlivening shelter, together with two callow youths to whom I'm too bored to expand, nowadays. Even this poor roof was very nearly denied me, as the rooms were all booked; but this danger was happily averted. Had it not been, it is hard to say where I should have gone; Mrs. Walsh said I could sleep on her veranda, but better accommodation was unavailable owing to a crowd of strangers having descended on us for a farewell dinner to a railway-magnate, which takes place tonight.

Things go on quietly, and it is cooling off. I dined at the Neilson's on Monday, and there is this feed tonight, and I dine out on Saturday. Last Saturday I gave a little tea-party to Mr. & Mrs. N., a Miss McKenzie, who stays with them; Miss Woodhead, the Collector's sister; and Mr. Biden, a callow youth who is in her train; he is Berkeley's personal assistant, and I had to intercede with B. to get him off for the afternoon, as Mrs. N. insisted that he should come. B. said I was like a blooming old dowager, but let him come. We had the tea fight on the launch; it was a fine sunset, and a full-moon to follow, so it went rather well. I don't think there is much more of interest. I'm not doing much work to speak of, and am looking for my post every morning with great anxiety as to my orders. I hope I get Kohima, or Dibrugarh [Allan was competing for one of two new Assistant Commandantships]. The simple life is what I want; to drill the wily Gurkha again, to shoot, fish, draw T.A. (d'you know what that is, by the way? Travelling allowance, ten bob a day. This is paltry) and economise. Heigh-ho! May the Gods be kind.

Well, here's all that's good to you again. May you all be cheery and happy, and enjoy your Christmasses. I'm not sending any presents this year, as I'm very broke; and it is an impossible place to get any. I do hope you will all be equally ungiving.

Good bye for the present, and best love to you all from

Yours affectionately

Allan

After a two day hike from the nearest railhead Allan arrived at Sylhet in the Surma Valley in time for Christmas 1910, with carte blanche to sort out the 'Inefficiency, Slackness and Insubordination' that prevailed in the district police force – attributes, he noted ominously, that in Chittagong were not discouraged and 'did not cease at the native ranks'. One suspects that Allan was let loose on Sylhet to get him away from Campbell.

25 December 1909 Saturday

Rode Othello to church. Very small attendance. Little ride round by golf-course then back to bungalow. Campbell, Woodlands, Mecer, Stevenson, Martin, Florence to break-fast, likewise tea. Whole station (27) dined. Rather cheery event, gymknana and dancing. Bed at 2.

27 December 1909 Monday

Shot several Ghils from the launch. I got a few snipe. Good fun, but didn't have much luck with the duck.

31 December 1909 Friday

Beat for tiger with elephants. No tiger.

'The station' he wrote, 'consists of the head-quarters, offices, courts, etc. the bungalows of the Europeans, and the rest native bazaars and villages dotted about in bamboo jungle.' Allan's absurd description of the station's eccentrics is akin to a Gilbert libretto – a gentle mockery of a society that, as he well knows, includes himself.

★★★

Sylhet

Assam

9 January 1910

My dearest Family

I've not been good about writing lately, have I? And here am I in Sylhat, working like an 'oss, for the sake of doing something. My boss (Moore) is an awfully good chap, and it's a pleasure to work for him; he backs one up like one o'clock, and rejoices to see me wading in and making the constables' lives a burden to them, instead of trying to ride me off like my late boss did, in the interests of peace and slackness. He has given me the town, Reserve, and Head-quarters Police Station to work my wicked will on, and I'm doing my best to make myself unpopular. I must explain that, in this province, anyhow, the watch words of the Police Force has become Inefficiency, Slackness and

Insubordination; when I elicited this fact at Chittagong I found it did not cease at the native ranks, and my efforts at reform were not encouraged by my chief; 'au contraire'. So I got fed up, too, and enjoyed myself. Here, as I say, old Moore (sounds like the Almanac doesn't it?) pushes me on; and the constable's verge on mutiny!

This is quite a different station to Chittagong; it's the head-quarters of a larger and more important district, but there is hardly any town, as you would understand a town, and very few sahibs. It is technically Assam but really Eastern Bengal. Assam proper is the Assam Valley; this is the Surma Valley. We are very cut-off from the world here, at this time of year; in the rains, and hot weather, steamers run right up here; but now the normal way in is rail to Karimganj (about 32 miles) and in by road or country-boat. It generally takes two days for this part of the journey! The station consists of the head-quarters, offices, courts, etc. the bungalows of the Europeans, and the rest native bazaars and villages dotted about in bamboo jungle. Our society is:

(a) the District Commissioner, and his wife. Name Hazlett. Very nice, cheery, full of go, and entertain, etc. With them are her mother and father, Capt. and Mrs Goode. Capt. Goode was formerly Port Officer at Chittagong and I know him well by name. He was a bit of a character. He's a hearty old chap; awful bounder, but very amusing. Chittagong tradition hath it he feathered his nest pretty well while at Chittagong; and she is full of money. So they are very well off; they live in France and are now visiting round. She is a dear old thing, as deaf as a post, but full of beans. With the Hazletts also resides a Miss Good (a niece of the old man) who is young, full of conceit, and also a bounder. She is the only spin. here, though, so we have to make the best of what we can get. She is apparently going to rope in the Asst. Commdt. who also lives there (it's a rum menage, isn't it?) He is also a character; a bit dotty apparently. He is quite a senior I.C.C. man really; but as he has never passed any exams since he came out, he is still in a junior's job. He is long senior to Hezlett, (his boss!) and of the same year as Jeffries, the judge, who is drawing two thousand. Barnival, the A.C. draws eight or nine hundred! He isn't a bad sort but half-baked apparently.

(b.) the Supdt. Police, Moore, his wife, and son who is about 17 and an invalid which is why he's at home. Mrs M. is a very cheery, sporty old lady with the most beautiful white hair. She wears short skirts, is mad on bridge and snookers, and a splendid dancer in spite of a generous girth. We are great pals. She was a professional pianist, etc.

(c) The Civil Surgeon, Capt. McCoy IMS and his wife. He's very dark and she plain, dumpy, and no class. Very harmless both of them, however.

(d) Jeffries, the judge, with whom I live. He was Judge at Chittagong, before Chotzner, so I met him there. He is an exceedingly good-hearted little chap, but very quiet and retiring. He keeps three horses so I've fallen on my feet again! We get on very well, but he really is very hard to talk to. But he is, as I say, a really good chap; he ought to marry a good stamp of girl and then he'd just be right. As it is (I don't want to be nasty, but only to give you an idea) he is rather a finicky insignificant, little old bachelor.

(e) One or two planters who have gardens near. This is a planting district, but the gardens are mostly far from here; so the planters rarely come to headquarters; they have their own meeting places, and Clubs etc. dotted about the district. And there you are!

We have an additional judge here now, temporarily; he is a babu who married a white woman (country-bred). She is a big striking-looking woman; it's only a few years ago (I remember it in the papers well) when she brought a libel suit (as a spinster against the Judge of Mymensingh and horse-whipped him on his own verandah. He had been rash enough to try and prevent her 'contaminating' a married lady (whom tradition says, was considerably 'contaminated' already) and the recipient of his confidence had given him away. The moral being, I suppose, that contained in the song – 'Be careful, very very, careful, very, very careful, do!'

So you see, we're not a large or expensive station. (If I stay on, I can certainly save a good bit, but, of course, they're bound to transfer me or something. I should like to vegetate here a bit). On Christmas Day, Mrs Hezlett dined the whole station, and what with planters, etc. managed to beat up 27 of us. We danced and played silly games, and thoroughly enjoyed ourselves. On Boxing Day Jeffries and Hezlett took out the Commission (who was here) old Good, two planters and myself for a few days duck shooting etc. We went in a big launch, with a house boat attached, and had a very decent time, and got back on New Year''s Day. We didn't do very great execution but not so bad. We went after tiger too but they didn't show up. I've had 12 elephants for this so we were rather toffy. The only large beast we got in this way, was a big hen sambhur deer, which yours humbly plugged. I was wanting to go to Chittagong for the 'Week' (6th Jan) but it has been cancelled, so I shan't go just now.

Monday evening.

I meant to finish this off by answering your letters and thanking you all for your Christmas kindnesses; but having had a busy day, I have only just time to finish up anyhow, and get this off in time for the post. Have been busy since 6.30 this morning (it's now after 7) with the exception of 'brunch' from 10 to 11.30. I hope you are all fit and happy. Best love and best luck to all; I will answer your kind letters when I get a chance. I haven't been to the Club for three nights running!

Yours affectionately
Allan

A posting to the edge of Empire; in January 1910 Allan relinquished his Civil Police posting and was, at last, rewarded with the job of Assistant Commandant of the Lakhimpur Military Police Battalion stationed at Dibrugarh. Here, on the shore of the Bramaputra River in a 'country of infinite distances' (Angus Hamilton, In Abor Jungles) the 'wandering boy' arrived by boat (65 miles from Sadiya) with a Gurkha servant he had sprung from Sylhet gaol, a blind bull terrier and fewer debts, looking forward to leading Gurkha troops once more. The Military Police was formed after the Mutiny to replace the earlier, mutinous force and at the time Allan joined comprised around 5000 British and native officers and 170,000 sepoys in nine divisions. On the northern frontiers the Police comprised battalions commanded and trained by officers of the Indian Army. 'The life of the European Police Officer in India' wrote Angus Hamilton 'is passed in the open air, and is not unaccompanied by excitement and adventure, while blessed with opportunities for sport of all kinds. The pay is good; promotion is secure.'

Even now, Dibrugarh seems an astonishingly long way from anywhere, pressed into the bottleneck of an alluvial plain 450 miles long and 50 miles wide with the Himalaya to the north and the Assam ranges to the south and east. In 1910, even the flat country near to the river was an impenetrable, dense jungle of leeches and disease; the military maps that Allan would have used faded into nothingness at the edges, marked 'unexplored territory'. But this was Assam where, on the rich soil and for endless miles, a vast amount of private British and European capital was invested in the tea crop – an investment reputed to be Europe's greatest by far. In 1838 the first 12 boxes of Assam tea arrived in London; by 1910 there were more than 750,000 'coolies' working 400,000 acres of plantations, most of them for white owners. As Allan describes it: 'The white population consists of a handful of officials amid hundreds of square miles of howling natives.'

Steamers carrying tea to Chittagong for export crowded the Bramaputra River – a mile wide at Dibrugarh. The tea gardens themselves were 'as isolated as Australian sheep runs' and yet the planters came to Dibrugarh and made it 'pretty and prosperous' with an excellent hospital, a race course, golf club, a branch of the Assam and Planters Stores and a District Club 'from where dispensed a generous hospitality somewhat stronger than the cup that cheers.' (The planters' hospitality was revered and feared).

In this farthest corner of the Empire, British interests were served by British justice enforcing the rule of law amongst a vast pool of indentured labourers, administrative genius and military presence. But even the British Raj had its limits and here they were marked by a line drawn on the map of hills and forests beyond which British protection was no more than notional and British subjects were not allowed. Beyond the line numerous ethnically related and constantly warring tribes were mostly left to their own designs as semi-independent subjects. Semi-independent; which meant that should the Chinese enter from the north they would be considered as trespassers on British sovereign territory and ejected. It was the Great Game adapted for the north-east frontier with a smaller British presence but the same practical approach to divide and rule in which chieftains were paid an annual bounty to rebuff Chinese approaches and acknowledge, for what it mattered, British dominion. Behind the line they were free to pursue old allegiances and rivalries unless and until the Pax Britannica was so jeopardised as to threaten the bigger interests at play, at which point the deputy commissioner would assert political control by punitive, military intervention. Certain tribes mostly inhabited the British side of the line; the Nagas lived on both sides; others almost exclusively in the 'wilds' beyond, but alliances were ever-changing and often struck with a particular chieftain or village.

It was in this fascinating, half-explored land – the 'forgotten frontier' of the Abors –that Allan sought to satisfy his appetite for adventure, in his longed for military posting to the north. In August 1910, a good 18 months earlier than hoped for, he was gazetted a captain. Can we detect a different kind of tone in the following letters? Has Allan gone a tiny bit doolali?

Chittagong
18 Janr. 10

My dearest Family

You'll be surprised to see me back again on the old pitch. The fact of the matter was that I was summoned down to give evidence in a case on Monday (yesterday); I arrived on Saturday morning, and having done my part, am now enjoying a few 'days casual on the bust' as our Mr. Kipling puts it [see below].

I arranged my departure from Sylhet so as to catch the train on last Friday by which mine ancient enemy, Bonham-Carter, the Inspector-General of Police was travelling from Shillong to Dacca; and bearded him in his saloon; with the I shall be very grateful. My pay will be slightly more than at present, until Aug. when my Captaincy will increase it. He informed me I should be transferred within 10 days or so to be an Asst. Commdt. of the Lakhimpur Mily. Police Battn. which is at Dibrugarh; the vacancy occurring thro' the absence on sick-leave of Lt. Beeman. The matter has to be referred to Govt. of India, but in the meantime, B.-C has asked the local Govt. to post me pending orders. He further gave me to understand that before Beeman returned, there would be a nice vacancy at Kohima (Naga Hills Mily. Police) waiting for me and the work will be more pleasant. It's true that Dibru. is an expensive place, as it is a very gay station; but as the battn. has about 20 detachments, I hope to spend a lot of time on tour, earning T.A. So I have another 2 years (or 3 with extension) to look forward to in this Province.

I seized the opportunity also of holding the old man down until he granted me 7 days C. L. to be spent here; I had applied some time previously for 10 days to come down for the 'Week' (you know what a 'Week' is, don't you?) but as the week had been cancelled, owing to a death from plague (imported) and B-C hadn't answered my application the matter had fallen thro'; but as I was here (and drawing T.A. for the journey) I thought I might as well have a bit of leave too. Old Craven is putting me up (at the Keeley Institute) and the Neilsons are as good to me as ever. Others profess gratification at my speedy return, and all are very polite.

So poor Sylhet has about seen the end of me. I will return there, of course, to pack up etc. but my labours to make things uncomfortable for the Force there will abruptly cease. I'm sorry in a way, but there you are. I hope to gather a bit of moss in spite of the adage.

Many thanks for your letter of 22 Decr. Glad the tea arrived and was acceptable. Is it really good? What is this about Kitty going back so soon, & why? I'm rather surprised. Thanks for the other news & Podgie's note. I've no more time to write, so excuse myself

Your affectionate 'wandering boy'
Allan

P.S. As fit as ever, thank goodness. Same to you, and many of 'em.

A Ballad of Burial, Rudyard Kipling
Recollect a Padre must
Mourn the dear departed one –
Throw the ashes and the dust.

Don't go down at once. I trust
You will find excuse to 'snake
Three days' casual on the bust.'
Get your fun for old sake's sake.

Letts No 46 Rough Diary

Saturday 5 February 1910
Arrived Dibrugah 3 pm. Dunbar met me. Went to live with him. Wrote letter and posted.

Tuesday 15 February 1910
About 3 am waked by approaching storm. Turned out Bahadun and tried to fix tent. When storm burst everything went; B and I (in pyjamas) sat out in sheets of rain and tried to hold her up without much success. Passed off and we lit fires, wrapped ourselves in the few dry things and waited for day. Went out and shot a Brahiminy. Left by boat with B about 10.30 back to Dibru about 1.30.

★★★

Dibrugarh
21. 2. 10

Dear Ma and Pa

I think it's time I sent you a letter again, after writing the last few weeks to the other members of the family. Your last fine favour to me is (mamma's) of 27th Jan. giving the news of Kitty's departure again for Mexico. Wasn't it a pity that our visits could not have coincided? I was rather surprised to hear that she was going back so soon, as I thought she would stay longer through the cold weather – I mean winter – excuse my Anglo-Indianisms.

Many thanks for the *County Timeses*; I'm surprised and pleased that J. D. got in again; but how he has the nerve to sit as a Liberal beats me, or how the b_Rads. can vote for him.

So you've been skating have you? It's pretty cold here, the last few days (do you notice how far I am from the paltan? We are just in the extreme corners of the Frontier and wet too, though, of course we are 20 or 30 miles from the hills. I was out in camp for a couple of nights last weekend and had to turn out and hold my tent up in a raging thunder and hail-storm clad only in my pyjamas; when it was over the only dry stitches in my camp were my dressing gown (which I assumed) and two of my blankets by the aid of these, and some wood by them from a neglected boat hard-by for a fire, we shivered it out till morning. No ill effects ensued. What's going to happen to the Govt. now that they're in again? Will then be another General Election? The things must be quite exciting, the noo. [The Liberals had won massively in the 1906 election with a mandate for social reform and state welfare – a mandate subsequently frustrated by the Lords. In November 1910 the Liberals threatened a Parliament Act to permanently curb the powers of the upper house – it got through by a whisker.]

It's a decent place, and I'm very comfy and like the work; and my boss is quite tractable. [Sir George Duff-Sutherland Dunbar of Hempriggs, 6th Baronet Dunbar, Commander of the Military Police, Assam, who was mentioned in despatches from the forthcoming Abor Campaign and went on to fight in two World Wars. Allan describes him a 'bit of an ass' but Dunbar shows tact and loyalty to his Assistant and Allan does admit 'He is really awfully good in the way he lets me have my own way in most things.' Allan was to become great friends with Lady Sybil Dunbar who joined her husband at their shared bungalow and tragically died six months later.] I don't know many people here yet; I'm not the Society Pet that I was at Chittagong, as I go out very little.

My skipper and I have a quite decent bungalow, and I run the servants and Commissariat etc. I generally go on Parade about 6.30 (Standard. That's about 7.30 local time) and get back to an early brekker about 8.30. After that I write and see to the house etc and get to office about 10 and am there till 1. Then we get back for Tiffin. After that, I may, or may not, go on 3 pm parade with the recruits, or play hockey or go for a ride, on Dunbar's pony (yes, I have another free horse – he never goes near it) and generally go to the Club about 6.30, or else stay home and write letters. At the Club I bridge; or twice a week, dance; we dine nominally at 8, which generally means 8.30 or 8.45 (isn't it a shocking hour?) That is one of the characteristics of this province. We, most of us, in the towns, think in Standard time; the real time is one hour <u>later</u>; fancy dining at quarter to ten! It was just as bad in Chittagong …

Our bungalow is raised off the ground on pillars. My personal staff now consists of the bearer-bhit-cook; and Gurkha that I caught at Sylhet; my orderly, another Gurkha. I've had such awful bother to get a decent servant, ever since my Almora boy went back from Chittagong. There was never any question of his staying of course; he only came to see me settled, as those people won't leave the Hills. I'd had him about 3 years. Since then, I've had 5; you don't get the same stamp of man on this side of the Bay as you do up in India proper. Here, being scarce, they are frightfully over-paid and independent. The chap I've got now is the third experiment of importing from the Calcutta agency that I tried. The others went back in double quick time. This is a rather respectable sort of old devil; a Punjabi Mohammedan, but he's doing a month, which is unheard of; the Almera lad I told you of, was getting 11 when he left me; I started him on 8. The Gurk is not much good, being stupid, even for a Gurkh, which is saying a good deal; I picked him up out of Sylhet Jail! Partly because I was sorry to see a Gurk stranded there, partly because it's a good, if extravagant thing, to have a dependable champ [like] that and attached to one, when one moves from place to place so much; (being a foreigner himself, he's not likely to chuck in his job because you leave a place) and partly for his physique, which is very sturdy. He was in the Lushar Hills Military police and got 18 months for hammering his subadar; I wrote to his C.O. about him, and he said he'd be glad to see him employed again. Billy will be interested to know that his name is the Gurkhali equivalent for her old friend, Sherebahadur; it is Bhagbir. They both mean Brave Tiger which is inspiring. The bearer's name is Asphan Dayalshan which is also sonorous. The orderly's name is just Bahadur – meaning Brave. He's a good able chap, and very useful; wish my old ass, Bhagbir, was more like him. These, with Venus my Bull-terrier (the deaf 'un; have I told you about her? She's a good-looking and well bred beast, but rather wayward and a deaf dog is not much use. Old Johnson was blind, you remember?), make up my personal incumbents as the house-servants I have, with the khansama, the masalchi (male kitchen maid, or scullion!) sweeper, dholin (washer man) mali (gardeners), etc. I give you the list because these details fill up the letter and may interest you, showing what life in the Shiny is like. I felt most chuffed the other day, out with Bagbir loaded with guided guns and knives hanging on behind, hacking through rough heavy jungle. We have to use elephants a lot in these parts, as the few roads are only by courtesy.

Well, nummore. Best love to all I hope you and all is fit as this old sinfulness.

Yours affectionately
Allan

★★★

Dibrugarh
Assam
25. 4. 10

It seems very long time since I wrote you, someone I have to acknowledge receipt in the interim of your kind favour of 17th and 31st ult. and several newspapers, including one in which George laid bare the hideous secrets of his past, and looked so pretty in the pictures.

No, mamma, I'm not going out and wasting my substance in the way you hint; in fact, the necessary company indicated in the parable would be hard to come by in Dibru; but apart from that, am leading a godly, righteous, and sober life. Well, if not the first two, anyway the third; I've just finished my dinner-peg (I'm writing after dinner) and that's my 'first today'; and will for probably be my last, unless I sit up much later than I expect. Oh, I'm very good; and though I haven't yet succeeded in saving any money, I'm sub-scribing quite a lot to paying off debts. The total is still formidable; I reduced it to paper recently, I thing I never have the pluck to do before! And last month I paid off Rs.550, which, considering my pay and allowances come to 555 less income tax and deductions, is rather a record isn't it? How's it done, you ask? The soldier's friend, my dears; good old T.A. I haven't quite made my 200 T.A. this month but close on it, and I'm going to try to complete the turn round before the 30th.

Wharryer mean by your dark saying about people taking all I give? I'm not giving much these hard times. Life is a continual dual a la mort with my bearer and the cook; they have to sit up at nights thinking of ways to get round the sahib.

I have a great deal of work to do, and am very happy in consequence. It may interest pah to know that this battn. is in a pretty low state of efficiency. The last Cmdt. was a 'charming fellow'; used to every Gymkhana and race-meet etc. in the place, and presented with an enormous silver bowl as a testimonial from the residents when he left; pershonally, to quote the illustrious Phillup, I should like to present him with the toe of an ammunition boot, except that cleaning up after him gives me an interest in life. However, Dunbar and self mean to have things ship-shape before we are done, and the prairie is on fire, I tell you. I think most of the men and native officers appreciate our efforts, though it has brought trouble to the doorsteps of a few on 'em! At present, besides my ordinary work (training recruits, doing Adjt. and inspecting the numerous outposts) I am retraining the drill-staff from the very beginning and also the whole of the N.C.O.s of the battn; and introducing 'bundobast' [contract or agreement] into a very go-as-you-please sort of system. Well, it's all very rewarding sort of work, the men are keen enough, though they are inclined to think I'm a sort of Fee-fo-fum to whom the blood of a wretched N.C.O. is a necessary daily sacrifice.

What a blow about the Logan girl; I suppose it's too late now, but she was too good for what's his name. I'm rather sorry I didn't have a shot myself now; she was a nice girl.

Although this place is supposed to be expensive by living quietly I find it quite cheap. (Dunbar has asked me to go on living with 'em when Lady D. comes out in the autumn, which will mean continuance of the sober life). There is more T. A. to be made, the shooting is better, I shall be able to play polo, and I shall know the ropes; and besides all that, I have my heart in the job, and want to see this is a damn smart battalion. So I hope they'll be able to leave me alone.

Did I tell you of the Dr. Findlay? I went out to hunt tigers with? Well, as 'a little return' he has sent me a most scrumpchuous thermos flask, which bears my tea when I'm on the wing. I was out a good deal last month and this month I was up at Sadiya (map please) twice; it's right near our frontier, and the guards round it are quite interesting. I returned last time from Sadiya by boat all the way; 65 miles down the Brahmaputra – did it in 11 hours too. This is good going at 8 annas a mile, isn't it?

Well, nummore. Best love to you all, and hoping you are as fit as this old flesh.

Yours affectionately
Allan

★★★

Tiger hunt. 'He looked about the size of Europe (he was only 10 yards off) and was indeed a noble sight ... Well, it was an experience, but it's rather sickening.'

Dibrugarh,
Assam
4th April 1910

My dearest Pa, and Ma, and Podgie,

An awful thought has occurred to me that I never wrote to thank the latter dear child for her kind present to me on Xmas day; did I, or did I not? About that time, my rapid alternations from place to place, etc. so mixed up my correspondence that I cannot mind whether I did or not; but either way, I hope she doesn't think I'm not grateful for the kind thought, because I am; and the little book is so useful that I wonder I never got one before. I used to have to search through piles of untidy papers (the heredi-tary instincts are strong in me) before I could find an address; now the 'where-is-it?' accompanies me everywhere, and I note with the greatest business punctuality such items as 'the Duke of Devonshire, Carlton Club', 'Masich Cigarettes, Dott, Wellesley Street, Calcutta.', 'Tottie, c/o Doorkeeper, Piccadilly Hotel', 'Vet for Bull-dog, Ashdown, Middx.' etc. etc. (Note: some of these items are slightly exaggerated!) and can look 'em up at once. I wish someone would send me the family birthdays, so that I could enter them, too. I have asked this a thousand times.

I beg to acknowledge receipt of Mamma's letters of 24th Feb. and 3rd March; also a *County Times* last week, and to give thanks there for. I see poor old Cap. Myttar is dead, so suppose George is now the squire. I should think the community lose some ability by the exchange, and do not gain much in the way of polish.

How's the Prince's visit getting on? Will George (our's) get an M.V.O. or anything of that sort, for holding the bridges steady while he crosses 'em?

My stable companion Dunbar and I get on all right together; there's no use trying to disguise the fact that he's a bit of an ass, but he's very good to me, and we can work together very well, as he is quite amenably good-natured. If I want a thing done in a certain way, a little tact generally ensures that it's done so. His wife will probably come out in a few months, and, if I stay on, he wants me to live with them. I dare say I shall take it on, as I'm beginning to steady down, and married life – I don't mean that, life in a married family would be good for me. If course, it has its drawbacks, but I dare say I could stick it for a bit, and it wouldn't be a bad thing in a way.

You will be very glad to hear that I am very <u>abstemious</u>, and have been for some time now. I generally drink soda for lunch (!) and limit myself to a peg before, a peg at, and a peg after dinner, this has been going on for <u>months</u>. Isn't I clever?

I like Mamma's way of saying that Elliott 'was doctor to the tea-planters'. If you had any idea of the size of Assam, and the number of tea-gardens, you'd larf as I do. I hap-pened to meet one lady who knew them rather well, as I told you. She lives only <u>five hours</u> by rail from here, and is therefore a sort of next-door neighbour.

I've been to church since, twice. Once at Chittagong, on Easter Sunday nought nine; partly to please Mamma, and partly to please Mrs. Walsh who paraded me as a natural curiosity up the aisle; and once at Sylhet, on Christmas day last, when on my arrival, the congregation consisted of two missionary ladies, these being struck dumb by the arrival of so dangerous a blade as your servant, the psalms resolved themselves into a dialogue between the parson (also a missionary, and very Owen-Morganish, if you take me) and me; I thought it was up to me to see the thing through, and talked about wombs and harlots as if I had been brought up for the Church, in fine sonorous tones. The arrival of some less bashful ladies, about the first lesson, relieved me of the burden of the responses; and I retired into my shell, and read *The Maxims of La Rochfoucould* (spelling uncertain) in a tasteful prayer-book-like binding and generally gave the impression that I was an earnest young feller. I would have kept up my good resolution of going to church last Easter Sunday to please Mamma, but was out in the junghole.

I hope poor pa gets his motor car all right, and doesn't bump his nose again driving it. Is the nose quite well now? It was nearly so when last I heard.

Things are going on nicely here, thank you. I'm living pretty cheaply, and even saving a little. I am getting Cox to send you £7.3.7 this week, which please apply as follows, <u>immediately</u>. Please don't bank it or anything, but just pay it off direct.

£5. 0.0. to George Evans (make him send a receipt.)

£1.4.0 to Turner for the Fox-pad.

3.9 to 'the Wilson Vety. Medicine Manufacturing coy., Ashford, Middx.

£7.3.7.

If you will do this, and tell 'em who it's from I shall be greatly relieved.

There is a globe-trotting doctor here (or was until a day or two back) named Findlay. George, (my stable companion), made rather a lot of him, as his wife is a bit of a toff, too. (George is an awful snob, you must know, and seems to find his title a size large) to wit, Lady Sybil Findlay (she was a Tollemache, or something like that) and also they are pretty lucre-ish. So George promised Findlay (who's a very decent chap) to provide a tiger for him to shoot, on an island about 12 miles up the river, as Findlay who has shot most things, has never seen a tiger. Well, George found he had other fish to fry; had to go down to Tezpur, partly to chase T.A. (which is his shining goal) and partly to chase some skirt or other. So he tells me to take Findlay off to this place Chark for a week, do him and myself well, and charge it up to him. Which, as Harry Lauder says, 'I certainly did do, without the slightest (hic!) hesitation.' I took out 100 Gurks, 5 tents (besides the men's), a cook, scullion, two servants, my orderly, two mighty hunters from the lines, four boatmen to do a daily post, and generally fixed ourselves up like lords. Findlay was very pleased, and we got rather matey. He's quite a nice chap, and very interesting, as there are few parts of the globe he hasn't visited. Well, we spent several days arranging the beats, and then started beating; there were tigers about but I didn't succeed in honking me up to the guns; it was very interesting and we enjoyed it all right. But poor Findlay didn't get his shot, although we tried all sorts of things. We wouldn't fire at anything except tiger, on account of disturbing the noble hannimile. Findlay had to leave on Friday. (Good); I stayed on till Monday, and then shot a big pig, one or two hog-deer, and duck, snipe and jungle-fowl. On Easter Sunday I got fresh rehabar [from Persian *Rahbar*, 'guide', hence traces] of a kill quite close, and sat up that evening. The weather had been atrocious all the time; poorin'o'rain, but it was a fine evening for a change, with a misty moon. About 7.30, when I had begun to give him up, my lord suddenly turned up. Whoo! I was excited. He looked about the size of Europe (he was only 10 yards off) and was indeed a noble sight. He was very suspicious. I tried to get on to him (I had a double.470 high velocity belonging to Dunbar) but I could not get a sight on him. When I raised my head a bit, I could see my barrels, but as soon as I put my head down to the butt, I lost 'em, and couldn't tell whether I was coming at him or Timbuctoo. This went on for some time, and then he winded me and cleared and went off, as I knew, to go round behind me and see what I was, and how employed. I sat very still, I assure you. My machan was only 9 or 10 feet high and open at the back. For half an hour I never moved an eyelash, and cursed my fate, making almost sure he would spot me and get out; but about 8.15 he turned up again on the other side of me; and after a few more attempts to get a sight on him, I fired more or less blindly. Oh! The language!! I found afterwards I broke a hind leg, but from the way he chewed about, and swore, I thought I'd got him through the loins. Well, he banged off after he had exhausted his vocabulary (I wasn't able to get in a 2nd barrel) and I felt rather pleased with life. Waited half an hour, and then sneaked out of the jungle very quietly, and so home to camp. Met one of the elephants ½ way coming to find me. Ordered them to be ready at 4 a.m. and turned in. At 3 a.m. I woke with a start, and found the heaviest rainstorm that we had coming up. Goodbye, tiger, says I to myself, and sure 'nuff, before we could begin to search, not only was there no chance of a blood track, but the foot-prints even of the buffaloes were washed flat. I was awful fed up, and came in that day. I left a couple of men out, in case the vultures found him, but they came in on Saturday, and said he had crossed to the N. Bank, dragging a hind leg. So endeth my first tiger. Well, it was an experience, but it's rather sickening.

I must wind up now. I'm very busy these days. George an' me gave a dinner party last Wednesday; rather a snob, with our band in attendance, etc. The Findlays; one Elmes, a planter, who is an old friend of theirs; Mainwairing-White of the 120th, rather a nice chap; and George an' me. We did 'em rather well. On Thursday I dined with the Bentincks, the Deputy Commissioner. She is rather a saucy little puss, but country-bred. On Friday, the Bentincks roped me in again for pot-luck; we played Auction, at which I'm getting rather keen. It has a great vogue here. Tonight we dine the Bentincks, a spin, and one Hore (I don't mean what you mean) who is Adjt. of the 120th. Its another rather snob affair. Band again, etc. We dine at 8, it's twenty to now and George is yelling to me to get my trousers on before Mrs. B. arrives.

So farewell. Best love. All's well, hope you're the same,

Yours affectly,
Allan

★★★

2nd May 1910
Dibrugarh
Assam

Dear Billiam

It doesn't take much, by the way, for mamma to be *glad* about the reform of my character. Instead of being properly confounded and amazed, she merely adjures me to become a 'total abstainer'. Lumme, some people are never satisfied and the expression used is such an unpleasant one. It always makes me think of a person who not only does not drink, or smoke, or eat, but also denies himself the satisfaction of the 'Ty Bach'. Why mortify the poor flesh, after all? There's quite enough unpleasantness banging about in this old world of sin 'without going out of one's way to hunt up trouble'.

More good news for the old lady: I went to Church last Friday, for the Memorial Service [For Edward VIII, who died 6 May; his horse had won at Newmarket earlier that day and his last words were 'I am glad']. A lot of people came in, and the place was full of fair women and I'll have you know I fairly knocked 'em in my gleaming panoply of war. Poor old King; so sad to think he has gone.

There's an old flame of mine turned up here. Did I ever tell you of a nurse who came to Almora to nurse Mrs. Allen, the District Commissioner's wife? Mrs. A. was a weird bird and quite dotty; she thought it was *so* dull for a nice girl at Almora, not knowing a soul; and it would be *such* a kindness if I (who had dropped in to have a look round) would come round sometimes and cheer her up and take her for walks of an evening. At which the gallant Bill, encountering the 'nice girl' with merry brown eye (she really was a 'nice girl'), replied courteously 'Pas demi' and it was all as easy as falling off a log. They used to pull my leg about it and had deals at Almora; 'thoroughly trustworthy' was the great draw. Well the 'nice girl' is stationed here now and we had a great bukh about old times the other day.

Yours
Allan

★★★

Dibrugarh
Assam
11.7.10

Dearest Mamma

(You see this is a specially addressed letter this week, which is a great honour. You must pass on the news, however!)

You and my other worthy parent must be in town now; I hope the old man enjoys his Bisley and gets a bull's eye. It's very sporting of him, and I expect there will be one or two even in that gathering of select shots who will find who is the King of Glory yet. The best of luck to him; and may you both enjoy your visit.

Yes, I'll be careful of the nurse, thank you, the designing minx. She's been away a long time now, but is coming back. She's a nice girl, though not so young as she was, like poor Bill.

Yes, it seems certain I shall stop on here for a year or so, and I'm pleased at the prospect. My skipper has been up at Shillong interviewing the tin-hats, and says all is well, and that he has been buttering me up to them. I must say, I do a fair amount here, and he would miss my guiding hand in the majority of daily matters. This entre nous, of course. He knows it, and so do I; and the value of velvet -glove is appreciated by both of us. He is really awfully good in the way he lets me have my own way in most things. At present to all intents and purposes, I run the battalion, while he goes in for bigger questions of improvements, organisation etc; I am too busy with detail etc. to mix up with them much at present. I'm frightfully busy these days, from dawn till dewy eve. But enough bukh about shop; it's a labour of love anyway. So, I'm not a total abstainer yet, and don't know what Lord Chesterfield had said about it. But am a very good boy, considering.

When Dunbar was in t'other day we had a little dinner-party (I still housekeep) ourselves, and the superintendent of Police, with his new bride, a pretty and charming girl. We were very frivolous and did not break up till 12.30. He has a past, of which I know, but don't expect she does! A woman I knew had an 'affaire' with him a few years back; she has been writing to me, to pump me about the bride. Being a tactful person sometimes, I led her to believe it was a broken heart seeking consolation. Well, <u>she </u>has consoled <u>herself</u> once or twice since she threw him over, so there's no need to waste sympathy on her. But it will comfort her to think he is still faithful! I <u>am</u> getting a beast, ain't I? – but it's rum the odd ways one gets to know bits of other people's histories.

Well, no more except best love to all.
Yours affectionately
Allan

★ ★ ★

'I am 31 today and a gallant Captain.' On 18 August 1910, Allan was gazetted Captain in the 3rd Queen Alexandra's Own Gurkha Rifles. He took a month's leave, travelling down to Chittagong to play golf, ride and make up parties on the river and, on 14 September, celebrate his 31st birthday. His letter home announcing the promotion is understated, though he must have been thrilled to pass on the news and especially to his father.

Chittagong
E.B.
14.9.10

Dearest Family

I'm afraid I missed last mail; while I have two of your (mother's) letters to answer. It being my birthday, and mail-day, I feel I must try and get you a line, though there doesn't seem much news to communicate. I expect to hear from you tomorrow, by the way. The mail gets in here in Mondays, but my letters go to Dibu first of course.

Well, I am 31 today and a gallant Captain. Did I tell you that I had been in the Gazette of India, 'subject to His Majesty's approval', as usual? The date is the 18th of Aug, I think. I'm still down here, you see, though my leave approaches its end. I leave for Dibu and work on today week. It has been very pleasant. I golf a good deal, and get asked out a lot to dinners, breakfasts, rides, drives, etc. etc. People are very kind and I could do a lot more of that sort of thing, if I liked, I think. Both my host and hostess have had spells of seediness since I've been down, but at present are fairly well, though she won't be right until she goes home, which will probably be next April. This is a bad climate if you're at all delicate, and she has had a bad year of it. The baby, however, flourishes, and is a fine and bouncing boy, with a devil of a temper; all same like mamma. We've had two babies on the premises, by the way, most of the time; another woman got very ill, so Mrs. N. took the baby; it used to howl all day, and most nights, have convulsions, and diarrhoea, and fight with Sonny. So things were lively.

We had another dance a week last Monday; again we were all dined at the Club before it. Another two or three nights we dined out and bridged that week; and twice we went on the river in a launch; and teach.

Today, we go down to the jettas and have tea on a ship; tomorrow, we dine at the club, and bridge. On Saturday I dine at a bachelor party; and there are innumerable other little things that I have forgotten. Golf fills up the chinks. So I've been enjoying my leave, and having no spare time.

So Amy's married, is she? Well, I expect somebody will be led a dance.

Well, I've no time for more just now, so will close.

Best love to all, and best luck
Yours affectionately
Allan

★★★

On a river steamer
22. 10. 10

Dearest family

I'm off into the wilds and have just found that if I'm to get a letter to you this mail I must write it now; so here goes. I'm on my way to a guard of ours called Harmatti, which is near North Kakhimpur, in order to make preliminary arrangements for this 'yer expedition against the Daphlar. Harmatti is to be our base; we collect there etc and start off on 8th Nov. into the hills. We expect to be back at Harmatti in about a fortnight. We are taking up 100 rifles. Williamson, the Political chap at Sadiya is in charge; Dunbar and myself are going with the Escort, and one Hore, the adjt. of the regt. at Dibni, has got himself attached as Intelligence Officer. The objective of the expedish is to punish the Daphlas for raiding into our country, and recover some elephant catchers whom they have bagged as slaves. Thanks to the way the Local Government find fit to jaw, back-talk and for regarding so serious a step as the movement of 100 men (they've been at it about 6 months!) and the close interest which our able Indian Secretary of State has in matters which he can know dam' all about, and it's not probable that the expedition will serve any very useful end, or attain any very definite result; our friends the enemy are expecting thus, and being persons having a respectable amount of intelligence will withdraw themselves and their belongings to places where we cannot follow them, until such time as the extremely limited transport gives out (money cannot be spared for such purposes; it being required to build sedition centres in the shape of colleges down in Bengal) and we withdraw ourselves. However we get a chance of seeing some new country, so are pleased to go. Williamson and I are fore-gathering here and going to have a look at routes, etc. I have 25 rifles along; I also have to see about getting our people from the river up to Harmatti. They follow down with Dunbar in about a week. Lady D. wants to come too, to see us off. Then Beeman (did I tell you he was back?) and she keep the nest at Dibru warm until we return, about the beginning of Decr. Then I go up to Sadiya. I <u>cannot</u> remember what I have told you, or not told you. Did I tell you that we are trying to get sanction to increase our Sadiya detachment to 200 rifles? The idea being that in that secluded spot, without outside distraction in the way of duties etc and on its excellent training terrain a really first-rate British officer (me) will be able to knock 'em into such shape that the perambulating Abor will tremble with fear, and they will be available as a striking force at a day's notice. Sort of movable column, in fact; <u>under</u>, as I have hinted, a specially selected officer. H'm. As a matter of fact, I believe Beeman and I will take it in turns to be up there, but I go first.

I think I have described Lady D. do you? She is an exceedingly amusing person, and makes us all laugh immoderately with the jokes. She's about Billy's age, rather plump and quite good-looking. She doesn't cotton to Dibru society much; I'm not surprised, as there really are damn few presentable women close at hand, and it must be hard at her age to adapt herself to enjoying a new style of acquaintance.

By the way, I'm sending to home a chest of Assam Tea, made by a peculiarly expert feller near Dibru. It ought to be good. It's very strong (Broken Orange Pekoe) and should be made with freshly boiled water, allowed to stand eight minutes (or less if preferred, then swill round and pour off the tea leaves into another pot. Don't forget the water should not be allowed to go on boiling more than a minute or two once it comes to the boil, or the tea will be spoilt. There are 65 pounds of it; and as this seems rather a lot for you, I should be glad if you would have three neat boxes made, of about 10 pounds each, and send one to Becky, one to Maude, and one to Aunt Loo as a Christmas present. The rest is my Christmas present to you. I hope you're very fit and happy I'm wunnerful thank you. I expect my letters will be a bit irregular now for the next month or so, so don't surprised. Best love to all.

Yours affectionately
Allan

In Pursuit of Daphla Kidnappers

In the following letters Allan describes his pursuit of Daphla tribesmen who, deep in the jungle, had kidnapped and enslaved government-endorsed elephant catchers. After months of political prevarication he is instructed to lead a force of 100 men and accompany Noel Williamson, the Political Officer in a punitive expedition against the kidnappers, who have refused to pay a fine. Using a map that was 35 years old and with little detail Allan set out up a 'boulder-strewn, swift river and through jungle which had to be cut through' to establish secure depots, with several days' hacking, leech-ridden march between each. Leaving Williamson at the first depot, Fort St David at the confluence of the Borpani and the Dibrang rivers (whose sources were still disputed), Allan decided he should continue 'into the unknown' to reconnoitre the country. The two men had never taken to each other – 'it was love at first sight but the other way round' – and when Williamson demanded Allan stayed at St David a row erupted. Allan presented his papers: no, he was not under W's command and would proceed as he saw fit, moving on to establish a route and depots that might put the party within striking distance of the kidnappers' village. If the mission failed or turned into a fiasco Allan's head would be served on a plate. If he succeeded, with the backing of his commanding officer and an apology, he might look forwards to better things.

Letts No 46 Rough Diary

Wednesday 2 November 1910
At Fort St David, very busy preparing camp and defences.

Friday 11 November 1910
Fort St Andrew. Up at daylight. Column, after lot of fiddling about, started at mid-day and left me alone. Offered W a species of apology which was accepted. Dunbar very gratified which is what was required.

Friday 8 November 1910

Climbed more hills and got eaten by more leeches. Must be losing pints of blood daily. Column came in unexpectedly about 2, 3 o'clock having accomplished their mission, recovered the two slaves, done a lot of damage, shot two Daphlas for certain and bringing 17 prisoners. Very busy inded getting them all bedded down.

19 November 1910 Saturday

Found Dunbar in dusters about too much rations to take down. Pointed out that W had told me not to worry about them so D asked me to go over and see him. He lost his temper as usual and denied everything until I dragged it from him step by step. But he wouldn't own up.

★★★

Fort William (in the wilds)
24 Nov. 1910
& 25

My dearest Guv'nor

I'm afraid I've been very bad in the matter of letters lately but as a matter of fact I have had such a devil of a lot to think of, and have been so busy. However having now a few spare hours, and it being a month to Christmas, and am killing two birds with one stone, by writing to send you my best wishes for a happy Christmas, and a Merry New Year, and to tell you all about it, as I'm sure you'll be dying to hear. It's a long narrative, but here goes.

In the first place let me explain that the Daphlas (Assamese name) are one of the small independent races of Hill savages who border our North-East Frontier, which in Assam lies along the foot of the Himalayas, and is a vague and much disputed boundary, lying for the most part in that No-Man's land of impenetrable forest. Their particular bit lies between the Akas, and the Hill. Mins and Abors, which names you will probably find on the map. They are a small people, but in common with the rest of their kind have for ages levied toll on the wretched Assamese of the plains; in fact to this day the Govt. pays them all 'posee' (subsidy) nominally to assist a pauper people (they have practically no government, you know) to maintain a force which will prevent their unruly spirits from raiding, but really as a recognition to their early rights of blackmail. The country is highly precipitous, and covered with dense jungle; there are no communications, except the beds of the mountain streams; where nominal paths exist between villages they are so precipitous as to be impassable for anything but an active man. The jungle is practically untraversable, except here and there. Of course by cutting, one can make a mile or so a day, an an active man, used to jungle work can get about by knowing the country, using the river beds, and elephant paths, and also freely using his dao, or kukri or axe or whatever his national tool may be (Assam is a country of mixed races, I can tell you. On this expedition there were some 7 or 8 separate and distinct languages spoken over the fires of a night, although the force was so small). Well, the Daph has been getting his tail up during the last few years; there was a big expedition which over-ran their country about 35 years ago, but since then they've not been touched; and all these tribes require punching about once in a generation 'lest they forget'. The policy of Government invariably encourages their forgetfulness; but I digress. In this case, after one of their little raids, in which they carried off the couple of Assamese who were employed elephant-hunting, as slaves (all our friends here are great slave-holders) they were far more truculent then is usual in these frequent occurrences. They not only refused to pay the fine which Govt. inflicted, or to give up their slaves, but even to say they were sorry. This is, against the rules of the game; Govt. will let 'em play hell for years provided they will pretend that they're sorry and send in driblets of the ridiculously small fines imposed, presumably with the 'peace at any price' idea; but this defiance eventually stirred up even E.B. & A. Local Government, and the India Office, and after months of tearful trying to get out of it, it was decided to send a small party to try and get the slaves, and punish the particular villages who had bagged 'em. No soldiers, oh dear no; nothing aggressive; merely 100 military police to arrest law-breakers, and above all, the expenditure must not exceed a particular sum (very small) as the rest of the revenue is urgently required for building more colleges for Babus in E.B. and new houses at pleasant stations for the L.G. Very well then; 100 military police under their officer (me); the whole under the orders of a civilian, which brings us to Mr Noel Williamson; a strong character with something of a reputation at Shillong. He is the administrator of the Sadiya Frontier Tract, (which has nothing to do with the Daphlas, but they couldn't find anybody else for the job) and his reputation is for dealing with savages, exploration, and for being 'a masterful man'. I don't think he is particularly intellectual, but he's undoubtedly a good man at his job; and certainly a good selection for this particular show, if it were not for the fact that both my skipper and myself have been rather against him for some time. It's not so much my skipper, as me; from the first it's been a sort of love at first sight between us, the wrong way around. We are thrown together officially at Sadiya, to a certain extent; and I think have both gathered that we have no use for each other; I think we both think the other thinks too much of his own opinion! When we heard that he was to be in charge, there was dismay in M. P. circles at Dibru; I think Govt. which has an inkling of the situation, tried their dam'dist to find somebody else, but couldn't do it. However we made up our minds to try and get the thing through, both without giving W. a chance to pick holes in us (I ought to mention that one of our great causes of offence is that he damned the battn. in heaps on a show which he had before; before our time, but it does not tend to amity; they certainly were pretty bad in those days, but we believe that what really did the damage was the W.'s own 'masterfulness'; apparently the chap in command of the men let him curse and rag 'em about; one thing that Johnny Gurk will <u>not</u> stand from an outsider, even if he will from his own officers, which is not always) and without having 'friction' with him. We really made up our minds to swallow a lot, in order to get things through.

Now take your little maps (large scale, if possible) and see if you can find the Dibrang river running into the Brahmaputra from the North. I'm afraid you won't be able to, but it's about Long. 94° degrees. Up the Dibrang, where it crosses our Frontier, where we have an outpost and about 8 miles above Harmatti, the river Borpani runs into the

Dibrang from the S.W., flowing along in between a low outlying range of hills, and the main system of the Himalayas. All the country beyond our boundary, up to the Dibrang is uninhabited, and practically unknown jungle. It's only traversed on very rare occasions by the wandering elephant-hunter, and the occasional Daphla, who can come into Harmatti down the Borpani and trade. His home is much further up, in the higher hills; and his usual route to the plains (particularly of the particular ones we wanted to get at) is down the Poma river, which runs roughly parallel to the Dibrang much further west. But still, they could get in to Harmatti in the cold weather (which means the jungle is more possible, and the rivers traversable) and did; and it was a wily idea of Dunbar's (who has devoted months to working up routes and schemes for this show) to get in by the Borpani and catch the Daph. on the hop. Very well, then. Now it was very obvious that the sum which Government sanctioned for transport for the show, would not admit of our getting to our objective at all, unless we dodged 'em in some way. So W.& Dunbar laid at their heads together, and evolved the plan which has come off very successfully. Of course in this country coolie transport is the only thing to be thought of; but Dunbar had gathered by arduous inquiry from elephant-catchers etc that it would be barely possible to manhandle small boats up to the Borpani to the confluence of the Bahor river, which would be about 3 days from Harmatti and only a couple of days over the watershed into the Poma Valley, and our truculent Daphla friends. The expedition had orders from Govt. to commence from Harmatti on 8th Novr; but they thought if we could get all our supplies etc to Baharmukh (the point just mentioned) before they started, it would be a very much easier to make a show against the enemy; in fact, the only chance. Very well then.

On 20th of last month, I left Dibrugarh with 25 rifles, to go to Harmatti, make all arrangements for our force coming down to going on, and if possible, and I thought it practicable to try and sees Baharmukh to defend it before our people got to Harmatti first week in November. W. was also coming down to reconnoitre to make arrangements, and I was to render him every assistance I could, and above all, be careful not to quarrel with him! Dunbar was, of course, going up in command of the 100 rifles, but I was to accompany him, although not officially sanctioned by Govt.

Well, I met W. on the steamer going down, and although I could see him trying, at times, to avoid being nasty, we began to clash almost at once. We were both trying to swallow what we didn't like in the other, I think, but he didn't succeed as well as I did. After I made all my arrangements for getting the force to Harmatti etc and he had got his bundobast going on 25th he said he was going up the Dibrany and Borpani for a couple or three days; I said, 'could I come', and he said 'right oh'. We were to start the next day. Next morning, I was just ready to start, when I got a chit from him, ordering me to stop at Harmatti, because he had omitted to make arrangements to carry on his show there, and there would be no one to open his telegrams, etc. I was furious; according to our orders the show didn't begin until the 8th and I considered myself, according to my instructions absolutely on my own in the preliminary arrangements. I was in the middle of the letter telling him politely but definitely to go to the devil, when I thought better of it, and went down to parley with him instead. I thought to myself that if I could get him to do as I wanted without saying I wouldn't take his orders, I would swallow the rest, according to my instructions; in other words, if he liked to think he was giving me orders, he was welcome, so long as I carried out my job, and didn't fight. So I persuaded him that it would be better if I came, and I dug up a planter who said he'd open telegrams, etc. Mind, knowing my bird, I was perfectly aware that if I told him I couldn't take his orders, there would have been a 'breach of diplomatic relations' and he would have said 'You don't come up the river with me, either'. And if I'd said 'All right, I'll go on my own he'd have said the political situation does not admit of that and forbidden me to cross the Frontier. And I could not have gone in the face of that; so all my instructions would be bust. This incident was a precursor of several more of the same rating. As I say, he's not particularly bright and wanted me to do all sorts of things which were not the best that I might; he kept ordering me to do them, but by diplomacy I persuaded him round to seeing a better line, and things went on fairly well. We went up the Borpani a bit, finding that the difficulties of getting along had been much underestimated, and the going (for the pioneers, so to speak) was extraordinarily slow. We only got up what is, now that the path is broken and the way known, a march and a bit. It took us 3 days hard work, and then he had to turn back, and go down and get on with his arrangements. We decided to form an advanced depôt at the confluence of the Borpani with the Dibrang, as a preliminary step; with the men I took up with me (15) I was to prepare a defensible camp, and receive our samples by boat from Harmatti, while he went in, and sent up his stuff etc. (I must mention that he was arranging all transport etc, from Harmatti, while we had to get everything of ours to that point). All our people were to come on to this advanced depôt (christened Fort St. David, out of compliment to me) as they arrived. Very well then. By the time W. was ready go in, and we'd got some more men up, and my working parties were getting well going, it was time for Dunbar to arrive at Harmatti with the larger part of the force (the last 50 men, and he had instructed me to go meet him there, in order to tell him what had been done, put him up to the ropes etc. Mind, it's 5 days for a letter from Harmatti to Dibru. Besides this, I had several very excellent reasons for wanting to go down to Harmatti for a few hours; and there was no reason why I shouldn't, as far as I could see, and a great number why I should. W. who had been getting very grumpy (seeing, I suppose, that I was getting everything asked for, in spite of his efforts) said he wished me to stay at Fort St. David's, when I told him I proposed going in. I asked him why, and he brought out some reasons which I was able to show him didn't work. He was dying to say that he thought the men shouldn't be left by themselves, but he didn't dare; and I was quite satisfied that they'd be all right for the short time I was away. However, he was obstinate; I abandoned the question two or three times, to try and find him in a better temper but I got him eventually at a wrong moment and he lost his hair, and said 'We won't argue about it. You'll have to stay'. After that of course there was nothing for it; I kept my temper, and explained that I was not under his orders, but if he would show me any reason why I should be required there, I'd stay, and oblige him. As I explained he merely got angrier and flew to the paper. 'Was I under his orders, or not'. Politely but firmly 'No'. The reply to this was somewhat illogical, being a written order to stop. By this time he was shouting; so I didn't argue the point with him any more, and followed him down a few hours after. Poor Dunbar he didn't know what to do. He knew I was perfectly right, but with W. boiling with rage, and me a mere understrapper, he had to make some concession; so it was decided that I was greatly to blame for not having shown my orders to W. give my reasons in writing (I did, fully, so poor old D. couldn't use 'em) and apologise to W. for not having done so. Before I'd made up my mind about doing the latter, though, I finished my work at Harmatti (it's a good job I <u>did</u> go in. Dunbar was laid out by fever, and there'd have been a fine hash if I hadn't been there) and go back by river to Fort St. David. For a couple of days I continued fortifying it, and then D. came up and joined me. He told me W. was still fuming, and swore he wouldn't speak to me when he came up; and had ordered Dunbar put me in command of the advance depot when the show actually commenced. (I had calculated on being fired out of the whole thing when I bearded him; my presence at all was sub-rosa, of course, and he had me; but I decided that I'd put up with that rather than with any more of his lip). D. was furious at being ordered to put me there, but didn't want to go to Government about it; I believe I could have made him fight it if I tried, but preferred not to drag him into a row more than was necessary; he was very grateful, I believe. I simply refused to discuss the advisability of his taking the matter up, and asked him to decide for himself. So he decided, as he put it to 'sacrifice' me, which I think was certainly best; my not being authorised to be there cut the ground from under our feet. So leaving matters in status quo, off I went again the next day (the 4th November, I think) with 25 men and 4 days rations, into the unknown to try and get to Baharmukh. On the third day I got to a place which I thought might be it. (it was really just halfway) and formed another defensible camp (where I now write this, in fact which we called Fort William (compliment to our leader!) You must recollect that this country is so covered with jungle, that it is impossible to get a view in any direction; the only map is 35 years old, very barely outlined, and quarter-inch scale; and there was practically nothing to decide one's position by except the time one was travelling and the compass. As the greater part of the travelling was done up a boulder-strewn, swift river, and through jungle which had to be cut to get through, you would understand that the former guide is a very vague one. After two days at Fort William, the site which the men prepared, I continued to reconnoitre the country; I've got little bites from leeches and 1000 of ants and blisters. I came to the conclusion that I was not at Baharmukh. So thinking the matter out I determined to take the responsibility on myself of going on, and trying to make a third depot. Fort William was quite as far as supplies, etc. could manage in one day from Fort St. David, even after the path was made, and the ground is known, while the river was still practical in the direction we wanted to go. So though I couldn't get into communication with D. on the 8th I took half the men and profiting by my two days reconnaissance, did a devil of a march, went up to Baharmukh, came to the conclusion it would not do, returned about an hour down, and built Fort St. Andrew (compliment to Dunbar! These were all his names; St. Andrew was to have been William but the latter was named before I found out it wasn't the place) at a most advantageous spot for the final rush for the Poma (coming back, at the column came in from the

Poma in one-day.) So by the time the coolies and main advance came up the river with W. I had the whole thing nicely cut and dried, in nice marches with a post at each halt. Harmatti 2 Fort St. David, one day; Fort William second day; St. Andrew third day; and all the stuff up and ready in the latter as Dunbar kept boosting it up behind like the devil so there were no flies for N.W. to pick over that. Lord, I did sweat for those days; it was generally, 12 o/c before I got to bed. I was up before daylight, and never had a wash or a shave or took my clothes off all the time, and enjoyed it all. When Dunbar caught me up at St. Andrew on the 9th (he was urged on by W. who in a devil of a stew; said I was exceeding my instructions, and God knew where the feller would be getting to! To which he received the reply that my boss was quite satisfied with the way I was carrying out my instructions and that he had every confidence in my ability and discretion!!) He said I looked like an Australian settler; as I had a beard, and was out of my boots, and in rags, and cooking my own food, he was justified in his observations. Well, W. (and the other white man on the show, one Hore; adjt. of the regiment at Dibru; worked the oracle at Shillong and got put on as Intelligence) rolled up on the 10th with his coolies, and the rest of the men and off they went on the 11th for the Poma. During this time when W. & I were together at St. Andrew he wouldn't speak to me(!) but as I was dam' busy (Dunbar leaves everything to me when I'm on hand and I had to get the whole thing, as far as we were concerned, started) it didn't matter much. Dunbar again spoke to me, and also informed me that his wife had sent a message to me, asking me to make the amends honourable; so when the coolies were loaded and the men fallen in, and all just moving off, I went to W., and said W. I want to apologise to you for not showing you my orders. He said 'Oh, very well then, this matter ends there' (I don't think) and discussed with me amicably the work until he left. So off they went, leaving me and 25 rifles to hold St. Andrew I mussed about, finding plenty to do there until they turned up rather sooner than was expected on the 18th with seven prisoners and their mission accomplished. It seems that everything went perfectly; the Daphla were taken by surprise, and although very confident and truculent at first showed no fight when smitten on the head, and told to come along. We got the two slaves, burned two villages and all their grain, slaughtered all their cattle, beat out their crops, shot one of them who was trying to get into camp at night, and another who tried to bolt, bagged a large proportion of the men 'wanted' and returned to St. Andrew, leaving them gasping. So you see W. scored off me heavily; but I expected that.

Well, when the return journey from St. Andrew was coming off on the 20th it seems there was a hitch about transport; both W. and Dunbar had far more supplies at St. Andrew than they had reckoned on, and there wasn't enough transport to get 'em down again, our boats had been dismantled as soon as the stuff was at St. Andrew, to save expense; and there was only the coolies to take us down. I was out all day on the 19th with 25 men, trying to find another village in the neighbourhood (no luck) and got back to camp after dark. I found D. rather pained; W. had had a hit at him over having more rations there than he should have, and saying they would have to be destroyed; and here at last was a flaw in our bundoblast, in fact. I said 'But dammit, the feller told me he could do with all of it' and went on to recite the conversation I'd had with him before our disagreement.

D. said 'But he never said anything about that' and eventually asked me to come over and see W. I said 'right oh' and over we went. Eh, lads but there was a row; the masterful man fairly blethered, and denied the whole thing. I kept cool, but bit by bit forced admission after admission out of him; everything in fact except the crucial point, which he denied any recollection of. The result was that D. told him that as he said he didn't remember, and I said I did very clearly he was going to take my version, and act accordingly; and would trouble him for transport or sanction to destroy the surplus on his authority. So God knows what will happen now; I expect there'll be a glorious row; it's only my word against W.'s and he's the bigger man and boiling.

To save destroying the rations, I thought out a rather ingenious (though I says it as should not) scheme to bring 'em down, which D. proposed to W. (didn't say was my idea though, as it would have been kiboshed at once!) and which he accepted with very ill grace. So here you see me still in Daphla country (though far from any probability of attack) with 50 men, eating surplus rations like a devil; tomorrow I move on down the Borpani to join Dunbar at Harmatti on 28th and catch our steamer on 29th ford Dibru. I have been building rafts of bamboo; 12 of them and have two boats; so tomorrow will be quite a nautical show. I've been singing 'The lively little lads in Navy Blue' all day. [A song by Harry Dacre, popularised during the Boer War.]

I'm sorry to be going in; I do love this primitive sort of life, and to be out in the wilds with the men on my own. I'm quite comfy; we have princely houses of bamboo, and palmetto leaves, I'm camped on the junction of two streams, with a cliff on two sides of me, and the other closed by a patent of my own, which I mean to call the Hutchins Unrushable Perimeter. It's made of bamboo spikes, and barbed wire, and nearly has my life every time I go near it. I've been out all day today, doing a reconnaissance on my own for fun. The old map shows that in 78 there was a village up the small river I'm camped on; the guides we had said they'd never heard of it so I thought I'd go and see for fun. Of course, you've no conception of what this means; looking for a needle in a haystack is a fool to it. I suppose the catchment of the stream is about 12 miles by four or five; the whole of it dense jungle (and most Assamese under-growth is pitted with forms of the most ingenious type; while the forest trees are festooned with creepers ranging in thickness from nothing to a thing as thick as your arm; I don't know what this type of plant is called; isn't it 'liana'? I only know the native name. I started at 7.30 with 10 men, my old map and the compass. Waded up the river (principally boulders) until about 11 (my watch is bust, so I can only judge time by the sun) and then turned right-handed and climbed the ridge. It sounds simple, but the ridge (which is I suppose is about 600 feet above the river) is so densely covered, that you can't see there's any ridge from the river! After cutting and slipping and fighting till about 1, I reached the crest; hairy work; bloody, in all senses of the word, in fact. And had only gone about 10 yards when I stumbled over an ancient mortar (for grinding corn) and found signs of an old clearing, and a path. Not bad pioneering, considering the circs. I'm quite bucked about it. Got back about 4, very done, and sore; picked off the leeches changed, had a bath, and tea, and made arrangements for tomorrow. (I have about 70 or 80 leech bites on my two legs; and not at square inch of whole skin on my hands!)

So the expedish is over. I've made a fool of myself, I suppose, by kicking against the pricks. But I'm quite khoosh; one can't have everything, and I've kept my end up with the blighter, anyway, and have had a month or six weeks which I shall always look back to as top hole. Though I says it as shouldn't, I've done a devil of a lot of useful work for the show; even W. couldn't spare me from the preliminary part, though I'm sure that he'd have tried to get me away if he could have seen how to get on without me; and enjoyed it all.

I hope you will not be worried about my being so cantankerous. I really feel I did my best under the circs. and that it was just bad luck running up against W. He's an impossible chap to work under; I've had since to into-seed to stop my skipper having a turn up with him, but that was all right I'm glad to say.

The 30th

Well, here we all are on the steamer, approaching Dibrugarh, where are we shall arrive tonight some time. I haven't seen W. who had gone away into camp on the North Bank before I got down to Harmatti. My voyage down was a sight to be seen; 12 rafts drifting on the Dibrang in the morning run, with the Gurks singing joyous songs and were in a dug-out eating cold sausages and chapattis, and drinking hot tea out of a thermos flask all. Fore-gathered with Dunbar and his crowd at Harmatti, and made a long march (which rather sewed up some of the prisoners) next morning, getting to the river (Subansiri) in the evening. Straight on board the lugger (in this case, a feeder steamer, and next day down the Subansiri, and across the Brahmaputra to the mouth of the Dharnsiri. There we caught the big steamer on which I write this. And now on home; how long we shall be there, can't say, as usual. I handed over my census rights to Beerman as I couldn't find the time; and now am all for getting on to Sadiya as soon as possible, for our proposed training there, for our movable column. I think I've told you about this idea; we want a striking force of about 200 men kept, fully trained there; and I'm to do it. Mamma asks if it is a nice station! Well opinions would be divided as to that; the majority would probably say 'no'. At present there is a dett. of about 70 MPs under a Native officer there: a draft company of Native infantry; a sort of bazaar, a bungalow, a Post and Telegraph office; an American missionary, and (last but not least), the Assistant Political Officer (who runs the Frontier tract) Mr Noel Williamson, Esq. It should be at least interesting when I get there! Joking apart I'm rather in love with the prospect; it's practically like living in the wilderness. But I shall be on my own; training is the part of my work which I love; I have several outposts to visit and earn T.A. over and hope for a rattling good time in the way of shooting and fishing and a quiet life. W. is the black spot; but I hope that we shall be able to keep out of each other's way. I shall have to watch it, but trust to find a modus vivendi. There are some who envy me the job; and many who will look commiseratingly at me about it! But as I agree with the former, all is well. I must bring this lengthy episode to a close. How you, old guv'nor? I hope you are getting on all right and enjoying life. What is the news about the motor-car? It will be a great thing for you in your work; you must learn to drive it yourself. Here's my very best wishes for a Merry Christmas and a Happy New Year; I hope that my little offering of our local products will have arrived by the time you get this and that it will give satisfaction. May you all enjoy it, and the rude health of which I am always guilty. With much love.

Your affectionate son
Allan

★★★

Letts No 46 Rough Diary

Monday 28 November 1910
Marched with 50 men and prisoners at 6. Halted 2 hours and fed. Long and dusty march but got through in good order except one or two of the prisoners who were a bit tucked up. Got 'em on board steamer (which made 'em weak) and so to dinner and bed.

★★★

Dibringarh
18. 12. 10

Dearest Mother

Just a line to tell you that all goes well, and thank you for your letters and papers, which are always most acceptable. So J.D. [J.D. Rees MP] has handed in his portfolio, and now tries a flight on the other side? Well I wish him luck, though it's a poor chance in that constituency isn't it? I'm afraid that this will be another unsatisfactory election; our system of party Govt. seems to have broken down with all the various freelances beginning to form parties. I'm very fit, thank you, as usual, and hope you're all the same. The weather is delightfully cold and fine, and we're all beginning to blossom out of our cold season. I'm just back from a trip to a place called Doomdooma still snorting, and seeking the blood of your progeny; he has now annoyed my skipper into unleashing me and as he is asking for trouble, he is now going to get it. So I'm as busy with my trusted pen as I was with my little hatchet a few weeks ago; and if the Lion of Sadiya (as Lady D. calls him) doesn't find he's stuck a snag this time, my name's not B.H. His rage at my temerity has delivered him into mine hand, I think; of course, he's got a good backing, and I've none (except D.) and will carry some lead; but methinks he's up against it. Nous venons. And things should be interesting when I go up to share the delights of solitude at Sadiya with him, which event should take place within the next week or so. I'm trying hard to get away. I think that's all; it's a week to Christmas, and I've missed writing nearly all my mail letters. Did I tell you that the fools of agents had gone and messed up sending your tea off? But it's coming. Best love, and best wishes.

Your affectionate son
Allan

★★★

'I'm very khoosh (that is, contented) here'; with the backing of Dunbar (and no doubt Lady Dunbar behind the scenes) and an apology, Allan survived the row with Williamson pending an investigation and meanwhile was rewarded with the job of training a 200-strong striking force for jungle warfare. He is based in Sadiya – with Williamson.

Letts No 46 Rough Diary

1 January 1911
Enter on this year in a chastened mood. Wish I felt cheerier. 1911 doesn't look like a [good year] for Bill. Serve him right! Hope it has good luck.

The next day, after breakfast with Lady Dunbar, Allan left Dibrugarh for Sadiya. The cool and beautiful days of January cheered him and in a letter to his sister Billy he writes:

2 January
I'm very khoosh (that is, contented) here. There's no one to worry me, and I have an unusual taste for my own company. And am frightfully one-idea'd on the subject of my work. I love training; I ought to have been a school-master. So no day is long enough for me; even in Sadiya, for living in which place people look at me commiseratingly and say 'Whatever do you do with yourself?' I go to bed early, of course, as I can't work after dinner, and get up early; but somehow the rest of the day seems to dwindle away. It's a pity my inclinations were never diverted into more profitable channels; the work I do is mostly it's own reward, and isn't really paying. But I can't help it. we want a striking force of about 200 men kept, fully trained there; and I'm to do it.

In these deserted spots, one can give rein to one's overflowing sentiments without being interfered with – can in fact indulge in what someone nearly described as 'a sentimental diarrhoea' so your poems have had a fair chance. Thank you, fair sis.

I went on shoot last week just beyond the Frontier with one Gibson who stayed with me a few days. Got nothing of any importance; I shot a small sambur and we got some duck. But I had 'one crowded hour of glorious life' which I'm not anxious to repeat. Got lost in the jungle for that space of time; brrrhh it was horrid. When I dug my way out again, I was very done up, and very pleased to be clear. They're not good jungles in these parts to take liberties(!) with.

There's not many females who I'd ask to share the delights of Sadiya with me; but as Welshpool has been unable to disturb your mental balance, I feel you've had a good preparatory training, so to speak.

★★★

Sadiya

29.1.11

My Dearest Becky and Roney,

Many thanks for your kind Christmas letter and good wishes, which in spite of your forebodings (it's a mistake to over-forbode) reached me in good time, and assisted to cheer me on the festive day. I hope that. 'ere this, my tribute of this land's produce, the tea, will arrive to grace your board; to cheer, but not inebriate. I was glad to hear of, and think of, you being down at the old nest at Christmas time; in spite of the drawbacks, it is still the centre-point of the House of Hutch, and one can't help having an affection for the old place which has seen so much of the rum ingredients which make up that not altogether unloveable clan. Who's like us? Dam' few!

Has Roney got the motor-car yet? It will suit him down to the ground; I wish I could see him getting into it in an overpoweringly professional topper, a 'coat of skins', and his best bedside manner.

George, also, apparently has ambitions to hog about the roads; just fancy him at his time of life. Can either of them afford it? It would seem that taking income for hen-cumbrances these days, it ought to be me that sports the motor. I am drawing a fairly respectable screw, and the odd half-a-crown a week here and there doesn't make any difference. But you never knew such a place as Assa for getting rid of money with no result. Nowadays I really have no vices worth mentioning, and live like a pig in the middle of a howling wilderness; and still manage to get rid of the (roughly) £600 a year I draw without trembling. Where the devil it goes, it's hard to say; of course, I do pay off about half of it to my [debtors]; the remainder, one's servants get. They're a loathly tribe; rottenly inefficient at everything, except knowing just how much you can stand without going through the dire trouble of sacking them. They're absolute geniuses at that. Still, I suppose one oughtn't to grouse; I'm very happy on the whole, and have to take very little thought for the morrow, or deny myself much in reason.

Have you realised where my humble habitation is at present? I am now located on our extreme N.E. frontier, with about 150 of our boys. Putting me here is the last resort of our skipper; coming to the conclusion that as long as we had to train at Dibrugarh, where we were at the mercy of every inspecting officer, and civil official who wanted a party for this, that, or the other, we should never have a man sufficiently trained to bring credit on us, he sez to me, sezee, 'Hutch, my boy, bag all the best you can, and go with 'em to Sadiya, and twist the tails off 'em!. So here you see me, in this deserted spot. The only other inhabitants are goddam natives (nearly all foreigners in these parts, by the way, immigrants, and traders, etc.), the Assistant Political Officer (mine own familiar enemy, who runs the 'Frontier Tract'), and American missionary and his wife. Truly can I cry with the Psalmist, 'Lover and friend hast thou put far from me; and mine acquaintance out of my sight'. But some of these absences have their advantages, and I love the job. There's no one to worry me; and training is the part of my work I like best. Then there's shooting, on which I'm always keen. I'm just back this moment from sitting up for a tiger. This morning, two Nepalese settlers loafed into the compound (I live in the dak-bungalow here), and having been rescued from Venus my bull-terrier, announced that a tiger had killed a cow in their village about 4 miles off; and as I was a notorious generous feller, would I give them some buckshish for telling me? Very well, then. My batman, (and our familiar friend; a dear chap) sepoy Dakman Gurscary is summoned to the council; his strong resolute face lights up at the news, and in a few moments he is off with his rifle, to reconnoitre. I get on to my bicycle, run down to the lines, give a few orders, back, have some grub, change into the filthiest and raggedest old khaki clothes you can imagine, and off after him. Through the bazaar, then two miles of grassy, bumpy track through the jungle. This is the road to one of our outposts, and therefore well cleared. Otherwise, anything but one's feet would be out of the question as a means of locomotion. Then a river about as big as the Thames, but a mere flea-bite in this country of giant streams. The ferryman puts me across; and then another two miles, and Dakman is again on the tapis. We screw through a few hundred yards of high grass and jungle, and there is the poor cow, looking very dead, and partly eaten. Dakman and I skin up a tree; a few blows with the ubiquitous kukri; a little 'knotting and lashing' with the rough creepers which abound, and there is a place for me to sit. Dakman slips down and withdraws, to fill in the time hunting jungle-fowl and such small game. I sit, and sit, scarcely moving to scrape off ants and mosquitoes and pests. The jungle is very still when one sits like this; one can hear the noise if one turns one's head or lifts a hand; while a falling leaf makes a crash which gives every pulse in one's body a jump. Suddenly, there's an animal by the kill; no, not a tiger, though he would have appeared just as silently. It's extraordinary how a wild animal in that crackly sounding stuff just seems to suddenly materialise out of nothing. When you've seen him, you can see him plainly enough; and hear every movement; but the instant before there's nothing, absolutely.

This time it's a jackal, and a handsome, glossy, alert beast he is, though one's idea of a jackal is not of anything very handsome, is it? But on their own ground, any wild animal will show up to advantage. Well, one sits on, till the light goes; now and again a movement or a sound will give one that instant or so of wild, choking, excitement which is the object of the whole game, as far as I understand it, but nothing happens. At last, when the carcase of the poor ol' cow is no longer visible, I slip down my tree (another moment or two of excitement here, in the dark, in spite of my common sense which tells me that the tiger would be a dam' sight more frightened than me if we did bump against each other), pull out my kukri, and stumble and crawl through the thorns until I find a path, then into the village, where there's a little crowd of Nepalese round a fire; in the middle, Dakman and my other batman, Santabir, who has come out to bring my bicycle home; both very superior and dignified to the common herd. A chair is produced; I sit down in the midst to warm my frozen limbs, and drink tea out of a thermos flask. The crowd watches with interest, and a simple bucolic conversation goes on, in which I take part (I'm rather hot stuff at Nepalese). Then a knowing old face bursts through the circle; the crowd gives way respectfully before the waving trunk and enormous feet. From the darkness above the intellectual forehead, comes a thud and the mystic words, 'But! But!!' and Hathi the majestic kneels down, almost in the fire. I go a journey round his proportions, find an enormous outlying foot somewhere in the outer darkness, and with its help, skin up. A lurch, and we're off, thump, swish, through the jungle till we hit the road. The Oriental figure, in a blanket, on the elephant's head is not communicative; neither am I. We simply plod along the road, through the river, and so home, to a bath, and solitary dinner, after which, bed. This sort of thing happens about twice a week, and is my main relaxation, which is my excuse for inflicting it on you. Send it home, will you? I know Mamma will revel in it. Well, goodbye; sorry to have been so prosy.

   Best love to you all, particularly the kiddies,

Your affectionate brer,
Allan

                                      ★★★

Sadiya
Assam
12. 2. 11

My dear Guv'ner

I've not written you for some time; nor for the matter of that, to dear mamma; but this week will draw pen to your address, and you must both participate in the boon, as the babu says. Many thanks for your letter in reply to mine. I'm glad the descriptions interested you; I was sure they would and it's good to pour out the things one is immersed in to some appreciative soul. The expedition has been warmly praised on all hands, and my skipper has given me a good 'chit'. What N.W. [Noel Williamson] has said about me in his report I don't know, as I've not seen it; as it will puzzle him to get at me over anything, I surmise that his revenge will be a high obliviousness of my services, which will be a thing one can"t object to. My row with him drags on its weary length; I like it in a way, though I can see it can't do me much good. Did I tell you that subsequent to our return, a sense of his wrongs impelled him to write a very unguarded letter, which delivered him into my hand, to my great delight? He practically called me a liar, which gave the opportunity for a forward movement, and the powers that be are now confronted with the old problem of the upstart (me) with a strong case against the tired old servant (him) who's made a bad break. It's worrying 'em some, but they'll find it hard to get at me. Of course the military are rather the weak side over here; perhaps you know that in India the civilians can never forgive the military man that he holds a commission and is usually sublimely unconscious of anybody's superiority to himself; the result is perpetual war. And here it's all civil. But still, I'm not down-hearted; they can't get at me, and must bow the knee in this case.

   There's no news; I'm as busy as ever with my detachment; from dawn till dewy eve I'm poking my nose into every petty detail of interior ceremony and training, and trying to (a) minute a system of internal administration to serve as an example for the rest of the battalion; and (b) to train a striking force that shall be able to wipe the floor at a moment's notice with any tribe that may require it. The first is a nuisance, and the second a labour of love; both highly necessary and offering some promise of success. My skipper is up here for the moment; a rest to a certain extent, I believe; and also I think he likes to be with me. If it were not frightfully conceited I might say he seems rather to lean on me, and after a long tour, such as he's just been on, to thrash matters out with a fellow can cry on for sympathy and advice. Just fancy coming to me for the latter! I'm afraid I've let him down once or twice, but I've been useful to him on other occasions.

Lord, what a bubbling letter; it comes of being so much by oneself, I suppose. Please burn when read, without showing to anybody except ma. Best love; I'm very fit.

Yours affectionately
Allan

★★★

Sadiya
18.2.11

My dearest Mamma

Your last letter was dated 27th Jany. and said the tea had not arrived, which I am sorry to hear, as (strange though it may seem) I paid the uttermost farthing for everything to your door ages ago. It's unusual for me to pay for a thing <u>before</u> I get it, ain't it?

I don't know why you accuse me of gadding about; the Doomdooma dance, I suppose, which cost me my railway ticket, tips to my host's servants, and another chip off my already somewhat jagged reputation only. Cheap at the price, I should say. No, I'm not gadding any nowadays, dear mamma, though the money still seems to melt in an extraordinary way. Still, my income exceeds my exes slightly, and I'm paying off a bit month by month. I did not even go in to Dibru. for the 'Weeks' which is just over though my skipper and his good lady urged me not to be so conky; in fact my aforetime acquaintance would hardly recognise poor Bill now.

There's one bit of news that may interest you; it's probable that I may very shortly accompany the civilian in charge of the North Lakhimpur sub-division on a tour among the Hill Miris up the Subansiri River which will mean, if it comes off, a very interesting and pleasant expedition into practically unknown country (some of it quite so) and possibly important geographical discovery. Also, an unusual amount of T.A. and cheap living for your dutiful son. The Hill Miris border on, and are very like the Daphlas, but have always been well affected; and the Subansiri is one of the much disputed over and mighty tributaries of the Brahmaputra. It may take us into Thibet although the contention is that it is the Tsang-Po is now practically disposed of. I don't know whether you have ever heard of the vexed question of which is the main stream of one of the biggest rivers in the world; i.e. the Brahmaputra. It's practically certain that the Thibetan Tsang-Po runs into it, but <u>where</u> is the mystery, owing to the difficulties of the intervening country, and tribes. It has even been alleged that the Tsang-Po ran into the Irrawaddi, but the popular theory now is that it is the Dikong, another giant to the west of me. The branch on which I at present live is really the Lohit; not the main river at all, though it's a trifle of some 2 or 3 miles from bank to bank here; it's been called the Brahmaputra for ages, the name which should really be the Dikong's if the Dikong is the Tsang-Po. Follow all that?

I'm glad your 'bonds' are going so well, and hope you will make a fortune to leave to your struggling son! We <u>all</u> seem to be on the make in our old age – particularly Billy!!! I <u>think</u> that's one to me. I see that she's been going it again at the Newtown Ball. Damme, she wants me home again to turn a forbidding eye on the forward swains. You should have seen them wilt in 1908, when the unpleasant looking brother lurched across the floor, to what we call out here the 'Kala pagah' or 'dark place'. By the way, you might inform her that I was the other day told by a competent critic, that I had 'the most fascinating smile of any man', etc. etc. which is another proof, if such were needed, of her being badly placed in our little race for popularity.

No time for more, except my love to all.
Your affectionate son,
Allan

★★★

Dibrugarh
Assam
2.4.11

My Dearest William

Thanks for kind remarks re tea; but how alliterative mamma becomes. The sentence regarding the tender tea-taster tasting tip-top tea is terminologically terrific. Talking of tea, some people seem to think a planter ought to distribute tea gratis to all applicants. The chap I stopped with the other night got a chit from his local postmaster (babu, of course) saying 'Dear Sir, Please send me some tea, which I have learned to drink.' He wrote back 'Dear Babu, Please send me some stamps, which I am learning to lick.'

I send you a couple of native letters, for your edification. One is from our Qr. Mr. a very clever chap. Some of it is <u>intended</u> to be humorous. The other is from a young babu; rather a decent sort of youth, for a babu.

Best love to all. Tell 'em I'm very lusty.

Your affectionate
Allan

Murder and Pursuit

Noel Williamson may have been a stubborn and difficult man to work with but he was also dutiful and curious. His duty was to create good relations with the hill tribes in his district, the crescent-shaped, half-known valley at the foot of the Himalayas, that they might nail their flag to the British staff. At the very least he needed to know what the Chinese were up to and which tribal chiefs could be encouraged to repel them. Williamson was also a skilled cartographer and wanted a decent map of his district. He especially wanted to find the waterfalls of the Tsang-po river.

An earlier expedition had stumbled upon inter-tribal fighting so violent that Williamson turned back at Kebang on the Dihang River – the edge of terra incognita. But he had made other successful, though less ambitious tours and in the spring of 1911, raised a new expedition to explore Abor country 'to the inner line'. It wasn't just curiosity: there were rumours of Minyong tribesmen cultivating land on the British side of the line and Williamson saw an opportunity to levy tax. He set off with a Dr Gregorson. Was he confident that they would be well received by the tribes, or did he want to show Allan that he had no need of his protection? Whatever the reason, Williamson dispensed with a Military Police escort and instead took a gramophone, a magic lantern and a medicine chest. Gregorson was a company doctor on a tea plantation; a decent man, he saw an opportunity to carry medical care to the natives. Amidst rumours of smallpox the party skirted potentially affected villages. On the Dihang River they met a party from Kebang and hearing Kebang was infected, declined hospitality there. Then, without the requisite permission from Government House, they crossed the outer line into tribal lands. At Sissin, no more than a stockade in a clearing, Gregorson stayed to treat the sick of the expedition. Williamson carried on, his rifle tucked away in his bedding. At Komsing (Allan calls it Kinseng) he was welcomed by his Minyong hosts and shown to his quarters where, as the bath was being prepared, he was hacked to death. His party was massacred. The cook shot himself with his last cartridge. Five escaped and one, a Gurkha, was chased by dogs for three days until reaching Sissin; he found Gregorson's camp abandoned to vultures.

It was shocking. The Times *reported it as 'The Assam Frontier Outrage': 'There were about 1000 of them. They uttered their war cry and suddenly poured into the house and attacked us with spears and daos.'*

Lancelot Hare (Lt Governor of Assam and East Bengal) and Maj General Bower (O-in-C, Assam Brigade) held a council of war and agreed that reprisals must follow – properly planned, prepared and executed in the cooler weather – and the murderers brought to justice. In April Bower toured the region and planned his campaign. There would be two seven-pounder guns, No 1 Company King George's Own Sappers and Miners, a detachment of 31st Signals, 1/8 Gurkha Rifles, 300 troops, 4000 coolies and 400 of Allan's Lakhimpur Military Police armed with Maxims. Such a force would make two columns to support each other and confuse the enemy, and make and hold fortified positions where signals and supplies could be maintained and replenished. Men would carry 60lbs of kit and officers 30lbs plus Burberry gabardine, khaki tunic, brandy flask, writing kit and Kodak.

*Meanwhile and immediately on hearing news of the murders, Allan raised a force of 60
men to pursue the killers and, with Dunbar's permission, in torrential rain moved by boat
up the Dikong River. Where the fast-moving river leaves the hills he secured a base, Camp
Pasighat, and there joined forces with Dunbar to 'wipe out the villages concerned' before the
Government could intervene. Alas and to Allan's disgust, the Commissioner of Police and
'a rotten specimen of white man' ordered them to go no farther – thus giving the quarry
time to boobytrap the jungle paths and make secure behind stockades. 'Please report at once
where Hutchins is and what he is doing stop' read one signal, 'he must not make extended
tours or burn villages without permission.'*

*In fact Allan's liberal interpretation of orders shortly found him with 50 men on a
reconnaissance mission beyond the outer line and 'a quarter of the journey to Kebang'.
He reached Mishing and destroyed the village. The repercusions were entirely predictable:
he was both reprimanded – 'Don't do it again' – and attached to the flanking column
that would benefit from his experience of the route. For Allan, the flanking column was a
punishment – a poor second to the main show.*

Letts No 46 Rough Diary

Wednesday 5 April 1911
Went off with Douglas to Saikhowa Ghat. Heard there of Williamson being cut up by
Abors. Shoved on to Sadiya and got on with matters. Raining like hell but at it till about
10. Principally at the 'press' after boatmen.

Thursday 6 April
Up at 3. Left Sadiya by boat with 60 rifles and a fleet of boats. Met Dunbar and Bentinck
at Saikhowa, handed over boats, got stores etc and got off again with 60 rifles and six
boats for Dihong … didn't get camped till nearly mid-night, the big boats (2) giving a
lot of trouble.

Friday 7 April
On up Dihong at 6. Travelled all day.

Saturday 8 April
On up Dihong at 5. Kansung caught me up and I joined his party. Camped about 2
miles below Pasighat at 3.30. Got an arrow into the camp during the night. [Abor
arrows were armed with poisonous aconite, deadly nightshade or, it was said, with the
rotting flesh of their enemies.]

Sunday 9 April
Moved on to Pasighat. Bagged couple of men over the arrow incident. Reached
Pasighat about 10 and Dunbar caught me up. Made a camp. Rather good position.

Camp Pasighat
(At Gorge of Dikong River)
Upper Assam
Thursday 13.4.11
Saikwaghat Friday 14.4.11

My dear Guv'ner

Having a day of leisure after some quick happenings, I chew my pen to give you the history of the events which have landed me at this spot, where I'm likely to be for some little time. You will probably have heard of the death of poor old Williamson from the papers; he was cut up by the Minyong Abors up this river on 31. Poor chap; they planted him at last. The I.G. of police was coming up this month to inquire into our differences, but I expect that will all be shelved now.

I had better give you some explanatory notes. The Abors are the most powerful and independent of the tribes along our N.E. frontier. They are very similar to the others (Daphlas, Hill Miris, Mishmi's, etc) but more so, and have always given more trouble. The others funk 'em like anything. They have several tribes (Minyong, Bor Abor, Padani[?], Passi, etc. etc). Of these, the Bor Abor is top-dog, and his big villages, far back in the hills, give the policy to be pursued by all the rest. How far back his country extends, of course nobody knows. There are probably more Abor tribes, still wilder, behind him this side of Thibet. I expect we'll know soon now. His frontier this side is the foot of the hills, and lies on both sides of the Dikong river, which is unexplored from here to Thibet, where it is supposed to be the Tsang Po. Though many attempts have been made to follow it through, none has ever succeeded. We have had two or three expeditions against the Abors, but owing to mismanagement and dam shillyshallying of government (whose treatment of these tribes is too contemptible for words) they have all taken the knock more or less, and the Abor has kept his tail waving at the Sarkar. If you can get hold of St. John Mitchell's 'Report on the N.E. Frontier of Assam' it will give you all this much better. The last expedition in '94, was a fiasco; it tried to get to Danurshi, the stronghold of the Bor Abors, but turned back and a post was cut up by treachery.

Williamson was always moving about among these tribes, and was very good in his handling of them. About 18 mos. ago he went up the Dikong to Kebang, the capital of the Minyong Abors; and this year went up again. He was desperate keen on exploration, and of course, the tracing of the Dikong is a bait that would lure most people with a leaning that way. The ostensible object of his trip was to find how far the 'zone of Thibetan influence' extended, and nobody knows what's behind. This time he took about 30 Nepalese coolies, and a tea-garden doctor from near Dibru, who is a pal of W's and very keen on Thibetan subjects. The Abors lured him on and induced him to separate his party from Gregorson's (the doctor.) Then having got him across the Dikong and well up into the hills (further than any white man has ever been) they got him away from his men, and suddenly fell on him. At the same time another village did for Gregorson. They are treacherous swine; they had got him to go farther than he wanted to, they were so friendly, etc.

Well, that's how it seems to have happened; we've got it from a few of the coolies who managed to get clear, and after a week of starvation and misery, made their way down the Dikong to the plains.

Now for my part; I was going up to Sadiya and got to Saikhowa (on the S. bank, opposite Sadiya) about 10 am. on the 5th. There I found a telegram from Williamson's babu at Sadiya, saying that a friendly Abor chief (or 'garu') had come in, and reported that W.'s party had been cut up by Abors. I wired off to Dibru, and got across the river, and inquired. The annoying part was that our beautiful moveable column at Sadiya had been broken up a fortnight before when I went in to Dibru, and half had come in with me, bringing all the mobilisation equipment, etc. So I lost a day. However, I managed to raise 60 rifles and get 'em ready; and by working a 'press-gang' all night: succeeded in catching enough boats and very reluctant boatman to take them and their stuff down the Brahmaputra; and also for the party which Dunbar wired he was bringing from Dibru. So early next morning Thursday (6th.) I set forth down the river with my 60 stalwarts, and a regular fleet of country-boats. We put into Saikhowa, Thursday 6th, and there was Dunbar with Bentinck (the Deputy commissioner, a ripping good chap; full of spirit) and about 100 more. Dunbar told me I could go on, so after handing over all the boats but 7 (which held me, and the 60) and picking up mobilisation stores, I biffed on down the river, and turned up the Dikong. And so, sweating blood, (it rained practically all the time from the day I left Dibru) I pushed on up to here (which is where the Dikong leaves the hills) closely followed by the rest. I got here on 9th. Sunday and started a defensive post. Dunbar & Bentinck caught me up the same time, in a light boat, and we soon had 150 men here. We meant to leave 50, and make a rush with 100 on 11th, wipe out the villages concerned (we kept getting news of all about it from the wretched coolies we picked up on the way) and be back here by 18th. It was far the best way from all points of view; moral, and practical; and we could have done it on our heads; and the effect would have been most exemplary. Both Bentinck and Dunbar, knowing the ways of Govt. and the Commissioner (who is a rotten specimen of white man) in particular, were rushing all they knew, while the heads of Departments were wiring wildly in all directions, to all sorts of people, trying to find out what was happening. But the few hours delay at the start did us; we had to stop a day here to make the defences, load up etc. and on the evening of the 10th. one Horse (Capt. 120th. Infy, who was with us on Daphla show, and very keen on all matters connected with the hills) who is about on leave, caught us up, and asked to be taken along. With him he brought a telegram; we knew it was all up when he produced it, and sure enough 'No advance beyond Pasighat till further orders'. So here we are, 150 of us, within 3 or 4 days of Kebang, doing nothing, while Government scratches its head, and wonders whether it really ought to do anything; and the Abors carry off their grain and belongings to the jungles, and prepare their stockades, and set traps, and panji the paths, and generally play hell undeterred. If we'd gone straight on, we'd have caught 'em on the hop like we did up the Bozpani. And the rainy season has set in, when movements in the hills are supposed to be impossible. So they' will very likely keep us here till next cold weather; but we hope that Bentinck's representations (poor chap; he is frightfully sick at being stopped) may induce 'em to give us our heads again, in which case it will not be so bad, though more difficult, and less exemplary, of course. We took out 50 men on a recon-naissance the day before yesterday, and actually did a quarter of the journey to Kebang, and returned to camp, during the day! These chaps could no more stop us than fly; with 100 men one could march from Bhutan to the Khamti country, if they would let one. But they prefer to shilly-shally, and send up people who know dam'all about it, and play into the Abor's hands. It's really miserable how weak Govt. is with these people.

I'm improving our post; we have about 50 Abors in camp, belonging to the Passi villages just above us. But no treachery this time, I trust. They're sick as be-dam'ed. Bentinck simply sent for the 'garus' who thought they'd better come, as they live so close. They came with a tail of about 3 or 4 hundred. Bentinck said he wanted 40 coo-lies; in the usual Abor way, the big garu said, 'Oh yes; perhaps he'd be able to see about it in day or two'. Bentinck said he'd like 'em now, and that the garus could stop in camp to look after 'em, and see they didn't misbehave. 'Oh, quite impossible; we'd get coolies all right, in time'. They were mad when Bentinck simply said 'My order' and they found they had to comply. You must understand that an Abor has never done anything he didn't want to since he's been born. The big 'garu' nearly threw fits when I got Betinck to tell them to give up their dhaos; in fact, he became so obstreperous shortly afterwards that when B. had gone I chastised him. This restored confidence, and we get on all right now. They have been very useful in building the defences; and have not so far tried to escape; which, seeing that every possible avenue is stopped by a man with a gun is per-haps not surprising.

The camp is a rather good position on a sand-bank between the river and one of its wandering arms. There was a sort of square hollow in the side of a big sand-hill which I pitched on. There is the river behind me, a line of sand-hills round the hollow, and in front of that a great expanse of stones, which besides being open and noisy, prohibit anything but a slow crawl over them. A better obstacle would be hard to conceive. I have a stone wall all round, an abattis in front of that, and two trip wires, as well as the spikes left in clearing the foreground of the tough grass. A sepoy got one of these bang through his calf yesterday, so I don't suppose they'd be much joke to charge through. The only weak spot is the upper end which is too far to watch at night from camp; so I have a picket in a sangar there at night.

Well, I think that's all. We shall probably go on up soon, and I don't see how Govt. can help giving these chaps their lesson this time. It ought to be a biggish show, and I ought to see the cream of it. Try and get J.D. to keep his eye on it, and go for the Govt. if they try and climb down again. The representative of the British Government has been treacher-ously murdered on a peaceful expedition by a people who have defied Govt. for 50 years, and harried our subjects with impunity all that time; and unless they get a severe lesson are certain to be encouraged, as they have been in the past, by the laxness of the local Government. So J.D. might make a row in the papers if they don't sit up. Anyway they seem to be pretty well compromised now, by our presence here, which is a blessing.

The catch-word in the camp now is, 'inspiring confidence'. The Commissioner wired Bentinck he thought it would be a good thing to keep some men here to 'inspire confidence in the neighbouring tribes. As this came just after my having kicked the chief of the 'neighbouring tribes' in the butt, we thought it rather apt, and we 'inspire confidence' in all sorts of ways now.

Well, best love. I hope you're all fit and having a good time. Don't be surprised if you don't hear from me for some time; this is a most inaccessible place, and I'm very busy.

With love
Yours affectionately
Allan

★★★

Letts No 46 Rough Diary

Tuesday 25 April 1911
From last entry at Pasighat forget to write up but from (I think) 19 came up daily to Balek with 50 men and made a stockade assisted by Abors. Very hot weather.

Tuesday 9 May
Balek. Found orders from Dunbar in card box (!) telling me to meet Dorward at Pashighat tomorrow with 100 coolies. Just in time. Moved into new house (upper floor). Men moved into new barracks completed today.

Sunday 21 May
Marched from Remi through Khemi villages to Ledum and about 1 and half miles up Misheng road. Very wet again.

Tuesday 23 May
Took 60 men. marched with party thro' Misheng to Ledum. Destroyed former. Two alarms during the night.

Thursday 25 May
Marched right into Balek. Sort of triumphal progress, glad to get back. Gave the men a pig and some liquor.

★★★

Balek

31st May 1911

My dearest family,

You ask why I left Sadiya, as I had 'been appointed for 5 years', you funny old thing. I have been appointed Asst. Cmdt. of the L.M.P. Belton – whose jurisdiction and area extends from the Naga Hills to the Bhutanese border, round the extreme N.E. frontier, and serve all over it. Sadiya is one of our detachments.

Dunbar had a scheme (I've told you all this before) to train a lot of extra men at Sadiya, instead of at Didur, and sent me up to do it. When the cold weather (training season) was over, the extra men and I naturally returned to headquarters (Dibur). As a matter of fact, this movement was accelerated slightly, because Dunbar go the jumps about the way W. and I were scrapping, but it was all in the natural course of events. Have you got it now?

By now you will have learned that I was <u>up</u> the river; very much so, and the 'swollen state' that Podgie has got hold of from somewhere gave your li'l brother and his 'sipakis' a good old gand at pulley hauling up the rapids. It was like the Borpani again; I am going to apply for a commission in the Marines after this. We're soldier, sailor and policeman (as Bentinck calls us, to rag Dunbar) all in one.

I'm proud to hear of Billie's prowess with the long bow; she showed great promise in that direction. The gentle Abor has also been instructing me how to loose a shaft; in fact, I had a practical illustration from the wrong end the other day. They are fairly useful; bow, cord and arrow are all the ubiquitous bamboo; the proper arrows have iron heads with about 2 inches of poison round 'em; but they shoot in a different style to us. The snappy thing seems to be to wrap one leg round the other and lean forward; the bow is held diagonally, not straight up. I must send you some arrows to see; I bagged a lot at Misheng the other day. Their cross bows are quite useful, and shoot a long way.

Now for a yarn about my reconnaissance. When we were at Pasighat, I think I told you that General Bower (at present commanding the Assam Brigade). You should remember that I am a civilian at present, and am not under him in peace time, and the commissioner came up to have a look at things, before abandoning matters for the rains. We had a sort of council of war and I was summoned to attend it. The General had his map out, and gave us a rough outline of his plans, in case he had the command of the show next cold weather. Among other things, he put his finger on the map, and running a line up through a big village called Ledum, away to the West of here, he said, 'Of course, we know nothing of what's here. We haven't even got the real situation of Ledum. But there's a report that there's a road from there to Kebang and we want information all about there (Ledum). Now, for that we must rely on you gentlemen' (indicating Bentinck, Dunbar and me). I said nothing to nobody, but thought a helluva lot. Kebang is the big village which runs Abor policy on this side of the Diharg for several days up; and is now known to have been the instigators, and part perpetuators of the massacre. It has enormous influence, and all the rest funk it like the devil. So does Govt.! There've been two expeditions against it, which have failed (one didn't stop till it got back to Dibur!) And Govt. thinks it a devil of a place. Now, I have theories, very different to the accepted one, as to the size of the columns required to work in these hills. So thought I'd try them practically, if I got a chance. Of course, I didn't let on, or they'd have stopped me; but one day, when I'd got my fort here pretty snug, etc. I biffed off with about 90 of the boys. I thought I'd have a look at the General's road, as an excuse, and if Fortune favoured me, I'd be on to Kebang before thay expected me, knock hell out of 'em, burn their blooming metropolis, and come home again, and larf at their elaborate arrangements for punitive expeditions in the hills. Howsumdever, as you will see, a bit of bad luck spoilt my little game. Of course, what I really turned back for was the fact that if I went on there was bound to be a fight, in which we should have had to lose a few men; and then Government would have started asking questions, and I should have had to admit I was waging war on my own account, so to speak. And should probably have got into bad trouble. I'm still confident I could have taken and destroyed the dam' place, and been back only a couple of days later; but you can't make omelettes without breaking eggs, and the eggs wasn't mine, so to speak. So came back. Of course, I expect the reconnaissance will be pretty valuable, and I've lost no men; and the impression made (looking at it as a demonstration) has been tremendous. As you'll see, Ledum has been eating out of my hand, and it's attitude was causing Govt. great anxiety for the safety of the border in that direction.

I daresay there'll be a bit of a shine, particularly about the village I burnt, but they'll have to pat me on the back. The first thing anybody knew about it was of course, my report, which I send herewith. I also took the precaution of sending a copy privately, by same post, to poor old Bower, and asked him to back me up; so when the Commissioner and LG. start asking me what the devil I mean by it, I'll say it was the perfectly correct thing to do, and refer 'em to their military adviser, the G.O.C.! I should love to see their faces when they get the report; of course, I'd no business to do it, but I was certain I could, and now it's done, what can they do but say the information acquired is valuable?

I was only just in time; when I got back I found a letter from Dunbar saying he wanted me in, and must relieve me. Nothing to do with this, of course, as nobody knew of it.

But he seems to have some scheme on, which, as usual, he won't divulge until he sees me. Beeman, I hear, is going on leave; perhaps that is something to do with it. A man from the Dacca M.P. Battn. is to have this place, with men from his own batt., my little fort that I made with my own hands, so to speak, will now know a stranger's care; and the Abor villages, over which I ruled with the autocracy of a Czar, will bring their morning's offerings to another's door. Boo-hoo! Joking apart, I hate going; I've made the blooming place, and these people understand me now, and everything goes like clockwork. But it can't be helped. Dunbar says I'm to have it again for a month before the show begins, but that don't console me.

Well, no more at present. Excuse writing being worse than usual; I had a bit of an operation in the morning After I got back, but they couldn't find the thorn, and now I have a big ulcer on the back of my hand; and 16 others in various places! I nearly 'went off' after the operation, dam' funny. He had been chopping for about five minutes, without hurting me much, and had given it up. We were talking, and I was telling him where it had gone in etc. when I suddenly announced I was going to faint, and he just grabbed me in time. Very odd, wasn't it?

Best love to all,
Yours affectionately,
Allan

P.S. My report was bowdlerised of course. The whole thing, from beginning to end, like our presence here, is merely 'force majeure'. My 'invitations' and 'requests' etc. were orders, backed up by 95 of the true and brave, and 'reluctance' of any sort was overcome by the readiest means. Information was obtainable only by the fear of death and other persuasion. So you must read between the lines. The whole place is in Kebang's pocket.

★ ★ ★

Dibrugarh
25.6.11

Dearest Family

Lor knows when I last wrote to you; it seems an age, and I have a score of letters, *County Timeses* etc. to thank you for. Anyway, behole me now at HQ. once more, with the liklihood of remaining here for the next 2 or 3 months, anyway. We all look forward to an expedition about Septr. or Octr; its hard to see how even Morley [Viscount Morley of Blackburn, Secretary of State for India who in fact had already been replaced] can wriggle out of it, though I bet he does if he can. Get J.D. to keep a fatherly eye on the proceedings. Govt. has already disowned poor old Williamson and his works, I see from an 'inspired' article in the *Pioneer* yesterday. Not only this Abor expedition, but also his recent Mishmi one, which was aided and abetted by the L.G. himself. It really makes one sick to have to serve under such a contemptible Col; they treat every one the same in a job like old W's. 'Go on' they say 'Do your damndest; if it comes off, well and good; if it don't, we disown you'. W. had been doing these semi-authorised trips for years, and everyone liked it, and said what a fine chap he was. Now they call his crossing the Outer Line a 'grave breach of standing orders'. Same with my Kebang trip; if there had been an 'accident', they'd have wanted to know what I meant by going. Even old Bower (the Gen. who gave me as broad a hint as possible, cast me off and damned me I hear, on some garbled report he'd got in through an ass he is employing as Intelligence. Luckily I had taken the precaution of sending him a copy of my report at once, so when he got that, he patted me on the head, and said what a good boy I was. So that's all right. Still we hear rumours that the dovecotes are much fluttered in high places, as evidenced by a telegram from Govt. to Dunbar, which was duly brought out to me by runner, me being peacefully engaged in shooting on the grass lands near the Dikong at the time, having been relieved Balek, and wandering quietly down to Dibru. It said 'Please report at once where Hutchins is, and what he is doing stop he must not make extended tours or burn villages without permission'. I larfed some when I got it, as I had reason to believe that my successor, (Robertson, or the Dacca Mily Police) was at that moment burning another village that I had sworn to do for. They do get excited at Govt. H.Q. when these brutal and licentious soldiery gets away from a telegraph wire.

It's quite likely I get an official reprimand over Misheng [see 6.7.11]; but I didn't expect any better, and they'll probably make it up to me some other way if they do sit on me.

Balek is to be relieved again the beginning of next month. Dunbar is going to take a turn this time; I'm afraid it won't suit him, though. That sort of thing is not his métier Lady D. is going home; but has been very ill the last week, and the question now is whether she'll be well enough to go in time. If not, I don't know who'll go to Balek; not me, I'm afraid, as I've a feeling that my worthy chief is not keen on my identifying myself much more with that spot. He's terribly frightened of any of his underlings becoming too prominent, so to speak; he wants to make a reputation himself out of this show.

When I got back, he was away and Mrs. Robertson (married about 3 months; and very young; awfully nice, but quite a babe) was stopping with Lady D. When the latter was taken ill, the duties of head of the family sort of behoved on me, and I had a fine time of it, including 2 nights sitting up before we got a nurse. You see, Lady D. is a large and determined person, while poor Mrs. R. is as I've said, very young, and naturally rather diffident towards her hostess; so I used to insist on Mrs. R. going to bed, while I sat on the verandah. If anything was wanted, I'd arouse Mrs. R, who would see to it, but when the patient at last got a bit lightheaded and obstinate, I had to go in myself and insist on her taking her medicine etc. Don't it make you laugh to think of your off-spring doing the heavy father to two married women? Of course, I'm great pals with Lady. D, so it wasn't like a stranger; but still it's rather an amusing situation, in a way, though the poor lady's illness is rather serious and worrying us all. Her husband is back now, and they've a nurse, but her temperature won't settle down. The doctor says it's malaria.

How did your London trip go off? And did you get safely back with the motor? I hope it's a nice one; you must all cut an awful dash in it. Let me know what it's like, and all particulars.

George asks questions about the campaign etc. which I find hard to answer. Distance in miles is rather difficult, even in an explored country, when all the rules are on end, so to speak, and really don't matter much when it's a question of thickness of jungle, swiftness of current etc.

Pasighat is, at a guess, 35 miles up from the junction of the Dikong with the Brahmaputra. Aren't the hills on your map? Because it's at the gorge. Balek is 5 or 6 miles W. from there. Nobody quite knows how far Rui is; say (another wild guess) 40 or 50 miles straight from the gorge. It's on the L. bank, you know. The arch-offenders, and boss-village is Kebang, you know, about 30 miles up on R. bank. What place Rui holds in the policy of the Abors is unknown; some say it's bigger, and independent of Kebang; others say it runs with it. It sent messengers to me at Balek, declaring its innocence of complicity in the murder and asking for peace. We have failed to get any evidence implicating it so far, though Williamson was on his way there, by invitation of its chief, when he was killed. Its complicity is one of the problems of the affair. W. was killed at Kinseng, the next village, and according to all accounts, at the active instigation of Kebang, the leading village of the Abors known as Minyong. Rui is also Minyong, by the way.

As regards what you ask of my 'fort'; it stands on a ridge; or spur in the middle of the Pasi group of villages. On 3 sides a very steep and difficult, stony drop of about 150 feet; the 4th or upper side is level and open. On one side, it is commanded at long arrow range from the next ridge, which is much higher. This is the weak spot, though it would only allow of sniping, and perhaps fire-arrows (which I have never heard of among these people.) During an attack it (the next ridge) would be valueless, and untenable. The reason I call it 'weak' is that it's a flaw in the perfect serenity of our defences; a sniper up there might pot a lucky shot at someone crossing the square in the middle. The stockade varies in height from 12 to 20 feet, made, in places, of bamboo, and in others, of timber, tied with galvanised wire. It has a banquette inside, and is loopholed every yard. It also has a light gallery running round the top, inside, in order to prevent anyone who reached the face of the stockade acquiring immunity from his proximity (that's good, ain't it?). It is about 200 yards, of irregular outline, and is surrounded by a high-wire-entanglement at about 5 yards distance. On the upper face, I have also digged a ditch. There are two gates; the main one down the hill, and the side one over the [?] whence we draw out water if beseiged. At present, we run our water out of a village higher up, in bamboo pipes. I see your start of horror – 'Pizen!' Yuss, papa, but it's been carefully thought out by a very able mind. Mine, in fact! You see, if Roying (the village concerned) wished to poison our water, they could; but it's so arranged that they'd only get some of us, and then Roying would be poisoned by the rest. Likewise, the men of [?] take a little water daily from us, for their stomach's sake. If we had a separate pipe, as at first insisted on by D.C., Comdt, and Medical officer, it would be a deal easier for anyone to monkey with it, as the same great brain pointed out; and if we use the 'siege' water supply continuously, we run a very good chance of getting disease, as the village stands on its bank, higher up. So it's the best budobast I could think out, and caused me many an hour's reflection.

The whole thing's a compromise, of course. I wanted a beeooutiful peak, much higher up, the topmost pinnacle of the highest village, which had a water-supply, uncontaminated, just below it. But the D.C. wasn't for it; it meant the removal of 3 or 4 houses. Dunbar, who has a way of putting things to you that you can't get out of, ses to me 'I leave the selection entirely to you. The place you say is certainly the best, but unless you' (you is good, ain't it?) say you can't find another that will possibly do, I do not wish to force the D.C.'s hand by insisting'. So I tells him, of course, I could find 40, but he keeps harking back to what he said, and knowing exactly how to manage ole Bill, eventually gets a fairly good site, without having had to force the D.C. or having the responsibility of having selected an imperfect site!

I'm afraid I'm a bit hard on him; he knows I'm no good unless he lets me alone to do things, and I dare say that's really what he was at; but he's such a deep bird that I always expect hidden motives. Anyway, he gave me my head all through, and let me do what I dam' please, and there are very few bosses who'll do that. And I'm not half grateful enough to him, most times.

Well, I must close. I find here another copy of a report which will interest you. I had another try to get a biff at the Kebang lot, but just missed it again. Robertson gave Kengging the 5 days, and then went and socked 'em. His report says 'I found the village deserted; and the inhabitants had evidently fired the houses before they left.' Ha-ha! I know who fired the houses – the wily old dog. I larfed considerably over his report because it seems they had again laid a trap; i.e. a pitfall about 8ft. deep, with 3ft. bamboo spikes. The Gurks weren't having any again, and went round it but when he came back, a lurking Abor trying to bolt in a hurry, went bang into it, and spiked hisself. So their traps seem to sour on 'em, so to speak

Well, best love to all, and best wishes.
Yours affectionately,
Allan

How did the coronation go off, and who saw it? Here I went to church, and a garden party.

★★★

A Death

Letts No 46 Rough Diary

Thursday 26 June 1911
Buried poor Kitty [Lady Sybil Dunbar]. Awful day. Went up to bunglaow afterwards then went to Bentinck's and saw Dunbar. Eventually went down with him to ghat.

★★★

Dibrugarh
1/7/11

Dearest Family

It's rather a subdued son who writes this time. Lady Dunbar died last Wednesday, in the most unexpected way, and as we had become the closest friends, it has been rather upsetting. I've told you how bright and charming she was; and she was pleased to consider me the most reliable and trustworthy of her friends, and we had no secrets from each other. She got bad fever suddenly, and although we are used to that sort of thing, and didn't worry about it much, she suddenly went up to an enormous temperature (109°, the doctors have it) and in spite of an exceptional constitution, died before any of us were more than worried about her having so bad a time.

Everything afterwards was trying too. Of course, I was only too anxious to do what I could, but her husband was so upset that I had to do everything by stealth, and get her buried in spite of him. And it's the rains, and everything is flooded; and we had a job to do it decently.

However, it's all over now, and things are better; but it makes a big gap. We were awfully fond of each other, and one misses a pal of that sort. And she made rather a figure here, and everyone misses her.

We packed her husband off, and I'm here now up to my eyes in the next Balek relief, and all the accumulated files which poor old Dunbar passed on to me. He'll be away for 6 weeks, and the mantle of Commandant descends on my shoulders. So I have to skip round. I'm going back to live in the old bungalow; I'm not afraid of her poor little ghost, and he's not made up his mind whether to keep it on or not. So I'm going to keep it warm till he does. At present, I'm at the Club.

No more now. Best love to all; I'm getting on famously. My debts have become quite small, and the I.G. wrote a D.O. to Dunbar the other day re the Abor business, finishing up: 'I am glad to hear Hutchins has done so well. Please give him my congratulations', which being interpreted means 'When the row comes on, melad, I'm backing you'. So that's all right.

Yours affectionately
Allan

★★★

Dibrugarh
6.7.11

Dearest Family

No particular news except I'm very busy with the July Balek Relief. By much cogitation and energy have reduced the whole thing to rather a tricky result, and think it will work rather well, and be <u>cheap</u>, which is what they look at. I'm Offg. Cmdt. and very important! But it's been a sweat. Off to Sadiya day after tomorrow, taking Robertson's wife up to be ready for him (he's going to be at Sadiya now for a bit.) Meet Dundas (W's successor) and drive down the river with him to our base on the Brahamaputra on the 10th. I've forgot to tell you that we've abandoned the Dikong, owing to the rains, and have cut a road through the 30 miles of jungle between the Brahmaputra and Balek, from a point (called Kobo, N.B.) about 5 miles lower down than the mouth of the Dikong. We keep a post at Kobo. One party of my relief and the rations, comes up the river from Dibru to Kobo; I meet it there and go up with it, returning again with a party coming down. I expect to be back in Dibru about 18th. I'm back in the old bungalow; it seems very empty when I'm in it, which isn't much.

Govt. have whitewashed me over Misheng; we were awfully surprised to get a 'confidential' (so please don't talk about it, or you may get me into trouble) in which His Honour, 'after carefully considering all the circumstances of the case' was pleased to consider that 'Capt. Hutchins had handled his men well, and got out of a difficult situation in a skilful manner'. Also that 'Capt. Hutchins was justified in the action he took' for a variety of reasons. But – don't do it again; was the last para.

I think old Bower (who it appears will really have the show in the Autumn) must have stuffed in a good word, as I hoped for.

So once again do we escape the consequence of trying to do one's work! Balek has done me well, on the whole I think I've established a reputation in a small way, in a few useful quarters, and having not paid any bills during the time I was there, have just been having a regular field-day, paying off creditors. Toosie will be pleased to hear that I've just paid over £100 worth of debts this month. In fact, am solvent. Now we begin to save, and be virtuous. Lord, how dull it'll be. But I want an awful lot of things so perhaps I shan't 'roll' for a bit yet. This show in the autumn will probably make me unable to receive Billy, if she is coming, before Christmas; but if she means business, tell her to be ready by then.

Best love to all; I'm fit, as usual, and hope you're the same

Yours affectly
Allan

Waiting for a launch at Kobo; 'Extortion, robbery, criminal intimidation, causing hurt, mischief, etc. etc. are a few of the sections of the Indian Penal Code I'm rendering myself liable under.'

Letts No 46 Rough Diary

Saturday 15 July 1911
Waited for *Curlew*. She arrived in evening, without coal.

Sunday 16 July
Sent *Curlew* to Saikhowa for coal and awaited her return.

Wednesday 19 July
Went up on *Curlew* with stores. At it all day. Rather exciting at times. Eventually left in jolly boat about 5pm on to Kobo 6.45. Found Webb there.

★★★

15.7.11

Dearest Family

Behold your little son temporarily in the wilds again, endeavouring to carry out the monthly Balek relief which a paternal, though bat-eyed Local Govt. have insisted on, in the interests of the men's health. As matters stand at present the whole thing will have taken about 3 weeks to complete; in a moment of temporary aberration I've been trying to save the aforesaid Govt. money, with the result that I've been left in the lurch, with practically no transport to do the job. Lemme explain; I am here on the Brahmaputra's bloody bank (excuse alliteration) on the N. Bank at a spot due south of Balek, and hence we have made a road of sorts (3 marches) to that abode of bliss. I made a bargain with the steamer-agent, and decanted my parties for Balek, and their rations etc. with great success here; and also sent off the people coming out thereof to their respective lairs, by means of a feeder-steamer I had asked the Civil authorities to provide many elephants to take the stuff up; and at the last moment they produced 2! (Perhaps you don't know that now owing to the height of the rivers, we can't get up the Dikong; hence all this trouble). So I'm once more at my old game of trying to play a sort of chess with parties of sepoys, coolies, odd boats, and elephants in order to work the stuff up somehow, and keep every one employed continuously. It's very like the problem of the boat, the river, the fox, and the goose, and the bag of corn, and requires severe mental gymnastics. Of course, a flood comes along to make it more interesting, and a launch I wired frantically for from Dibru, and which is reported to have left on 13th. is still in the unknown. I came up here to go up to Balek, and see Beeman, who is taking his turn there, comfortably installed; but when I found the state of things that the transport (or lack of it) had caused, I had to chuck that, and confine myself to running things round here. Of course, the local villagers (Miris, Abors, and Assamese) are in a blue funk, and have to be 'caught', as they term it themselves, before they'll do anything; so I have to fly from one village to another, bullying the head-men, and assist them to maintain their very sketchy authority over their people. This, I would point out, is not my department, but is an entirely civil job; but as Dundas (Williamson's successor) is sick, and the D.C. 60 miles down a flooded river, it devolves on me, though of course I do it at my own risk. I larn the villagers, and fine 'em goats, and swear I'll break up their happy homes, and put the elephants in their crops, all without a semblance of jurisdiction, except that Dundas is a good chap, and said 'Do whatever you like' when I left him in his bed at Sadiya. The results have been hopeful but legally speaking, of course I'm liable to all sorts of pains and penalties. Extortion, robbery, criminal intimidation, causing hurt, mischief, etc. etc. are a few of the sections of the Indian Penal Code I'm rendering myself liable under; but it's all in the day's work and I don't expect there'll be anybody with sufficient pluck to say anything; particularly as I always promise to come back in a few days, and always make a point of arriving unexpectedly. My most signal triumph has been the arrival of a Miri interpreter; he bolted from Robertson at Balek, and R had been unable to get him back, as he had fled to the jungles. I went to his village and made myself unpleasant, and said he was to be produced; and yesterday morning, a Miri rug was sent to camp as a peace-offering from him, and shortly afterwards, having thus prepared the way, he came in and 'surrendered' as the police reports have it. As there had been several attempts to get him, I was rather pleased about it; of course, one could no more catch a man like that than a particular fish in the river. So it's a testimonial to my powers of moral (!) persuasion.

Well, I'm afraid you've got rather a dose of 'shop', haven't you? My pen's run away with me. I'm hung up at this place (Kobo) and can't do anything more till the launch turns up; so have some time to inflict all this on you.

There's no news, I'm afraid, and your recent letters are at Dibru, (where, by the same token, I ought to be; I tremble to think of what the I.G.P. is saying about our office, as Robertson – the Dacca M.P. man attached to us – is at Sadiya; Beeman at Balek; old Dorward, our 'European Subadar' gone up there too with the guns, to put them in, he being an old gunner; Dunbar on leave, and me stuck here.) Have I ever told you of old Dorward, our very present help in time of trouble? He is the last survivor of a grade which used to be extant in all the Assamese M.P. Battns; the 'European Subadur', or sort of Hony. Lt,. or Sergt-Major; a most useful bird, and one of the best. Originally a Sergt. in the Garrison Artillery, he married a Lady's maid, and got this job; and as he does not change like Cmdts, and Asst. Cmdts, sort of holds the battn. together. Whenever I'm out of the station and want anything done for certain; I write to Dorward; failing him, Mrs. Dorward, who is just as reliable. They are both mines of useful knowledge, and can turn their hands to practically anything. Mrs. D. is at present looking after Satan and Venus for me; she also runs the club catering, and is the adviser of most of the ladies of the station, who always fly to her when in trouble. She hasn't an H to her name, and is <u>not</u> a beauty; but one of the best. A real Tommie's wife.

Well, as I was saying, your letters being at Dibru, I can't answer them; the most startling events I can think of at home, being the arrival of the motor, which, by now I trust, is comfortably installed, and getting used to its new surroundings. The hay, I take it, is in, and the roses blooming like mad; are you having a good summer? The weather here is – seasonable; i.e. damnable; it's hot as h-l, and rains continuously. The rivers are all up, and the country a bog.

How's the family? And is Billy thinking of coming out some time? Mrs. Robertson, who's a dear little creature, has been urging me to get her out, so that they can console each other, and keep house together, while Robertson and I pursue the Abor in his lair next cold weather; but it seems rather like dying one's whiskers green, so to speak. However, if she wants to come out, there's an 'opening' for her, so to speak, during the uncertainty of my movements until Christmas; and as the latter are never very definite, we may go on putting it off for ever, as things go at present. So if she's ready, she might be thinking of making a move as soon as the weather's cool enough; say about September. Let's have your views.

I will now say farewell for the present. This seems to be quite the dullest letter I've ever written, but ideas don't seem to flow on this watery lair. Good-bye for the present, and best love and best wishes to you all.

Yours affectionately
Allan

P.S. Mamma will be pleased to learn that a lady complained to me the other day that I was 'so old-fashioned, and prim, and proper', so you see there's hope for the prodigal yet. I don't' think that Billy has yet been accused of arriving at this moral altitude, has she?

★ ★ ★

Letts No 46 Rough Diary

Monday 24 July 1911
Dibrugarh. Got wires from Beeman at Balek. Apparently he very ill and Cornelius dying.
Dined at Hawkes's, also ran with Webb (with me in Bentinck's pumps!). Played cricket!

★★★

With Dunbar on compassionate leave Allan, as acting District Commissioner is invited by
the Lieutenant Governor – 'a rum old bird' – aboard his 'yacht' for an unwanted jolly.

7.8.11

Dearest Family

I'm afraid I've missed the post again, as well as having been bad as regards correspondence lately. But have been busy. I think I told you of how I got hung up at Kobo; when
I got back there was a deuce of a lot of accumulation etc. and then the Lt-Governor
[Lancelot Hare] came on 28th. That day we all had to put on our fancy dresses and
go and meet him; on 29th. there was a sort of a public address to him in the morning
(fancy-dress again) and the Assam Branch of the Indian Tea Association dined him in the
evening. I forgot to say that as Dunbar was away, I have to represent the M.P. at these
affairs with the other district heads of departments (Ahem!) On Sunday fancy dress
again, to call on him and he gave an official dinner in the evening; and in the afternoon
I had a heart-to-heart talk with the Commissioner, who came up with him, as did all
the blooming officials in the province, apparently. As I also had to find time to shoot an
elephant that didn't <u>want</u> to be shot (they're awfully wily, and he spotted there was some
game up as soon as I appeared, and gave no end of trouble before I handed him his little
parcel). I had a busy Sunday. On 31st Monday I had to go and see His Honour's private
Secretary, and Depy. Comm. and the latter entertained everyone to dinner again. On
the next day, I had to interview the Secy. to Govt. (Revenue & General Depts) who is
the bloke who really <u>is</u> Govt. as far as most of us are concerned, and then leave by train
with H.H., a few of the bugs, and the D.C., for Saikhowa. Here we got on board H.H.'s
steamer, and yacht; the latter is a sort of barge tied on to the steamer, and is really awfully
pretty & comfy, I went because he was going to look at Kobo, and wanted to talk Abor
matters etc; but as a matter of fact, he merely wanted to get away and loaf; he is a rum old
bird, his time is up, and his health is poor; so we lived an exceedingly gentlemanly life
until we got back to Dibru. 3 days later, and 'shop' was practically barred! How Bentinck
[Arthur Bentinck, Deputy Commissioner] & I cursed; we both had heaps to see to at
Dibru. and had to charge after the old bird on his dam' lotus-gorging for 3 days!
    After getting back, we only had to go and see him off next day, and then shake hands
with each other and say 'Thank God, that's over'. He's a costive old devil, and never
considers anybody. Still, he backed me up over one or two things (including Mishing)

so I can't complain. This is a footling Govt. in this Province, but he's not as bad as some of them, and it's not an easy job to run with hysteria at home as well as among his lieutenants. And I think a new spirit is creeping in in one or two depts. Let's hope Sir Charles Bayley [Hare's replacement] will be a plucky I larn the villagers, and fine 'em goats, and swear I'll break up their happy homes, and put the elephants in their crops, all without a semblance of jurisdiction, un. I hear it's likely.

The new man at Sadiya is Dundas, [Robert Dundas, whose father Donald had been DS of Police at Berhampore, Bengal] another policeman; and a very good selection. He's excellent; poor old Williamson's virtues without his 'masterfulness'. I don't mean to imply that he's not as strong as they make I larn the villagers, and fine 'em goats, and swear I'll break up their happy homes, and put the elephants in their crops, all without a semblance of jurisdiction, em; but opposition doesn't make him lose his head. He's had the same training as W., savage tribes all his service, until two years ago (isn't it a show-up for the incompetency of the accepted methods?) they dug him out and brought him down to Dacca of all places, to fight Babu sedition. How he hated it; but he made the babus sit up; and when he asked for Sadiya, although they begged him to re-consider it, they practically had to give it him. It's a side-track, of course; but as he says, fancy wanting to be a D.I.G. of police when you can have a job like Sadiya.

Lord, what a lot of shop; and I expect you're wondering what the deuce I'm talking about.

Nowadays, what with your motors, and whatnot, you seem to be doing as much gadding about as I am. What a tremendous run you had in the car home, and how you must have enjoyed it. I'm glad it's a success, and that you are finding it an acquisition.

Pa keeps urging me to precaution with regard to Abors; I beg to assure him that I am not of a rash or negligent nature, and should be seriously annoyed if an Abor got a chance at me through my fault. My future movements are uncertain as ever, and I don't even know yet whether any of us will beard the Abor in his den. But it's probable we go up, with the expedition I may go back to Balek shortly.

My hand was well months ago, and was <u>not</u> an arrow. So mamma's anxieties may be relieved, as I understand they are by now re our Kitty. Was the Investiture a success? And did the motor behave? [The investiture of Edward Prince of Wales at Caernarfon Castle, 13 July 1911.]

I wish mamma would not talk rot about burning villages, etc; there is a damn sight too much of that spirit abroad without finding it in a respectable family. I don't think any decently intelligent people are unnecessarily cruel, but confess that if there's any burning, killing, or ravaging to be done I prefer that we should do it to someone else rather than allow them to do it to us. Perhaps if my tender-hearted parent would write to Williamson's sister she might sympathise less with the ill-treated Abor.

Well, no time for more. Many thanks for all kind letters, news, newspapers, and good wishes. Best love to all and best luck

Yours affectionately
Allan

Letts No 46 Rough Diary

10 August 12 August 13 August 14 August 1911
Sick.

Tuesday 15 August
Mrs Bentinck came and took me for a drive.

★★★

The Times *26th August 1911*
   The Abor Expedition – Tribes bent on resistance
   Reports from the Abor country state that the tribes there intend to offer resist-
ance to the expedition which is to be despatched to avenge the murder of Mr
Williamson, and are busily engaged in blocking the passes and building stockades.
The leaders are boastful and are anxious to kill the so-called white sepoys. The
tribes on both sides of the Dihong River are evidently joining the Abors.

★★★

Dibrugarh
Aug 27th. 11.

Dearest Family,

I'm afraid, from the accumulation of home letters I find on my desk, that I've not been
a very good correspondent lately; but my busy-ness caused by my skipper's absence was
followed a few days before his return by an attack of what the doctor called influenza,
which laid me out for a bit. I know I missed last mail, but think I wrote the one before,
though my head was rather queer at the time and I don't remember much of what I
told you. I was laid up for a week; nothing much in the way of temperature, but aches
and pains, and inability to eat, or think, or anything. Then Dunbar came back and after
a few days I got on to a steamer and took a two days' run down to Tezpur, on the river;
our local specific for all ills, and very good, too. I stopped at Tezpur two or 3 days, as I
was waiting to bring up a friend of Dunbar's to pack up poor Lady D's belongings; a
Mrs. Phillips, wife of a planter, a pleasant woman to meet.
   I got back a few days ago, and am going up to Sadiya for a day or two on Tuesday. I
am much better; in fact except for very slight weakness, am all right again. We are giving
up the old bungalow; Dunbar is going to the club, whilst I'm going to chum with
O'Sullivan, the S.P. whose wife is in the hills; not a very interesting companion, but a
good chap, and an old acquaintance of mine. This will take me on to the expedition, on
which I am expecting to go. It seems certain that we shall have a force of M.P. in it, now.
   Well, that's enough about here. Many thanks for all the home news, in which I take

as much interest as ever. You have had a tremendous lot of visitors lately and must have been an enormous gang at the Show. I was surprised to hear you had had this at W'Pool; it must have been a very good thing for the town.

Thanks for all your kind inquiries and advice re my health, wealth, and occupations. The first is satisfactory, the second better than usual, and the third promising. I must try and get hold of a map for George to follow my peregrinations on, tho' it's not easy to get 'em even for ourselves, of a suitable description This country is very unmapped; you must remember that there are huge stretches of uninhabited jungle, which handicaps survey work.

Well, I must away. I am sending you some photos to look at; please return, <u>carefully packed</u>. The ones of the Daphla Show were taken by poor old Williamson; the others by Bentinck, the D.C.

Did you read in the papers about the 'Abor's abortive attempt' on Balek? It's funny reading; it's all based on a yarn brought in by same Abor to Meklamuddi Saw-mills, and in my opinion, is pure fabrication. At all events, I can certainly show it is grossly exaggerated.

Best love to all, and hoping you are all keeping fit

Yours affectionately
Allan

★★★

Dibrugarh
2.9.11

Dearest Family

Many thanks for your kind birthday wishes which arrived in good time! And reminded me that I had forgotten to send the same to our Podglet, as usual. I hope she'll excuse me this time, and take the will for the deed.

Well, we're getting on, ain't we? I feel a hundred myself, and am very bored with waiting for this damn expedition to start. I'm never really contented these days except when out in the jungle with lots of things to do. Dibrugarh feds me up.

There's a few rumours, etc. of the expedish, but nothing very definite for me, yet. We shall move up about the last week in October, apparently, but what I shall do (if anything) hasn't yet transpired. It seems there are to be one or two 'missions' to other tribes, subsidiary to the expedition (this is strictly confidential, N B.) and I forebode that I may possibly be given one of them; in which case I shall miss the medal, I suppose. However, it's no use worrying until things are settled; nous verrons and Dunbar says I'll go on the main Expedish.

Webb [Lieutenant Allan Bonville Webb who later served in France] is staying with me for a few days; he's a great lad, in the 5th. Gurks. He came up to these parts on leave; then when the trouble began, he worried everyone for a job, and eventually got the billet of attending to Balek communications, and for the last 3 or 4 months has been living in the jungles on the N. Bank. He never has any kit, or food, and leads the simple life for preference; we all rot him about it, and tell him he's never really at ease unless he's sitting in a pool of water eating boiled rice with his fingers. But he's a very good chap, and we all like him. He came in unexpectedly the other day, and came to stop with me as usual; as Bentinck said when they met, 'Floated down on a log, I presume?'

Yours affectionately
Allan

★★★

Dibrugarh
10.9.1911

Dearest Family,

No news again to speak of, 'cept that we received your kind birthday letters, for which I am grateful, and thank you kindly for the good wishes contained therein. 'I am an old man, Mr. Bailey; an old man'.

Things chew on, and it seems that I'm to go on this expedish. But to play what part is not yet known. We're taking 300 of this battn., and will form part of a composite M. P. battn. on the show; though again what our task will be, dunno. We have 'opes that they may give us a little turning movement on our own along a route partially reconnoitred by an intelligent and promising young officer (me) last May.

My skipper has got the hump badly, because Major Bliss of the Naga Hills battn. Is going to command the composite battn. He (Dunbar) had hoped for that himself, but they apparently thought him too junior.

Poor Beeman has got the hump, too, and has been transferred down to Lungleh, at the back of beyond in the Lushar Hills. He has got it badly in the neck over his little kicking over the traces up here; I'm sorry it's so severe, tho' he certainly has only himself to thank.

Well, no more at present, except best wishes. I'm feeling very fit, and now that the beginning is imminent, and I know that I'm going, much cheerier. We go to Kobo on 26th, the rest follow and we should advance about the middle of October.

Best love all round, and best wishes. Thanks for your desires that the expedish should go well; I <u>might</u> get a chance of throwing dust in the owd General's eyes. It's all possible.

Yours affectionately,
Allan

★★★

Dibrugarh
17.9.11

Dearest Family

Just a hurried line to tell you that all is quiet on the Shipka Pass, and that your offspring is well and busy preparing for the fray. The bustle of military activities already begins to be felt at Dibrugarh, and the forerunners of the storm in the shape of various supply officers etc. are in our midst. We (the L.M.P. contingent) have to be at Kobo by the 26th. of this month, and the rest of the other contingents by Oct 6th. We shall probably all advance from there about the middle of October.

I was much shocked to hear of my aged parent driving motors up hedges, and trust he'll be more careful in future. I congratulate him on his escape from physical or financial damage.

No time for more, except best love and good wishes

Yours affectionately
Allan

★ ★ ★

Letts No 46 Rough Diary

Friday 22 September 1911
Left for Kobo with A Co. travelling with Webb. Gotto Saiskhowa and camped at ghat. Dunbar and Ballantine came up from Kobo in Curlew in time for dinner.

Saturday 23 September
Left for Kobo by *Curlew* 7am with A Co, Dunbar and Ballantine. Got there about mid-day. Busy arranging camped men.

At Kobo Camp

General Bower's plan of attack required massing troops and support at a suitably secure base on the north bank of the Brahmaputra. Until such a base could be built supplies coming up by steamer from Calcutta, a two-week passage, were held on barges at piers off Dibrugah, where the river was a mile wide. It's said the troop boats were so densely packed that men took turns to lie down.

4000 coolies were recruited from Naga tribes. Christened the 'heavenly terrors' in the messes, the five-feet tall Nagas wore only bark loincloths and cane helmets. They would be allowed to carry a spear but only for their own protection and when Bower ordered them not to take the heads of the enemy they wore 'an air of unrelieved depression'. The Nagas were there to carry and fetch, not fight.

About 50 miles further on from Dibrugah near where the Dihang River runs south

from the Himalyas into the Brahmaputra, Bowyer chose his base and Beeman, with
Allan's detachment of Lakhimpur MPs, the Pioneers, Sappers and Miners – and elephants
– created a stockaded fortress out of nothing, with lookout towers, a well, hospital and
telephone link, all done in atrocious rain and floods. Bower arrived by steamer with
1/8 Gurkhas and was shown to brigade headquarters on 'The Mall'. Allan's force was
occupying 'Scotland Yard'.

Kobo Camp
Nr. Dibrugarh
10/10/11

Dearest Family

Well, here I am at last, properly mobilised with the Expeditionary force. So far, so good, but we are full of grouses. It seems as if we are to get a little column to ourselves round to the W[est]. after all, but our chances of having a decent show seem remote, as we are only to be let loose if really required; a contingency which seems remote to me, though those in high places dilate on the difficulties and dangers. They have to, to justify their existence!

Well, it's all in the lap of the Gods, and orders vary so constantly that it's no good being despondent, and meeting trouble half-way; but one can't help feeling sick at the way they're treating us. I feel that, if we really get no show after all; I can never face the men again; they rely on me absolutely, and if all their agony and bloody sweat results in our being kept out of the fun, I shall get back to my regt. as soon as I can.

Well, enuff of that. I'm sending you a map and hand-book, which I hope will placate George, and which I hope he'll not talk about too much, as it's not intended for general consumption. You will see that I've marked such items in the book as I contributed, and that they form quite a part of it. The map is the best at present, but *very, very* sketchy still. Col. Macintyre does not command the show, but General Bower. Col. Macintyre is a great pal of mine; a genial old cove. He's base-commandant and Inspector of Communications. He's been using the M.P. here (who were under my command until Dunbar came up 3 days ago). as everything from protective troops, intelligence, etc. down to sappers and miners and conservancy inspectors. They've depended on us for everything, and now send regular regts. to oust us when it comes to getting a chance.

I've got a camera lately, and have had some decent results. I will send you some snap-shots. You'll see we've been hard at it clearing this camp with the 32nd. Pioneers and 1st Sappers and Miners. It was all virgin jungle; high trees and the thickest undergrowth; now it's a huge clearing nearly a mile long, laid out in streets, etc. with Norton Tube Wells at each corner, and bands playing of an <u>evening</u>, and all life and bustle. The streets are named by some humourist on the staff; our lines are bounded by Scotland Yard, Bow Street, Piccadilly, and Pall Mall.

The Mess (you'll see a photo of this, and the lines, etc; the best in camp, and all your humble's work) is full of visitors (old pals from India etc) and I've been full of work. So

I must close. Many thanks for your last letters and paper, and best love to all. I'm very fit, and still hoping to get an opportunity to see something
Best love to all
Yours affectionately
Allan

★★★

20 October Friday
Off at last. The 2nd GR full of themselves but energy ill-directed and poor bundobast all round. Camp about 4.30.

22 October Sunday
Marched by columns thro' Magnang & Dorlek to Mekang. Camped there.

23 October Monday
Went on reconnaisance to Ledum. Found it empty. Got back to Mekang at 8.30.

25 October Wednesday
Marched column to Ledum. Camped there.

27 October Friday
Took out a column to occupy Mishing and improve road. Slew a couple more Abors.

On 20 October Allan left Kobo with the column bound for Ledum – the heart of Minyong Abor country – following the route that, according to the offical account, 'Capt Hutchins had followed in his reconnaisance the previous May'. Essentially the Ledum column was a feint, made to keep the Abors busy in the direction of Ledum and thus protecting the flank of the main column. Under Lt Col J Fisher, the small force would pursue a more direct route on higher ground than the main column, which would pursue the enemy up the Dihang valley to Kebang.

The column 'moved off silently at dawn' and taking a silent salute, 'were swallowed up by the mysteries of the jungle' (In Abor Jungles). It was an impressive display of stealth for a force comprising 1000 men, 2 companies of 2 Gurkhas with a 7-pounder, a party of 32nd Pioneers, 300 MPs with a Maxim under Allan and a corps of Naga coolies, 14 elephants and a field hospital.

★★★

Camp about 6 miles south of Baliming village
25/10/11
(address 'Abor Field Force')

Dearest Family

Behole me here, alive and kicking. We're a detached column of us (L.M.P. 300) with Dunbar, Masters self and one Fathiner, a planter's doctor, who has volunteered and is a very good fellow and a double coy. of the 1st 2nd Gurkhas; all under the command of Lt. Col. Fisher of the latter regt. We've been sent off here to manoeuvre about Ledum; how far the manoeuvres will lead to glory remains to be seen. We still hope, but the idea is that we merely demonstrate; the rest lies with the gods. Ledum, poor devils, daren't submit, but are afraid to fight; so they've abandoned their village, and we move up there tomorrow. We went yesterday, and found them 'Not at home', but were ready to raise a scrap, and returned to our convoy.

The main column is marching up to Pasighat. The idea is that they take Kebang and then we go in to Pasighat and follow them up and join them for the rest. But we hope for something to happen here first.

We're on very light scale and spoiling for a fight.

Many thanks for your letter of 28th. Sept. safely to hand; also Podgie's, and the cutting from the paper. Col. Beynon is not with us, or on the show at all. I was glad to get all the news; just fancy, Gladys Davies is going to get married tomorrow; and Susie, I see from your kind *County Times* was married off the other day. They'll all be gone soon, the friends of me youth.

Well, no more at present. We've had a slack day today, after 4 hairy ones; I got back from the 'battle of Ledum' at 8 pm last night. Have you any idea what marching through the jungle at night is? I think we should have been at it until now, but that rescue parties with lamps turned out from camp to meet us.

Best love; all's well, and I hope you're all blooming
Yours affectionately
Allan

The force reached Mishing village, considered an Abor stronghold, and burned it.

Camp Mishing
Abor Hills
(Abor Expeditionary Force)
1.11.11

Dearest Duch and Doy

How are you all this long time? The latest from home says you're all fit, and blowing, as it leaves me at present I don't think I ever thanked my big brother for his kind efforts on my behalf re Cousin Mue's wedding present; from all accounts the latter gave great satisfaction, and I'm much obliged for the care and skill shown in its selection; and apologise for not having said so before. All's very well with yours humbly nowadays; I am on the Ledum Column of the force, and it looks as if we should have some fun after all. This camp is where Mishing village was once; there's little trace left now however, except the cultivation. We have had a few brushes with some Abor in which they [took] the worst of the exchanges. Jungle as damnable as ever, though the weather is good. We have a beautiful view up here, across the valley of Assam, right away to the Naga Hills on the other side. We're marking time here a bit, trying to get orders out of G.Q.C. to go ahead; in the meantime we wander out daily, and pursue the lurking Abors around.

   Excuse a hurried line, but not much time nowadays.

Best love, and best wishes
Yours affectionately
Allan

★★★

Letts No 46 Rough Diary

Sunday 5 November 1911
Mishing. 2nd Gurkhas again in luck. Went out towards Kebang and found a stockade, traps etc and had quite a scrap. Burned the village.

Wednesday 8 November
Dunbar and me went with small column towards Sidaw, marching for Kerang while the 2nd with another column went round by Ledum. They got there and burned it. We turned down a tributary of Sidaw. Brother Abor got a Kabar, who strayed off the path, with a gun, to the intense disgust of the natives.

Thursday 9 November
Worked up to Sidaw village. Found a bad place with lots of stone-traps. Then a devil of of a storm of rain and hail. Miserable cold. Found a stockade (empty) below Sidaw.

11 November Friday

Still wet. Went out towards Kalashing, reconnoitring. Saw a couple or three Abors but failed to pick 'em up. Got in sight of Kalashing and saw most of the Gallong Country. Very interesting. Back to camp E of Sidaw.

Camp Mishing (still)
17th. Nov. 1911

Dearest Family

We're still here, you observe. Our activities have extended in several directions, and we are still waiting the word to go in and do something. We hope to be allowed to co-operate with the main column if it gets far enough forward for co-operation to be useful. As things go at present, if we went on we should have it all to ourselves, so we've got to hold back. But we wander North, East, and West, and make roads, and pull down the obstructions which the Aybor puts up for us, and occasionally get a bird, which is more than the Main Column does, anyway. So far we've had all the fun, such as it's been; it includes the taking of one defended village, anyway, away to the west, where we didn't expect to find opposition. We occasionally get a hairy day's marching. The other day, Dunbar & self went out with 100 rifles, and the Abor succeeded in getting a wretched dooly-bearer, who strayed off the path – a bold fellow (Abor) slew him with a gun, to our great surprise, as they have few guns. That is our solitary casualty up to date on the force, if you exclude one Naga scout whom an officer of the 8 mistook for an Abor and boldly biffed him one, but we got the fellow with the gun next day.

We're getting wily as regards stone-shoots, etc. and I think the Abors are some fed up with our refusal to walk into traps, etc. They're an awful sweat to construct, and when we simply find 'em, break 'em up, and proceed, it galls a leisure-loving people considerable. I spent two hours the other day in pulling down a heavy stockade, and hurling it bit by bit down a precipice. It was a labour of love; each log and brick as it went down made me think 'The blighter who fetches that up again, will have to sweat some.'

We had an awful storm t'other day; I was Advance Guard, and had just 'guessed' the existence of stone-shoots in front of me, and was sending up. It came on in buckets, with hail intermixed and oh – so cold. [?] to get across [?] dam' place in front, and after that, in the worst of it, lost the path, and we were regularly held up. Talk about being miserable – brrhh. However we found the path, and after a teaser of a cliff with a stockade on top (unoccupied luckily) the sun came out, and I found a topping camp, and all smiled again.

Thanks for the news and gossip. I'm glad to hear that you are hale and hearty as can be and that all goes well. Just fancy – it's nearly Christmas. [Time] seems to fairly buzz under the bridges these days. Well, no more except best <u>love</u>.

Yours affectionately
Allan

Letts No 46 Rough Diary

Saturday 18 November 1911
Took det. of 100 C & B cos to Dosing for reconnaisance & road-making. I shot an Abor on the edge of the village but thought he got away.

Sunday 19 November
Sent D. and most of column road-making towards Mishing and took one section up the Yemseng road. A hell of a climb, damn unforgiving. Came down again about 2.20 feeling rather tired. Heard the Abor I shot yesterday was a Kelabang man.

Monday 20 November
Feeling rather cheap … Scott and I went off to Kelabang. Both a bit off colour, & glad to get back to camp.

21 November Tuesday
Marched back to Mishing, feeling very 2 1/2d. Soon as I got in, went to bed. Doc says I've fever. Wrote report.

22 November Wednesday
In bed. Worse! Damn!!

★★★

To the Officer in Command, General Hospital, Dibrughar,
date unknown

Dear Sir,

I would feel extremely obliged if you are able to give me a few details of my dear son's death, Capt. Allan Hutchins who I understand died in the hospital at Dibrugah after a dreadful journey down from the Abor country. Do you consider that the journey hastened his end and had he … experienced any suffering?

Yours
Mrs G Hutchins

★★★

The Club
Dibrugarh
Assam
23 Feb 1912

Dear Madam,

I received your letter last mail, asking for some particulars of your son's fatal illness.

He was admitted to my hospital in the evening of the 29th November last, he had been ill for some 10 days, and had been sent down to me from the front as it was thought that that would give him the best chance of recovering.

The hardships of war have unfortunately to be shared by the sick as well as the healthy, and it was undoubtably your son's best chance of life to get into a hospital without delay.

Unfortunately after his arrival here, he rapidly became worse and died in the morning of December 3rd. His mind was wandering when he arrived here, and the day after his arrival he became delirious and remained so to the end. He expressed no wishes and left no messages as he had no lucid intervals.

Here he received every care and attention that could be derived, he was nursed night and day by trained English lady nurses, and there was nothing that could have been required in his case which was not at hand. I think it will comfort you to know this, and that nothing the doctors could desire was lacking.

He suffered no pain from first, either physical or mental.

Please accept my very deep sympathy, in your great loss.

Yours very humbly
G Church Capt. Indian Med. Service
OC Gen Hosp Dibru.

★ ★ ★

Dibrughar
Assam
29 December 1911

Dear Miss Hutchins,

In answer to your letter of last mail and to give information of your poor brother.

Poor fellow when he left here for the Expedition, he was in the best of health and spirits and one of the finest young officers to take part, his whole mind and soul was in his work and what little time he was here in the Battalion he was liked and respected. He had been at a place called Mishing and was sent down to Kobo and I am afraid they kept him there too long or else he must have got cold as he was brought here in a high fever, suffering from Double Pneumonia. He was brought in on the 29th and died on the morning of the 3rd, being unconscious all the time and delirious and I believe from what I heard it was all about what he and the men were to do by the General's orders. I did not go to see him as nobody was allowed to, but they thought he <u>could</u> have recovered, but I am afraid he was left too long at Kobo without proper attention as there were no nurses there. His bearer I must say was very attentive and the poor lad was very cut up at his funeral. He was laid to rest in a pretty cemetery, with full military honours by the side of poor Lady Dunbar.

I am afraid I have not been able to you very much news of your poor brother, but my husband is still at Mishing. I only get little news and I am very anxious about my husband. When they heard of your brother's death they were dreadfully shocked and could hardly realise it.

Believe me, yours sincerely
Jane Drummond.

★★★

Winforton House
Hereford
8 August 1913

Dear Mrs Hutchins

I knew your son very well in Assam, where we worked together for a long time and I liked him immensely. His death was to me and to all his friends the saddest part of the whole Abor expedition, as he more than us all had done all the rough pioneering work which made the expedition possible, and we knew he had sacrificed himself to his sense of duty and indomitable energy.

Yours very sincerely
AB Hay. Webb

★★★

County Times

12 December 1911

LATE CAPT ALLAN HUTCHINS
TRAGIC DEATH IN INDIA

The very many friends of Lieut-Col Hutchins, County Surveyor of Montgomeryshire, and Mrs Hutchins, will be grieved to learn of the sudden sorrow in which they have been plunged by the death of their soldier son, Capt. Allan Hutchins, which was telegraphed on Sunday last from Kobo, the base against the Abors in northern India and in which the young officer was a prominent figure.

Captain Hutchins, who was a qualified civil engineer, had had a very successful military record, full of exciting experiences and this sudden termination at the age of 32, to so promising and brilliant a career, is truly tragic, and it was a severe blow to the family to learn of the death, seeing that his letters home were invariably cheerful and full of the spirit of his duties ...

Appendix: The Hutchin's Ancestors – D'Oyleys, Cliffords and Percys

The Hutchins (or Hutchense) family are direct descendants of William the Conqueror through the D'Oyley, thence Percy, families. The D'Oyley pedigree itself stems from Nigel D'Oyley and his brother Robert, who became the 1st Baron Hooknorton of Chislehampton; from Liseux, Normandy; the brothers were commanders in William's army when he landed on English soil in 1066. Robert supervised the building of Oxford castle and was gifted countless manors and lands in England. Coincidentally, Robert's great niece, and one of the chief movers of this book, lives in a house built on land gifted to Robert. The home of Sheila Shaw (nee Hutchins) and her husband, Tony, stands in woods near Missenden Abbey, at the head of the Misbourne valley in Buckinghamshire.

Of later D'Oyleys, John, MP for Woodstock and captain of the county troop was knighted by Charles II in 1666 and became the first baronet of Chislehampton – five miles south east of Oxford. Sir Cope D'Oyley, (1571–1633), is remembered in a side-chapel in Hambleden church, Oxfordshire, where effigies of his wife and ten children humbly kneel, and where Yvonne, not knowing of her family connection, sang in their shadow as a choir member for many years and where two of her sons and a daughter were married. The second baronet, also John, married Susanna, the daughter of Sir Thomas Putt of Combe in Devon. It is through the Putts that the Hutchins descend from two great martial families: Clifford and Percy. The Cliffords – Lords of Skipton and Earls of Cumberland – were intimates to a succession of kings, combatants in the Wars of the Roses, feared, trusted, hated. John Clifford, 9th Lord of Skipton (1435–1461) fought at the Battle of Wakefield in 1460 as principal commander of the Lancastrian force. He was just 25 years old when, after the battle and surrounded by Yorkist dead, he was knighted for his part in the slaughter.

It is said that John had the head of the Duke of York put on the gates of York. Worse, that John stabbed the Duke's teenage son after the boy had surrendered, crying 'by God's blood, your father slew mine and so I will thee and all thy kin.' Thus John acquired the title 'Butcher' – a man considered 'detestable' by both Lancaster and York whose wife Margaret lived in fear of her life and the lives of their five children. But was he the ruthless murderer of York's son? Shakespeare in Henry VI portrays him so but

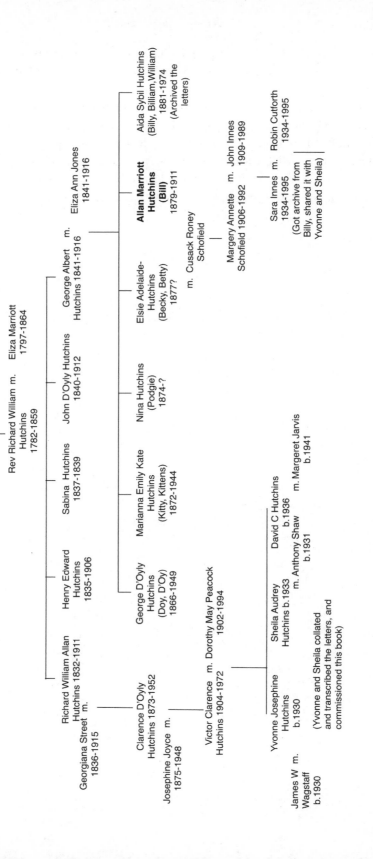

William Hutchins 1710-1779 m. Margaret D'Oyly d.1771

Rev Richard William Hutchins 1782-1859 m. Eliza Marriott 1797-1864

Richard William Allan Hutchins 1832-1911 m. Georgiana Street 1836-1915

Henry Edward Hutchins 1835-1906

Sabina Hutchins 1837-1839

John D'Oyly Hutchins 1840-1912

George Albert Hutchins 1841-1916 m. Eliza Ann Jones 1841-1916

George D'Oyly Hutchins (Doy, D'Oy) 1866-1949

Clarence D'Oyly Hutchins 1873-1952 m. Josephine Joyce 1875-1948

Marianna Emily Kate Hutchins (Kitty, Kittens) 1872-1944

Nina Hutchins (Podgie) 1874-?

Elsie Adelaide Hutchins (Becky, Betty) 1877? m. Cusack Roney Schofield

Allan Marriott Hutchins (Bill) 1879-1911

Aida Sybil Hutchins (Billy, Billiam, William) 1881-1974 (Archived the letters)

Margery Annette Schofield 1906-1992 m. John Innes 1909-1989

Sara Innes 1934-1995 m. Robin Cutforth 1934-1995 (Got archive from Billy, shared it with Yvonne and Sheila)

Victor Clarence Hutchins 1904-1972 m. Dorothy May Peacock 1902-1994

Yvonne Josephine Hutchins b.1930

James W Wagstaff m. b.1930

(Yvonne and Sheila collated and transcribed the letters, and commissioned this book)

Sheila Audrey Hutchins b.1933 m. Anthony Shaw b.1931

David C Hutchins b.1936 m. Margeret Jarvis b.1941

gives John good reason for revenge: according to Shakespeare, and to recent historians, five years earlier at St Albans the Duke of York captured and had killed John's own father.

Henry John Clifford (or de Clifford) married Elizabeth Percy and into the family of Henry de Percy, Harry Hotspur 2nd Earl of Northumberland, dubbed a knight by Richard II at his coronation, who defended the north lands against Scottish invasion with diligent, merciless violence. At 24, he led the closing scene of the siege of Berwick and left no man alive. Later he joined with Henry Bolingbroke to depose Richard (and lead him to the Tower) and place Bolingbroke on the throne as Henry IV.

Bibliography and Further Reading

Conan Doyle, Arthur *The Great Boer War* (1902, London)

Gilmour, David *Ruling Caste: Imperial Lives in the Victorian Raj* (2005, London)

Glancey, Jonathan *Nagaland: A Journey to India's Forgotten Frontier* (2011, London)

Gould, Tony *Imperial Warriors* (1999, London)

Hamilton, Angus *In Abor Jungles* (1911, London)

Jackson, Tabitha *The Boer War* (1999, Basingstoke)

Judd, Dennis *The Lion and the Tiger: The Rise and Fall of the British Raj, 1600-1947* (2005, Oxford)

Keay, John *The Honourable Company: A History of the English East India Company* (1991, New York)

Kipling, Rudyard J *Barrack-Room Ballads* (1890, London) *Collected Verse* (1907, London)

Lee, Christopher *This Sceptered Isle 55BC-1901* 'Empire' (1995, London)

Packenham, Thomas *The Boer War* (New York, 1979)

Powell, Millington *On the Track of The Abor* (1912, London)

Wilson, A.N *The Victorians* (2003, London)

Official Records:

Records held at the Army Museum, Templar Study Centre, Chelsea, verified Allan's appointments and movements.

The Anglo Boer War Museum in Blomfontein released valuable photographic evidence.

Websites:

www.angloboerwar.com

www.britishempire.co.uk

www.thegurkhamuseum.co.uk

For the history of the British in South Africa and the Boer War Thomas Packenham's *Boer War* is both detailed and entertaining, there is nothing to touch it. Tabitha Jackson's *The Boer War* throws new light on the black experience of the war and the miseries of ordinary people, including soldiers, caught up in it. Arthur Conan Doyle's *The Great Boer War* gives the contemporary, Imperial perspective. So does Kipling, but with empathy and wit. There are several versions of his collected works. For newly-researched and often very specialised information the Anglo Boer War website www.angloboerwar.com is a good opening to on-line research. A.N. Wilson's *The Victorians* gives context to Britain's involvement in South Africa and India.

For civilian life in Imperial India David Gilmour's *Ruling Caste Imperial Lives in the Victorian Raj* is fascinating. On the Ghurkhas, Gould's *Imperial Warriors* is a good read and, unlike most books on the subject, neither patronising nor gung-ho. For the most obscure part of Allan's experiences, in Aborlands, there are three contemporary sources: the Official Account in the Army Museum, London; *In Abor Jungles* by Angus Hamilton; and *On the Track of the Abor* by Powell Millington. In *Nagaland: A Journey to India's Forgotten Frontier* Jonathan Glancey shows the fighting still goes on.

Right: 'I have the honor to inform you that your appointment to The Imperial Yeomanry as a Second Lieutenant has been sanctioned ...' Allan's commission, February 1901.

9th February, 1901

2nd Lieut. A.M.Hutchins
5th V.B. S.Wales Borderers
Clive House,
Welshpool.

Sir,

I have the honor to inform you that your appointment to
The Imperial Yeomanry as a Second Lieutenant has been sanctioned by
the Secretary of State for War and will appear in an early Gazette.

2.   You should report yourself without delay to the Officer
Commanding The Imperial Yeomanry at Aldershot on Thursday next the
14th instant showing him this letter.

3.   I enclose a copy of Army Order (Special) of 17th January,
1901, for your information.

4.   In accordance with the Queen's Regulations para 653, you
should provide yourself with the following books:-

"The Queen's Regulations & Orders for the Army."

"Manual of Military Law."

"Regulations & Instructions for Encampments & Cantonments."

"Field Service Manual, Mounted Infantry."

"Cavalry Drill or Infantry Drill."

"Rifle & Carbine Exercises."

5.   I also recommend to your careful perusal the "Manual of
Saddles & Sorebacks," (Publishers, Harrison & Sons, St. Martin's Lane
London), and "The Regulations for Mounted Infantry."

6.   It has been ruled by the War Office that Officers whilst
serving in the Imperial Yeomanry, can only have the rank and wear the
badges of the position they hold in it.

Index